Pennie Foster-Fishman

RESEARCH IN
COMMUNITY SOCIOLOGY

Volume 9 • 1999

VARIETIES OF COMMUNITY SOCIOLOGY

RESEARCH IN
COMMUNITY SOCIOLOGY

Editor: DAN A. CHEKKI
Department of Sociology
University of Winnipeg

VOLUME 9 • 1999

JAI PRESS INC.
Stamford, Connecticut

CONTENTS

LIST OF CONTRIBUTORS

Dan A. Chekki

Department of Sociology
University of Winnipeg

Wayne K.D. Davies

Department of Geography
University of Calgary

Torry D. Dickinson

Women's Studies Program
Kansas State University

A.L. Sinikka Dixon

Department of Behavioral
Science
Canadian University College

Raj S. Gandhi

Department of Sociology
University of Calgary

Fran Klodawsky

Department of Geography
Institute of Women's Studies
Carleton University

Patrick C. Jobes

School of Social Science
University of New England
Australia

Karin Palm Lindén

University of Lund
Sweden

Leonard Nevarez

Department of Sociology
Vassar College

Graham Marsh

School of Social Science and
Planning
Royal Melbourne Institute of
Technology Australia

William Michelson

Centre for Urban and
Community Studies
University of Toronto

Ivan J. Townshend

Department of Geography
University of Lethbridge

Tomas Wikström   University of Lund
                                            Sweden

Lee L. Williams   Department of Sociology
                                            Indiana University Southeast

STATEMENT OF SCOPE

The *Research in Community Sociology* series aims to publish recent research on various dimensions of communities. The volumes in this series include discussions of theoretical and methodological issues, empirical research, case studies, as well as analyses of micro-macro linkages. Special focus will be on cross-cultural, comparative, interdisciplinary, and critical studies on community structure/ change, problems, policy planning, and related issues. Thematic edited volumes and monographs will form part of this series.

ACKNOWLEDGMENTS

The *Research in Community Sociology* series expresses gratitude to the following colleagues for evaluating manuscripts during the 1998-1999 period. Their reviews of manuscripts have been a valuable service to authors and to the discipline.

Mark Baldassare   Nancy Klos
Tom Carter   Lyn Lofland
Karen Duncan   Joel Novek
Cathy Fillmore   Jake Peters
Parvin Ghorayshi   Randy Stoecker
Bud L. Hall   Laurel A. Strain
Sandra Kirby   Michael Weinrath

The editor acknowledges with thanks the assistance of Laureen Narfason, George Hamilton, Lesley Murphy, and Lou Lepin in preparing this volume.

Dan A. Chekki
Editor

MANUSCRIPT GUIDELINES

GENERAL INSTRUCTIONS

PAPER: Type or print the manuscript on **one** side of standard-size, or European equivalent, paper. **Do not** use half sheets or strips of paper glued, taped, or stapled to the pages.

TYPE ELEMENT: The type must be dark, clear, and legible.

DOUBLE SPACING: Double space between all lines of the manuscript including headings, notes, references, quotations, and figure captions. Single spacing is acceptable only on tables.

PERMISSION TO REPRINT: If you are using material from a copyrighted work (e.g., tables, lengthy quotations, figures), you will need written permission from the copyright holder (in most cases the publisher) to use this material. **It is the author's responsibility to obtain the reprint permission.** A copy of the permission letter **must** accompany the manuscript.

TITLE PAGE: The title page includes 5 elements: (1) title and subtitle, if any; (2) author(s); (3) abbreviated title to be used as a running head consisting of a maximum of 70 characters, which includes all letters, punctuation, spaces and the approximate word count for the manuscript; (4) complete mailing address, phone, fax numbers, and e-mail of each author; and (5) list of acknowledgments, credits, and grants.

ABSTRACT PAGE: Provide an abstract (about 150 words) headed by the title. Omit author(s) names.

TEXT: Begin the text on a new page. The sections of the text follow each other without a break. Headings and subheadings in the text indicate the organization of the content. Keep the text of your manuscript anonymous for peer reviewers.

APPENDICES: Begin each Appendix on a separate page, with the word "Appendix" and identifying capital letters centered at the top of the page. If there is only one Appendix, it is not necessary to use an identifying letter.

NOTES: Notes that are mentioned in text are numbered consecutively throughout the chapter. Begin notes on a separate page and **double space** them.

REFERENCES: Follow the American Sociological Association (ASA) Style Guide. Please consult a previously published volume in the *Research in Community Sociology* series.

References cited in text **must** appear in the reference list; conversely, each entry in the reference list **must** be cited in text. It is the author's responsibility to be sure that the text citation and reference list are identical.

<u>**Important**</u>*:* Foreign language volumes, parts, numbers, editions, and so on **must** be translated into their English equivalents. Both the original language and the English translation will appear in the references. Authors **must** transliterate or romanize languages that do not use Latin characters (e.g., Greek, Russian, Chinese, Arabic, etc.), along with their English translation. A comprehensive resource for this is a publication issued by the Library of Congress, titled *ALA-LC Romanization Tables: Transliteration Schemes for Non-Roman Scripts*.

TABLES: Tables are numbered consecutively in the order in which they are first mentioned in text. Begin each table on separate page. Do not write "the table above/below" or "the table on p. 32" because the position and page number of a table cannot be determined until the page is typeset. In text, indicate the approximate placement of each table by a clear break in the text, inserting:

TABLE 1 ABOUT HERE

set off by double spacing above and below.

FIGURES: Figures are also numbered consecutively in the order in which they are first mentioned in text. Indicate the approximate placement of each figure by a clear break, inserting:

FIGURE 1 ABOUT HERE

set off by double spacing above and below. All figures must be submitted in a form suitable for reproduction by the printer without redrawing or retouching. Figures should be no larger than 4 × 6". If a figure exceeds this size, it should be large enough and sharp enough to be legible when reduced to fit the page.

Type all figure numbers and captions, double-spaced, on a separate page. When enclosing a figure in a box, please **do not** include the figure number and caption within the box, as these are set separately.

For identification by the production editor and the printer, please indicate your name and the figure number on the back of each figure. "Top" should be written on any figure that might accidently be reproduced wrong side up. Staples or paper clips should be used on any figure. Scotch tape should **never** be used to attach figure copy to another page as tape edges show up as a black line in production. Art will not be returned unless otherwise indicated.

Manuscripts are evaluated by the editors and other referees. Submit THREE copies of your manuscript and a disk. Your paper should not exceed 50 pages. Address all editorial correspondence to: Professor Dan A. Chekki, University of Winnipeg, Department of Sociology, 515 Portage Avenue, Winnipeg, R3B 2E9 CANADA; fax: (204) 774-4134; e-mail: sociology@uwinnipeg.ca; see: http://www.uwinnipeg.ca/academic/as/sociology/guidleines.htm

DISK PREPARATION GUIDELINES

1   Use a word processing program that is able to create an IBM compatible file. Macintosh files are acceptable. (Macintosh files should be submitted on **high density** disks only.)

2.   Use 3½ inch, double (low) density or high density disks (preferably high density). **NOTE:** If you use double (low) density disks, be sure that the disk is formatted for double (low) density. If you use high density, be sure that the disk is formatted for high density. Unformatted or incorrectly formatted disks are unusable.

3.   Structure the manuscript according to the Guidelines. Print one (1) copy for copy-editing/styling purposes. Be sure to **DOUBLE SPACE** this copy, including the notes and references.

4. The entire chapter should be in one (1) file. **Do not** make separate files for text, notes, and references. If necessary, tables may go in a separate file.
5. All manuscripts must have **numbered pages**; all tables and figures must be placed **at the end of the chapters**; placement lines must be indicated for all tables and figures (e.g., PLACE FIGURE/TABLE X HERE).
6. Submit the word processing file with your printed copy. Please indicate on the disk which word processing program and version you have used (e.g., MS Word, WordPerfect 5.1, 6.0, 7.0, etc., Word Star, WordPerfect for Windows, MS Word for Windows, etc.).
7. All text files must be spell checked and stripped of any and all graphics (graphs, equations, charts, line drawings, illustrations, or tables). Text files must be marked as to the placement of **all** graphics. Please send a **separate** graphics file as either **tiff** (tagged image file format) or **eps** (encapsulated postscript) and indicate which format has been used on the disk. We will still require **camera-ready copy**, whether or not material is also supplied in a graphics file.
8. **PLEASE** be sure that the manuscript and disk submitted match. If the material on the disk has been updated, please print out a new copy of the manuscript to be sure you are submitting the correct version.

PART I

PARTICIPATORY ACTION RESEARCH
AND COMMUNITY CHANGE

PARTICIPATORY RESEARCH, KNOWLEDGE, AND COMMUNITY-BASED CHANGE: EXPERIENCE, EPISTEMOLOGY, AND EMPOWERMENT

Lee Williams

ABSTRACT

Participatory research is an organizing strategy and research methodology composed of five related processes: participation, research, action, education, and reflection. In this paper, an interactive framework is developed to understand participatory research as an empowerment strategy. The framework is based on three dimensions of power (decision making, nondecision making, and control of consciousness), three types of empowerment (advocacy, organizing, and transformation), and three forms of knowledge (representative, relational, and reflective). These ideas provide an outline for an analysis of the Yellow Creek Concerned Citizens' struggles to deal with a toxic creek. Excerpts from in-depth interviews ground and connect the elements of participatory research to the forms of power, knowledge, and

Research in Community Sociology, Volume 9, pages 3-40.
ISBN: 0-7623-0498-7

empowerment embedded in people's experiences with community-based change. The success of the approach in promoting empowerment and change is in the fact that people with a problem produce and use multiple forms of knowledge to understand and transform their circumstances.

We are dangerously close to creating a situation that effectively denies the knowledge creating abilities of most people in the world. The ever-increasing domination of a large majority of the world's population comes not only through economic exploitation, but also from the power of elites to control, manipulate, and monopolize knowledge. Most often research in the sciences is seen as a process in which an "objective expert gathers information," "in an "objective manner," "to prepare an objective report," "to objectively solve whatever problem(s) may exist." It has results, generally by way of recommendations, produced with little if any real consent and participation of the "subjects" involved in the research. Power over what knowledge is produced, how it is produced, and how it will be shared is maintained by experts and their powerful patrons. "Knowledge that the researcher produces is deposited in the scientific storehouse from which, supposedly, policy-makers, corporate executives, and other would-be social engineers draw requisite techniques for administering to, managing, and manipulating unwitting and pacified populations" (Park 1993, pp. 3-4). Usually this type of activity, done by an outsider, "comes back in the form of power forged with what has been taken (or stolen) from the people who participated in the research. Often it comes back to exploit" (Arnold et al. 1991, p. 165).

Participatory approaches to research, on the other hand, are democratic strategies for generating information and learning used by individuals, groups, and movements working for social change. Many forms of participatory research (PR) try to strike a balance between collaboration and participation. Depending on the needs of the community and the skill levels and politics of professional practitioners, the projects may be more or less participatory and liberatory. Most notable among these types of PR are: participatory action research (PAR), participatory rural appraisal (PRA), participatory learning and action (PLA), participatory evaluation research (PER), empowerment evaluation (EE), action research (AR), collaborative research (CR), community-based research (CBR), and feminist research (FR). Other authors have compared and contrasted these ideas and presented detailed accounts of the distinctive features of these approaches.[1]

For the purpose of this paper, the main concern is with liberatory PR, rooted in the work of practitioners like Fals Borda (1981, 1985), Hall et al. (1982), Kassam and Mustafa (1982), Lewis et al. (1990a, 1990b), Maguire (1987), and Tandon (1981, 1988). Ownership of process and products are two of the practical differences between traditional, collaborative, and participatory research methods. In traditional research, power, control, and ownership are maintained solely by the expert, university, or funding agency. In collaborative research approaches power, control, and ownership are shared between communities and experts. In liberatory PR the community is in control of and owns the research, education, and action processes. In a rather gross oversimplification, it is to say, traditional research serves the expert(s), collaborative research serves the cooperating groups, and participatory research serves the community.

Liberatory PR is an organizing strategy built around people's participation in solving problems by producing information, knowledge, and action. The approach breaks down the barriers between knowing and doing by putting people traditionally thought of as "research subjects" in charge of investigating and transforming their own world. Fundamentally, PR is about whom has the right to speak, analyze, and act. The goal is to empower people to build democratic organizations and movements to bring about needed changes in society. PR is a process where grassroots people and organizations can sharpen community knowledge through careful and strategic analysis of various kinds of information. Community members can gain critical thinking skills for improved problem solving and decision making at multiple levels. They can also build better and more solid relationships within and between community members and groups. Ultimately, participants in PR can develop in themselves the capacity to determine and address the root causes of problems and issues in their lives and communities.

This paper will deal with two important questions about PR. (1) What do participants gain by participating in PR? (2) What can researchers, educators, and organizers learn from the experiences of participants in PR to improve the theory and practice of the approach? The path toward answering these questions begins with an overview of the basic elements of PR and continues with definitions of and a discussion about the concepts of knowledge, power, and empowerment. I then develop an interactive framework that describes the process of participatory research as an empowerment strategy. These ideas are used to present and discuss the case example of the Yellow Creek Concerned Citizens' (YCCC) struggle to deal with the effects of a toxic creek. Excerpts from in-depth interviews with YCCC member's highlight the types of power, knowledge, and empowerment found in their experiences with community-based social change. Finally, the theoretical and experiential are joined to offer a discussion about what researchers, activists, and organizers can learn from people's experiences with PR in community.

PARTICIPATORY RESEARCH: A BRIEF OVERVIEW

PR is more than simply a set of research methods. It is a theory of knowledge, a strategy to produce knowledge, and a philosophy of social change. Development practitioner and educator, John Gaventa, put it this way:

> Participatory research attempts to break down the distinction between the researchers and the researched, the subjects and objects of knowledge production, by the participation of the people-for-themselves in the process of gaining and creating knowledge. In the process, research

is seen not only as a process of creating knowledge, but simultaneously, as education and development of consciousness, and of mobilization for action (1993, p. 34).

The theme of the "subject/object dialectic" and the process of "conscientization" (growing critical consciousness), based in the work of Freire (1970, 1973, 1978, 1985, 1998), inform this stream of PR (Hall 1994; Park 1993). In this view, inclusive, participatory, and popular knowledge production provides the impetus for learning, understanding, consciousness-raising, and action. "Participatory research is above all a critique—built on a critical analysis of assumptions underlying knowledge derived from historically shaped and politically beholden institutions" (Heaney 1993, p. 46). The strategy is a flexible and experiential approach to personal and social transformation that aims to demystify the process of creating knowledge.

There are five major elements in the PR process: participation, education, action, research, and reflection. Reality finds these categorizations quite fluid with more overlap than separation. PR practitioners have generally shied away from rigid models of research process, although they have developed rigorous and demanding methods and approaches to knowledge production. PR has tended to remain imprecise on issues of methods because of other considerations. Hall (1994, p. 4332) identifies some of the more prominent factors as:

the origins of the issues, the roles that those concerned with the issues play in the process, the emersion of the process in the context of the moment, the links to action, the understanding of how power relationships work, and the potential for communications with others experiencing similar discrimination, oppression or violence.

In addition he says, "participatory research is based on the epistemological assumption that knowledge is constructed socially and therefore approaches which allow for social, group, or collective analysis of life experiences of power and knowledge are most appropriate" (Hall 1994, p. 4333). What this all means is that in PR there is no rigid methodological orthodoxy, rather the idea is that the content, issues, and ways of doing should flow from context.

Participatory researchers have used an eclectic mix of scientific research techniques to investigate a host of social problems and issues. Useful methods have included among others, group discussions, public meetings, research teams, surveys, community seminars, fact-finding tours, collective production of audio-visual materials, popular theater, interviews, oral histories, document research, archival research, and educational camps. Most strategies for investigating the world are amenable to a participatory approach and no research method is useless in the quest for liberating knowledge. Most liberatory PR follows a similar process and philosophical bases, but the different social contexts and problems along with the strengths and weaknesses of participants influence the approach. Whatever the strategy it must be appropriate to local, cultural, economic, and political conditions. Participatory researchers make efforts to ensure that methods complement rather than supplant indigenous forms of expression, communication, discussion, and decision making. Research methods may be used only once or quite often during the process. Participants need to give thoughtful consideration to which methods to use and when. The goal in the PR process is to build on people's experiences to generate and use multiple forms of knowledge to understand present circumstances, envision a better world, and work toward improving people's lives.

THREE TYPES OF KNOWLEDGE

Based on a modified version of Jurgen Habermas's sociology of knowledge, Park (1993, 1997, Forthcoming) offers a framework that allows us to see the efficacy of PR in terms of its ability to produce multiple forms of knowledge. The perspective provides an opportunity to think more broadly about knowledge than ordinarily conceived in the positivist scientific framework. Habermas' critical theory postulates three kinds of knowledge that underlie human conduct in society. Park, somewhat departing from Habermas' terminology, calls these "representative," "relational," and "reflective" knowledge. According to the theory, each kind of knowledge goes into the human cognitive constitution, making it possible for social beings to relate to the world and one another to act as a group. In this scheme, all three branches of knowledge are science. However, the term science (often appropriated by positivists, especially in western countries), refers almost exclusively to representative knowledge.

Representative Knowledge

In its extreme form, the production of representative knowledge is the method of inquiry embraced by most natural and social scientists in the West. The basic thrust is to explain how things work through the development of empirical theories by testing and refining those theories based on observable and representative data. The logic of the method entails the separation of cause and effect and a dualist understanding of researcher and subjects; the researcher as an acting and active agent and the subject as a passive object that is acted upon. The validity of representative knowledge is understood pragmatically by testing whether it works to control, predict, adapt, or produce something tangible in our larger social ecological system. Practitioners follow a number of distinct and generally, orderly steps in the quest for "objective" knowledge: problem identification, hypothesis formulation, literature review, data generation, data analysis, and publication of results. In this model, the researcher is in charge of each step in the process. The only place subjects are involved is in answering predetermined questions so researchers will have some data to analyze and explain in order to develop answers to the problem(s) they defined.

Less powerful people, however, cannot dismiss the important task of producing representative knowledge, for they too, must have knowledge of how the social world operates. There is a need to know, in some systematic way, how people feel, think, behave, and relate to one another, in order to create conditions for a good society. The Appalachian Land Ownership Taskforce Study (1981), an early and very important example of PR in North America, offers several insights into the potential of grassroots people to produce and use representative knowledge for social change.

The land ownership project was conducted by a coalition of community groups, scholars, and individuals associated with the Appalachian Alliance. The 7-volume study involved a great deal of fieldwork in which grassroots researchers spent many tedious hours transferring ownership and taxation data from county tax rolls onto coding sheets. Organization and computer analysis of the survey data took several months of collaborative work, as did editing the county case studies. After much labor and the involvement of at least 100 people, the land ownership report was released on April 3, 1981. What the process accomplished was a study that was one of the most comprehensive surveys of land ownership patterns and related impacts in the United States. It included a survey of corporate and absentee ownership and related socioeconomic data for 80 counties in six states. The report contained extensive case studies in 20 counties, demonstrating the impact of ownership patterns on such things as jobs, environment, housing, local power structures, taxes, education, and services.

Although a grand revolution did not occur based on the participatory research of the land study, a great many individual, organizational, and structural changes attributable to the project are identified by Gaventa (1981), Gaventa and Horton (1981), and Horton (1993). They include the effective training of a number of grassroots researchers, the creation of a network of action-oriented individuals and groups, and education and action around land ownership issues at multiple levels (local, regional, state, national). Gaventa (1981, p. 130) writes, "a citizens based research process can be used both to gain information needed for action and to educate community leaders, link communities facing common problems, coalesce local organizations, and serve as a spark for change. In Appalachia, the groups involved in the project will use the information they have acquired to continue to combat land ownership problems. And, in the process of getting the information they need, they have gained more strength for the battle." All of this was achieved through the process of producing representative knowledge.

When representative knowledge is pursued collectively and based on the needs of community-based people, as evidenced above, this knowledge can be used to critically and directly challenge traditional power relations in society. The research methods pursued by most social and natural scientists, however, cannot accomplish this task because they fail to recognize or value the special "interactive," or "relational" nature of knowledge.

Relational Knowledge

Relational knowledge makes human community possible. This knowledge does not derive from analysis of data about other human beings but from sharing a life-world together—speaking with one another and exchanging actions against the background of common experience, tradition, history, and culture (Park 1997). Relational knowledge centers on understanding through interpretation and interaction. The logic of the method is to merge self and other, and enter the social world to first understand the other from the perspective of the other and then through the self. This form of knowledge establishes and creates meaning and communion between fellow travelers on the planet. Sharing and creating common understandings establish validity, for it is in community that we come to create meanings and understand other human beings. Interactions and activities, in which we talk with others about personal feelings and listen with interest and supportiveness, substantiates relational knowledge.

Relational knowledge has a number of different facets. Collins (1989, 1990), hooks (1984, 1989), Walker (1988, 1989), among others, offer insights into the role of relational knowledge based on ideas labeled "third-wave feminism" (Madoo Lengermann and Niebrugge 1996, pp. 468-470). These writers are distinguished by the fact that they aim their critical effort not only against sexual ideology and the unequal status of women, but more broadly at all systems of domination. Central to this perspective is that the truth about power is best discovered from the vantage point and experiences of oppressed people (both women and men), whose accounts must therefore be uncovered through dialogue. It is to validate the voices, experiences, and knowledge of the subaltern first, not last (Spivak 1989; Chambers 1983).

Collins (1989) uses the idea of dialogue to emphasize the importance of relational knowledge within the "social construction of black feminist thought." She states: "For Black women new knowledge claims are rarely worked out in isolation from other individuals and are usually developed through dialogues with other members of a community. A primary epistemological assumption underlying the use of dialogue in assessing knowledge claims is that connectedness rather than separation is an essential component of the knowledge-validation process" (1989, p. 763). Collins goes on to describe this dialogue in terms of an interactive network.

> The widespread use of the call and response discourse mode among African-Americans exemplifies the importance placed on dialogue. Composed of spontaneous verbal and nonverbal *interaction* between speaker and listener in which all of the speaker's statements or 'calls' are punctuated by expressions or 'responses' from the listener, this Black discourse mode pervades African-American culture. *The fundamental requirement of this interactive network is active participation of all individuals.* For ideas to be tested and validated, everyone in the group must participate. To refuse to join in, especially if one really disagrees with what has been said is seen as "cheating" (1989, pp. 763-764 emphasis added).

For Collins this networked dialogue among African-Americans serves the function of validating what I term here as relational knowledge. For our purposes, it is also important to see the emphasis on the participatory nature of the knowledge validation process. It is done face to face and listeners are considered to be "cheating" if they refuse to join in the conversation, especially if they disagree with the speaker. For author and activist June Jordan (1985, p. 129), the language used by Black people assumes, from its inception, that there are at least two human beings involved in the process—the speaker and listener and both active. This way of thinking about knowledge turns the epistemological assumptions of representative knowledge producers on their head. Rather than de-emphasizing dialogue, connectedness, participation, and multiple vantage points during knowledge production, they each inhabit a place of central importance.

Canadian sociologist and ontologist, Dorothy Smith (1987, 1990), has written about similar themes emphasizing what she terms the "bifurcation" and "relations of ruling" between social scientific discourse and the everyday world of experience. In her papers, she directly articulates how to fashion a social science that transcends the established frameworks for producing the representative knowledge of enlightenment science. She is concerned with developing:

> a sociology which does not transform those it studies into objects but preserves in its analytic procedures the presence of the subject as actor and experiencer. Subject then is the knower whose grasp of the world may be enlarged by the work of the sociologist (1987, p. 1).

For Smith, the researcher must be located on the same critical plane as the subjects of the research. In other words, some sort of common understanding, or relational knowledge, is necessary to equalize power and alter traditional relations of ruling. Smith (1990) argues for social research practices that are interested in, begin from, and value particular sites in the world and that value and integrate experiential and relational knowledge into the analysis and depiction of everyday life.

Author and activist, Vijay Kanhare (1981, 1982), provides an example of the impact of relational knowledge in organizing and mobilizing through PR with local women in India. The "Adivasis" (tribal people) became landless laborers during British rule in the Dhulia District of Northern Maharashtra State. Women "Adivasis" suffer multiple oppressions. They get lower wages than men, have to do all of the work in the fields and all domestic and childcare tasks. Sexual harassment by the farmers is rampant, beatings by drunken husbands are common, and male laborers keep the women from participating in wage negotiations. Community activists took the initiative to set up a three-day education camp so that landless women laborers could begin to develop an awareness that their problems were particular to them as women. Activists proposed the camp to villages during night meetings. Many villagers expressed doubt: "What can we talk about for two whole days?" "We cannot express ourselves well." The men asked: "Who will cook and look after the children?" (Kanhare 1982, p. 24).

Women came to the camp from 15 villages. In opening the sessions the activists explained that they thought a women's camp was necessary in order to increase women's participation in the laborers' movement by encouraging them to take action on women's problems. Early in the camp, some felt very shy about speaking before such a big gathering. Some felt they should not discuss their personal problems with a group. For many, it was a novel experience to stand up and tell their names and villages without anybody to threaten them. After their initial efforts to speak, they became bolder and their self-confidence increased. As one women explained: "We never thought we had the strength to speak in a gathering of 150 women, that we could shout slogans in front of and against the *maaldars* (the rich)" (Kanhare 1982, p. 24).

Many of the women described their villages and the sexual harassment they suffered from rich farmers and the watchmen of the crop protection societies. Pretending to suspect a theft, watchmen would search through the women's clothing. As the women spoke, they began to realize that the problems they thought were isolated and personal were, in fact, social problems. They collectively identified their problems as women as sexual harassment by the rich, wife-beating, and bootlegging. A woman from a nearby village spoke: "We complain that the men drink liquor, that they become corrupt due to drinking. We complain that they beat us up. We want to do some things about this problem. Our village is small, but it produces hundreds of litres of liquor and they beat us up. We women of Karankheda are not organized. Can the other women help us? We need help" (Kanhare 1982, p. 25).

The women at camp decided to help. They cordoned off the village so that no bootlegger could run away. They broke all the liquor pots and bottles and warned that any bootlegger or any man who drank and beat his wife would be severely punished. They said that the Karankheda women were not alone anymore. By building their relational knowledge into collective critical consciousness of themselves as oppressed women, they were able to struggle not only against the rich farmers but to support each other in struggles with the family against alcoholism and wife-beating. Following the camp, groups as large as 50 went to villages and encouraged women to organize and punish husbands who beat their wives. In later camps, women looked at the "elder" system, in which older men make judgments about divorces, marriages, remarriages, and fines with respect to sexual relations. They discussed myths about the male-dominated value system, such as the myth that women became unholy during menstruation.

By producing relational knowledge through dialogue these Indian women learned about their shared oppressions and started to grasp the complexity of their struggle for equality. To put it in Collins' (1990) words, they began to understand the "matrix of domination" and they organized themselves to do something about it. The relational nature of knowledge suggests that there are many different versions of reality for there are many different realities in which people live. All of these realities should be explored and each should be regarded as producing a more complete, less distorting, and less perverse understanding than can science in alliance with ruling-class activity. However, in order to effect social change, relational knowledge needs to be connected to reflective knowledge that leads to critical consciousness and action.

Reflective Knowledge

Reflective knowledge means that people not only come to understand the causes of their miseries which can be dealt with instrumentally, but "by reflecting on these causes as being historically rooted in human actions, they also come to realize that things do not have to remain the way they are and that they can engage in actions to transform that reality. Critique thus turns into will to action and action itself" (Park 1993, pp. 7-8). Reflective knowledge is about values. The logic of reflective knowledge understood as critiques that inform values, which inform critiques through dialectical relations. Reflective knowledge establishes critical meaning, emancipation, and social justice through the development of individual and collective autonomy, responsibility, empowerment, and freedom. It is learned through popular education and its validity is created through individual and collective social action.

PR is based in the interests of oppressed groups; it is about producing reflective knowledge in order to transform consciousness. The process involves people in critical analysis, so that they can, potentially, act collectively to change oppressive structures through participatory, creative, and empowering methods of practice (see Epstein 1991, 1996; and also evidenced in Kanahare's example cited above). The term popular or participatory research defines this approach and its practitioners promote "conscientization," or critical consciousness, as an essential element of this type of research. The process involves a reflection/action/reflection dialectic through which critical consciousness and conscience develop. Adult educator, Paulo Freire (1970, 1973, 1978, 1985, 1998) developed an analysis for understanding this process based on three levels. The three levels—intransitive, semi-transitive, and critical transitive consciousness—sometimes exist in discrete pure states, but primarily they overlap. Educator and scholar Ira Shor (1992, pp. 112-135), whose work guides this discussion, provides an excellent synopsis of Freire's perspective.

Intransitive consciousness denies the power of human beings to change their lives or society. Divine forces control the intransitive person. They think that what happens in life and society are controlled by all-powerful deities, their chosen earthly representatives, or by dumb luck and accidents. People with intransitive consciousness accept and even celebrate the status quo. A person with semi-transitive consciousness believes in cause and effect and in the human power to learn and to change things. The semi-transitive individual does not connect the pieces of reality into meaningful wholes, but rather acts on parts in a disconnected way. This unintegrated view of the world does not perceive how separate parts of society condition each other, or how a whole social system is implicated in producing single effects in any one part. Semi-transitive thought is partially empowered because it accepts human agency in the making of personal and social change. This type of thinking is reformist insofar as it leads to partial or contradictory changes. The final stage, critical consciousness, is what allows people to make broad connections between individual experience and social issues, between single problems and the larger social system. This stage is when people have developed the ability to produce and use reflective knowledge to make social changes.

A concrete example from an earlier paper on popular education by Williams (1996) offers some insight on reflective knowledge in PR. During a 1993 gathering at the Highlander Research and Education Center,[2] one of the workshop participants who was involved in the Appalachian Land Study, shared a story about a community trying to do economic development. The story illustrates both the process of "conscientization" and the role of reflective knowledge in PR.

> A group of people in a small rural community felt that they needed to do something to develop new ways of making a living in the area, or the community itself was in danger of failing. Community members knew what they needed to do, but were unsure what tactics and strategies would help the community to remain viable. The first solution was that industries must be recruited to locate in the area. The first tactic to emerge was that the community needed to clean and spruce itself up, then companies will certainly want to come here. An intensive cleanup effort was mounted (trash removed, rubbish burned, vacant areas fixed up, etc.), yet no companies decided to locate in the community.

> The next tactic was to start their own industry based on resources within the community itself. But major obstacles to this strategy included a lack of land and capital, as well as the wrath of local companies already in existence who make their livings in conjunction with the absentee land owners and their managers. At this point the people began to move from blaming themselves for their problems (e.g., we must clean up our community) to dealing with the underlying power issues that were hindering local development: absentee land-owners controlling over 75% of the county; several local coal and timber operators controlling nearly all of the rest. It was only after these initial attempts at local development were tried and failed that the opportunity for the critical analysis of structures became possible within this particular community (Williams 1996, p. 103).

Although some missteps may happen in the long-term struggle for social justice, opportunities for critical learning take place at each juncture of the reflection/action dialectic. Rather than internalizing the oppression, or blaming themselves, the people in this small community began to perceive and resist the larger social structures that were controlling their human agency. This insight only developed as they educated themselves and actively struggled to make changes in their community. Only when multiple forms of knowledge are combined can people alter unequal power relations in ever widening contexts.

THREE DIMENSIONS OF POWER AND
THREE EMPOWERMENT STRATEGIES

Social critic Manning Marable, in his book *Crisis of Color and Democracy,* offers a concise and apt definition of empowerment for an analysis of PR:

> Empowerment is essentially a capacity to define clearly one's interests, and to develop a strategy to achieve those interests. It's the ability to create a plan or program to change one's own reality in order to obtain those objects or interests. In other words, you shouldn't say that a group has power, but that, through its conscious activity, a group can empower itself by increasing its ability to achieve its own interests (1992, p. 3).

In judging whether empowerment through PR is effective, we should understand "who are empowered" and "how their power is used." If those who gain from the process are outsiders who exploit, or local elites who dominate, certainly effect should be questioned. But if powerless people, by doing PR as a conscious and creative activity, increase their ability to achieve their own interests, empowerment can said to have been created. If indeed the possibility that a state of empowerment exists and that there are effective strategies at the grass roots to foster this transformation, we must first clearly understand that this is so because power seldom completely suffocates resistance movements. Places and spaces where democracy is practiced and transformative learning and action accomplished always exist even in the most oppressive of social structures (see especially Evans and Boyte 1986).

In order to understand how to develop people's capacities to be active and empowered participants in the struggle to build democratic social structures several questions emerge. "What organizations and approaches are necessary for creating and sustaining a democratic citizenry?" "What capacities do people require to carry out this work?" "How are they to be developed?" Answers to these questions are located in the work of Gaventa (1982, 1988, 1993, 1995). Gaventa's analytical scheme (see Table 1) is useful for understanding the social change strategies that people can employ to gain power. The framework outlines the general nature of power, several forms of powerlessness, and three different empowerment strategies that grow different forms of democratic participation in society.

Advocating

The first dimension of power equates with the pluralist model of democracy. Power is a product of who wins and who loses on clearly recognized issues in a relatively open political economic system. The lack of participation in this model is a nonproblem signifying the contentment of the citizenry with the status quo. Where citizens choose to enter the political arena and exert power, they may do so as others have done by organizing into interest groups and associations. Many

Table 1.   Power, Powerlessness, and Empowerment

	1st Dimension of Power	*2nd Dimension of Power*	*3rd Dimension of Power*

Power A	• Open Systems
	• Who Wins and Loses
	• Clearly Recognized
	  Issues
		• Mobilization of Bias
		  Against Participation
		• Nonissues
			• Shaping of
			  Consciousness About
			  Barriers and Issues
			• Hegemony

Powerlessness B	• Lack of Resource to
	  Compete Effectively
	• Nonparticipation due
	  to Individual Barriers
		• Lack of Resources
		• Nonparticipation Due
		  to Systemic Barriers
			• Uncritical
			  Consciousnes
			• Internalized
			  Oppressions

Empowerment Strategy	• Advocacy
	• Issue-based
	• Professional Leadership
		• Mobilization and
		  Organizing on Key
		  Issues
		• Organizer Leadership •
			• Emancipatory
			  Education
			• Critical Consciousness
			  Indigenous Leadership

Source: Gaventa (1995).

progressive organizations concerned with issues at the grass roots (e.g., the "big ten" environmental organizations) use advocacy-based approaches to social change. Those who practice this strategy are often professional activists or alternative experts who may often not be effected by the issues they advocate for. In this approach, the skills citizens need to build democracy have much to do with:

> learning to advocate for a particular issue, to influence the political process through established institutional means such as voting, lobbying, writing ones' congressperson, or joining an organization...learning how to mobilize resources (votes, funds, expertise) to influence decision-making in the policy arena, to collaborate and bargain, to challenge technical policy questions.... However, in this arena, capacity building [empowerment] is less concerned with questions of expanding political participation through direct organization, or through the development of grassroots political education and political knowledge.... This becomes a form of politics 'for the people,' not one 'with' or 'by the people' (Gaventa 1995, pp. 6-8).

Mobilizing and Organizing

The pluralist vision of an open, participatory society is important, although the assumption that it actually exists in everyday politics has been widely challenged on a number of fronts. The challenges related to the mobilization of bias and non-decision making prevalent in our political economic decision-making process (see Bachrach and Baratz 1970; Bachrach and Botwinick 1992; Crenson 1971; Johnson 1996). The key for understanding power in this perspective is not about who wins and loses on key issues, but is about analyzing how certain issues and actors are kept from getting to the decision-making table in the first place. Some issues are organized into politics while others are organized out. The process of empowerment in the second dimension becomes one of organizing people to bring their grievances into the political process. In everyday terms, this becomes the politics of community organizing found in the traditions and work of people like Saul Alinsky (1946, 1971).

The practice of grassroots community organizing has flourished over the last several decades. Gary Delgado, in a recent report, argues that there are now over 6,000 community organizations in operation in the United States. He suggests that they are mostly "local, unaffiliated groups, initiated out of local residents' need to exert control over development in their communities" (Delgado 1993 in Gaventa 1995, p. 10). In social movement terms, empowerment in this arena becomes a process of resource mobilization, of building funds, members, communications, and tactics that allow previously quiescent groups to act directly upon their concerns. Thus, while the competencies found in the first dimension of power have to do primarily with effective advocacy on key issues through established interest groups:

> the competencies in the second dimension of power add to these the emphasis on organizing greater participation by those who have been excluded, and on getting previously latent issues and players on the political agenda. But while the mobilization and building of grassroots organizations has been critical for educating citizens in the skills of democracy, this approach, in its narrowest forms, also has its limitations for dealing with the broader issues of power (Gaventa 1995, p. 11).

Transforming Consciousness

Some community organizing approaches see the development of people's knowledge of themselves and of the operation of the political economic system as a necessary and integral part of any social change strategy. Their concerns about political education, critical analysis, vision of what is possible, and basis in participatory values get right to the core of the capacities necessary for dealing with the third dimension of power. The second dimension of power analyzes and highlights the ways in which power operates to "prevent grievances from reaching the table." However, the approach is still tied to the pluralist notion that the exercise of power must involve conflict over clearly recognized issues and grievances. Political scientist Steven Lukes (1974), and then others (Gaventa 1982, 1995; Williams 1997) have challenged this approach. They argue that the most effective and insidious use of power is to prevent conflict from arising in the first place. The powerful may exert their power by influencing action and participation upon recognized grievances. However, they also influence people's "consciousness and awareness of such grievances through such mechanisms as socialization, education, media, secrecy, information control, and the shaping of political beliefs and ideologies" (Gaventa 1995, p. 14).

The skills and competencies for empowering citizens to challenge this third dimension of power involve strategies of "awareness building, liberating education, promotion of critical consciousness, overcoming internalized oppressions, and developing indigenous or popular knowledge" (Gaventa 1995, p. 15). While theorists have been able to articulate quite clearly the more pragmatic skills of advocacy and organizing, this approach to empowerment remains somewhat murky due to the debates about false consciousness and the like (see Scott 1985, 1990). Gaventa (1995, pp. 21-22) suggests when dealing with the third dimension of power that:

> self analysis by those affected of their own reality in order to change it becomes an important stage in the process of building democratic citizenship…[and must include] processes of education for critical consciousness, the recovery and development of people's knowledge as a basis for action, and the modeling and promotion of democratic values in organizational development…. With such an approach, the role of the political activist becomes that of a facilitator and educator, rather than the organizer or advocate.

In order to be effective agents of social change people need to develop skills and capacities that allow them to address power at all three levels. The desire to make social change obliges people to develop the capacities to advocate for issues. It also means that people need to be able to organize and build lasting participatory organizations to gain a voice at the decision-making table. In addition, people must develop critical consciousness in order to pursue equity and justice for all. Being involved in producing representative, relational, and reflective knowledge is one way to develop these capacities. PR is an approach to change that embraces all of these elements in order to transform oppressive power relations.

AN INTERACTIVE FRAMEWORK FOR PARTICIPATORY RESEARCH

When grappling with issues of power and empowerment it is clear, at least in participatory and experiential modes of investigation, that research, education, action, and reflection are each empty without being connected to the other. The advocates of participatory research make no pretenses that this alternative investigative approach will, by itself, create a revolution. Rather, by emphasizing power sharing in knowledge production and stressing the collective analysis and working out of problems and solutions, PR reinforces and builds the capacities of powerless individuals, groups, and communities to make social change. By learning through doing, people can strengthen their awareness of, and belief in, themselves and their abilities and resources for organizing, educating, acting, and thinking critically.

Figure 1 outlines an interactive and epistemological framework between power, empowerment, knowledge, and the elements of participatory research. The point is that successful social changes are based on the ability of people to empower themselves in each of the areas. Attention to each of the three dimensions of power, knowledge, and empowerment is essential if PR is to build people's capacities to overcome powerlessness. From a pluralist framework that focuses on the decision

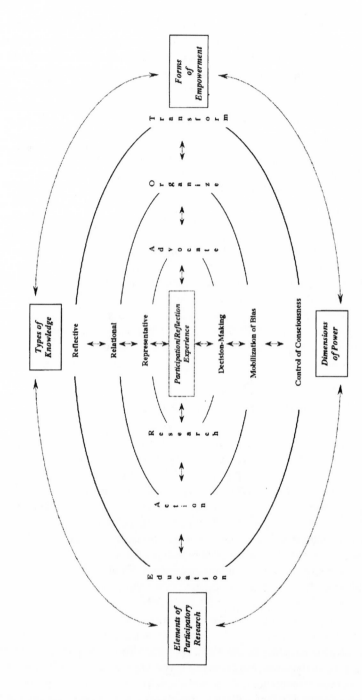

Figure 1. Power, Knowledge, Empowerment, and Participatory Research: An Interactive Framework

making process as it actually occurs (the first dimension of power), the emphasis is on building the advocacy skills necessary to influence decision-making and decision makers on key issues. An informed and empowered citizenry needs concrete information, or representative knowledge, to advocate for or against particular issues and agendas in order to influence and alter the process in their favor. Thus, the elements of PR that are most important are participation in the research process and, consequently, reflection on the process. This does not mean that education and action have no role in building the capacity to advocate; of course they do. Rather, research is the central activity that produces representative knowledge in order to advocate. Education and action supplement the process.

The second dimension of power suggests that our political system is not as open as we might believe and that barriers are constructed that hinder authentic participation at the decision making table. In this dimension, empowerment means promoting people's participation in decision-making. In order to build the skills of citizens to challenge this form of power, energies must be directed at mobilizing and organizing broad-based and participatory people's organizations that can gain access to the political arena. As access grows people's capacity to turn nonissues into issues increases. Who participates is as important as how to participate effectively. Thus, action and reflection are the elements of PR that help to bring relational knowledge to the forefront and research and education add additional ingredients to this mix.

The third dimension of power raises questions about how the values, views, culture, and knowledge of community-based people are shaped. This in turn raises more questions about the perception of grievances and the possibilities for acting upon them. So, if we are empowering citizens to deal with the third dimension of power and questions of knowledge, culture, and consciousness, what people are participating about becomes the critical variable, and the forms of political education and awareness building the crucial change strategies. To challenge the third dimension of power, people need to develop the capacities to be active in their own efforts to make change and understand the context in which they are acting. To do that, education is necessary in order to more thoroughly understand the workings of the global social-political-economic system, envision a better world for dominated and oppressed people, and put those visions into action. It is by combining experience and critical education that people begin to learn the true nature of the oppressive structures they are challenging. They can begin to understand the matrix of domination as they connect different forms of oppression together, in turn becoming more critical, and upon reflection, able to devise better strategies to overcome powerlessness in all its forms.

The third dimension of power also suggests that researchers must enter the murky waters of socialization, media, culture, knowledge, information control, and the shaping of beliefs and ideologies in order to understand the nature of power. This approach resembles Gramsci's (1971) ideas about hegemony. Specifically, it highlights the Marxian notion that the prevailing ideas of any era serve certain interests over others. If culture and the construction of consciousness are important to resistance, how does this translate to the political work of using participatory research as a tool for empowerment? A first step is to understand the process by which resistance is developed and codified. This involves the specification on how free spaces for participatory research are created, defended, and multiplied. It is only then that we can begin to move from an analysis of individual resistors to the socialization of resistant knowledge production practices. Most of the political life of subordinate groups is to be found neither in overt collective defiance of powerholders nor in complete hegemonic compliance, but in the vast territory between these polar opposites (Scott, 1990, p. 136). Participatory research offers one vantage point where free social space exists to carry out and grow the discourse of resistance with people's experiences, knowledge, and culture. The case of the Yellow Creek Concerned Citizens offers a number of insights into the process of PR and provides an experiential basis to ground the theoretical and epistemological framework discussed here.

THE YELLOW CREEK CONCERNED CITIZENS

The project takes place along the Yellow Creek, which flows past the town of Middlesboro, KY and consequently by the Middlesboro Tanning Company before it empties into the historic Cumberland River. Up until the mid-1960s, the company tanned hides with vegetable dyes that were biodegradable. They colored the stream but did not seem to have any toxic side effects. Occasionally, wastes tainted with dye were released in such massive amounts that they killed a number of fish by using up the oxygen supply while decomposing in the creek water. However, compared to what was to come this was something the people could at least live with. In 1965, the company introduced a chrome tanning process, based on the toxic element chromium. Along with that, the tannery also began to use some 200 additional chemicals and minerals as it moved from a vegetable-based to chemical-based tanning process.

Beginning in 1980, a group of residents of Yellow Creek, Kentucky opposed the Middlesboro Tanning Company's negligence and lack of concern for community health. They believed that someone should be held accountable for the effects of the disposal of hazardous substances into the municipal sewage treatment plant and thus into Yellow Creek. Toxins from the tannery overran the city's sewage treatment plant poisoning the water supplies of all those that lived along the creek. City officials and company owners denied the problem and worked to cover it up. Thus, the residents formed the Yellow Creek Concerned Citizens Organization (YCCC) to fight for their rights and, in a real way, their lives.

With the help of the Highlander Research and Education Center, YCCC used the Freedom of Information Act to develop information on the company and chemicals involved. They worked with university researchers and scientists to determine the extent of the poisoning. In the process the members of YCCC conducted community health surveys, videotaped waste dumping, city meetings, group activities, and actions, and educated themselves and others about community environmental health. Their own work along with studies by the Center for Disease Control (CDC) eventually revealed that leukemia rates along the creek were more than five times the national average. The rates of miscarriage and birth defects were equally alarming, as were a number of other types of cancer and the unlikely occurrences of a variety of highly unusual diseases. As a direct result of this community-based PR project, the residents along Yellow Creek were able to get a safe water line to each home and eventually win a class-action suit against the tannery. A jury of their peers found the tannery company owners guilty of gross negligence. They, along with the city of Middlesboro, were ordered to provide for a multimillion dollar health fund to monitor, identify, and treat the effects of the poisoning in the Yellow Creek community.

Participatory Research, Advocacy, and Representative Knowledge

The production of representative knowledge guides many PR projects. This is so because representative forms of knowledge are the only kind establishment institutions and structures will validate. As will be seen in the struggles along Yellow Creek, the science of the people was at first disregarded by political decision makers but eventually was proven to have produced better knowledge than that provided by the tannery or the city. During a workshop on PR at the Highlander Research and Education Center, activists Sheila and Larry Wilson shared a number of experiences and observations based on their 20-year involvement with YCCC. They provide an overview of their work and highlight some of the activities that proved, in their view, to be essential in the ultimate successes of this PR project.[3]

Yellow Creek is a little creek that flows through where I [Larry] was born and raised. I am the fifth generation of family on the same property there. The creek is 14 miles long from the point of discharge and there is a leather tanning company located upstream in the county's largest town. Middlesboro has a population of 10,000 people or 1/3 the population in the entire county. As the water came downstream from the tannery, it was black, red, blue, white, and green water, it was all colors. We had a very colorful creek, but it came at a very high price: dead fish, a dead creek, dead farm animals, and dead people.

As our farm animals grew sick and eventually died we started talking to the neighbors about it and found that people had been concerned about water from the creek for years. We had been gone from the farm for about 15 years and apparently a great deal had changed. So we wondered about what we could do. When we began to look, we found out that a lot of awful things seemed to be going on: pregnancies with still-borne babies, lots of miscarriages, something in just about every home along the creek. At first, we were mainly concerned about the farm animals, recreation, and the lack of fish in the creek. When we first began to realize people were dying, we thought there must be something we can do. We hate to be accused of doing popular research, or whatever you want to call it. We have never used those words on Yellow Creek. One reason for that is that we had been researched to death up there as long as I can remember: sociologists, cultural anthropologists, psychologists, government officials, you name it, they came and did research on us. My dad had a saying about all those researchers; he said, "Son, figures don't lie, but remember liars sometimes figure." So, we had a lot of distrust of what we call hard research.

Then after we had been working for awhile on the problems with our creek we were asked to testify before the re-appropriation of the Clean Water Act in 1982. We had no idea what we were going to talk about. Here we had a chance to go to Congress, you know the big house, because there's where you get results because everybody knows they have the power to make things right. Right?

So in order to have something to tell the Congress, we went door to door in our community. Yellow Creek has about 300 households and around 900 to 1,000 people. When we started talking to people, the first thing we did was organize; we started sharing information and gathering information, I guess that might be research too.... Anyway, we tried to learn what it was that was going on. So we were asked to testify, and I don't even remember we had around, I don't know how many members, but at this time, we have 450 people out of the 900 or so in the community. But we went door to door to look at these birth defects that Sheila was talking about; "Our Problems In Pregnancy," we called it. What we discovered was something different: a lot of children had leukemia. So we checked with some of the national cancer registries to find out what the incidence rates for leukemia were. Ours seemed to be double what it was for the nation. So not knowing any better we went up to congress with a couple of van loads of people and said, "We have got twice the amount of leukemia as other places, you've got to do something about it." Our own congressional representative then told us, "We can prove that is wrong." Now this was very objective; "We can prove you are wrong." So our congressional representative called the Center for Disease Control (CDC), they came up and did a survey, and boy did they prove us wrong. They found that we did not have double the amount of leukemia: we had 5-7 times the normal rate!

Here is where we have trouble talking about this, because first, what we have had to do is figure out a strategy of what we wanted to do. Then we have tried to discover what we needed to learn in order to actually do what we thought we wanted to do. Then we had to learn what information do we need to be armed with in order to do this work. To do this work and to try to share it with the rest of the community so that everybody in the community was involved and understood. So organizing, educating, and research are intermingled, and we find all of them to be inseparable, so if we misspeak, you academics please forgive us. But, we came back from our trip to the Congress and we did a health survey door to door. Out of the 900 or so people along the creek we interviewed 97 percent of them face to face. Then we collated the data and worked with some students from Vanderbilt University to analyze it. This time our research showed similar problems to the leukemia one with every health effect you could think of. We had something like 10 times the normal cancer rate and on and on.

During this same time, we contracted with attorneys to help us address our grievances legally and they wanted experts to furnish the information we needed for our court case. Now we had a long history of everybody feeling put upon and knowing these expert types always took something away from us, not helped us. We know that despite how poor we are, we have some of the world's richest deposits of coal, oil, natural gas, timber, and water, and people were always coming in to "help us," and what they really were doing is "helping themselves to our stuff." So we didn't trust anyone, and when they wanted to hire experts, our group insisted that they not, we would do that: we will hire the experts. So here's a bunch of people, most without a high school education, going out and interviewing all these PhDs, MDs, etc., and saying, "No we don't want you to work for us we want this person." I remember one of those instances. The group went to the University of Kentucky; the lawyer came up with the idea that we had been psychologically damaged. He was going to get a psychologist so he could claim it in court. So the first thing is that this psychologist said is, "We will have to design a special study down there because everybody knows that people in Eastern Kentucky are functionally illiterate." So our delegation got up, walked out, and said we don't want him, he is prejudiced. We did this interview process with all of the experts that worked with us. In fact, we had to teach our lawyers that we were always to be a part of the research or anything that needed to be done.

Another interesting story is that this fellow, an aquatic biologist who had been doing a study for months and months along the creek. He had set up stations, very scientific, all down the creek at different points and he was checking aquatic life, sediments, and chemicals in the water. He had his control station upstream from the discharge point of the tannery, or at least above the main pipe that ran from the factory. One day he called me. He had been doing this for months now; he had been coming up there twice a week taking these samples and analyzing them. He said, "There is something wrong up here at my control station." I said, "What is it?" He replied, "Well, what appears to be raw fecal material and toilet paper are floating by. What is it?" I said, "Where is your control station?" He told me and I said, "Well, it is probably raw fecal material and toilet paper." Right upstream from where he had his control station is where they bypass all city sewage including tannery wastes when the water treatment plant is overloaded. Thus his data was all wrong and he really had no controls for his study. So he had to throw out all the data and start months of work over again. We decided that next time we had better help him pick the spot for his control station. So we had a lot of that going on.

Where this process really came to a head was in the first trial. As we told our attorneys, our biggest goal was that we wanted everybody in the community to tell their stories to a jury of their peers. We didn't care if we won or lost at that point. If we could get to do that, we would be happy, and their job was to get us on the stand. Well the first thing the court did was to not allow us to use the health survey that we had worked so hard on. But remember everybody in the community knew about the survey and participated in doing and analyzing it. What had happened is that it had sensitized people to know about the types of illnesses that they should watch out for in the community so every time somebody got sick they would relate that to the creek and would debate whether or not it had caused that illness. So when they got on the stand, it was somewhat accidental in a way, but everybody started talking about the diseases. We had two cases of Kawasaki disease, whose ratio should be one in every several million, several cases of Krohn's disease, Wagner's disease, Graves' disease, which Sheila has also, and things like we had babies being born with spinal defects, like spina bifida.

When our doctors and experts came on and took the stand the lawyer said, "All these people have testified about all these diseases and the effects they have had on them. What diseases would you expect in a population that lived so close to these chemicals?" Well, he started to name them: Kawasaki disease, Krohn's disease, Wagner's disease, the very ones the people had testified about earlier. Because they had learned and were in a way experts about the health impacts of the creek because of our health survey and the information we tried to share with others, these sensitizing experiences and their effects on the community proved really important to our success. Then when the aquatic biologist got up on the stand, he had done embryo studies on aquatic life, and showed these big color photos of these grossly deformed fish that had been hatched in Yellow Creek water. They all had the same spinal defects in those fish that the women were talking about in their children.

We have had a number of results, some good and some not so good. The medical fund, a clean creek, and having fresh water to drink are some of the tangible results. So are a number of other community organizations linked either directly or indirectly to our organizing efforts in Yellow Creek. Our community has worked to elect officials that are sympathetic to our causes and help us to solve our problems instead of cover them up. Some of the other results were not as good, the violence: we were shot at, our brake lines were cut, the whole nine yards. So all of the results weren't good either. Nevertheless, we have had a whole lot of success and we hope we don't have to but would do it all again if we needed to!

According to adult educator Juliet Merrifield (1993), an active participant in the YCCC project, doing the survey as PR had some important effects on the members of YCCC and on the community of Yellow Creek itself. Doing the survey gave members of the group a reason and incentive to call on each household along the 14-mile stretch of creek. They had the chance to sit down and discuss not only health issues and concerns, but also many other problems community members were experiencing. Through the project the leadership in the organization was broadened and strengthened. A number of the major activists on the survey were local women who became better informed and more vocal and confident in advocating for their work. The PR approach allowed the group to mobilize resources from within and outside the community connecting two broader issues and structures. The study itself provided concrete information not formerly controlled by the community. They found a statistically significant association between ill heath and exposure to creek water. They used that information to persuade local, state, and federal officials of the seriousness of the situation along Yellow Creek. In fact, they found cancer rates 2-3 times the national average while local and state officials claimed their findings inaccurate. When the Center for Disease Control finally came into the community many months later to carry out an official health survey, they did find out that the community's statistical analysis was indeed off. The real rate of many cancers among local residents was nearer to *seven* times the national average! Based on this PR project and a lot of effort and will on the part of many, the citizens of Yellow Creek have since won a long court battle. Things will be better for future generations of people who live along Yellow Creek. Although, for the adults who have had to live through, the children who had to grow up with, and the yet unborn, who will bare the ill effects of this contaminated brew, this "victory" hardly makes up for the unrelenting health problems faced by families on the creek.

YCCC also developed representative knowledge at another level by using video cameras, content analysis, and collective learning. This method also created relational and reflective knowledge at a number of levels. During interviews, YCCC members Clyde Smith, Larry Wilson, and Gene Hurst, each talked about the important and valuable roles that video documentation served in their work.

Clyde: *I don't think I did anything much; I was just along for the ride mostly. I got a video and took some videos of some of the council meetings had up here in Middlesboro and things of that sort. I left all the dirty work to the other people. I guess John Gaventa is the one that gave me the idea to get a video camera. We had these hot discussions in these council meetings and he had that video camera; it would kind of help council members to stay in line when they were looking on. So I thought, well, John and them can't come up here every time there is a meeting, so I went and got a camera and started attending the meetings and filming them myself. That way we would have it for a record too. And we did that and we filmed a lot of them, didn't we Larry?*

Larry: *Clyde probably did almost 100 percent of our documenting in terms of public meetings and actions and things. That is back when video cameras were not common. He may have had the only one in the county*

Clyde: *I know one thing: I used one up, you know one of those old big ones with the power packs you wore on you hips. Heck, it pretty near took two people to carry it all. Well, I used it up you know; the color went bad. Then I finally got me one of those little ones.*

Larry: *Clyde would set that big old camera up before council meetings and they would think he was from the TV station or something and treat him real well at first. Reverse intimidation you know. Another thing good that came of that camera was that we could show the film back to each other and we could use it to critique ourselves. You know there was a missed opportunity to make a point and the like, and we could see how they would change questions and shift subjects on us. Then we could make sure we were better prepared next time. You could also show people the film and see people actually doing things and have a better impression than just hearing someone else tell you about it. Many people in our group couldn't always go to the council meetings and they could watch the film and get just as mad as we did and often times pick up on things that we didn't.*

Clyde: *Sometimes we would use the camera when we were having get- togethers just among ourselves; I would film that too. In addition, when we had a bunch of people organizing for clean water up the road, I did some things for them too. We took some pictures of the creek running black, documented releases, fish kills, and some of that. You see they are from over the mountain and they were trying to organize themselves to stop some strip mining that was going to pollute their drinking water supply. So they asked our group for some help and I was interested in that too, because Cannon Creek is where my drinking water comes from. So I attended their meetings and tried to help them learn how to do some of these things we did with the video.*

           You see, I wouldn't ask when I would go in to start filming; I would just go in, set it up, and put the burden on them to stop me. That's been another use of the video to help us document trials and things, court hearings, cause hearings, temporary restraining orders, trials and the like. We documented them and shared them with others. You know trials are intimidating and we could get people to see them in progress and maybe start participating. Also it was good to watch and see how they misled you or got you off the point you were driving at and got away with it. Then the next time they can't get away with it so easy. You just can't measure how important that is.

Gene: *You know your own words being fed back to you sometimes don't make a good meal. I think one of the reasons we have been able to do what we have done for such a long period of time in terms of not only dealing with the chemicals, but also fighting our government, is that we taped every word in our own meetings and with all the officials we ever talked to. We took videos of all our dealings with people in power whenever we could. You know*

> *people in power are so used to dealing with individuals and they want you to believe that they are interested in your well being. We were able to show those videos to those same people still in government 10 years later and let them hear their very own words from 10 years back. We were comfortable with that because we had it all on tape; we had the patronage, the lies, and the stories. We actually fed it back to them and make them live by, or change their words. It was very effective and served us well.*

Video documentation served to produce useful representative knowledge on a number of counts. It proved useful for self-critique, reflection, and individual and collective learning by the members of the organization. Video analysis documented and helped increase the ability of the group to hold people in power to the words they spoke in public forums. The method also offered a way to share events, actions, and activities with members who could not participate. Inside the community, the videos have provided concrete evidence of this story as a form of people's history and culture. They also provide a way for others from outside the community to learn from the YCCC experiences. Not only did the video documentation produce representative knowledge, it also offered some initial insights into the roles of relational and reflective knowledge in participatory research. Reflective knowledge, or critical consciousness, was being generated as people used the videos to learn about themselves and when they were used to challenge people in power to hold their words. By using the videos to share experiences with other members, relational knowledge was being created with other members, rather than denied them simply because they may have had to work or take care of family.

Experience, Mobilizing, Action, and Relational Knowledge

The ability to create and use relational knowledge played a large role in the YCCC movement. Sheila and Larry Wilson traced the early aspects of the organizing efforts in Yellow Creek to experiential and relational knowledge. They understand the origins of the effort to be tied to the first attempts to use people's experiences with the creek and relationships with each other to mobilize local people to address the problem. Then they began to figure out how the decision-making process actually operated.

Sheila: *The first research piece for me was just looking in the state files and records and realizing how much documentation they had already and then realizing what we had been living through with them knowing about it. So that fed wanting to know what else there was. How much more is there that they know? What all do they know that they have never told us? But that's not really the first of what I would call research. The first was really talking to neighbors and finding out what other neighbors knew and had already done to try and clean up the creek. That was our very first.*

We found neighbors who had documents where they had written to the state and complained about the creek and from that we wanted to know how many neighbors had this stuff. We wanted to know how many people had written individually to the state or questioned it or whatever. Putting all that together was really the first research we did. How many of them had stories about livestock and pets dying, or changes that they had seen in the creek? That was the very elementary part of it.

We did this for a period of several weeks or months before we even openly announced that we had an organized group. We were meeting over in the Sugar Run Picnic Area on a weekly basis and people would bring letters that were written in the 50s and 60s and news clips from the 30s and 40s. That's what made us realize that there probably was a file somewhere at the state with these letters in it.

Larry: *You see as far as we knew when we started we were the only community-based environmental group in the world. We didn't know that anybody else had done it or was in fact doing it at the same time we were. We weren't even thinking of it in those terms. We never considered the fact that there were any other communities that faced this sort of situation and tried to confront it in an organized manner. We have heard about a lot of them since then, you know: Times Beach started about the same time we did and a bunch of others before and since. But we didn't even think that there might be a group in Love Canal. It wasn't as if we were saying, boy, do we have something here that is unique and we are going to invent the wheel. The fact is, we just didn't know anyone that was doing it and so we just started to make our own way. We didn't have any models or anything. So everything we did involved research because we were operating in that vacuum of ignorance, or unawareness.*

The other or next major sort of research we had to do was really trying to figure out who had the responsibility for monitoring this problem in our creek. Who had responsibility for enforcing the laws? What was that structure? What role did the city government play in this? You see we never even considered them to be a part of this. It was in a USEPA hearing that we first learned that the enforcement responsibilities lay with the little city of Middlesboro. You see we didn't know that and the EPA said you need to talk to the city about this. They hold the permit for this kind of dumping because the tannery dumps into their water treatment plant.

So we then we went directly to the City Council. But you see we didn't even know that at first. We had to learn the hierarchy, the structure. Then we had to learn what a permit meant. You mean there is some sort of permit that is written that says they can do this? Then we had to learn who monitors that. We were astounded to learn that the city monitors it themselves. In other words, the fox is in charge of the hen house. You know we couldn't believe that stuff.

Clyde Smith, a life-long resident along Yellow Creek and the videographer for YCCC, helps to demonstrate the impacts of relational knowledge on an individual. Clyde had a great deal of experiential knowledge about the condition and effects of the toxic creek. However, he did not know how to use that information to change the situation. It was not until he began to share his knowledge and experiences with others that he began to understand that maybe there was something to be done about the creek; critical consciousness was evolving.

Clyde:　*I remember one time in particular that they had a really big fish kill, the dogs were dragging them up in the yards, and it really stunk. It don't take much of that to make you want to do something, but if you don't know what to do there is nothing that you can do. You see it began really when I was a boy back before this organization ever started. I would see the creek running black and would have to swim in it if I was swimming and I did. When you would go fishing hoping to catch some fish, you would get down there and it would be running black. Then you would just have to turn around and come back home—unless you could find a clear stream that was running into it. Then you might catch a few. I was mad and aggravated with them then, but I thought there wasn't anything I could do about it so when this organization started up I hopped right on that thing as soon as I heard about it. I figured it was going to be the only chance I had to do something about our creek. I was already interested in the thing when it started so when it did I was ready to go.*

We had a state game warden that lived just down the road and he tried for a number of years to do something about it himself, but he didn't get very far. Then we had this state senator, he tried to stop it, and he didn't get very far either, because you see he didn't have enough help. When this group started, I didn't know if that would work or not either, but it looked like the best chance that we were going to have. We all jumped on the bandwagon and it worked. It has been a long struggle, but it has worked. You know it's hard to do anything with the politicians and business folks. You know they have got the power and they band together and you can hardly do anything with them you know. But since I have been involved in YCCC it's made me realize that there is something you can do when you join together and start at it the right way: some things can be done.

Clyde moved from being a singular individual with a great deal of folk knowledge about a situation, to a person acting in an organized way to mobilize with others to make change for the better. Relational knowledge provided the impetus for the seeds of reflective knowledge to grow. Clyde's experiences also serve to show that relational knowledge is not enough to make social change. Representative and relation knowledge must be connected to reflective knowledge in order to produce action and intended consequences. Hotense Quillen and Gene Hurst offer other meaningful examples of the role of relational knowledge in the YCCC struggle.

Hotense: *You see, we were a part of this all the way up and down the creek; you*
            couldn't help but be a part of it. Up until we did our survey, I had never
            been up and down the creek like that before. I had run up and down it as
            people would you know, but not house to house and place to place. That was
            real exciting because you could discuss much more than just this with the
            people. You could begin the discussion because you knew their folks, or you
            knew someone that was connected to them in some way. You could go in
            with this conversation, and that would lead into your health survey. If we
            had used students, or professionals to conduct our survey, it would have
            never happened. Strangers can't come into a community around here and
            get the kinds of information we got about people's personal health.

Gene: *The women who did the interviews saw it as they went up and down the*
            creek. They began to see patterns that some of the rest of us didn't.

Hotense: *When we were doing this, all we were seeing was one disease after another*
            in the same household, in the same families, all the way up and down the
            creek—and there we have got 14 miles of it—and you could see that we had
            the same diseases coming up in every community. You could see that, espe-
            cially after you had been through the surveys so many times, as you were
            coding them and what not. You almost had to see it.

Gene: *The women that did the interviews realized what was happening as they pro-*
            gressed up and down the creek, but they also began to see some other things.
            Like in the time of a great deal of rainfall a lake actually forms where Yellow
            Creek runs into the Cumberland River. This thing can extend for a mile and
            a half back. Your gardens and your low lands and stuff are all under water.
            It stands there for several hours and in some cases up to a day before it goes
            back down. So this water became stationary, backwater if you will.

            At that time, if the rainfall was heavy enough, all of the lagooning system,
            and in some cases the entire wastewater treatment plant, would be under-
            water. At that time, the wastewater plant also had a seasonal permit, which
            meant that if you had an extra 3 feet of water in the creek, you could throw
            anything you wanted, in any amount into it. Hotense and the other women
            picked up on it that things are much worse along the creek where this water
            is standing and soaking into the ground, and into the wells, and into peo-
            ple's homes in some cases. They figured out that they had a more severe
            problem down there.

Through their knowledge of their neighbors and community, YCCC interviewers were allowed access and to ask questions and get answers that strangers likely
would not have been able to get. It also allowed a 97 percent response rate; an
almost unheard of rate in most traditional science. Although the community-based
health survey was never allowed to be used in court as evidence, it proved to be a
tool that generated all three forms of knowledge and was quite important for
empowering people at multiple levels. The interviewer's ability to be on the same
"critical plane" as the interviewees helped to produce and access knowledge that

would otherwise have been unattainable. The bifurcation between the researcher and the researched was nonexistent, as they were in this example one and the same people. The researchers were and are from the community carrying out the investigation. People's experiential and relational knowledge of the community served to benefit the investigation, not take away from it. The importance of common knowledge of the community and the life experiences of those with a problem cannot be underestimated. In this example, it also helped those involved to begin to see patterns in the data they had collected. Relational knowledge provided the impetus for further research, education, organizing, mobilizing, and action. Then when powerless people combined their experiential and relational knowledge with representative knowledge to mobilize against the powerful, reflective knowledge and action was generated. It was then that some success was gained in altering oppressive institutions and structures in order to serve the community base.

Putting It All Together: Learning, Empowerment, and Reflective Knowledge

Trying to clean up the creek had a noticeable impact on many people active in YCCC. Community members came to new critical understandings of the social, cultural, political, and economic systems. In individual and collective ways they have taken more control over their own lives, have clearly come to define their own interests, and are working to achieve those interests. They may not have power, but they certainly are becoming empowered and developing reflective knowledge through their experiences with participatory research. Sheila Wilson described her path toward more critical consciousness.

> *You know I went into this thing thinking that all we had to do was tell the people who had the power to do something about our poisoned creek about it and they would fix it. But then I began to see all these things that the state and the tannery knew about and had known about all along, and that they still weren't willing to do anything about it. That they could sacrifice a certain number of people's lives for one company and that was OK. But OK for whom? Us that live on Yellow Creek, or the tannery and the city? That made me realize really quickly that the most renewable resource is people and that we are cared the least about. So I guess when I really started understanding how the system worked and how business, government, and the legal justice system keep people powerless is by trying to access them and then trying to get them to work for us rather than those in power.*

For Sheila a deepening critical awareness emerged and arrived through experience, education, and reflection. Gene Hurst and Hotense Quillen, in a running exchange during an interview, talked of experiences that helped to transform their thinking and behavior.

Hotense: *It would take a blundering idiot to not see what's going on in terms of our
             health survey. I mean, you go in and everyone is telling you the same thing.
             You can't keep hearing that without getting concerned about it. But accord-
             ing to the professionals, you aren't supposed to get concerned about it. But
             if you are a human being how can you help it?! Doing each interview just
             gave us more proof that we were right about what we were doing and that
             we were going to succeed in what we had taken on. We were going to suc-
             ceed because we had to; it was too important: there were people dying, chil-
             dren dying with leukemia and people with cancer all over the place. The
             residents along Yellow Creek had those kinds of problems that were directly
             associated with the kinds of chemicals that were in our creek.*

             *My involvement in YCCC changed my whole thought process. First, it
             changed me politically from nothing to something because you have got the
             same thing either way you go. We are the country and we should be telling
             these folks what to do. What's changed me the most is how just knowing
             about our problems, more than maybe I want to.... I also see the lackadaisi-
             cal people that don't do anything about it. Even my pop will say, "Well they
             were elected to do something about it." But I know now that most of them
             don't give a damn about us country folk anyway.*

Gene: *When this whole thing started, and this year makes 20 years for me, I was
             angry. Some part of my growing-up years enjoying the creek had been taken
             away from me and it had been taken completely away from my children and
             grandchildren. When I got into YCCC, I wasn't angry anymore; I was
             scared. You know we here in Appalachia have always had a deep appreci-
             ation for the federal government. If they said it was OK, it was OK. What
             you realize growing up in rural Appalachia when you see the politics you
             see, you know that things aren't as they should be. Each county in Kentucky
             is like a little feudal system within that boundary. When I started, I knew
             that about the county but the state I wasn't as familiar with. As we went on,
             I began to see there wasn't much difference in how they did things either. It
             was a continuation of the same process; might makes right. I mean, if you
             have the power, the control, the money, whatever, regardless of who you
             hurt, or what it might effect, that's always right. Then when the federal gov-
             ernment got involved, we found that we just had another layer of the same
             onion. It looked the same; it smelled the same. You take off each layer and
             it is just the same.*

Hotense: *For example, when the EPA sent their attorney in here to investigate, he
             began to make such comments. He made more fun of our new high school
             and said things like, "if it weren't for the house that would be a nice piece
             of property." He was just an ignorant son of a bitch and to send him in here
             to make fun of us and to think this is what we have got helping us really
             makes you mad.*

Gene: *The first trip I made to Frankfort, Kentucky, the state capital, on business
             for YCCC, was quite a learning experience. We have always known that in
             Kentucky you have these sort of two states, the bluegrass area, and then us*

over here in the mountains. We walked in and met the lieutenant governor, and to be patronized by the very institution that should be helping you is an incredible thing. You know they actually said thinks like, "Mr. Wilson and Mr. Hurst, we realize you are from the mountains and you just have to understand that's the way we do things here." I don't know what the word is: "patronized," I guess is best. That was probably the biggest thing I learned up to that point. I just found out the feelings of our political people, what they think about us, our environment, and our lives. and I don't think I like what I learned. They still have that attitude today. We had a severe problem, not just for us but people 50 or 60 miles downstream who were drinking this stuff. We tried to tell these people from the state what was going on and they just kind of pat you on the head and say you'll hear from us. Just go on back down there and we'll handle it, which at this point we don't believe any of.

Let me tell you the first thing that strengthened us is that we did the health survey. It was all taken and all computed and showed us what was going on. But, before that was ever released, the Secretary of Natural Resources went public and basically said, Whatever it says it's wrong, it wasn't sanctioned by us and the people who did it were not professionals. So regardless of what it says it isn't worth anything. In other words, what she was saying was that she really didn't care what our study said. She disowned every part of it and would not accept any part of it, just because local people did it. It didn't make any difference what we found. In fact, before we did our survey, she said that the state would take care of it, but of course they never did. You know as a state, if you don't recognize a problem you don't have a problem, but once you recognize it you have got to do something about it. It took us almost 5 years to get a state official to admit that our problems were coming straight from the water treatment plant by way of the tannery.

Hotense: *We watched night after night, taking pictures of raw sewage and sludge going in. We had a state inspector here and it rained. He saw what they did in terms of emptying the lagoons and the sludge ponds and stuff going right into the creek... but he went back and wrote his report and said everything looked like it was working just fine to him! Well what are you supposed to do when the professionals tell you that stuff and then you see your neighbors dying.*

Gene: *It is a hard lesson when you learn that you can't trust your local businesses, or the federal, state, county, and then local governments to do what is right by you.*

It is only when this shiny, thin veneer is stripped away from the surface of the political economic system that people begin to achieve more critical awareness. Larry Wilson also talked about what he learned through his experiences with participatory research.

What I learned from doing this kind of work is that I want a revolution. I think the only way to get one is to create a better understanding about why we need it in the first place. That means we have to have some information to work with about conditions and possibilities and about how to work differently and to do things differently. And I am talking about a revolution that changes the structure so the capitalists don't own the system and that grassroots folks do have some control. So as long as we keep trying to work at that concept we can't help but work in a way that includes participation and a way for people to act to change their own worlds. Doing participatory research offers those kinds of possibilities to people. The chance to work for an active democracy and to make changes in their own communities. To experience and get the kinds of knowledge about how the system works and develop ways to change it. That's what I have learned.

I can't think of one aspect of my life that hasn't been changed by this process. From what I buy at the store, to what materials I read, to how I view the news on television. The subtleties of news commentaries that used to indoctrinate me that I would have never seen. I can't think of any aspect of it. The relationship between Sheila and I. I can now see what a chauvinist pig I was and still am sometimes. But now I see it and am trying to get over it and do something about it. You know we are indoctrinated to be that way and all of this process has helped to bring that out.

Consciousness and empowerment were certainly increased in members of YCCC; reflective knowledge was grown and used in individual and collective ways. Their experiences serve to show how grassroots people can go through the process of making a private trouble into a public issue. It began with individuals understanding there seemed to be a problem with dying farm animals. They then moved toward a common understanding among a large group of community members that indeed a problem existed with their creek. They used multiple forms of knowledge to mobilize the community, learn about their problems, and then began to do something about them. After organizing themselves, YCCC began a research effort to see and assess local health conditions. By chance, they were actually given the opportunity to present their case to a group of people with some power to help them in their struggles: The United States House of Representatives. During testimony, their community-based and participatory research was ridiculed as "biased" and hardly the kind of "hard data" that could influence decisions at that level. When the official experts from the Centers for Disease and Control arrived on the scene to do some real science they, rather than invalidating the community's research, instead affirmed their findings. The knowledge produced by the community proved to be very influential in winning their court case on a number of counts. Thus, a community organizing effort rooted in experiential and relational knowledge evolved into a full-scale research endeavor. This combined with participation in action, education, and reflection helped to empower individuals to effect change. In a number of situations, the community was able to use their knowledge and experience to improve expert research, but more importantly, they used it to change their own lives and circumstances. Put another way, when working for social change the questions asked by the pluralists—who makes decisions and how—are indeed crucial ones that need be answered during the early efforts of any group doing PR. As suggested by the second dimension of power, people must be keenly aware of the mobilization of bias and nondecisions at structural levels. Thus, people need to learn why issues are not on the decision-making table. This is necessary in order to mobilize and do effective actions that can give voice to people's grievances. In addition and most importantly, we must also deal with the control of consciousness and hegemony identified in the third dimension of power. Critical and popular forms of educational practice that are rooted in people's experiences help to overcome this aspect of power.

SUMMARY—PARTICIPATORY RESEARCH AND COMMUNITY-BASED CHANGE

Popular knowledge, political learning, and people's culture are all crucial elements in the process of community-based problem solving and democratic social change. By combining them to deal with community problems, people are involved in producing and using multiple types of knowledge. They are also building the capacities to advocate, organize, and transform consciousness. Each of these activities in turn helps people and their organizations act upon their issues and organize against the mobilization of bias in decision making. Education that builds on these experiences and helps people to develop connections between their own reality and the socially structured world moves people toward understanding the nature of domination in the global system. Knowledge produced in this fashion can empower participants, and in many instances, provides a much more thorough understanding of the world, than that developed by researchers using traditional scientific methodologies.

What I have tried to demonstrate is that each dimension of power implies a strategy for overcoming powerlessness, in turn implying the competencies, skills, and knowledge needed to make the strategy effective. Participation in and reflection on research, action, and education help people to produce representative, relational, and reflective knowledge in order to advocate, organize, and transform consciousness. Each element of PR has primary, secondary, and tertiary functions in the effort to alter the power of elites. Participation is critical at every level of PR. In well done projects like YCCC, participation by those effected by a problem is an integral part of each facet in the process. Moreover, all members of the project will critically and systematically reflect on all aspects of the work as an ongoing process and occasionally in times of more concerted and purposeful individual and group reflection. The idea is to assess whether the work is having the desired impacts and if not, to revise it.

For the folks in YCCC, participation in research blended into education and then into action. Participation in research was to do action and education. Participation in education was to do research and action. Knowledge, learning, and transformed consciousness were gained and produced through critical reflection that was an inherent part of everything. The elements of PR fade one into the other, one out of the other, ever changing and evolving in a chaotic and tangled, yet visibly successful empowerment and change strategy. Overall, we must conceive of the participatory research process as interactive and cyclical moving between participation and reflection.

The multiplicity of activities PR entails are happening to people all at once. Individual and collective critical consciousness, and skills and capacities to make change are improving and spiraling upward. I understand it as if an individual or group were inside a tornado in terms of imagining how PR works at its most basic level. People are producing multiple forms of knowledge and challenging power at multiple levels. People are increasing their skills as active participants in their daily and civic lives, empowering themselves, and growing their consciousness while attempting to transform social structures. PR is a process that is in constant motion, impacting individuals and collectives who practice it and the structures and institutions they encounter at different times and in different ways. The process corresponds to the proverbial same river you can never step into twice. Each time you dip into a PR project the name of the group may be the same, the people may be the same, the tasks may even be the same, but the individual and collective consciousness of the people doing the work is never in the same place again. Thus to paraphrase Chinese philosopher Lao Tsu, the sum and substance of PR is not found in the telling or showing; it is only fully understood by being involved in it!

PR is a strategy for building awareness, mobilizing for action, overcoming internalized oppressions, and addressing the structural, relational, and ongoing nature of unequal power relations in society. The essence of PR as an empowerment strategy is in the fact that it combines participation in research, education, action, and reflection. None of these elements are treated as discrete units and divided up according to area of expertise, or the most rational division of labor. Rather, a host of PR practitioners are indeed correct when they find that it is the combination of these processes that is a major strength of PR. John Gaventa, in an interview with John Forester (1996, p. 1) captures this idea.

> You see lots of things happening all at once. In any one of these meetings, just with a tape recorder like we have now, we would have gotten incredibly powerful information and data. So you're documenting knowledge. But you're also producing networks: people are making connections, making relationships with each other, which is strengthening for them, and we are also talking about action. All those things are happening simultaneously—which I think is the essence of the participatory model. It's about knowledge production, about education and capacity building and consciousness, and about action all at once. But, in our traditional

research model, or the "research for change" model, you do the research, and that's one piece. Then you educate people, and then they take action. It's linear. In participatory research, this happens all at once.

ACKNOWLEDGMENTS

Thank you to Randy Stoecker and an anonymous reviewer for their insighful and helpful comments and suggestions that improved this paper. Thank you also to John Gaventa, Helen Lewis, and Peter Park for encouraging my thinking about participatory research and empowerment and for allowing me to borrow liberally from their ideas about participatory social change. A special debt of gratitude is owed the members of the Yellow Creek Concerned Citizens for sharing their experiences with me and for participating in this work.

NOTES

1. For excellent overviews see the following: participatory action research (Fals Borda and Rahman 1991; Park et al. 1993; Stoecker and Bonacich 1992, 1993, participatory rural appraisal (Chambers 1997), participatory learning and action (Petty et al., 1995), participatory evaluation research (Rugh 1992; Williams and Park 1999), empowerment evaluation (Fetterman et al. 1996), action research (Kemmis and McTaggart 1988a, 1988b; Greenwood and Levin 1998), collaborative research (Nyden et al. 1997), community-based research (Murphy et al. 1997; Sclove et al. 1998), and feminist research (Bloom and Britzman 1998; Collins 1990; Fonow and Cook 1991; Maguire 1987).

2. Highlander Research and Education Center is a residential adult education center founded in 1932 in Monteagle, TN, by Myles Horton and Don West, and relocated to New Market, TN in 1972. Highlander is committed to the belief that people can learn to take charge of their lives and circumstance. Their goal is to advance participatory democracy through an educational program based on popular education and participatory research. For more information on the Highlander Research and Education Center's history and approach to social change see Adams (1972, 1975), Glen (1988, 1997), and Highlander Research and Education Center (1989).

3. Throughout the remainder of the text, quotes from members of YCCC are in Italics. In this part of the paper, voices merged as Larry and Sheila spoke during a workshop, so rather than dividing their words, I have chosen to weave them together. At other points in the text, quotes are labeled with the speaker's name as the conversation ensued during in-depth individual and group interviews conducted with members of YCCC in 1995-1996.

REFERENCES

Adams, F. 1972. "Highlander Folk School Getting Information, Going Back and Teaching It." *Harvard Education Review* 42(4): 433-456.

_____. 1975. *Unearthing the Seeds of Fire: The Idea of Highlander.* Winston-Salem: John F. Blair Publishers.

Alinsky, S. 1946. *Reveille for Radicals.* Chicago: University of Chicago Press.

_____. 1971. *Rules for Radicals: A Practical Primer for Realistic Radicals.* New York: Random House.

Appalachian Land Ownership Taskforce. 1981. *Land Ownership Patterns and Their Impacts on Appalachian Communities,* Vols. 1-7. Washington, DC: Appalachian Regional Commission.

Arnold, R., B. Burke, C. James, D. Martin, and B. Thomas. 1991. *Educating for a Change*. Toronto: Doris Marshall Institute for Education and Action.

Bachrach, P., and M.S. Baratz. 1970. *Power and Poverty: Theory and Practice*. New York: Oxford University Press.

Bachrach, P., and A. Botwinick. 1992. *Power and Empowerment: A Radical Theory of Participatory Democracy*. Philadelphia: Temple University Press.

Bloom, L.R., and D.P. Britzman. 1998. *Under the Sign of Hope: Feminist Methodology and Narrative Interpretation*. Albany: State University of New York Press.

Chambers, R. 1983. *Rural Development: Putting the Last First*. Essex: Longman Scientific and Technical.

_____. 1997. *Whose Reality Counts? Putting the First Last*. London: Intermediate Technology.

Collins, P.H. 1989. "The Social Construction of Black Feminist Thought." *Signs: Journal of Women in Culture and Society* 14(41): 745-773.

_____. 1990. *Black Feminist Thought*. Boston: Unwin Hyman.

Crenson, M. 1971. *The Un-Politics of Air Pollution: A Study of Non-Decision-Making in the Cities*. Baltimore: Johns Hopkins Press.

Epstein, S. 1991. "Democratic Science? AIDS Activism and the Contested Construction of Knowledge." *Socialist Review* 21(2): 35-64.

_____. 1996. *Impure Science: AIDS, Activism, and the Politics of Knowledge*. Berkeley: University of California Press.

Evans, S.M., and H.C. Boyte. 1986. *Free Spaces: The Sources of Democratic Change in America*. New York: Harper and Row.

Fals Borda, O. 1981. "Science and the Common People." Pp. 13-40 in *Research for the People, Research by the People: An Introduction to Participatory Research*, edited by D. Folke. Linkoping: Netherlands Study and Development Centre for Adult Education.

_____. 1985. *Knowledge and People's Power: Lessons with Peasants in Nicaragua, Mexico and Colombia*. New Delhi: Indian Social Institute.

Fals Borda, O., and M.A. Rahman, eds. 1991. *Action and Knowledge: Breaking the Monopoly with Participatory Action-Research*. New York: Apex Press.

Fetterman, D.M., S.J. Kaftarian, and A. Wandersman, eds. 1996. *Empowerment Evaluation: Knowledge and Tools for Self-Assessment and Accountability*. Thousand Oaks, CA: Sage Publications.

Fonow, M.M., and J.A. Cook. 1991. *Beyond Methodology: Feminist Scholarship as Lived Research*. Bloomington: Indiana University Press.

Forester, J. 1996. Transcript from interview with John Gaventa on his experiences with participatory research. In *Profiles of Participatory Action Researchers*, edited by J. Forester et al. Ithaca: Einaudi Center for International Studies and Department of City and Regional Planning, Cornell University.

Freire, P. 1970. *Pedagogy of the Oppressed*. New York: Continuum.

_____. 1973. *Education for Critical Consciousness*. New York: Continuum.

_____. 1978. *Pedagogy in Process*. New York: Continuum.

_____. 1985. *The Politics of Education*. South Hadley, MA: Bergin and Garvey.

_____. 1998. *Pedagogy of Freedom: Ethics, Democracy, and Civil Courage*. Lanham, MD: Rowman and Littlefield.

Gaventa, J. 1981. "Land Ownership in Appalachia, USA: A Citizen's Research Project." Pp. 118-130 in *Research for the People, Research by the People: An Introduction to Participatory Research*, edited by D. Folke. Linkoping: Netherlands Study and Development Centre for Adult Education.

_____. 1982. *Power and Powerlessness: Quiescence and Rebellion in an Appalachian Valley*. Chicago: University of Illinois Press.

_____. 1988. "Participatory Research in North America." *Convergence* 24(2-3): 19-28.

_____. 1993. "The Powerful, the Powerless, and the Experts: Knowledge Struggles in an Information Age." Pp. 21-40 in *Voices of Change: Participatory Research in the United States and Canada*, edited by P. Park, M. Brydon-Miller, B. Hall, and T. Jackson. Toronto: OISE Press.

_____. 1995. "Citizen Knowledge, Citizen Competence and Democracy Building." Working paper presented at the Political Economy of the Good Society Conference on Citizen Competence and the Design of Democratic Institutions, Washington, DC, February 10-11.

Gaventa, J., and B. Horton. 1981. "A Citizen's Research Project in Appalachia, USA." *Convergence* 14(3): 30-41.

Glen, J. 1988. *Highlander, No Ordinary School*. Lexington: University Press of Kentucky.

_____. 1997. *Highlander, No Ordinary School*, 2nd ed. Lexington: University Press of Kentucky.

Gramsci, A. 1971. *Selections from the Prison Notebooks*. New York: International Publishers.

Greenwood, D.J., and M. Levin. 1998. *Introduction to Action Research: Social Research for Social Change*. Thousand Oaks, CA: Sage Publications.

Hall, B.L. 1994. "Participatory Research." Pp. 4330-4336 in *The International Encyclopedia of Education*, edited by T. Husen and T.N. Postlethwaite. New York: Pergamon Press.

Hall, B.L., A. Gillette, and R. Tandon, eds. 1982. *Creating Knowledge a Monopoly? Participatory Research in Development*. Toronto: International Council for Adult Education.

Heaney, T.W. 1993. "If You Can't Beat 'Em, Join 'Em: The Professionalization of Participatory Research." Pp. 41-46 in *Voices of Change: Participatory Research in the United States and Canada*, edited by P. Park, M. Brydon-Miller, B. Hall, and T. Jackson. Toronto: OISE Press.

Highlander Research and Education Center. 1989. *Highlander: An Approach to Education Through a Collection of Writings*. New Market, TN: Author.

hooks, b. 1984. *Feminist Theory: From Margin to Center*. Boston: South End Press.

_____. 1989. *Talking Back: Thinking Feminist, Thinking Black*. Boston: South End Press.

Horton, B.D. 1993. "The Appalachian Land Ownership Study: Research and Citizen Action in Appalachia." Pp. 85-102 in *Voices of Change in the United States and Canada*, edited by P. Park, M. Brydon-Miller, B. Hall and T. Jackson. Toronto: OISE Press.

Johnson, G.S. 1996. "Toxins! Tocsin: The North Hollywood Dump in Memphis, Tennessee—A Community's Struggle Against Environmental Racism." Ph.D. dissertation, University of Tennessee, Knoxville.

Jordan, J. 1985. *On Call: Political Essays*. Boston: South End Press.

Kanhare, V.P. 1981. "The Struggle in Dhulia: A Women's Movement in India." Pp. 110-117 in *Research for the People, Research by the People: An Introduction to Participatory Research*, edited by D. Folke. Linkoping: Netherlands Study and Development Centre for Adult Education.

_____. 1982. "India: Tribal Women Organize." Pp. 24-25, 35-36 in International Council for Adult Education (ICAE), *Participatory Research: An Introduction*. New Delhi: Society for Participatory Research in Asia.

Kassam Y., and K. Mustafa, eds. 1982. *Participatory Research: An Emerging Alternative Methodology in Social Science Research*. New Delhi: Society for Participatory Research in Asia.

Kemmis, S., and R. McTaggart. 1988a. *The Action Research Planner*, 3rd ed. Victoria: Deakin University Press.

_____. 1988b. *The Action Research Reader*, 3rd ed. Victoria: Deakin University Press.

Lewis, H.M., S. O'Donnell, and the Ivanhoe History Project, eds. 1990a. *Ivanhoe History Book*, Vol. 1: *Remembering Our Past Building Our Futures*. Ivanhoe, VA: Ivanhoe Civic League.

Lewis, H.M., and the Ivanhoe History Project, eds. 1990b. *Ivanhoe History Book*, Vol. 2: *Telling Our Stories Sharing Our Lives*. Ivanhoe, VA: Ivanhoe Civic League.

Lukes, S. 1974. *Power: A Radical View*. London: MacMillan.

Madoo Lengermann, P., and J. Niebrugge. 1996. "Contemporary Feminist Theory." Pp. 436-486 in *Sociological Theory*, 4th ed., edited by G. Ritzer. New York: McGraw Hill.

Maguire, P. 1987. *Doing Participatory Research: A Feminist Approach.* Amherst: Center for International Education.

Marable, M. 1992. *The Crisis of Color and Democracy: Essays on Race, Class, and Power.* Monroe: Common Courage Press.

Merrifield, J. 1993. "Putting Scientists in Their Place: Participatory Research in Environmental and Occupational Health." Pp. 65-84 in *Voices of Change: Participatory Research in the United States and Canada,* edited by P. Park, M. Brydon-Miller, B. Hall, and T. Jackson. Toronto: OISE Press.

Murphy, D., M. Scammel, and R. Sclove, eds. 1997. *Doing Community-Based Research: A Reader.* Amherst, MA: The Loka Institute.

Nyden, P., A. Figert, M. Shibley, and D. Burrows. 1997. *Building Community: Social Science in Action.* Thousand Oaks, CA: Pine Forge Press.

Park, P. 1993. "What is Participatory Research? A Theoretical and Methodological Perspective." Pp. 1-20 in *Voices of Change: Participatory Research in the United States and Canada,* edited by P. Park, M. Brydon-Miller, B. Hall, and T. Jackson. Toronto: OISE Press.

_____. 1997. "Participatory Research, Democracy, and Community." *Practicing Anthropology* 19(3): 8-13.

_____. Forthcoming. "People, Knowledge, and Change in Participatory Research." *Management Learning.*

Park, P., M. Brydon-Miller, B. Hall, and T. Jackson, eds. 1993. *Voices of Change: Participatory Research in the United States and Canada.* Toronto: OISE Press.

Pretty, J.N., I. Guijt, J. Thompson, and I. Scoones. 1995. *Participatory Learning and Action: A Trainers Guide.* London: International Institute for Environment and Development.

Rugh, J. 1992. *Self-Evaluation: Ideas for Participatory Evaluation of Rural Community Development Projects.* Oklahoma City: World Neighbors Publications.

Sclove, R.E., M.L. Scammel, and B. Holland. 1998. *Community-Based Research in the United States: An Introductory Reconnaissance.* Amherst, MA: The Loka Institute.

Scott, J. 1985. *Weapons of the Weak: Everyday Forms of Peasant Resistance.* New Haven, CT: Yale University.

_____. 1990. *Domination and the Arts of Resistance: Hidden Transcripts.* New Haven, CT: Yale University Press.

Shor, I. 1992. *Empowering Education.* Chicago: The University of Chicago Press.

Smith, D. 1987. *The Everyday World as Problematic: A Feminist Sociology.* Boston: Northeastern University Press.

_____. 1990. *The Conceptual Practices of Power: A Feminist Sociology of Knowledge.* Boston: Northeastern University Press.

Spivak, G.C. 1989. "Can the Subaltern Speak." In *Marxism and the Interpretation of Culture,* edited by G. Nelson and L. Grossberg. Urbana: University of Illinois Press.

Stoecker, R., and E. Bonacich, eds. 1992. "Why Participatory Research?" *American Sociologist* 23(4): 5-14.

_____. 1993. *American Sociologist* 24(1).

Tandon, R. 1981. "Participatory Research and the Empowerment of People." *Convergence* 14(3): 20-29.

_____. 1988. "Social Transformation and Participatory Research." *Convergence* 21(2-3): 5-18.

Walker, A. 1988. *Living by the Word.* New York: Harcourt Brace Jovanovich.

_____. 1989. *The Temple of My Familiar.* New York: Pocket Books.

Williams, L. 1996. "First Enliven, Then Enlighten: Popular Education and the Pursuit of Social Justice." *Sociological Imagination* 33(2): 94-116.

_____. 1997. "From Common Sense to Good Sense: Participatory Research, Power, Knowledge and Grassroots Empowerment." Ph.D. dissertation, University of Tennessee, Knoxville.

Williams, L., and P. Park, eds. 1999. *Sociological Practice: A Journal of Applied and Clinical Sociology* (special edition) 1(2) June.

REUNIFYING COMMUNITY AND TRANSFORMING SOCIETY:
COMMUNITY DEVELOPMENT EDUCATION AND THE UNIVERSITY

Torry D. Dickinson

ABSTRACT

Thirty years after the first women's studies and Black studies students called for the university to actively participate in the transformation of community life, many teachers and students are now engaging in community development education (or community action research). The university's involvement in community-based research and service learning has reintroduced many of the old debates about the extent of the divide between the university and the community. Based on my involvement with four community-based social change programs (which I explore here), I argue that university classrooms and community-based social change environments often share common educational processes. These often involve peer-centered, multicultural learning activities that lead to learner-designed social change approaches. A selected review of research on peer learning circles in both university and community-based settings demonstrates that learner-centered, social change approaches have been utilized in both environments. As I worked with four social

Research in Community Sociology, Volume 9, pages 41-63.
ISBN: 0-7623-0498-7

change organizations, I discovered that social change actions often emerged from peer-centered learning activities. Then, as I outline five educational models for involving university students in community development education, I examine these models in relationship to qualitative research issues and social change processes.

SOCIAL CHANGE IN THE CLASSROOM

Democratic and egalitarian learning processes in the university and in other community settings share many educational elements in common: learner-centered education, applied learning on social change, the development of multicultural relationships and knowledge, the naming and definition of social problems by marginalized and disenfranchised groups, the development of social solutions by cross-cultural groups, the individual and collective empowerment of community members, and the formation and implementation of social alternatives that transform larger communities and societies. All of these are elements of community development education, or community action research that involves community residents and students in solving their social problems.

In this paper, community development education is presented as a way to link academic work on social change with social change activities in more informal learning contexts. My understanding of community educational pedagogy is discussed in relation to the intellectual work of bell hooks,[1] and in relation to similar educational approaches developed by Myles Horton and Paulo Freire. Through an examination of "civil society" in the United States, I briefly explore the theoretical, historical, and contemporary significance of an important social site where community development education sometimes takes place. Then I examine four of my own experiences with community development education, where similar—but slightly different—social change models were employed. Within the university context, five models for enabling students to study social change in the community are discussed: (1) public policy education, where interested parties resolve public conflicts; (2) individually tailored community action research projects of one to two semesters in length; (3) targeted internships, where all students study a related area in depth for one semester; (4) service learning, where students' limited community work substitutes for an academic classroom assignment; and (5) overseas travel courses that examine social change. I conclude with some final reflections on the social change classroom and the study of global change.

Recently the American Sociological Association and the National Women's Studies Association have developed a renewed interest in ethnographical and service learning research, reintroducing a long-standing debate about the extent of the split between the university and the community. Over the last three years, and in the coming year, many journals, conferences, and university departments will have addressed the apparent divide between academic and community organizations. Those academics who have not been teaching and conducting community action research may find themselves participating in a debate about the gap between the university and the community for the first time. Because so many schools are just beginning to move forward with service learning and enhanced internship classes, and because few community organizations reach out to schools, relationships between these two spheres are still evolving.

Based on my research, I see community development education as social change education that contains both applied and theoretical elements. If one considers the integrated knowledge acquired from both classroom and hands-on social change environments, community development education can be found in both university and community-based classrooms. Theoretically (although perhaps not historically), there is no easy divide between the university's classrooms and those of the community. They reinforce each other, and they both contribute to the cumulative development of knowledge about social change. Rather than seeing faculty members and students as tied to an elite-minded sphere that is outside of real life, I see teachers and students as members of communities, and schools as community institutions.

Education in college classrooms can come to life for students if educators start with the idea that the university is part of the community, and community organizations are invaluable sites for collaborative learning about social change. When examined from an historical perspective, "forgotten people's studies" (as they are called in the Gulbenkian Commission's report; see Wallerstein and Gulbenkian Commission 1996)—are taught in disciplines like sociology, and in multidisciplinary programs. These areas of study have been based on the understanding that academic studies, autobiography, culture, community, and applied social change experiences are all useful sources for helping students and scholars acquire knowledge about the social hierarchy and processes of social transformation. When women's studies, Black and Africana studies, Chicano studies, ethnic studies, and related programs were being initiated in the academy almost 30 years ago, considerable emphasis was placed on thinking about how to change the world. But, over the last 20 years, too few schools have valued community learning experiences. Also, universities' community-based activities often have been disconnected from curriculum. Because the university often has de-emphasized the importance of hands-on social change research, students have missed some of the excitement associated with qualitative research; and the needs of encompassing communities have been neglected in many urban and rural areas.

In addition to addressing social inequality, schools have recently become much more aware of the need to create sustainable, ecological, and alternative development patterns. Today many service learning projects engage in collaborative efforts that explore how ties between the university, community organizations, state agencies, and community-oriented businesses can benefit each other.

By strengthening the connections among classroom work and education that takes place outside of the classroom, applied researchers have demonstrated that educators can help students become effective professionals. Also, as community-based educators have shown throughout the century, the academic arm of the university can help research and even solve community problems. The social sciences, history, education, and multidisciplinary programs now are paying closer attention to learning processes that take place in community settings. In many cases, social service planning sessions, community speak-outs, community needs assessments, and nonprofit board meetings, for example, serve as informal classrooms. Educators in community-based and university classrooms are working together more closely, allowing all learners to understand and address historical and contemporary barriers that face different social groups and inhibit general community development. By fully engaging university students in academic work on social change, teachers can help successfully promote societal transformations. By conducting academic programs partly in more informal learning settings, teachers are enhancing formal learning experiences in the university classroom.

Social scientific and multidisciplinary programs can lead the way in creating academic learning experiences that enable the university to serve the communities of which it is a part. The gulf between the university and the community may not be as large as we fear it to be. As we explore our apparent separation, we may find that it is not so hard to teach students about social change practices. A shared pool of knowledge often is revealed, especially as activists rely on common, participatory learning processes. The examination of any differences in formal and informal learning settings may provide a way to consciously weave together different strands of community life that may have become artificially separated through institutional arrangements and divisive ideologies.

Getting educators and learners to assume that "all spheres are theirs," at least in a general way, is a tall order for educators in both informal learning and university settings. Unfortunately, the divide between the enclosed spaces of ivy-covered universities (including land-grant state universities which are mandated to serve the public) and other service organizations and groups has not always narrowed in recent years, even with federal and state initiatives to reward institutional collaboration. University teachers often are intimidated by the practical, real-life knowledge displayed by policy advocates and program operators. Sometimes faculty members are afraid (with reason) that they will be penalized by the university if they link their scholarship with real-world concerns.[2]

On the other hand, educators in informal learning settings often feel "put off by" and not included in activities at the university. Some of these fears are based on negative experiences with others, and some are based on assumptions that developed simply because people did not try. These tensions between teachers and practitioners often surface, demonstrating that effective collaboration takes a lot of practice and requires a new set of knowledge.

Since 1975, when the state began going through a fiscal crisis, schools became defined as major players in the process of coordinating service provision, developing shared ownership for social problems, and designing social solutions, such as developing new ways to promote job-related successes for students. Some teachers already understand that social advancements for students, their families, and communities can begin with curriculum and program development on a variety of social change-related topics. Social change learning experiences in the university may include: classroom-based leadership development for students, academic programs that include community study, and the establishment of sustained school-to-work and undergraduate-to-graduate transitions. A central part of community development is the development of people, and of learners of all ages. In the *unified community*, the university and their encompassing regional networks benefit when everyone has the opportunity to reach their potential.

The social change field is open, and teachers do not have to feel constrained by rules made by others. There are no rules that limit or clearly define the roles that teachers and students, social work professionals, educators, and volunteers can play in the process of conducting education for social change. This is partly because there is no strict divide between social change activities that take place in the university-centered part of the community and the social change activities that are organized by community-based, state-wide, regional, national, and global organizations. Educators who want to do more than talk about social change activities can now invent new ways to help students learn more about meeting their own needs, and the needs of others who are in informal educational contexts.

THEORETICAL FOUNDATIONS OF CRITICAL EDUCATION

My work on community development education has been influenced by my practical work in this field, and by bell hooks (who was influenced, in turn, by Paulo Freire). Freire conversed and debated extensively with Myles Horton, a community educator who founded Tennessee's Highlander Folk School 60 years ago. Horton's Highlander Folk School has been renamed the Highlander Research and Education Center, and it is now located near Knoxville, in New Market, Tennessee.

Myles Horton's work reflected the community organizing values of many pioneers in this field, and he influenced many critical educators who teach today.[3] Horton stressed the importance of creating true democracy, and not false and limited political liberalism. He writes: "To have democracy, you must have a society in which decision making is real, and that means replacing, transforming and rebuilding society so as to allow for people to make decisions that affect their lives" (Horton 1990, p. 174). Part of this, he stipulated, means ensuring that profit maximization does not take precedence over democratic decision making. Horton described the educational process in New Market, TN as one where adults learn about their personal interests, work with others as part of a learning group, and then make democracy work for them (see the interview with Myles Horton in the film "You got to Move" 1985). This early educational model contains many strands that closely resemble key elements in community development education.

An excellent example of the Highlander's educational and organizing approach is provided by the women, men, and children who lived in Bumpass Cove, Tennessee in the early 1980s. This community began organizing to fight the secret toxic dumping that had been taking place in the landfill near their homes. Although the Highlander Research and Education Center had included community members in their educational workshops, women began the cycle of community development education when they started to recognize that their children were becoming chronically ill. As this group of mothers began to identify and prioritize their needs, men from these households also started the process of determining whether illegal wastes were being trucked to the nearby landfill. The men videotaped the trucks' movements at all hours of the night and the women conducted archival research on what toxic wastes had been buried in the landfill over a 7–year period and what the effects of certain chemicals were. Following a flood that sent barrels of chemicals into the creek, both the women and men blocked the small dirt road leading to the landfill, stopping the trucks. As this community assumed more responsibility for its own destiny, the women started the long process of beginning to believe in themselves and in each other. Each woman stopped seeing herself "as just a housewife, a nobody" and started to recognize that the lack of a high school education did not prevent her from establishing democratic, community-based procedures for saying what should happen in Appalachia ("You Got to Move" 1985).

The method of analysis used in critical education is described by Paulo Freire (1985) in *The Politics of Education*. Not only did Freire meet and share ideas with Myles Horton in the late 1970s and 1980s, but Freire also served as a mentor for bell hooks.

As a literacy educator in Brazil, Freire was greatly influenced by the Brazilian extension service's goal that everyday learners should become experts at directing and transforming their own lives. Brazilian rural workers, who had never learned to read, became the center of the learning circles (or self-directed learning groups). The educational process began when the adults identified key concepts in their lives, which related to the landowning class, the work they did, and their culture. As they learned to read these key words, the adults learned related concepts, contributing to the widening of their world. The learners empowered themselves by linking reading, social analysis, and eventually, social action together.

Because Freire was concerned with educational processes in the classroom and in community settings, his writings and teachings encouraged many social scientists and educators to consider the relationships between scholarship, teaching, and social change practices. "History is made by us," and "history makes us while we remake it" (Freire 1985, p. 199). People's reflections become real when they act, he wrote. Through critical education, the act of knowing helps to transform the real world, and helps learners create their own world (Freire 1985, pp. 4-8, 124-125, 158).

Freire encouraged the development of circles of culture, or small learning groups that engage in critical thinking. Through praxis or cultural action, these circles enable learners to experience a reintegration and to develop a new cultural synthesis (Freire 1985, pp. 34, 155, 168, 176). Because of the comprehensive quality of critical thinking, which leads to a critique of all institutions and relations, this pedagogy offers circles of learners the opportunity to reintegrate their lives and community life in profound ways. In learner-centered environments, classrooms and small groups of learners can become learning circles.

Radical pedagogy, according to bell hooks, includes critical, feminist, and anticolonial orientations.[4] In *Teaching to Transgress*, hooks argues that teachers should create participatory learning experiences. To help students acquire knowledge about how to live in the world, teachers must "connect the will to know with the will to become" (hooks 1994, p. 19). An important part of this process is embracing multicultural relations and focusing on who speaks, who listens and why. Describing Freire's work "as living water to me," hooks places emphasis on theory, which "helps you understand what is going on around and within you" (hooks 1994, pp. 50, 59).

Believing that social struggles must be rooted in theory, hooks writes, "[m]aking theory is the challenge before us." For example, if we develop a feminist theory that addresses women's pain, she writes, "then we can make mass-based feminist resistance struggle" (1994, pp. 65, 75). Although I agree that personal testimony contributes to theory formation, the development of feminist or anticlassist social change theories in the classroom often has little to do with the development of social movements.[5] Grassroots and globally-related feminist struggles around the world often reflect social relations and social choices that we still do not understand; even involved participants may not understand how their social action affects changes in the wider set of social relations that make up societies. Many struggles are waged successfully even though participants did not start with theoretical formulations. Often activists are just beginning to understand one aspect of their situation when they start to fight for change, but their understanding grows as they engage in the process of remaking the world.[6]

By encouraging learners from different social groups to talk about and transform their intimate relationships that are created by social hierarchy, hooks is leading her students and readers through the needs identification and strategy development stages of the learning cycle. hooks compels learners to see that "it's all tied together"—patriarchy, racism, heterosexism, white female domination over black women, and capitalism, and that it is all part of a global system (hooks 1994, pp. 95, 53). As part of efforts to transform society, hooks argues, relationships need to develop in an integrated setting, where European-Americans accept that they, too, need to deal with racism, and where all learners are involved in the collective task of breaking barriers (hooks 1994, pp. 63, 101, 106, 110).

By preparing students for learning in more informal, social change settings, hooks encourages educators/learners to recognize that classroom learning, dialogical learning, and social action reinforce each other and contribute to each other. Her theoretical and dialogical approach prepare learners to integrate these learning processes together. Often engaging in constructive, controversial discussions with scholars and public figures, hooks correctly insists on the necessity for multicultural communication and problem solving in classroom settings and in public dialogue (hooks and West 1991). hooks' educational work and writing helps to prepare feminists to engage in cross-cultural dialogue, which is an integral part of community development education in classrooms and in more informal settings.

We learn from Horton, Friere, and hooks that community development involves: democratic participation in identifying and solving problems; learner-centered change based on the connection of theory with everyday life; and the creation of social movements through multicultural interaction and multilevel social analysis of gender, ethnicity, and global stratification.

When we introduce students to community development education in the *united community* (which includes university and non-classroom learning environments), we are asking them to work in a context where many forms of struggle are waged, and where many innovative (and too often disconnected) programs are developed to benefit people who have unmet social needs.

Students can be invited to study struggles that develop in multiple social sites, including the workplace, the state, and civil society. Many struggles take place in the amorphous "public" social sphere that develops outside of, but in relation to, the global economy and the state.[7] Civil society often is considered "the space of uncoerced human association" (Walzer in Fisher 1998, p. 11), but we are reminded that civil society often is despotic (Yeatman 1980). Civil society's boundaries overlap into the private sphere of households, into the public sphere of the state, and—partly through state-regulated unions—into the public sphere of the for-profit business world. Household members participate in social networks (as members of informal support networks or as nonprofit volunteers, for example) that form part of civil society. Nonprofit organizations often involve community board members, at the same time that they receive governmental contracts and grants and do state work. Many local, statewide, and national organizations are structured as nonprofit groups, where social change work, at least partly, takes place in what can be considered civil society.

As part of changes in civil society, students can study attempts to create and transform informal social institutions, such as local markets, small businesses, cooperatives, self-help networks, local clubs and organizations, independent community-based organizations, and religious groups. Many social change efforts try to increase people's power by creating social alternatives to large-scale businesses and the state. Educational theorists and practitioners in both university and community-based contexts have demonstrated that peer-centered learning circles have helped learners to understand how they can contribute to the formation of social change approaches.

Massive global changes have been taking place in the last 20 years and students need to be prepared to understand the changing context of social change movements. The last 20 years of global history in both the north and the south has been characterized by an intensification of working people's struggles, including those that take place in civil society. As part of these struggles, community development education has emerged during the last two decades partly because many learners have felt the need to define their needs, to invent long-term solutions, and to work on successfully implementing these solutions.

Twenty to thirty years ago social movements prepared students to think about changing work and public policy (as well as social consciousness), but today's movements often are directed at restructuring labor's reproductive relationships (Mitter 1997, p. 171). These efforts, which partly take place in civil society, may be directed at "reclaiming the commons" or creating sustainable living conditions where considerations about economic growth do not override efforts to meet human need. Sounding like one of Freire's students, Dalla Costa (1995, p. 11) writes that "women now represent the new outposts for interpretive insight, denunciation, and initiative, in a reversal of priority from production to reproduction."[8] By extending the classroom outward, and by bringing the community in, we are asking our students to be ready to think about, and to even participate in, the creation of new social paradigms, new definitions of civil society, and new ways of remaking the world.

INVOLVEMENT WITH COMMUNITY DEVELOPMENT EDUCATION

Although work with Oakland's Displaced Homemaker Project began helping me understand community change, I did not recognize how much I understood until I worked with the Cooperative Extension Service. This is the United States' largest volunteer-based organization, and many assume that it is simply a conservative dinosaur. I started working at the Extension Service because I wanted to think about how much employment and training programs were helping working people. Much to my surprise, the U.S. Cooperative Extension Service, based at land-grant universities, often centers it work around learner-driven, social change projects. When I worked as a statewide extension educator (specializing in aging, the work force, community development, cultural diversity, and public policy education), I began recognizing the importance of engaging universities and communities in the process of participatory education for social change. In particular, I began seeing that college students could participate in and help facilitate public policy education, which is the practice of bringing all community members into a common dialogue about a controversial public policy problem. Public policy issues might include conflicts over: access to water from a river, coastal access, adequate day care facilities, and oil spill and other environmental clean-ups.

I started to think about education as a lifelong process. I started to see lifelong learning as the relating of knowledge from everyday life, which partly came from community action work, to the process of understanding and transforming the world in concrete and diverse ways.

This is, of course, a part of theory building. I began to move from seeing the world as I thought I knew it through other people's theories; and I began to see and understand the world as I knew it, as learners around me knew it, and as other community members knew it. As I worked with diverse community-based groups, I saw that popular education and real, sustained community development go hand in hand.

In this section, I examine my experiences working with four social change projects that utilized community development education as one means of promoting social change. I focus on those program elements where people participated in the definition of their needs, and in the construction of ways to meet their needs. Although I have worked on other related projects, my understanding of community development education will be explored through my work with: Oakland's Displaced Homemaker Center, the Extension Service's Senior Community Service Employment Project in Maine, extended community action research projects carried out by students at the Western Institute for Social Research, and Kansas State University's future targeted-internship project on women's micro-enterprises and cooperatives, and its related service learning project (which forms part of course work for my courses on "Introduction to Women's Studies" and "Women and Global Social Change"). For each organization, I will identify the elements of community development education and consider how students and/or community members were able to promote social change through these projects.

Oakland, California: Displaced Homemaker Center

Meeting social activists who really care about people has made a tremendous difference in my life. My students laugh at me when they see how much fun I think it is to visit social change projects and to talk with the people who designed and benefited from them. Traveling to social change projects shows me how others have carried out education on social change. Visiting other types of organizations gives me new ideas about how to convert various social change strategies to different contexts.

Visiting organizations has also allowed me to meet some of the most amazing activists, who take on the world in really innovative and effective ways. When I was visiting the National Council on the Aging's office in San Francisco in 1983, I meet Jo Ann Wilder, who is an outspoken advocate for elders, women, and people who have faced interpersonal violence. When Jo Ann saw how much I was interested in social change issues, she told me that I had to meet Milo Smith, the cofounder of the first U.S. center for women who were re-entering school and the work force. When Jo Ann introduced me to Milo, my life really changed. Milo

Smith became my mentor and friend, and I permanently became involved in the women's re-entry movement. Milo Smith taught female and male feminists everything she knew about listening to women, supporting women as they conceived of social alternatives, developing long-term strategies for changing women's lives, and involving others in working with women. The women's job and school re-entry movement was a learner-centered one.

Just 25 years ago, re-entering middle-years women were largely considered "too old to be trained" and "unproductive," as far as many employers, universities, and employment and training officials were concerned.[9] Jobs for Older Women, which started in the East Bay, was one of the first grassroots organizations to begin helping divorced and single women who sometimes fell into poverty by the time they were 40 years old. Milo Smith formed a member of this pioneering group, which was based on the premise that middle-years women understood their situation better than anyone else. Because they understood the multiple dimensions of their situation, the idea was that they should be the ones to design the solutions. From this understanding, peer support groups emerged; this peer support group model was soon replicated when the group was reborn as Oakland's Displaced Homemaker Center. Some of the best people to help re-entering women, it turned out, were other re-entering women. These peer support groups helped women address the internal barriers (e.g., lack of self-confidence, inability to set and reach goals) and external barriers (e.g., discrimination against middle-years women, lack of institutional supports) that these re-entry women faced.

Integrated into peer support groups were peer advisers, re-entry women who had successfully navigated their way to greater self-sufficiency. By serving as volunteer peer advisers, women gained new leadership skills and remained in a supportive environment, which enabled them to become more stabilized. They were able to give back to the organization that helped them, and to pass on the skills that they had acquired.

Women formed this grassroots organization and its peer adviser support system to enable them to become socially, psychologically, culturally, politically, and economically self-sufficient. Many of the program elements that became incorporated into federal and state employment and training programs were developed in these peer support groups. The idea of comprehensive support services and one-stop service centers (which just became part of federal Department of Labor programs in 1996) emerged from the work carried out by Oakland's Displaced Homemaker Center. Peer support group and peer adviser programs also have been used by many community action agencies, youth programs, probation programs, and substance abuse programs. For example, just recently, Survival Skills for Women (a Manhattan, Kansas-based organization), which utilizes peer support and some peer adviser training, designed San Jose's YWCA peer support program that works to eliminate gang violence.

The Displaced Homemaker Center became a one-stop, comprehensive service center, as much as it could, during the years it received funds from California's Economic Development Department. After that, the center tried to get all state agencies and institutions to help re-entering employees and students by establishing special programs (at colleges, for example), and by creating one-stop service centers.

People who were going back to work or returning to school had many problems that needed to be addressed simultaneously before they could become independent. Individual needs had to be assessed and comprehensive support services needed to be accessed in order to meet individual and family needs. Because most re-entry women were responsible for taking care of dependents, it was essential that the entire family's needs were met. Comprehensive support services might include: housing, social service support (welfare), medical and dental care (including eyeglasses), individual or family counseling, drug counseling for a dependent teen, child care, transportation, job training, vocational or college education, goal identification, skills assessment, group stabilization exercises, and clothing for a job interview. The individual assessment process and the resulting comprehensive service plan addressed both external and internal barriers faced by re-entry women.

In addition to developing a broad social service and educational model, these peer support groups also identified ways that organizations needed to change if they were to meet the needs of re-entry women. Schools needed to accept middle-years students, job service offices needed to place middle-years workers, and veterans offices needed to recognize the needs of women who had served in the military. State legislatures and Congress needed to develop legislation that would recognize women's special needs that emerged from discrimination, and establish educational and employment programs that were targeted to meet women's needs.

The Displaced Homemaker Center and its advocates set the stage for the development of a statewide and national women's job and school re-entry movement. By demonstrating how to meet the full range of women's needs, the organization and the movement eventually transformed the ways that traditional employment and training programs and schools addressed women's and men's needs. It took more than 20 years for the federal government to set up one-stop career centers (where comprehensive support services are provided in one location); these government-funded centers developed as a direct result of the displaced homemaker movement's peer-centered learning groups.

At the heart of the center's invention of family support services was the learner-centered educational process, where women defined their individual and collective needs, and the solutions for their problems. One goal of the re-entry women's movement was to relocate service provision for re-entry women from the volunteer terrain of civil society to the state, including to its schools and universities and to its employment and training operations.

At the same time that Oakland's Displaced Homemakers Center secured sunset legislation in California during the mid-1970s to establish a comprehensive program to meet re-entry women's needs, advocates from this women's re-entry organization traveled to other cities and helped other women establish similar centers. Re-entry women—many from Oakland's Displaced Homemaker Center—became public policy advocates in California, Washington, DC, and in state houses all over the United States. A major transition took place, reshaping a peer adviser and grassroots movement into a partially state-subsidized, institutionalized set of services.

As a program volunteer, grants-writer, board member and archivist for the first Displaced Homemakers Center, I began working for the organization after it made the transition from a direct service provider to an educational and consulting group that prepared state agencies to assume more responsibility for women's welfare.[10] Many women and their families have been served because women's policy advocacy generated local, state, and federal support for new women's re-entry programs. As a result of the women's job re-entry movement, peer-adviser centered support groups and comprehensive support services became hallmarks of the national model for serving women and other disadvantaged groups.

Orono, Maine: Senior Community Service Project

The University of Maine's Senior Community Service Project, a statewide program that I managed from 1985 to 1987, addressed the training, schooling, and job re-entry needs of low income elders over the age of 55. Because older women tend to be impoverished more than men, 75-90 percent of program participants were women. This project, which was run by the Extension Service, was funded by the National Council on the Aging, a national nonprofit agency that administered about 60 similar projects for the U.S. Department of Labor. One goal of this project was to enable elders to become active, self-sufficient, community members in ways that reflected much more than economic self-sufficiency. Program participants were paid low wages to receive on-job-training at nonprofit organizations, where older women and men could update their job skills or develop new ones. Integral to the educational process was the idea that, in individual and collective contexts, mature women would be involved in assessing their own needs, defining their future goals, and helping to create social solutions for themselves and others. Learner-centered education for women was thus at the center of making social change happen.

Even though this project was constrained by bureaucratic procedures, regulatory constraints were minimized in this learner-centered educational context. The peer support group model was used in this project, but the peer advisers were paid, para-professionals who had once been on-the-job trainees at nonprofit organizations. Through the peer support group model, women in Maine were introduced to Extension's group-learning process, which is intended to result in social change for the community. These peer support groups formed the heart of community development education in this project. As they worked with women throughout the state, para-professional peer advisers helped other low-income women assess their needs and identify ways to meet their needs. The influence of the women's job and school re-entry movement was evident, as peer advisers helped to develop comprehensive support service plans to meet the needs that were defined by women and men in the program. In Maine, older women faced many of the same internal and external barriers that the re-entry women did. But additional barriers included some of the following: the lack of medical services in rural communities, the lack of public transportation, an inability to travel to work during the snowy months, and homes that were unheated or heated by wood stove (which was compounded by the discrimination directed against low-income women when their clothes carried the "woody smell" that came from wood-burning stoves).

The peer adviser group, who were elders over 55 years, confronted many dimensions of gender and age discrimination as they worked with other low-income, older people throughout the state. A central feature of their work was listening to what other women and men wanted for themselves and their families, and trying to help them meet their goals on their own terms. This was an empowerment model, one that enabled individuals and their communities to develop.

What did we learn together as we tried to increase women's and men's income-earning and educational options? The inadequacy of job placement services became obvious as older workers found themselves playing musical chairs with other job seekers (who often were other elders, youth with or without high school diplomas, displaced homemakers, and other economically disadvantaged women and men). The idea behind this program was to provide low wages to older trainees as they worked at nonprofits and upgraded their job skills, and then to help them make the transition to an unsubsidized job. As I helped women find employment, I recognized that self-employment or micro-enterprise could expand the number of available income-earning options, as well as do away with the "fixed" musical chairs situation, where one worker moves out of a job and another moves in.

In this employment situation, women often did not earn living wages after they received job training with nonprofits, but attended vocational school or college for a while, and then found what they once had identified as "desirable" jobs. This employment-focused social change model often did not contribute to a healthy cycle of community development because there were so few jobs. Furthermore, elders and especially mature women were very undervalued in the traditional job market. As I worked on this project, I began thinking about how community development education might be applied to create new work situations and to expand the pool of jobs, including through micro-businesses and worker-run cooperatives. I thought about how groups of displaced, marginalized, and underemployed workers could become involved in redesigning their work options, as well as implementing alternative economic relationships that could help sustain communities. The need for an expanded pool of jobs partly grew out of the analysis carried out by peer-centered support groups, who had realized that the development of micro-businesses was an important component of an effective employment program.

Berkeley, California: Western Institute for Social Research

The Western Institute for Social Research, where I taught on a part-time basis over a 10-year period, derived its original educational energy from the analysis of Freire's writings and the application of his ideas about theory and praxis to social change education and research in the San Francisco Bay area. The Western Institute for Social Research, a multiethnic institution with many working adults as students, is a small university that is located in a ethnically diverse neighborhood in Berkeley, right near the Oakland border. Originally graduate students at the University of California's School of Education founded the Western Institute as a classroom-without-walls school and held seminars at the University of California at Berkeley. Gradually, the school's operations became transferred to its current site on Sacramento Avenue. New educational approaches to studying social change were developed after the Western Institute obtained a U.S. Department of Education grant from the Fund for the Improvement of Post-Secondary Education (FIPSE) in the early 1980s.

At the Western Institute, one of the educational requirements is that all undergraduate and graduate students become involved in sustained, community action research that involves other community members. Individual students, who make their own decisions about their placements, usually work on community action research projects for at least one year. Learner-centered education at this school prepares students to help community members define and address their problems. Although students have different extended internships, they engage in small-group discussions about their community action research.

The Western Institute is the only school in the United States where students can earn a PhD in Higher Education and Social Change, an educational process that requires an applied and theoretical understanding of group-defined needs identification, program development, program implementation and evaluation. By practicing learner-centered education in classroom learning circles, students are gaining assessment and program implementation skills that they will use when they work with community members on community-action projects.

At the Western Institute, there are clear similarities between particular community-centered educational approaches (e.g., feminist education, multicultural education, and Africana, Native American, and Chicano participatory education). Typically there is not a big line drawn between the different ways that community-based education is applied. Some students apply this educational approach to community action projects that fight "neo-colonialism" and help to create new spaces in civil society for Native American healers, urban gardeners, young African-American males, or citizens seeking more democracy in South Africa today. Other students study prisons or youth authority systems, or the development of multicultural counseling practices. At this learner-centered school, gender analysis centered around the recognition that women and men are socially constructed in ways that have to do with much more than gender. In seminars, multicultural

issues were analyzed as an integral part of a broadly defined participatory pedagogy. All students were encouraged to speak from their own knowledge base, and
to explore how racism affected their individual research, their research with community groups, and the choices they made in their learning processes. Dialogical
learning around the issues of racism, sexism, ethnic and national identity, clas-
sism, ageism, and imperialism provided an important way for students to examine
issues and to learn from each other in small group settings.

Teaching at the Western Institute taught me how valuable it is to participate in
group research, and in community action research. Social change education at the
Western Institute reinforced my understanding that an examination of how social
barriers are created allows learners to create specific solutions that begin to undermine these barriers in comprehensive and innovative ways. Teachers are defined
as facilitators who support individual learners and who work with learning groups
in seminars. Teachers remain open to the learning process and do not see themselves as experts, but as learners who have completed certain stages in the learning process. Likewise, students are recognized as people who teach others, at the
same time that they learn. Through the community-based research that they do
with others as part of their education at the Western Institute, students acquire an
in-depth understanding of community action research. Learners are encouraged to
share theoretical and concrete knowledge about how to use group research as a
way to bring about social change. Peer-centered education and dialogical learning, which took place in both the classroom and in nonprofit organizations, were
reinforced in formal and informal learning environments.

Manhattan, Kansas: The Planned Women's Micro-Enterprise and Cooperative Internship Project and the Women's Studies Service Learning Project at Kansas State University

As a teacher of Women's Studies at Kansas State University (KSU), I have
worked on developing new approaches for introducing students to hands-on
social change research. Collaborating with KSU's Women's Resource Center and
KSU's Kansas Center for Rural Initiatives, I have designed a targeted internship
program that would prepare traditional and nonmatriculated community students
to support women who want to start micro-enterprises and cooperatives. Rather
than having students placed at completely different internship sites that have little
relationship to each other (as many internship classes do), all internship placements will help individual students and the class learn about how to develop different types of women's micro-enterprises and cooperatives. This internship class
is considered to be "targeted" because all community placements would, in some
way, relate to increasing women's self-sufficiency through the development of
micro-enterprises, cooperatives, or flexible business networks (where people
from related businesses cooperate together). When this project is implemented,
Kansas State students will be prepared to help community-based women start up

their own micro-businesses, and students who have taken the course will also be prepared to start their own micro-businesses.

This targeted internship class will be based on the pedagogical model of community development education. Students will work with a group of learners who identify women's micro-enterprise needs. They will design a program or plan to meet these needs, implement this program (or key aspects of it), and then evaluate the educational and social change processes.

When this internship class begins, students will attend one class each week and learn hands-on analytical skills in community settings for at least four hours a week. Even though student's hands-on community work will take place in slightly different contexts, all students will be able to study and analyze common themes. The processes of pooling their knowledge and examining their collective knowledge will be part of the class.

The project's goals are to expand work opportunities for women by supporting and creating micro-businesses, to increase women's income-generating options through the development of new micro-business models (cooperatives and flexible business networks), and by providing support to women in the program—as well as through annual conferences and publications—to strengthen women's economic networks and credit-granting mechanisms in the Great Plains region.

If women and other economically and politically marginalized groups are to become more sufficient, it will be necessary to create new alternatives to the historically established, stratified labor market, where too many groups find themselves locked into low-paid, essentially segregated employment in the service sector. Developing new bases of economic and political power may also enable more people to stay in small towns, which are slowly disappearing. As part of this project, we plan to share our knowledge with other schools, service providers, and policy makers. We plan to develop our understanding of strategies that have worked in the region, as well as to identify strategies that can be modified to meet the needs of groups in the region.

In addition to this project development work on women's micro-enterprises, I have developed two undergraduate classes ("Introduction to Women's Studies" and "Women and Global Social Change") that incorporate service-learning activities. Service learning is another educational approach that enables students to study social change outside of the classroom. As they engage in learning in more informal environments (where community development education takes place in different ways), students bring this knowledge back into the classroom and enhance their academic studies. Last year my "Introduction to Women's Studies" classes participated in the university's first cycle of service-learning classes that involved first-year students.

At Kansas State, service-learning programs are coordinated by the Kansas Center for Rural Initiatives, which has a 10-year history of organizing service-learning experiences. Teachers receive a lot of support and guidance—including educational workshops and information-sharing sessions—as we help our students acquire and analyze knowledge gained from service-learning placements.

Service learning is different than the two community placement models that already have been discussed: the in-depth, group-centered, community action research projects (the Western Institute model) and the targeted internship class that connects students who are participating in both related community placements (for 40 hours a semester) and weekly class sessions (the Kansas State Women's Studies model). Service learning is seen as a largely academic process, and not as a work experience situation. Rather than reading a book on how feminists bring about change, students learn as observers and participants in service placements for 10-20 hours a semester. Students work with other students who also are learning at the same social change site, which may be on- or off-campus. Students studying the same organization pool their knowledge and share their combined knowledge with the class.

In my classes last semester, seven groups of students observed and worked at different sites that contribute to an understanding of gender relations and social change. These sites included the city's Crisis Center for women; the Wonder Workshop's multicultural, learner-centered, after-school program for children; the Girl Scout's Be Your Best Program (which inspires girls to set their goals and go to college); the Boys and Girls Club (which provides supportive encouragement in after-school programs for low- to moderate-income youth); the multicultural, Douglass Center's Hand-To-Hand Program (which provides academic tutoring); the Flint Hills Job Corps (which helps high school students succeed in academic and vocational work); and Speak United, Manhattan's community organization that supports public housing residents and low-income people.

Each group of students began engaging in community development education when they sat down to discuss their interests and to decide what community or campus organization they wanted to study. One benefit of this collective learning process is that individual students did not need to spend a lot of hours working in a community setting, but yet they benefited from the hours that others spent.

Women's Studies students benefited from the small group service learning model, where they engaged in field study together. The field engagement process, which is entailed with service learning, provided another way to learn course content. As students learned individually and collaboratively in a social setting, they examined the impact of gender and other social divides and considered how social change organizations addressed key social issues. Students were encouraged to make suggestions for strengthening the social change approach that was used in the social change setting. Students thought about how to design new approaches for addressing the needs of women and girls, as well as other groups.

It also is possible for an entire class to learn together at one service learning site. With this service learning model, the teacher and the students travel to a community site. Classes that are organized in this way usually are more intensive, involve upper-division undergraduates, and require visits to community sites on three or four weekends during the semester. Although I have not tried selecting one service learning site for the whole class, my "Women and Global Social Change" students are doing service learning at related, fairly targeted sites that deal with women's self-sufficiency issues. Other teachers involve their students in one service learning site, either studying public use of the Kansas River, environmental preservation in a self-sufficient town, or public education through the development of a town's history museum.

Service learning process allows undergraduate students to begin reflecting on academic learning experiences that take place outside of the classroom. It gets them to share the knowledge they have acquired with the whole class. This learning model provides promising ways for teachers to help students become excited about creating social change through community development education. Service learning places the peer-centered learning process at the center of both classroom work and community-based learning.

COMMUNITY DEVELOPMENT EDUCATION: AN ESSENTIAL PART OF SOCIAL SCIENTIFIC RESEARCH

When applied in social change contexts, community development education involves community members in the process of defining and addressing their needs. Whether it is called community-based education,[11] experiential participatory action research, community action research, education for social change, or participatory strategies and methodologies (Smith and Willms 1997; Arnold et al. 1991; Thomas-Slayter et al. 1995), this approach calls for learners to become immersed in organizational activities. Becoming this involved allows students to learn how to work as professionals, carry out social change strategies in one setting, and acquire an in-depth understanding of how one social change network develops (Park et al. 1993).

Other kinds of research can help the student to examine his/her experiences in relation to other social change projects, and in relation to the changing social structure. Conducting slightly more distanced ethnographic and participant observation research on a related social change effort can provide insights into a student's community action research (Buraway 1991; Weiss 1994). Gathering contemporary and historical archival data on related community-based efforts, state-run projects, and workplace and neighborhood changes can help place the social change experience in context, and lead to a more critical evaluation of it. Conducting preliminary surveys of major employers, service providers, and community leaders in the project's neighborhood can provide a clearer picture of structural constraints and opportunities. Conducting semi-open interviews and oral histories with some of the individuals surveyed can broaden the student's experience, at the same time she/he acquires greater analytical depth. When educators look at the big picture, they can imagine studying communities within a broad historical and comparative framework; this framework helps learners to understand the unintentional and intentional human elements that are involved in social change transitions.

Furthermore, educators can connect community problems and community-centered social change strategies with global problems and global social change strategies. Social change approaches at both community and global levels include fairly spontaneous social actions and more sustained social movements, as well as carefully planned organizational efforts, which can be carried out by community-based organizations, state social service agencies, universities, and businesses. One way to connect the local and global is to organize overseas classes (from two weeks to one semester in length), where students have the opportunity to compare and contrast service learning in their communities with their study of social problems and social change models in other countries. The cross-national sharing of social change approaches has had a very positive influence on service delivery in the United States and in countries of the South. (For example, many women's micro-lending programs follow Bangladesh's Grameen Bank model, and provide loans to small circles of female micro-entrepreneurs.) An international perspective locates the solving of community problems within the context of global relationships. After all, community problems partly evolved within the context of global relationships. Community solutions may provide solutions in other parts of the world. Furthermore, they may lay the groundwork for future global relationships.

University educators can introduce students to the multiple layers where social change takes place. This requires preparing students to begin understanding global social change processes, the structure of the contemporary world, the barriers that particular social groups face, and how various organizations attempt to address and eliminate these barriers. Students should be encouraged to explore how effective approaches are in eliminating problems, including in both short- and long-term dimensions. Active learners need to explore options that they think might work more effectively. They should be encouraged to think about alternative visions of the social world. All these understandings about some of the essential elements—how to join others in a community project, how to meet needs that are invisible to many, how to work with others in a social change context, and how to envision better approaches—can come from engaging in community development education.

As committed as the United States is to democratic ideals and to social equality, true, full democracy and economic equality remain elusive. In structural terms, women and other disenfranchised groups have been excluded from social arenas where decisions are made about how society will develop and what the social priorities will be. Many of these key decisions have to do not so much with electoral process, but with decisions about how work is allocated and rewarded, and how groups of people are valued in relation to their work and in relation to where they live in the world. Social scientists, educators, and social service workers need to examine some of these "unconscious" and largely unquestioned decisions about how we live and what we think about each other.

One of the most expedient ways for educators and learners to develop a deep understanding of global and local transformations is to study and engage in social change practices. Academic study cannot uncover how we can change unequal social relations until teachers help unify the community by bringing the community into the classroom and the classroom into the community. Our books and articles do not tell us all that much about how to change the world, and teachers and students cannot know how to do this until we broaden our understanding of what constitutes the classroom. Likewise, social change educators and learners who work in more applied settings outside of the university can only benefit from a closer relationship with the university's teachers, researchers, and students. We all need each other, and given the similarity between some educational approaches, it is possible that we may be closer than we have thought. As educators and learners, we need to reach out to each other in more conscious ways and to think together about how we can learn new ways to understand and transform the world around us.

As a practitioner of community development education in formal (classroom-based) and informal (organizational-based) settings, I am committed to developing and implementing new models that are developed in multicultural, collaborative contexts. I am prepared to work with other teachers and learners in formal and informal learning contexts. I want to figure out how targeted approaches—which identify and relate important community needs—can be strengthened in particular locales and in various social contexts. A central element in community development education is the group decision-making process, which provides democratic and egalitarian opportunities for learners to choose and construct their pathways to the future. Many of these educational social change efforts now seem to be taking place in civil society, a critical site for multicultural transformations because civil society connects the family to the state and business. Wherever social change efforts are occurring, adhering to the democratic process is a very difficult thing to do; but it is the most important thing to do. This is something that the community's diverse group of educators and learners have taught us.

NOTES

1. When she does academic work, Gloria Watkins uses the name "bell hooks."

2. The California State University system now allows community service, along with teaching and research, to be acknowledged during the tenure and promotion process. This appreciation of the academic value of professors' community service is usual.

3. Myles Horton was influenced by Jane Addams of Chicago's Hull House and by Bishop Grundtvig, who was involved with Denmark's cooperative movement. Grundtvig proposed a "School for Life" to replace academic learning (Horton 1990, pp. 47-52). Rosa Parks was one of the more visible adult learners at the Highlander Folk School.

4.   For an analysis of how hooks' educational approach relates to Third World situations, see Florence (1998).

5.   I tend to agree with Freire's analysis of theory making. According to him, when a person thinks about the social world, that person moves between the totality and its parts, seeing the general and then the concrete (or seeing the concrete and then the general). Then the learner can move from the concrete back up to the general; or, for those who started at the concrete, the learner can move from the general back down to the concrete. Unlike hooks' idea that feminists should start by developing an applicable theory, Freire's formulation contributes to a more complex, concrete and useful understanding of how social movement theories relate to global social change (Freire 1985, p. 38).

6.   Many women's movements today relate to the reorganization of the global hierarchy, including gender relations. Women's protests often relate to wage and nonwage work, but their diversity is enormous (see Dickinson 1998).

7.   Civil society involves all residents of countries, not just citizens, and it develops in all countries, not just in the West. Limited definitions of civil society need to be questioned, including the one provided by Seligman (1992).

8.   According to Freire, key learning stages include: codification (abstraction), decodification (studying and defining relationships between abstract categories), problematizing (comprehending codification and beginning to see dialectrical movements), comprehension (understanding related dialectical movements and beginning to see what can be done), denunciation (identifying negative trends), annunciation (knowing what is needed and defining interventions), praxis (attaining unity between thought and practice), and critical consciousness (after trying to think and act, and after learning the lessons that come from this process, acquiring an intention toward the world and bringing about cultural action for freedom) (see Freire 1985, pp. 52, 87, 160, 172).

9.   Re-entering women thought the term "middle-age" was used by the public and by agency workers in a negative way. They invented the concept "middle-years women," hoping to recast themselves and the benefits of aging in a more positive way.

10.   I placed the archives of the Oakland's Displaced Homemaker Center (which closed in the mid-1980s) at the UC-Davis Library, Special Collections, University of California-Davis. This archive contains documentation on the development of women's services in Oakland. Records demonstrate the leardership role that the center played at subsequent displaced homemaker centers. Newspaper clippings from around the country document how this grassroots women's movement became a national movement. Records also show how this grassroots movement invented the service model that now is used by the government when its agencies work with underemployed and underserved people.

11.   Many learner-centered educational organizatons in the United States refer to their activities as community-based education; there is an Association for Community-based Education in Washington, DC.

REFERENCES

Arnold, R., B. Burke, C. James, D. Martin, and B. Thomas, eds. 1991. *Education for a Change.* Toronto: Between the Lines and Doris Marshall Institute for Education and Action.

Buraway, M. 1991. *Ethnography Unbound: Power and Resistance in the Metropolis.* Berkeley: University of California Press.

Dalla Costa, M. 1995. In *Paying the Price: Women and the Politics of International Economic Strategy,* edited by M. Dalla Costa and G. F. Dalla Costa. London: Zed Books.

Dickinson, T. 1998. "Preparing to Understand Feminism in the 21st Century: Global Social Change, Women's Work and Women's Movements." Journal of World-Systems Research.

Fisher, J. 1998. *Nongovernments: NGOS and the Political Development of the Third World.* West Hartford, CT: Kumarian Press.

Florence, N. 1998. *bell hooks' Engage Pedagogy: A Transgressive Education for Critical Consciousness*. Westport, CT: Bergin and Garvey.

Freire, P. 1985. *The Politics of Education: Culture, Power and Liberation*, trans. by D. Macedo. New York: Bergin and Garvey.

hooks, b. 1994. *Teaching to Transgress: Education as the Practice of Freedom*. New York: Routledge.

hooks, b., and C. West. 1991. *Breaking Bread: Insurgent Black Intellectual Life*. Boston: South End Press.

Horton, M. 1990. *The Long Haul: An Autobiography*. New York: Doubleday.

Mitter, S. 1997. "Women Working Worldwide." Pp. 163-174 in *Materialist* Feminism: A Reader in Class, Difference and Women's Lives, edited by R. Hennessy and C. Ingraham. New York: Routledge.

Park, P., M. Brydon-Miller, B. Hall, T. Jackson, eds. 1993. *Voices of Change: Participatory Research in the United States and in Canada*. Westport, CT: Bergin and Garvey.

Seligman, A. 1992. *The Idea of Civil Society*. Princeton, NJ: Princeton University Press.

Smith, S.E., and D.G. Willms. 1997. *Nurtured by Knowledge: Learning to Do Participatory Action-Research*. New York: Apex Press.

Thomas-Slater, B., R. Polestico, A.L. Esser, O. Taylor, and E. Mutua, eds. 1995. *A Manual for Socio-Economic and Gender Analysis: Responding to the Development Challenge*. Worchester, MA.: Clark University, Institute for Development Anthropology.

Yeatman, A. 1980. "The Classical Theory of Civil Society: An Analytic Critique." Sociology dissertation, State University of New York at Binghamton.

"You Got to Move." 1985. Film produced by Lucy Phenix for the Cumberland Educational Cooperative, MacArthur Foundation.

Wallerstein, I., and Gulbenkian Commission. 1996. *Open the Social Sciences*. Stanford: Stanford University Press.

Weiss, R.S. 1994. *Learning from Strangers: The Art and Method of Qualitative Interview Studies*. New York: The Free Press.

THE COMMUNITY OF
CIRCUMSTANCE—A TALE
OF THREE CITIES:
COMMUNITY PARTICIPATION IN
ST. KILDA, KNOX, AND LEWISHAM

Graham Marsh

ABSTRACT

Observed throughout this research, in the cities of St. Kilda, Knox (in Australia) and Lewisham (in England), was the potential for residents to participate within their local authority, but the right circumstances, or processes, had to be present for that potential to be realized and for community formation to occur. Such processes can lead to the establishment of what this researcher has come to see as a "community of circumstance." Such a community incorporates the ideas presented by the sociologist Max Weber of a community of interest but extends the concept. Weber's communities of interest may lie dormant with their potential to form being unrealized unless the individuals with similar interests have the desire to establish a community and the right circumstances and dynamics are present within their neighborhood or

Research in Community Sociology, Volume 9, pages 65-86.
Copyright © 1999 by JAI Press Inc.
All rights of reproduction in any form reserved.
ISBN: 0-7623-0498-7

networks to ensure a positive outcome. Residents as individuals or in groups had the potential to influence and certainly were influenced by the actions of other "agents" in local government, recognizing that the actual processes set in place could enhance or inhibit resident participation. The finding of Giddens (1984) "that [citizens] are dealing with other people, with institutions, with people having more or fewer resources, all of which will affect [their] capacity to achieve the desired outcomes" was true for the three cities. For those agents who coordinated and controlled the system, power was present to varying degrees depending on their resources. Much evidence was to be seen that ordinary residents who exercised their rights and brought pressure to bear on their councils could influence policy directions. However, participation was most likely to be present and successful when residents belonged to a community or network of like-minded fellow citizens. Confirmed in this research were the views that: first, the call to participation is answered by few residents; second, that participation is skewed toward the haves in society; and third, that interest groups are the power bases for the exercising of these rights and are fundamental to liberal democratic politics.

INTRODUCTION

The research that led to this paper arose out of my own role as an active participant in the then city of St. Kilda in Melbourne, Australia.[1] I should like to stress then that my own value position as a local, "left leaning" activist coloured this research although I did go to great pains to overcome this limitation. In the St. Kilda case study, the research style is almost that of action research. Being an activist first, and a researcher second, certainly influenced the early stages of the studies, particularly as it led me to pass negative judgment on those people who did not participate. As a participant observer in a number of St. Kilda's community organizations including the Australian Labor Party (ALP), I naively had high hopes, and assumed that if one informed the residents about the local needs, the reality and the justice or injustices of a situation then the people would come out and participate. The hopes were rarely realized and, after the early disappointment, I came to realize that this was in fact the norm for the city's citizens.

The aim of the research then took on a directional change. Rather than an emphasis on why people participate or why they do not (why should they anyway?), the prime aim was to explore through three case studies the *contexts* and *diversity* of people participating through communities of interests in local matters. The results are *not generic* but are historically and geographically (spacially) located in the three settings all showing different conditions of participation with some overlap, of course (i.e., they are idiosyncratic not nomothetic).

In a modern democracy every citizen has a democratic right to participate in the affairs of local government. We have the potential to do so through the ballot box; by standing for council or supporting candidates; by attending meetings, writing letters, and signing petitions; and by joining organizations that are able to wield influence on and within the council. For Anthony Giddens the potential is there for each of us to make a difference, no matter how small, to any circumstance. When this potential is realized in the area of participation and local government, we as citizens can be seen as exercising our democratic rights. "We each have the capacity 'to make a difference to a pre-existing state of affairs', to intervene or to refrain" (Giddens, 1984, p. 14).

However, this view of Giddens can not always be applied to participation at the local government level. Giddens here fails to recognize that not all residents want to, nor do they have the capacity to intervene. Many residents are intellectually, physically, or linguistically incapable of taking part in the formal proceedings often associated with participation. However, even when the residents are capable in these areas, the situation is not one where the majority of citizens do actually exercise this right and capacity apart from perhaps voting at elections.

Why is the opportunity so rarely taken by most of us "to exercise some sort of power" where publicly it should be easy to do so and where it should be likely that a difference could be effected, that is, at the level of local government? The following is an attempt to answer these questions on empowerment, in particular as it applies to three cities in two different countries.

WHY A COMPARATIVE STUDY OF THREE CITIES

While there are always going to be limitations with any comparative research, particularly when it crosses national boundaries, the potential is present to reveal the essential features and complexities of an issue and more so than if only one city was researched. In this study of three cities the potential was present to reveal both similarities and variations that existed in local governance and approaches to local communities, in the effectiveness or ineffectiveness of participation and the most likely participants in those cities. A study across time (1983 until 1996) also enabled changes to be noted within these cities. The research[2] that led to this paper was a comparative study of three cities: St. Kilda and Knox in Melbourne, Australia and Lewisham in London.[3]

WHY THE PARTICULAR CITIES, WITH ST. KILDA AS THE MAJOR FOCUS, WERE CHOSEN

St. Kilda

The interest in, and reason for, the research was twofold. First, I was a resident and have been involved in St. Kilda's community action groups since 1983, commencing with membership of the ALP and subsequently through involvement in a number of local groups which were particularly concerned with council policies and in the delivery of local health and welfare services. The most active participation was with a residents' group which acted, and still operated when the observations were completed, as an advisory committee to council. Originally it was called, the Community Development Advisory Committee (CDAC), and subsequently, the St. Kilda Forum.[4]

Second, interest in the research arose out of a desire to see if what was experienced in St. Kilda was an aberration or not. St. Kilda, in undergoing a process of gentrification, was attracting highly motivated and educated younger people, some of whom had recently fought planning and policy battles in other inner Melbourne suburbs. The suburb had always been a haven for articulate, artistic residents who (it appeared) wanted to keep their little piece of bohemia, preserving those aspects of the suburb which made it interesting. Many of these more articulate St. Kilda residents placed emphasis on the maintenance and provision of low cost housing and services that had attracted many of Melbourne's disadvantaged and less articulate residents to the suburb. Research was then widened into a comparative study using St. Kilda as the major focus while comparing the findings with later data to be gathered in another Victorian suburb—Knox—and Lewisham in London.

Knox

The city of Knox appeared at the commencement of this research to make an interesting comparison with St. Kilda. It was the largest, in population, of Melbourne's councils and thus was about one-half the size of those in London. It was said to be one of Melbourne's most stable and successful councils, mainly due to its chief executive officer at that time; and it was so different in the composition of its population that trends across local governments could be studied without bias toward inner city councils.

Knox had a more homogeneous population than either of the other cities. The majority of the population saw themselves as being relatively long-term residents who were Australian born, middle class, who owned their own homes on the 1/4 acre block, lived in families with children still at home, and who could be classified as swinging voters, although the council was generally a conservative one. Housing in most areas of Knox was relatively cheap and attracted first home buyers. It was not an itinerant population as was the case in St. Kilda and was often classified as a dormitory suburb where people worked elsewhere and came home to sleep and for their leisure activities. The Knox residents were seen at the time to be typical of residents across the fast growing outer Melbourne suburbs. The city contained older sectors which had been settled for many years and the new sections where orchards, farms, and market gardens had been recently subdivided for reasonably cheap housing blocks. There were some sections of Knox with much larger blocks and considerably more expensive houses built on them.

The contrast with St. Kilda where there always seemed to be some new, or old, controversy cropping up within a divided community made for what appeared at the time to be valuable comparative research. Would the residents in Knox (who were less educated on average than St. Kilda residents, who were busy bringing up families, commencing careers, and were generally—it appeared from the composition of the council and from studies performed on the city and its residents— much more politically conservative), participate in local government affairs to the same extent as residents in St. Kilda and Lewisham? Such a contrast appeared to be a valid reason to choose Knox as the third of the cities for review.

Lewisham

Why Lewisham? First, I spent three months living in Lewisham during 1986 and was able to stay there again in 1990 for another three months. Observations and follow-up interviews were subsequently carried out in 1994 over a 3-week period. It was, therefore, possible to conduct the research and be a participant observer, to a somewhat limited extent, over an extended period of time in Lewisham.

Second, information was received in 1990 that the Lewisham council had been described in the English Press as a "model Labour council using modern council methods." With Australian councils seemingly following and being influenced by the British trends in local government the chance to study a 'model' British council appeared to be too good a chance to miss!

Third and most importantly, like St. Kilda, Lewisham was an inner city with a high percentage of residents from a multicultural background living alongside the more traditional working class. Gentrification of sections of the city was also under way. Many pressures and changes were being imposed upon particular sections of the city as urban renewal was taking place. As with St. Kilda, there were residents of Lewisham who were living in more affluent, leafy suburbs, in stark contrast to the flat dwellers and others in the poorer belts of the borough. Useful comparisons, it appeared from a distance, could then be made with St. Kilda.

THEORETICAL APPROACH

The research focused on community participation in the development, monitoring, and evaluation of policies and programs that have a social impact on particular localities; it interprets the findings and builds a comparative analytic framework. For example, the policies, dynamics, and resources present in society which aid or hinder a resident's capacity to intervene and make a difference in the practices, activities, and events that occur daily in the life of his/her local community or suburb were examined in detail. Additionally, consideration was given to the actors involved, in the way their meanings of public participation are constructed. To what extent do these actors know why they act as they do? How are the political inequalities exhibited? How are the resources manipulated in the endeavors of the various actors to influence one another's behavior and the structures within which they operate? What are the social and material constraints faced by these actors in the process of participation?

There were considerable benefits to be gained for this research through approaching it from an interpretivist perspective. There were also considerable tensions involved. As the researcher, I had already placed myself in the position of the actor/participant and was thus able, as the research continued, to develop an understanding of the social world of the actor that would not have been possible by quantitative methods alone. In Weberian terms, it was possible to develop an interpretive understanding of the social action occurring within the three cities and "arrive at a causal explanation of its course and effects" (as quoted in Blaikie 1993, p. 37).

Because a major aim of this research was to provide a descriptive study of resident participation in three cities, participant observation and informal discussions were seen as being important tools for the achievement of this aim. I was able to experience first hand and thereby interpret the power plays between the various actors and the manner in which the structural forces aided or hindered participation. The subjective meanings and the experience of dealing with an indefinite plurality was dealt with as were the emotions, hopes, and fears of the actors. In Weberian terms again: *"Empathetic* or appreciative understanding [was possible]...Empathetic or appreciative accuracy is obtained when, through sympathetic participation, we can adequately grasp the emotional content in which the action took place" (Blaikie 1993, p. 38, emphasis in original). Such empathy was possible as I was an actor in the social action occurring in St. Kilda.

However, such intense involvement meant that the subjective meanings developed throughout this phase of the research and the interpretations of causal significance needed to be tested through other methods. It was possible only to observe fragments of the social action, and these were observed through my biased eyes as the researcher. The methods of positivism were used to compare my subjective meanings with those of other actors. They enabled the interpretations of residents who were normally not actively involved to be analyzed. The typicality of the observed participants could be compared with the background of the general populations, and my observations compared with those of other key participants.

The findings from the survey, observations, interviews, and content analysis were combined to compare the many interpretations that were presented during this study. Consequently, the degree to which resident groups were truly representative of the citizens generally could be studied and, most importantly, the reality for the citizen participant in St. Kilda was actively experienced and interpreted. Distortions inherent in the interviewing processes where the respondents answered, for example, seeking the interviewer's approval could be checked against the reality of the situation as I and others saw it.

The three councils' policies toward, and methods of dealing with, participation were placed under scrutiny along with an analysis of who were most likely to be the actors in the participation processes. After first conducting a review of the relevant literature from Britain and Australia, in particular, the study entailed the use of a variety of methods: observations as both participant and nonparticipant; in-depth, semi-structured and open-ended interviews with key individuals; surveys in all three cities using a structured questionnaire that was adapted to cover significant differences in what was offered by the three councils; and, analysis of the various local newspapers, council minutes and other documents, plus minutes and annual reports of various local organizations. The histories of the three cities were also examined to note changes, particularly those relating to the various fights for control of the councils and to see how power was distributed, if it changed hands, why, and what were the trends which may have impacted upon the particular councils at the time of the review.

THE POTENTIAL FOR PARTICIPATION: THE COMMUNITY OF CIRCUMSTANCE

Observed throughout this research was that the potential for residents to participate was present within the three local authorities, but the right circumstances, or processes, had to be present for that potential to be realized and for community formation to occur. Such processes can lead to the establishment of what I have come to see as a "community of circumstance." Such a community incorporates the ideas presented by the sociologist Max Weber of a community of interest but extends the concept. Weber's communities of interests may lie dormant with their potential to form being unrealized unless the individuals with similar interests have the desire to establish a community and the right circumstances and dynamics are present within their neighborhood or networks to ensure a positive outcome.

Residents as individuals or in groups had the potential to influence and certainly were influenced by the actions of other agents in local government, recognizing that the actual processes set in place could enhance or inhibit resident participation. The finding of Giddens (1984) that [citizens] are dealing with other people, with institutions, with people having more or fewer resources, all of which will affect [their] capacity to achieve the desired outcomes was true for the three cities. For those agents who coordinated and controlled the system, power was present to varying degrees depending on their resources. Giddens' recognition that influence is more than just a top-down process, that "all forms of dependence offer some resources whereby those who are subordinate can influence the activities of their superiors" (1984, p. 16) was true for these cities. Much evidence was to be seen that ordinary residents who did exercise their rights, bringing pressure to bear on their councils, could influence policy directions. However, participation was most likely to be present and successful when residents belonged to a community or network of like-minded fellow citizens.

The degree to which the resident not only desires to but is able to exercise his or her power as a citizen will often depend on the structures that are established by the local authority—whether the government is inclusive of the residents and open to critical participation by them or the degree to which empowerment exists. It will also depend on the material and other resources possessed and utilized by the individuals, as was noted by Ian Gray (1991) in his Cowra (a town in rural Australia), study. He wrote that

> possession of resources is a necessary precursor to the exercise of power. But it is not enough merely to have them: resources must also be deployed. Farming and business groups chose to deploy there's (1991, p. 186).

Gray continued by saying that

> Resources were deployed when what were perceived to be the interests of business, farmers or ratepayers appeared to be threatened. Under the popular technocratic model of bureaucracy, it was the bureaucracy which did the threatening (1991, p. 186).

In such circumstances, for those holding fewer resources and who have limited access to the bureaucracy and a limited understanding of how it operates, the achieving of influence in council concerns is slim.

Community

What is community? It is very difficult to categorize what is a community. Community is diversity (Bell and Newby 1971; Willmott 1989). Community is such a loose term. We use it often interchangeably with friends, networks, groups, voluntary associations, pressure groups, and even social movements. Within local councils generally it is often applied to the citizens living within the confines of their city or to neighbors who may not even know or talk to each other. In many situations neighbors may have no sense of belonging to, or connection with the city or neighbourhood—there is no "glue" within their geographic areas that bonds the residents together, which creates a unified force. Why should there be when all they may have in common is the closeness in proximity of their dwellings? For many people a feeling of community, of a common cause, of meaningful relationships with one's neighbors is lacking as their value systems, interests, and activities are different. Occasionally the promise that residents may be empowered through uniting with their neighbors has affect, but as these case studies indicate, even that promise fails to lead to ongoing participation. One last point on this would be that even when the neighbors do communicate with each other, feeling a common bond, this does not necessarily lead to participation in local issues and it was participation I was interested in.

My research confirmed that of Mabileau et al. (1989) who discounted the idea that individuals live in communities which are characterized by "a certain sense of solidarity and common identity" which are formed simply by living in a particular locality." They questioned this community identification theory which holds that in "such 'communities' residents are likely to have an intention . . . to act in certain ways towards one another, to respond to each other in particular ways, and to value each other as a member of a group" (1989, p. 190).

Mabileau et al. (1989, p. 190) believed that "a person's notion of a community is inextricably related to that person's ideological stance on a range of other values. Thus, the attributes of a community will be significantly different for a person on the left compared to someone on the right. Potentially, this should in turn affect the types of issues and actions taken in pursuit of community values." They also suggested the "possibility that locality and community are entirely irrelevant in the modern era . . . that people are moved by interests that transcend locality, with class, status or profession. Indeed, some may regard these as non-spatial communities" (1989, p. 191).

Within any one neighborhood or city there will then be many diverse communities, and within each of these there will be many diverse opinions. Each individual may belong to a number of unconnected communities even within the local council boundaries or, for example, within their ethnic group and yet have no meaningful relationships with their neighbors. My observations as a participant observer led me to draw the following conclusions: despite the best of intentions, policies, and publicity on the part of councils and local activists, communities will not form, nor will citizens participate, unless the circumstances are such that individuals will recognize the necessity of joining with other residents in a common cause and will be enabled in doing so.

Within the boundaries of the three local governments many potential communities of interest existed as the citizens had similar interests at stake that were under threat from local and other authorities. However, this potential to come together as a community with a common cause was, too often, not realized even when the residents had similar ideologies. Conflict was often present, as was the opportunity to compete for scarce economic, political, and social resources, all of which would normally assist in the development of communities; yet still many residents failed to establish themselves as communities and particularly to participate.

Community Formation and Participation

The actual circumstances present at a particular time within a person's life-cycle and in a particular local area determined: who the participants were at the level of local government and in local issues; how many people gathered, understood what was in their best interests, and contributed to individual and group goals and directions; what their responses would be and the effectiveness of these responses. Different responses were present in neighboring streets, not only due to conflict over ideological views and the support or nonsupport of proposed development, but because differences existed in the residents' commitment to activism. In some neighborhoods a single community formed centered on a particular issue; in others, separate communities, often at variance with each other, formed despite the issue being the same for both neighborhoods; while in others there was a complete lack of any cohesive response to a particular threat or issue. What was evident from my surveys in the three cities, was that not only did the majority of residents not form or join a community group to address an issue, 58 percent of them had never taken up any issue individually with their council. This was despite the fact that in the many of areas surveyed there were substantial issues needing to be addressed. The St. Kilda residents surveyed were the most likely to have taken up one issue or more, perhaps because they were the most highly educated of the respondents from the three cities.

Circumstances, including the mechanisms established by the council enabling participation and information dissemination, determined:

1. the composition, if one was formed, of a community of like-minded citizens at any one time;
2. how residents viewed their neighborhood (was it a temporary abode, a dormitory to go home to?);
3. the degree of conflict and competition for scarce resources present which might aid community formation;
4. whether empowerment of the less privileged existed;
5. whether any residents were aware of policies and proposals that may have affected them;
6. if residents who were aware subsequently contacted fellow residents;
7. the commonality of the residents including the ideological approaches present (for example, conservative, altruistic, or Not In My Back Yard (NIMBY));
8. the degree of community concern, competence, and the effectiveness of any submission presented by them;
9. the skills available to the community; and
10. the level of access they had to the council, and how comfortable residents felt in their dealings with the bureaucracy in particular.

While the composition of the community was important, it was not simply the "haves" who formed communities and participated while the "have nots" did not. While the "haves" are the most likely participants, these people have often been excluded from the participatory processes or they may have excluded themselves. Prior to the most effective participation of any citizen, occurring, the long-term full development of the citizen, particularly in the area of skills development, needs to be present; and many of the "haves" also feel that they are lacking in this field.

Changes in the 1980s and 1990s

In the 1980s and 1990s, the variety of actors involved in council processes has been broadened well beyond the cosy elite of the past where the ratepayers were basically the property owners of the municipality. The view of many councillors and officers (supported by many theorists of the past according to Carole Pateman) that certain groups of people were best excluded from the supposed democratic processes, has become less dominant during these decades. Male, middle-aged, middle-class, property owners dominated council concerns which were mostly related to property issues. Gray (1991, p. 49) noted that rural participants are required to spend much time and personal resources if they are to participate as, and perform the tasks of, local government members. Farmers, business people, and professionals "fit easily into the image of local government as property manager. The conservative ideal of local government is elitist rather than pluralist; it is seen as an organisation rather than as a political arena" (Gray 1991, p. 49). From my research in the three cities, the dominance and policy directions of this elite have been challenged with varying success in recent years and the structures and policy directions of many councils have been influenced by a new breed of activists.

THE CIRCUMSTANCES THAT ENCOURAGE COMMUNITY DEVELOPMENT AND PARTICIPATION

What then are these circumstances that are believed to be essential for the formation of a community of interest—the circumstances that encourage activists to come out of the woodwork? From the case studies, many residents were not always aware of why they were participants and would not normally participate, nor join in a community initiative, if the local circumstances had not led them to do so. For example, a neighbor or a tenants' association secretary with a strong and influential personality, coupled with knowledge of local affairs may bring together a whole street or block of flats to influence council policies. The type of area (e.g., whether the street is composed of houses or flats and whether these are rented or owned), can be influential in determining how many residents will be active contributors in any debate or proceedings and in the formation of a local community. Just as important is any access to community workers who may aid the development of an active residents' group. The standard and the stance of any local newspaper are also important contributors to the development of community formation and debate.

The size of the community of interest may be important—small may be less intimidating and more attractive to potential joiners—as Jones (1981) and many other scholars argue, but this is not always significant as a particular community could be a street, a local neighborhood, a block of flats or the whole of the city.

"Turn The Tide"[5] certainly extended its networks across the whole of St. Kilda and were eventually able to win control of the council with their allies. However, the research did confirm the studies of Parry, Moyser, and Day (1992, p. 14) and others that when resident involvement occurs it is most likely to be restricted to local issues, that is, those that have more meaning and understanding for the resident. Yet, it was also obvious throughout this research that proximity did not necessarily lead to a common approach to an issue. In some cases, resident apathy or a feeling of powerlessness meant that there was very little response, while in others conflict between residents was the norm and a number of communities of interest grew out of that conflict.

The intensity of feelings generated in any debate will also contribute to the willingness of residents to participate and form communities of interest. This intensity will vary from area to area and issue to issue and its level may be determined by the depth of solidarity present (in Weberian terms) among the participants. It may even vary within the individual over time. Such solidarity was to be seen in common sets of interests, values, and attitudes found among the members who made up the particular communities studied in this research. The more solidarity, the stronger the community encouragement was for the expression of views by its members. Solidarity may arise out of a response from external pressures or it may result from the residents' attachment to their local community. It may also be a combination of these two. A combination of the two led to community solidarity and action in all three cities.

For example, in Lewisham the proposed imposition by government for major road developments along the London South Circular brought out previously uninvolved residents[6] as did proposals for a waste incinerator in another part of the city. In Knox, a few, concerned residents formed community action groups to protest against developments at a quarry and over proposals to close a police station. In St. Kilda, developments in the tourist precinct and along the foreshore of the bay, in particular, brought many residents together, although this was often into warring groups. In all of these circumstances there was a perceived threat to the neighborhood and attachment to the same. It needs to be noted that the participation may have had successful outcomes at the time. The proposals were rejected or altered or the local members lost out at elections, but in the long term the problems are still not solved. It is impossible to drive around the South Circular; the police station was not relocated; St. Kilda is now being subjected to a 35-story development proposal for the hotel on its Esplanade. It is back to the streets yet again for the foreshore action group.

The type of community established will also vary according to the ideological stance of the participants. In all three cities interest communities formed around particular ideological orientations. In such cases the ideology was as important as the locality and, as Mabileau et al. (1989) wrote, the attributes of the particular communities differed according to the stance adopted by their members, or the perceptions of them by outsiders, for example, radical or conservative politically.

Most of all the desire to be involved has to be present for activist communities to form. Despite the best of intentions of social workers and others eager to empower the local citizens, unless those citizens want to be empowered, then the cause is lost. The resident as citizen has to see active participation as a priority and to believe that something can be usefully achieved by joining with others if that is involved or necessary. They as citizens have the right to determine who governs and whether it is "for" them or "by" them, but first the citizens need to accept that this can extend beyond merely voting at elections—if they do even that. Patterns of participation may vary according to how important the issues are perceived to be and according to the prevalent conception of community. The issue has to matter to them if they are going to take sustained action on it over time. Passion has to be felt about the issue.

Two examples providing confirmation of these findings were, first, when the St. Kilda CDAC executive had great difficulty in convincing people that issues were important; that, for example, their neighborhoods might be under threat from development or planning decisions; that it was in their long-term interests to band together and actively seek to influence the pending decisions. It was too late to try and do something when the decisions had been made, yet too often that was the situation many residents found themselves in when they finally decided to act.

Second, similar difficulties were experienced by me and my neighbors in our street when developments threatened the neighborhood amenity. Only a few residents joined together as a local community despite the issues or threats being the same for all. Even this limited solidarity did not continue beyond the period that the issue was addressed. In recent years there has been almost no protest despite greater intrusions into the neighborhood.

In Painter's (1992, p. 21) terms, many of the residents in both of these examples were passive participants, perhaps discussing the issues with families and friends, while a small minority were active, joining forces with fellow minded neighbors, standing for council, supporting candidates and "voicing grievances directly to authority figures" including councilors and officers.

For some residents in the three cities, participation at the local level was seen as being a waste of resources—the pond was too small—and they wished to concentrate on the larger issues within the state, national, and international arenas or in fields of special interest such as the environment, health, education, trade unions, service clubs, or business. The community of interest may have been present, as was the desire to be a participant; it was just that the resident wished to participate elsewhere than in local matters. Just as Miller observed in another city (in Munro-Clark 1992, p. 14), the really powerful actors who lived in St. Kilda, for example, executives of large companies and at least six sociologists and political scientists, seldom participated in local groups or activities possibly because they had other channels through which they operated or they had other major interests to follow within their limited available time.

THE PROCESSES OF PARTICIPATION

Also important for effective citizen participation was the attitude adopted by the council toward public participation. What Stoker (1988, p. 120) said of British councils (while the trend was more toward a principle of consultation many councils remained "enclosed organizations") was true for each of the three councils. They each had adopted the principle of consultation, but to varying degrees. In Knox the council and officers varied in their commitment to it, or so I was informed by one councillor and a number of staff members. Lewisham had established the most formal processes to ensure that consultation occurred. The St. Kilda council varied in its policy toward consultation. It very much depended upon which side of politics was in power and the formal processes were not as effective as in Lewisham.

However, in St. Kilda, even under the conservative councillors, consultation was present because a few officers were committed to such an approach. All chief executive officers spoken to, not only in Lewisham but at the other two councils as well, favored public consultation with some actively encouraging it more than others. Observed and reported in the surveys was the often fatalistic attitude of many respondents. A sense of powerlessness led to the belief that there was "very little that could be done about various issues so why bother trying." The vitriolic debate at a Lewisham tenants' meeting with council over "green services" was an example of the views expressed by those residents who felt frustrated in their dealings with the council. Council staff said that the residents should take more responsibility for their environment. The tenants said that when they tried to do this they were frustrated by council's inactivity. Two councillors present supported the residents and distanced themselves from any responsibility for council policy, blaming the council officers for the problems raised at the meeting. It was obvious to me as an observer, who had been taken on a tour of the estate by the senior housing officer, that in response to the residents' earlier demands, improvements on the estates and changes in council policies had occurred, yet these were not acknowledged by the tenants nor the councillors at the meeting. In other circumstances, when residents did attend public meetings, it was very difficult to involve them in any follow-up processes, even though the matters should have concerned them greatly. The Lewisham Pensioners' Forum discovered this when over 1,000 senior citizens attended a rally but only the organizers were willing to take action after the event.

The arguments were often put by many key actors in St. Kilda: "Don't hold a meeting on that [particular issue], the community is consulted (or meetinged) out," or, "it's too divisive." Yet in reality very few in the community had participated in the earlier meetings or been part of the consultation processes although they may have been divided over the issue. They may have been tired of receiving information in their letter boxes or newspapers (although many residents, it was discovered, never read such literature) but it was only those few who actively participated who were tired out. The methods used in consultation and community development need to be changed if more residents are to be informed, empowered, able to exercise their democratic rights, and take up issues of concern. Observations of much council community liaison indicate that such liasons are often more public relations—"this is what we are doing"—than dialogue or community development. Consequently, many residents appeared to be unwilling or even unable to address issues that may have concerned them. Such residents were unable to address these issues as they had inadequate access to information on what was occurring. Even when they were informed, they too often lacked the skills necessary to adequately deal with council over the issues.

For communities to develop and for public participation to occur, not all of these above circumstances needed to be present but, when too many of them were lacking, the intensity of any involvement was low or absent.

CHANGES TO THE CIRCUMSTANCES OVER TIME

Circumstances can and did change over time. The level of skills available to residents and/or their groups and neighborhoods developed as they learned through participation in the processes. Skilled activists were attracted to the particular interest communities or they may have been lost as people left or lost interest. As well, outside forces pressured the actors involved to take up a particular cause or to address an issue previously not on the agenda. This occurred in the 1980s in the area of Equal Opportunity that placed "new social categories firmly on the agenda of local government" (Gyford 1991, p. 8) and as new developments and policies of council and governments were seen as threats to neighborhoods and cities.

Resources also shifted from agent to agent over time, when for example, councils were overthrown; central governments changed the rules; workers, both government and nongovernment, moved or were moved; participation was encouraged or discouraged; and, alliances were formed and disintegrated. New alliances that formed in St. Kilda enabled the more traditional power holders to be voted out at council elections. Citizens of St. Kilda, largely unrepresented in the past, including representatives of that city's "have nots" were able to wrest control of the council from the more conservative councilors through networking, use of information and procedural knowledge. They were helped by changes to the electoral laws that made it compulsory for all residents, and not just ratepayers, to vote at the council elections. This empowered the many previously disempowered tenants in. St Kilda who were not eligible to vote.

Coupled with these changing circumstances from without, circumstances change within the lifespan of particular individuals and consequently resident participation waxes and wanes with variations over time and place as many of the commentators noted. Each individual's actions and areas of interest and activity may vary in intensity over time. They marry, have children, their children grow up and leave home. Old age catches up and health, safety and neighborhood watch take on more immediate concern rather than the education, leisure, local planning, or development matters of the past.

Residents may also be active participants in one city but move to another where networks encouraging participation are not present and they become nonpartici-pants. On the other hand, the opposite may occur and they move into a neighbor-hood where issues lead to, and neighbors support the concept of, participation and they become active participants. Job change may also lead to an increase or decrease in participation as time commitments may inhibit participation. Many activists eventually just suffer from "burn out" from too much activity and retire to a "quiet life" or their major area of interest is dealt with and they stop partici-pating. Networks may become represented in council and activism is conse-quently stifled as the residents have difficulty in criticizing their peers who they helped get elected. They may also lose their position on a community organiza-tion and consequently lose interest in participating. The opposite may be the case, as it was when I was co-opted onto the CDAC committee and my interest in par-ticipation grew rapidly, going well beyond that organization. My knowledge, skills, and expertise developed as I learned how to operate in one environment and then transfer the skills to others.

Encouragement and funding of interest groups by council and other agencies will also vary over time and place. For example, funding in Australia by Labor state governments working in conjunction with the councils from 1982 until 1992 provided many St. Kilda and Knox activists with the means and resources to establish community agencies and effectively continue in this work with a reason-able degree of security. Following the election of a conservative state government in 1992, such encouragement waned, groups struggled to exist, and the overall level of participation decreased. This decrease happened despite the local citi-zenry having more to fight for and against, such as withdrawal of community organization funding, council amalgamations, rezoning implications, and so on.

A similar change occurred in the United Kingdom with the withdrawal of funds to local groups following the demise of the Greater London Council and the rate-capping of councils. Community activists found it very difficult to con-tinue to influence decisions and policy due to the loss of resources, particularly of staff and office facilities. One obvious observation of all three councils was that community organizations, and councils for that matter, were less likely in the late 1980s and 1990s to be guaranteed continuity of funding. This had a profound impact on the ability of residents to mobilize in areas previously covered by them with the help of community organizations as there were now fewer resources available.

The British and Australian central governments' emphasis on a reduction in spending has also meant that financial matters are more often determined by those governments and less often by councils. The lowering of council rates, coupled with the balanced budget, were much more important to government than ensuring that any responsibilities centered on social justice were met by the councils. Autonomy of the three councils was thus taken away from them in the financial area. The state government in Victoria is in 1999 continuing the process of usurping the powers of council concerning important planning decisions where councils had previously wielded some degree of autonomy. In the 1990s many councillors, residents, and local activists expressed the feeling that it did not matter what they did, governments would simply overturn any controversial local decision. In Victoria councils are under threat in the 1990s as they fear that any nonconformity with state government policies by councils could lead to the firing of councillors who would again be replaced by commissioners.

In response to the earlier quote from Giddens, it was obvious throughout the years covering this research that individual citizens did have the capacity to make a difference to the pre-existing state of affairs, *if* they chose to intervene (Giddens 1984, p. 14). Not only did they have the capacity but many residents (and not just the traditional elites—the business people and professionals previously powerful in councils) did make a difference as they played their part in the production and reproduction of the system. Not all intervention caused political change within the system. Much of the intervention in the three cities actively supported the status quo. Only one of the councils lost power due to citizen action. Change most likely occured over peripheral matters, particularly planning concerns, rather than structural change or changes to the rules.

MAKING A DIFFERENCE

In the three cities there was sufficient community feeling present to ensure that incumbent councils were never really able to rest on their laurels. Conflict was to be found in all three cities between the various factions who saw council as important; but the vast majority of citizens were not involved in such conflict nor were they often aware of any. Relatively few citizens took public action that went beyond the confines of their locality. The size of the Lewisham and Knox councils possibly made it more difficult for residents in those cities to participate; however, there was no firm evidence to make this more than a possibility. Even with this possibility, in both of these cities, and even more so in St. Kilda, there were citizens who formed or joined networks and were eager to have their say and to stand or support others wishing to stand for election. These citizens went beyond talking to actively participating in the planning processes, which was the true form of participation according to the Skeffington Committee (1969, p. 1).

In St. Kilda the collective action that occurred through at least two "left of center" networks was one that was not a top-down process of council–assisted empowerment; it was action inspired by leaders within a number of networks who came together because they were unhappy with the empowerment processes among other things. They had worked through the local community organizations that provided the means of empowerment beyond the norm for most Australian cities, but they believed that these failed to adequately address the problems inherent in the system. With the emphasis on meeting the civil rights needs of the citizens, the rules needed to be changed if their objectives were to be met. The only way to do this was through control of the council.

In many ways this collective action could be said to be part of a worldwide trend or social movement. Citizens/residents—and particularly those living in the inner cities—seeking to establish new power relationships and influence groups were aided in their attempts by other changes occurring in their environments. Andrew Parkin in 1982 noted the mobilization trend which was occurring in many inner urban areas around the world at that time—that of the movement of sections of the educated middle-class into suburbs which had for many years been inhabited mostly by the working or poorer status groups.[7] It was a trend that aided the development of pressure groups, resident action associations, or social movements of various types. Such development ranged from support for left wing, social justice, community-related causes to ones centered on the rights of the self, of the individual over those of the community. The NIMBY syndrome was often espoused by these latter individuals. At the same time, cities also had ready access to potential activists who were concerned with what Jan Pakulski termed:

> the "eco-pax movement" (i.e., ecology-plus-peace). The movement is composed of a complex and interconnected network of organizations with a surrounding body of potentially mobilizable sympathisers. Its supporters inhabit a particular sociocultural arena focused on the highly educated, young, urban middle class (Waters and Crook 1993, p. 232).

In all three cities reviewed in this research there were such individuals and voluntary associations who were anxious to meet what they perceived to be their social obligations and duties. In St. Kilda, subsequent to winning control of the council, the progressive networks: were able to take on the mantle of power; changed at least some of the rules where possible; certainly changed the officers who would be responsible for implementing their policies; and implemented empowerment policies that met with varying success. However, voices of the underprivileged, for example, are still filtered through the voices of their representatives and the state government has been able to impose financial and planning restrictions upon the local authorities.

SOME NEGATIVE ASPECTS OF PARTICIPATION

What was obvious throughout this research was that the education processes important for participatory democracy (Pateman 1970, p. 44) and adequate and effective informing of, and consultation with, the community are still to be addressed despite the good intentions. Only a few residents are ever really aware of what is happening in their city, even in their local neighborhood, and citizens too often act and vote out of a lack of knowledge—according to myth as much as reality—and often do so successfully. There was the tendency in all three councils for many residents of all political persuasions to hear, believe, and act upon what they wanted to hear, believe and act upon despite the reality of the situation. The same was true for councillors who, generally, were more likely to accept the views of resident groups as being representative if they reflected their own philosophies. Three councillors interviewed agreed that this is more likely to be the case. It would appear that, like the residents, councillors also will see, hear and believe what best suits their interests.

While I am a firm advocate for citizen participation, the problems associated with its operations were only too obvious and the result often negative. Obviously present to me (as a biased observer to some extent) in all three cities were, just as Smith and Jones (1981, p. x) found, situations where: participation was used to divert, frustrate, and manipulate the community and proceedings; the methods that community workers used to promote participation were occasionally used for undesirable purposes; and, existing or aspiring elites of all kinds saw participation as an instrument to further their interests and empires.

In many cases the inadequacies of the processes lie with the citizens as much as with the council. If the citizens do not wish to be consulted, read the literature, attend meetings, be empowered then that is their right; however, they will continue to have their views unrepresented in the council and their needs unmet, unless, of course, their views are the same as those of the ruling group.

For those who were empowered, and it was most likely to be through participation at the level most near to home, there was the strong possibility that the individual participants were: better able to appreciate the connection between the public and private spheres; weigh impact of decisions made at all levels of government; and have "multiple opportunities to become an educated, public citizen" (Pateman 1970, p. 110). Motivated often out of altruism, a minority of residents in each city were able to participate in civic and altruistic associations, improving the welfare of the less privileged in society and improving the quality of democracy in their cities, which would confirm the views on altruistic activities of Salvador Giner and Sebastian Sarasa (1996, pp. 155-156). Altruism has been defined as: "regard for others, as a principle of action; opposite to egoism or selfishness" (the *Shorter Oxford Dictionary* on historical principles).

CONCLUSIONS

To conclude, if community formation is to occur, there is a need to look beyond the concept that locality and community are inextricably linked. The possession of a sense of community reflects "systematically the different experiences and social locations of residents" (Mabileau et al. 1989, p. 197). The circumstances have to be in place that will aid rather than hinder community development and these experiences need to be appropriate for the particular situation if individual residents are to form a community.

What is needed for success in citizen participation is that a community of circumstance has to come together with a strong desire to be involved and a common will and purpose. Within this community there needs to be among the citizens a sense of belonging, a feeling of identity with a community with a commitment to friends or place or cause or all of these which in turn leads to group solidarity—in other words, a sense of caring for one's community. It helps when there is a strong belief in the cause or in the organization's aims or in the validity of one's case as this can inspire others. If there are people with charismatic qualities present, that also helps to bring a network together, providing inspiration, leadership, and direction.

In all three cities there were many citizens who exercised their right to participate. Some were more successful than others; some did so out of a desire for individual power and control; some because their party or network encouraged them to, for example, run for council and they were so flattered they did so. Others participated out of anger at what was happening to their neighborhood or city; for some participation was a "one-off" event, and for others it was a life-long commitment. The most successful of the networks in the cities were those that had within their ranks individuals holding a variety of these reasons for their activism.

From my observations, what separated the most successful networks from the other activists in the cities (assuming success is gauged by effectiveness in influencing local affairs along with, but not essentially, longevity) was that they were joined with a sense of altruism, with a concern that went beyond the immediate needs of the individuals and group to concern for the welfare of fellow citizens. It was a sense of belief in the justice of their causes that motivated and enabled them in their activism. These altruists existed within all cities, operating from within political parties, but just as often not. They were often at odds with fellow citizens who emphasised individual rights while these altruists emphasized civil rights. Regard for others was their principle for action. Usually a threat to the status quo, in St. Kilda particularly, civil action led to these altruists challenging that status quo and assuming power, albeit, power shared with the bureaucrats. A community of circumstance, came together, captured the "spirit of the time" and changed the directions of their city through the processes of participatory democracy.

The most successful communities are able to draw "psychological strength from levels of motivation deeper than those of mere volition or interest, and [able to achieve] fulfilment in a submergence of individual will that is not possible in unions of mere convenience or rational assent...community is a fusion of feeling and thought, of tradition and commitment, of membership and volition" (Nisbet 1966, p. 48). Community formation and maintenance are aided when, as was the case with one local organizer, there is a sense of loyalty not just to friends but to a cause and a place, and a moral position is adopted. The strength of community feeling is very important then if the ordinary citizen is to be empowered, influencing the incumbent authorities. For a community to form and wield a degree of power, informed and skilled individuals must be involved with the time and commitment to bring together and maintain that community.

NOTES

1. It amalgamated with two neighboring councils to become the city of Port Phillip after most councils in the state of Victoria were forced by the state government to amalgamate in the early 1990s.

2. The research involved extended interviews with key actors in three cities, observations (as a participant when and where possible), and surveys of residents. The research was conducted over an extended period of time, finishing in 1996, thus enabling analysis of comparative changes across time (13 years in St. Kilda) and place to occur.

3. St. Kilda (population 46,000) is a cosmopolitan, bayside suburb in inner Melbourne which is now part of the city of Port Phillip. Knox (population 123,000) is situated in outer Melbourne at the foothills of the Dandenong Rangers and is a relatively new suburb. Lewisham (population 229,000) is an increasingly diverse city ranging from London's old docklands to newer, less deprived suburbs.

4. This group was established following the recommendations of the 1979 Bains Report on Local Government in Victoria with a left-leaning, but by no means radical, executive in 1983. It then promptly addressed issues going well beyond its supposed brief, as it became obvious that matters relating to finance and physical planning also had a social impact. The attitudes of the council officers varied, depending on whether the CDAC supported their proposals (which they often did) or not. The chief executive officer at that time maintained an outwardly friendly approach to the CDAC executive, but was highly critical of it when he believed it was intruding into policy areas which went beyond its brief.

5. "Turn The Tide" was a relatively radical local residents's group which had a significant impact on the transformation of the St. Kilda council and its policies during the period of observation.

6. The fact that many houses, some historic churches, and a few pubs were to be demolished to allow Mrs. Thatcher's retirement home to be by-passed was used as motivation to get the residents out.

7. This trend found in cities in Britain and Australian may not be so prevalent in American cities where reports abound of the white middle classes fleeing to the outlying, supposedly safer suburbs. They leave behind them decaying neighborhoods from which the poor cannot escape. The latter increasingly have to fend for themselves with often disastrous consequences for themselves and society.

REFERENCES

Bell, C., and H. Newby. 1971. *Community Studies: An Introduction to the Sociology of the Local Community*. London: George Allen and Unwin.

Blaikie, N. 1993. *Approaches to Social Enquiry*. London: Blackwell.

Giddens, A. 1984. *The Constitution of Society*. Cambridge: Polity Press.

Giner, S., and S. Sarasa. 1996. *Civic Altruism and Social Policy on International Sociology*, Vol. 11, pp. 139–159. London: Sage.

Gray, I. 1991. *Politics in Place: Social Power Relations in an Australian Country Town*. Cambridge: Cambridge University Press.

Gyford, J. 1991. *Citizens, Consumers and Councils: Local Government and the Public*. Houndmills: Macmillan.

Jones, M.A. 1981. *Local Government and the People: Challenges for the Eighties*. Melbourne: Hargreen.

Mabileau, A., G. Moyser, G. Parry, and P. Quantin. 1989. *Local Politics and Participation in Britain and France*. Cambridge: Cambridge University Press.

Munro-Clark, M., ed. 1992. *Citizen Participation in Government.* Sydney: Hale and Iremonger.

Nisbet, R.A. 1966. *The Sociological Tradition.* London: Heineman.

Painter, M. 1992. "Participation and power." Pp. 21-36 in *Citizen Participation in Government,* edited by M. Munro-Clark. Sydney: Hale and Iremonger.

Parkin, A. 1982. *Governing the Cities: The Australian Experience in Perspective.* Melbourne: Macmillan.

Parry, G., G. Moyser, and N. Day. 1992. *Political Participation and Democracy in Britain.* Cambridge: Cambridge University Press.

Pateman, C. 1970. *Participation and Democratic Theory,* Cambridge: Cambridge University Press.

Skeffington Committee. 1969. Report of the Committee on Public Participation in Planning, *Planning and People*, London: HMSO.

Smith, L., and D. Jones, eds. 1981. *Deprivation, Participation and Community Action.* London: Routledge and Kegan Paul.

Stoker, G. 1988. *The Politics of Local Government.* Houndmills: Macmillan Education.

Waters, M., and R. Crook. 1993. *Sociology One Principles of Sociological Analysis for Australians,* 3rd ed. Melbourne: Longman Cheshire.

Willmott, P. 1989. *Community Initiatives Patterns and Prospects.* London: Policy Studies Institute.

PART II

POVERTY, VICTIMIZATION, AND SOCIAL JUSTICE

POVERTY, GENDER, AND SOCIAL JUSTICE
VICTIMIZATION AND SOCIAL PROBLEMS IN RURAL PAKISTAN

Patrick C. Jobes

ABSTRACT

This paper discusses victimization and perceptions of social problems in rural Pakistan. Data were collected in 1996 through a survey of 160 rural Pakistan households. Questions on the interview schedule were derived from similar instruments currently used in the United States and Australia. The analyses offer a rare opportunity to consider victimization in a core Islamic nation. General discussions of social structure in rural Punjab are followed by elaborations examining how gender and stratification are associated with social problems, crime, and victimization. Substantive findings are presented after considering whether theories and instruments developed in First World settings are appropriate for studying poverty, social pronlems, and crime in the rural Third World. Conceptual difficulties encountered while conducting research in the Third World are considered, for example, the meaning of crime and the applicability of structural theories. Complex substantive issues related to the interpretation of crime and victimization in Pakistan are discussed. Serious

Research in Community Sociology, Volume 9, pages 89-122.
Copyright © 1999 by JAI Press Inc.
All rights of reproduction in any form reserved.
ISBN: 0-7623-0498-7

violent crime was found to be relatively common in rural Pakistan. In spite of the prevalence of serious crime few Pakistanis perceived crime as a major problem facing their households. Neither stratification nor gender were strongly associated with criminal victimization in respondent households or in perceiving crime as a social problem in Pakistan. However, women and poorer respondents were significantly more likely to believe that lack of opportunity was the most important problem facing their families. Strong support for a feminist theoretical orientation is provided. These findings imply that the concern for security, typical of First World nations, may be a luxury that people in the poverty of relatively high crime Third World settings can scarcely consider.

INTRODUCTION

Social disadvantage, victimizaton, and crime are universal social problems. The central research question of this paper is how being socially disadvantaged effects the likelihood of being victims to crime and of holding perceptions about social problems. Rural Pakistan, the site of this research, is a unique natural laboratory in which a caste system coexists with traditional Islam. The question is how being poor or female in a nation with immense poverty and gender bias affects perceptions regarding victimization. The differentiation in social structures and norms associated with social strata and gender contrasts to the West. The analyses are based on 160 personal interviews collected in 1996. They offer an empirical foundation for considering whether theoretical observations by western scholars are appropriate in the context of rural Pakistan.

A classic theoretical perspective underlies these analyses. Sociologists have long recognized profound distinctions between community and society (Durkheim 1947; Marx and Engels 1947; Toennies 1957) that lead to different kinds of crime and social problems (Schrag 1971), as well as to different kinds of responses to crime and social problems (Belyea and Zigraff 1988; Reiss and Tonry 1986). Differences between the First World (Core) and Third World (Periphery) make standard theories and analytic methods distinguishing community and society questionably appropriate (Wallerstein 1975). The classic theoretical perspective has been adopted for three reasons. First, the classic concepts are established in sociology for analyzing community behavior. They are based on historical and cross-sectional comparisons of theoretical and empirical interpretations that are compatible with recent orientations. Second, this research is exploratory. Couching the analyses in established theory provides a comparative framework for considering the structural differences within Pakistan. Third, the data are most suitable for structural analyses, whether conflict or functional in orientation (Taylor 1983). Research on rural social problems is rare in the industrialized world (Summers 1991). This research provides an unusual and unique opportunity to empirically examine rural problems in an Islamic Third World nation.

Several objectives guided this research. The first objective was to establish an initial empirical foundation for examining crime and victimization as social problems in rural Pakistan. This objective is closely tied to the issue of whether methodological and theoretical concepts developed in First World settings are appropriate for studying poverty, social problems, and crime in this rural Third World setting (Buttel and Newby 1980). The second objective was to examine the association of the "dual systems" (Agger 1989) of social class and gender with social problems, crime, and victimization. The data on victimization were generated from methods used in Australia, although Pakistan represents nations in the periphery (Bhaskar and Glyn 1995). Similarly, comparing differences within the polarized categories of gender and stratification, that exhibit a broad "gap" between the advantaged and the disadvantaged, will indicate the relative applicability of Western theories to this setting.

THE RESEARCH SETTING

Definitions of disadvantage describe human suffering. The differences in definitions require exercising considerable caution when deciding who are disadvantage to injustice and discrimination. In rural Pakistan, as for much of four continents, tens of millions of people have insufficient food, polluted water, and inadequate lodging for a healty life. For many, life involves a continual struggle to stay above the minimum. As long as people own a plot of land, most rural people have sufficient food. However, the ability to grow food is one of the few advantages enjoyed by many of the rural poor. By most criteria rural life is more disadvantageous for the poor. Eighty percent of Asian poverty occurs in rural areas (UNICEF 1995). Women are particularly at risk to poverty, extending problems such as malnutrition and poor health, into the generation of children they bear (Ward 1988).

Social services are largely absent in rural Pakistan, especially for women and the poor. Public education is minimal in most villages. Most adults are illiterate. Although improving, public health care, environmental protections, waste disposal, transportation, and communication facilities are similarly minimal by modern standards. Consumer items that require monetary exchange are luxuries beyond the reach of most people. Few people have much flexibility related to an exchange economy. The wife of a village leader spoke of her gratitude. After several years of saving, her family was able to buy a bicycle, which would allow her son to commute to a steady job fifteen kilometers away. The low modal and median incomes mask a much higher standard of living among a few residents with higher education, land ownership, and stable employment. Poverty in material terms should not be equated with cultural or moral poverty. Respondents often spoke of their wealth from traditions of family and faith.

Economic difficulties in Pakistan are severe. Globalization has made small farmers in Pakistan, as in most of the Third World, globally uncompetitive (McMichael 1996). They struggle to resist global pressures and to hold onto their land. During 1995 the annual income was about US $300.00 while inflation increased by nearly 20 percent. Subsistence farming provided a slight hedge against inflation, because at least some food could be grown, if a family owned even a small plot of land (Government of Pakistan 1996). However, fertilizer, soil additives, and fuels are expensive, making farmers vulnerable to inflation. Rural residents are becoming increasingly dependent on off-farm incomes to compensate for inflation and to permit upward mobility.

The poverty of opportunity implies being immersed in a social structure that offers little likelihood of increasing one's social position much beyond a level of survival. In a traditional culture such a level is the recurrent norm. In an industrializing world such a level becomes a ball and chain, dragging against opportunities. To remain in the same status with the same levels of production and income, implies being left behind in relatively deeper poverty, as the platform of the rest of the social and economic system is elevated. While poverty of survival has been identified for approximately one-eighth of rural Pakistan (Ali 1995; Ahmad 1993), poverty of opportunity reaches several times that many, depending on the standards that are used for comparisons (Government of Pakistan 1995). By economic criteria most Pakistanis are comparatively poor. Women are further deprived of occupational and educational opportunities.

Special attention is given to the opportunity structure related to stratification, that is caste, and to gender (Ward 1993). While the dynamics of disadvantage facing women in the traditional Third World are striking, societal support structures are stable. For example, single parenthood is endemic in the West due to a combination of high divorce rates and high frequency of illegitimate births. High levels of social problems among children of single parent families have been documented (Gottfredson and Hirschi 1990). This has become a severe multigenerational phenomenon (Vold, Bernard, and Snipes 1998, pp. 232-248). The dynamics of family structure and poverty in rural Pakistan are scarcely related to single parenthood, because divorce is rare and illegitimacy is almost nonexistent. This implies that explanations of crime and disadvantage popular in the West may be inapplicable in Pakistan.

Poverty in Pakistan, as through much of the Islamic Third World, is deeply established in a structure in which volition play s minor part. White (1994, p. 157) summarizes the interdependency of this life, "Where the group is the primary index of social life, elements of social life, elements of economic life—like money and relations of production—derive their meaning and their efficacy from the socio-cultural logic that informs life in general." Families are poor, generation after generation. The United Nations (1995) repeatedly recommends research and programs that may reduce the victimization of women. Women are poor in the context of intact families suffering from the combined absence of education, income, and land ownership. Women in other developing Asian nations generally also have lower education than men (Dreze and Saran 1995). While differences vary widely from one locale to another (191-195), they are generally coverging. In Punjab, India, for example, the percentage of literate men (76%) is only slightly higher than for women (69%). Illiteracy may be thought of as one form of victimization. It is an outright deprivation, as well as reduced opportunity. Women in the Third World, particularly in Pakistan, also are usually denied the opportunity to own land. Their land inheritance is given as part of the marriage contract (Agarwal 1994). Ownership and control of land are often equivalent to sufficient food to avoid starvation, to having a permanent home, and to some independence.

Family, Land Ownership, and Rural Poverty in Punjab State

Victimization and social justice in rural Pakistan must be understood in the context of family and land ownership. The extended family is the fundamental social unit in Pakistan. Family and the Islamic faith are the dominant institutions in Pakistani society. These characteristics probably affect how susceptible the family is to crime. Extended families are larger, which means that more members are at risk as victims. On the other hand, extended family homes rarely are empty, reducing their attractiveness as targets of crime. The extended family in Pakistan is an efficient unit for minimizing consumption and sharing the profits from production. Occupying a single house or enclave, large numbers of family members over several generations share everything from energy and consumer items to child and geriatric care. Because welfare programs are essentially nonexistent, the family is the primary source of support and opportunity At the same time, rigid informal control exercised by families imposes tight boundaries against the mixing of different strata. The advantaged consolidate, enhance, and perpetuate their wealth, status and power through arranged marriages and close family and caste connections. The poor are left a residual of ever-declining opportunity, less of almost nothing. The extended family allows a pooling of resources, permitting survival for the poor, or prosperity for the advantaged. Family members are expected to conform to strict roles and norms, if they are to share in family resources. In reality, survival is almost unimaginable for members, particularly women, who reject traditional roles and norms.

Ownership of agricultural land is the geographic and economic foundation in rural Punjab state, as in much of the agrarian Third World. Land ownership is widely dispersed. About 80 percent of the population resides in rural agricultural villages. Throughout much of history, land ownership was tantamount to prosperity and independence. Those advantages persist, although the levels of both prosperity and independence land brings are gradually being undermined. Population growth, combined with the fragmentation of lands through inheritance, have reduced the size of family farms. The median size of Punjab farms is only five acres. Even small farms often are composed of several very small plots, due to religious and traditional norms designating inheritance.

THE INDEPENDENT VARIABLE: SOCIAL DISADVANTAGES OF POVERTY AND GENDER

Poverty and Disadvantage

Social causality is a thorny concept that implies limited and specific knowledge that can be empirically established (Manis and Meltzer 1994). This research adopted the orientation that the disadvantages of being poor and female imply further disadvantages of being victim to crime and blocked opportunities. Literatures pertaining to modernization, crime, victimization, gender, and poverty are all so extensive that detailed citations are implausible here. More crucially, many of the finely detailed discourses on gender and poverty are too specific for these limited and general observations. While the review of the literature is deliberately brief, these findings contribute to the growing empirical foundations essential for comparative theoretical analyses of victimization and social problems in the Third World (Nowak 1989).

This literature review is divided into two sections. The first summarizes literature about poverty. The second addresses literature related to gender. Differences between Pakistan, as a Third World country, and the First World are implicit in the discussion. At the outset, it is important to address ethical issues. Issues of ethics are ancient to social science and are extraordinarily difficult to resolve. That scholars gain recognition and advancement through information and effort provided by informants and assistants is undoubtedly exploitive. Some scholars, such as Patai (1991) question whether ethical research on Third World women can be conducted by anyone other than themselves. Berik (1996) argues that such research can be ethical and effective. She conformed to the norms of her research setting, including obtaining approval of husbands, in order to conduct interviews with her respondents. Such conformity might be seen as unethical from an ethnocentric and feminocentric orientation. Aware of these ethical cautions, we believed that the questions and populations investigated in this analysis merited analysis.

The meaning of modernization in the late twentieth century is so complex that it almost defies accurate definition. The distinctions between mechanical and organic (Durkheim 1947), feudalism and capitalism (Marx and Engels 1947), traditional and rational (Weber 1958), and especially gemeinschaft and gesellschaft (Toennies 1957), convey relatively unlinear evolution into modernization, once industrialization beings. The complexity of this transition has been recognized by contemporary investigators in the developing world. Elias (1994) was among the earliest to recognize that developing nations in the twentieth century traversed a broad range of structural and interpretive categories. Pakistan is a quais-feudal nation with high gender and economic stratification. It also influences modern Islamic ideology, has nuclear weapons, and has had a woman prime minister. It is neither socialistic nor capitalistic. The historical foundations of the self-perpetuating stratification are beyond the perview of this research. That the social system favors strict informal caste control rather than individual freedom distinguishes Pakistan, yet the nation is coterminous with Western structures and ideologies.

Absolute and relative definitions were initially used to consider poverty in this research. An absolute substantive minimum implies insufficient food, water, and shelter to maintain health (Brown 1986; Miller and Holstein 1993). The analyses reported here use relative definitions, that can be based around any number of criteria (Sen 1992). One general parameter of relative poverty is the contemporary cultural yardstick by which it is gauged. Other parameters are the categories that are relevant to social justice, population, organization, environment, and technology (Duncan and Schnore 1959). These categories reflect more than minimal food, water, and shelter for survival. They include political variables, such as equal opportunity and representation. Any diversion away from the absolute meaning of poverty is by definition, a relative meaning. Both absolute definitions of poverty and relative definitions of injustice have conceptual and practical weaknesses. One way of thinking about absolute poverty is that along a continuum of economic prosperity, people who lack the essentials of life are absolutely poor. Furthermore, particular categories, women in this study, may be treated equally on a simple economic absolute scale, yet be highly disadvantaged in terms of education, employment, and other criteria (Sumner 1982). Some disadvantages many people endure may be left out when absolute definitions are employed. In 1998 the strictest standard might be the conditions under which the international elites live. A less stringent standard might be those typical for advantaged nations. These kinds of optima imply the hope of providing all deprived people with what is available by some contemporary standard.

Gender and Disadvantage

Literature related to gender and opportunity is so extensive and lively that a brief summary is impossible, This succinct review will address particular issues pertinent to this research. Most of the references pertain to general issues associated with gender and disadvantage, primarily because the literature about Pakistan is so limited. Extensive reviews and encyclopedias rarely mention Pakistan. The encyclopedic *Women and Politics World Wide* (Nelson and Chowdhury 1994) has few references and no chapter about Pakistan. Some contemporary issues cannot be discussed regarding Pakistan because no data have been collected that might help to resolve them. Other issues appear to be so obscure or irrelevant for the research at hand, that they are inappropriate to consider in any depth.

Dozens of particular issues associated with research and analysis of gender and poverty have been recognized. These are summarized here as four sets of issues associated with a dominant element of analysis. Overriding all of these is our fundamental endorsement of women's international human rights. Any distinction, exclusion, or resistance of fundamental freedoms on the basis of sex or marital status is objectionable to the author (Cook 1994). Pakistan has ratified the Political and Economic Covenants of the United Nations (Hossain 1994). Nevertheless, Muslim law offers numerous advantages to men with regard to marriage to non-Muslims and to multiple marriages. Less abstractly, the norms of extended family/caste system are more restrictive for women than men.

The following issues are pertinent and empirically important to our research. The functional versus conflict debate is among the oldest in social science. The debate is relevant for expressing moral outrage against hegemony, often simplified as First World and capitalist men dominating Third World and proletariat workers and women. As Chodorow (1978) and Johnson (1993) have made clear, the issue is much more complex. For most comparative analyses, the debate is largely irrelevant because both sets of theories acknowledge gender differentiation within societies. More pertinent are the intense debates about how social structures create and perpetuate gender differences. Blumberg (1984) contends that *the* cause of women's disadvantage is their failure to control production and surplus value. We begin with a moderate position on this debate. We contend that Pakistani women are at enormous occupational and educational disadvantage in a system under the control of men with the tacit acceptance by women. Pakistan lies in the middle of the "civilizing process," as discussed by Elias (1994), somewhere between fedualism and capitalism and more Gemeinschaft than Gesellschaft. Life in the rural villages, while clearly economic, is also passionately religious and familial. A facile presupposition that the economy determines other institutions is too simple. The complexity of village life involves a synthesis of conflict and functional structures.

Following Engels (1948) seminal classic, contemporary feminist scholars have insisted that gender should be considered in relationship to stratification. The issue is complex because women traverse the range of economic strata, yet suffer from occupational and economic disadvantages within each (Chafetz 1990). Male domination in a distinctly gendered division of labor appears to be standard in traditional societies with established structures of private property (Scovill 1991). Jacobsen (1994) contends the domination is due to greater mobility and physical strength. These factors coalesce in rural Pakistan. Male domination of properties and decision making is molded into the intensely economic extended family/caste system. Less than 14 percent of women in Pakistan are in the labor. The sex segregation index is 25, in the lowest quintile among nations. These figures are among the lowest in the world, and are typical of North African and Middle Eastern nations (Jacobsen 1994, pp. 420-429). Gender is clearly linked to differential opportunity in manners similar to the poor.

The issue of whether women have lower social status from a classic economic conflict perspective is complex. Women are part of the same extended family and caste system as are men. The representation of women in various strata is essentially the same as among men. Caste determines marriage partners, who usually are drawn within the extended family. First wives generally have higher status. Subsequent status, power, and wealth are allocated to individuals *through* the family.

Literature on modernization, particularly about changes in world values, is among the most current and succinct empirical and theoretical orientations for cross-national comparisons (Huntington 1996). The World Values Survey (Inglehart 1997) has shown that enduring familial and religious structures and norms persist despite economic development. Although secularization follows modernization, the relationship is multilinear. Sensitivity to differential treatment of women is among the last societal characteristics to modernize. In Pakistan evolution toward equality is in an early stage. We assume that most women will resemble the significantly lower education and occupation achievements of poor men. We are interested in whether those influences of disadvantage make the victimization and perceptions of women and poor men similar or whether economic status offsets the influences of gender disadvantage.

The World Values Survey (Inglehart 1990) has identified scarcity values, typical of poor developing societies, and security values, typical of wealthy developed ones. Developed nations have the luxury of being concerned with matters of security, like crime, equal opportunity, and environmental quality. Developing countries that lack economic and physical prosperity, like Pakistan, are much more concerned with material needs, that is, scarcity values. We are also interested in examining whether the poor and women in Pakistan are more concerned with scarcity values than are the wealthier and men.

Methodological issues are related to both empirical and ethical aspects of this study. Empirical challenges have been made that data on the Third World, in general, and about poor uneducated women, in particular may be unreliable and invalid if collected by educated investigators from the First World. Gunew and Yeatman (1993, p. xvii) warn to be careful about "who is permitted to speak on behalf of whom." The question of whether any outsider has sufficient knowledge, understanding, and empathy to engage in field research with any group is ancient in social science. Wolf (1993) has warned about the dilemmas of such work. Some scholars advocate such research. Notably Turkish, although American-educated, Berik (1996) defends her research on women rug weavers in Turkey as valid and reliable. We are sensitive to both sides of the issue. Every aspect of the work was conducted with local colleagues and assistants who understood and respected the local culture. Nevertheless, they were educated, while most of the respondents were not. Standard research procedures were followed to reduce empirically induced biases.

Differences between how men and women report victimization and how they perceive the importance of crime and other social problems are presented. These differences are then considered, controlling for the effects of land ownership, savings, and social status (caste). The purpose is to discover how gender and social stratification influence experiences and perceptions related to social problems and victimization. Research has indicated many women, whether in the First World or the Third (Chase-Dunn 1989) are reticent to discuss their victimization, especially at the hands of family members and partners.

Conflict and functional theories offer competing orientations of how structural factors underlay disadvantage. Both theories suggest that culture and poverty are linked. Classic authors most historically associated with these opposing orientations conducted extensive research in developing societies. Redfield (1955) took a strong functional position in the lineage of Durkheim, that stratification is an adaptive aspect of village life. Banfield (1958), following Redfield. maintained that where village culture was dominated by highly integrated and self-serving family systems, what he referred to as "amoral familists," social opportunities were gridlocked. Such systems prevented effective and adaptive change into a democratic and open market system. Lewis (1961) advocated a conflict perspective in the Marxian tradition. He maintained that people in poverty organized their lives rationally and responsively to survive within limited resources, largely controlled by an elite. Banfield implied that the family and community structures perpetuated poverty through their systems of beliefs and interactions. Lewis identified the broader societal structure as forcing adaptations made by poor families and communities.

These competing orientations both assume that norms, values, and adaptations of the poor are inextricably tied to social structure. Conflict theory further suggests that implemented changes in the polity and the economy increase opportunity and reduce poverty. The implications of Banfield's work are less optimistic. If polity and economy are normative reflections of the beliefs, values and interaction systems of the family, then any redistribution of power and exchange will be dominated by the family. Attempts to implement opportunities and reduce poverty may be only marginally and discouragingly effective. Except for Engels early work, these orientations, until recently, remained somewhat gender-blind. Although conscious of different roles and activities between men and women, they emphasized differences between strata. Lower strata were composed of disadvantaged men *and* women. A contribution of feminist research has been to identify the relative disadvantage of women throughout all strata. For example, Carlen (1988), while writing about women in Great Britain, identifies homebound women and women with children as one of the four categories of women in poverty who are at special social, if not criminal, risk.

The research assumes that the greater the differences between structural categories and how crime and social problems are experienced and perceived, the more the conflict orientation is supported. If structurally disadvantaged persons, that is, women and the poor, experience and perceive crime and social problems differently, then conflict, rather than consensus, is demonstrated within the social structure. If women and the economically disadvantaged are more critical of the opportunity structure, there is a foundation for disagreement and the potential for change in the community.

The theoretical distinction between liberal feminist and radical feminist traditions are relevant for these analyses. Liberal feminism, which is compatible with functional thought, assumes that equity of economic opportunity is the primary issue distinguishing the behavior and perceptions of men and women (Becker 1981). Men and women who are sharing work and being rewarded equally should be similar according to this perspective. The problem is defined as unequal distribution with the system, rather than the system of distribution itself. That women might enjoy equal status (caste) and economic wealth as men, does not mean that they have equal means for working toward those ends through education and employment. Radical feminism, which is within the conflict orientation, assumes that existing systems of distribution are inequitable between men and women in order to preserve patriarchy (Mies 1986). A partial resolution to this theoretical issue is possible through this analysis. If women, especially more advantaged women, consistently believe that issues of equity are more important than do their male counterparts, the implication is that the system is failing to provide sufficient opportunities. The cause may rest in the failure of an otherwise effective social system, or with the possibility that the system, itself, is fundamentally flawed. A theoretical synthesis of feminist theory with classic structural theories is attempted in the conclusion.

Finally, there are issues that are inappropriate to be considered further. While acknowledging the importance of these issues this research is unable to empirically address them. The first of these are theoretical. The issue of whether gender and stratification discrimination are based on biological foundations is not explored here. While sympathetic to biological notions of male hegemony (Allen 1989), we collected no data measuring the evolution of treatment of women and poor based on biological characteristics. The project assumed that differences in treatment and opportunities existed, and that those differences reflected the social structure and culture. Similarly, the question of rational choice is considered to be irrelevant for the research setting. As England and Kilbourne (1990) have pointed out, choices taken for granted by First World women, for example, whether, who and when to marry, or whether to attend school or to work, are essentially nonexistent in much of the Third World. Indeed, the meanings of choice between the two settings appear to be so epistemologically different that an entire project would be required to make sense of rational choice.

THE DEPENDENT VARIABLE: SOCIAL PROBLEMS, CRIME, AND VICTIMIZATION

Social problems, including crime and victimization, were treated as the dependent variable, the consequence of disadvantage (Clinard 1944). One of the most developed bodies of literature in criminology has studied poverty as a cause of crime (Harries 1971; Hagan 1989), a central issue to this discussion. More recent literature in feminist criminology has begun to investigate the effects of gender discrimination within the social justice system (Smart 1976). Perceptions of crime and social problems among both of these categories of the disadvantaged also are investigated in this research.

Contemporary theories of social justice maintain the poor experience a double disadvantage of poverty and of vulnerability to crime (Smith 1994). Such theories have been developed by Western scholars, primarily from liberal or socialist intellectual traditions (Quinney 1977). Their applicability to Third World nations that lie outside those traditions, has been examined less. It is possible that the pervasive influences of family and kinship structures and Islamic religious beliefs, for example, may modify the effects of income and wealth on the social problems they experience. Having been conducted in rural Pakistan, this research controlled for these influences through the selection of the location. If the relationship between economic inequity and social problems are not present in Pakistan, then Western theories of social justice and behavior may have to be modified for much of the Islamic Third World (Jamieson and Flanagan 1989). For example, the seriousness of rural vandalism demonstrated in Western nations (Alfano and Magill 1976; Cleland 1990) may not occur in Pakistan. As will become apparent, homicide data for the rural United States bear little resemblance to what will be reported here (Kowalski and Duffield 1990). No reference to international rural crime data was found. International comparisons between Pakistan and the West are limited and dated. For example, the Comparative Crime Data File (Archer and Gartner 1984) summarizes gender murder, rape, burglary, and theft data for Pakistan for only 1961-1968 at which time property crime in Pakistan was slightly lower and personal crime was slightly higher.

Three research questions guided how relative advantages from gender and wealth affect the perceptions and definitions of social problems. The first question was related to social advantage and victimization. Were women and the poor more likely to be victims? The second question was whether these two categories of the disadvantaged identified the same problems facing their families. Did sharing a common culture and location create a common pool of problems? As an alternative, did differential disadvantage introduce a different set of problems or a different prioritization among problems? For example, were rich and poor, and men and women, equally likely to mention inadequate opportunities or crime? The third question was whether crime was given the same valence in comparison with other problems by the disadvantaged. Did the strain of disadvantage and poverty make crime seem relatively less important to women and the poor? Or, did poverty or gender disadvantages create such increased risk and personal vulnerability, that crime seemed relatively more important to them? Were larger families or landowners more at risk, or more likely to perceive themselves to be? The resolution to these issues can partially be resolved by examining their relative criminal victimization. Were victims more likely to believe crime was a serious problem or to identify other problems?

METHODOLOGY

Following pretesting, an interview was administered to a systematic sample of 170 rural households drawn from Gughersingh, Harmonium, and Dholan Wala, agricultural villages located in Faisalabad District. One hundred and sixty respondents agreed to be interviewed during October and November 1996, creating a response rate of 94 percent. The district contains the densest concentration of agriculture in Punjab. Women respondents were interviewed by women, away from men. Men respondents were interviewed by men, away from women. Interviews took approximately one hour.

A quasi-experimental design guided the analyses (Cook and Campbell 1979). Multiple indicators were collected, each measuring a different component pertinent to rural poverty and to social problems and victimization in order to compensate for the weaknesses of any single indicator. Although complimentary, each measured a qualitatively different aspect of the dependent variables. The effects are cumulative (Zetterberg 1986). Several economic characteristics, including income and educational achievement, were measured to describe the sample in conventional terms. Following initial analyses, land ownership, social class, and household savings were selected along with gender, as the most discriminating measures of advantage. Measures common in the West, such as income per household, source of income, and the per capita income per household, dependency ratio, occupation and education of the head of household were obfuscated because of the complexities involved with the extended family structure and agricultural economy. For example, several well-educated, high income children might reside with parents (household heads) who were farmers with little education.

Farm ownership is a powerful and crucial economic indicator in rural Pakistan. Farming is notoriously difficult to classify as an occupational rank, hence the use of farm size as an indicator of stratification. Farm ownership was measured by whether the households owned property and by the number of acres owned. The number of acres owned were categorized as under .25, between .25 and 12.5 acres, and over 12.5 acres. Farm ownership is crucial to rural poverty, because it provides the potential for subsistence. Owning even a small plot of land can make an adequate food supply and a site for a home possible. Landownership also can provide income derived from agricultural production. The number of respondents who were not farmers was small for statistical analysis. The second measure of stratification was status. A self-reported global measure of social position, as upper, middle, or lower, was asked. These reflect castes, about which there is high agreement. The third measure was household savings. This simple economic indicator distinguishes between households that might have economic advantage, even when they own no land. Savings had a weak negative correlation with land ownership ($r = -.23$), and higher positive correlations with household earnings ($r = .46$).

Questions inquiring about social problems, crime, and victimization were sequentially constructed in order to evolve quantitative measures out of qualitative information (Newman 1997). First, an open-ended question asked what were, "the three most important problems affecting your family." This question established a qualitative context for the consideration of crime, as well as for unprompted subjective interpretations of family problems. The second question introduced the notion of crime through a self-anchored Likert scale. It asked how serious crime was compared to the worst problem mentioned in the preceding question. This question was followed by a series of questions about crimes committed against the respondent and other household members. These questions were drawn almost verbatim from the Australian victimization survey (Australian Bureau of Statistics 1994). A question about animal theft replaced the question about vehicle theft asked in Australia. Unlike offenses reported to the police, victimization surveys do not provide data based on precise legal definitions. Respondents provided general information that cannot be used to explore nuances of precise meanings of crimes. Respondents were asked to report how they and other household members had been victimized during the past twelve months and the past five years. When a crime was reported, respondents were then asked to describe it in detail. Their descriptions qualitatively enriched the information about the crimes. The survey, as a self-report, may diverge from officially reported statistics, although no official statistics were available for these rural areas (Biderman and Lynch 1991). All questions, except for the first, were pre-coded. Categories summarizing the responses to the open-ended question were developed through content analysis upon completion of the interviews. Measures for whether respondents referred to problems with crime, environment, or inadequate opportunities negatively affecting their households emerged and were added to the coding protocol.

Victimization data were treated in manners conventional to criminology. That is, social injustices, such as exploitation of poor laborers, were only listed as a crime if they were in violation of a law. They also were recorded as social problems, if they were mentioned. Unless otherwise stated, data are reported per respondent and per household. Multiple crimes against a single victim are reported as a single victim and a single crime. This conservative method of summarizing data may understate the actual amount of reported crime in order to allow more systematic tabulation.

The data are subject to cautions about comparing international crime statistics that have been made by Archer and Gartner (1984) and van Dijk and Mayhew (1993). The difficulties effectively compose a list of the range problems of research, compounded by the attempt to compare data from different nations. Differences in sampling techniques, question construction and translation, coding and rules for calculations, and the host of other definitional and measurement issues, are inescapable. However, these problems seem rather uncomplicated and intelligible compared to the cultural characteristics that underly the epistmological differences in meanings that respondents assign to crime. Local residents and colleagues who evaluated the questionnaire before it was administered believed that it was unlikely that respondents would honestly answer questions regarding victimization, particularly victimization of family members other than themselves. Their opinions, based on familiarity with the culture and experience with respondents in the area, were that the family is an extremely private institution about which little public admission is made. They believed that most serious crimes are committed in the context of caste/family vendettas, recurrent retaliations among known adversaries. Many legal violations, especially assaults by family members, are not perceived to be criminal offenses nor likely to be talked about.

Conducting this research made it possible to test their suppositions that crime in rural Pakistan would remain a "dark figure" in spite of a victimization survey. If gross differences in amounts of victimization occur between respondents and other family members or between victimization during the past year, as opposed to the past five years, then underreporting will be demonstrated. Underreporting might have occurred for several reasons. Respondents might have deliberately withheld information about crimes they knew had occurred. They also might not have considered behaviors to have been crimes, although such acts were legally defined as crimes. Respondents also might have forgotten violations, especially crimes that took place five years earlier. Reservations that this type of victimization survey might generate unreliable and invalid information have been noted by Travis, Eggar, O'Toole. Brown, Hogg, and Stubbs (1995). The sample size is small. Multiple victimizations of a person or a household, particularly around a single incident, are difficult to specify. Questions related to sexual offenses are especially unreliable because of reluctance and culpability of respondents (Coleman and Moyniham 1996). Despite these reservations directed against studies of this type, the alternative would have been to not conduct the research. Although the sample was small, the response rate was very high. Fortunately, the traditional agricultural homogeneity of rural Punjab may not require as large a sample as more diverse populations might require. This research is only a starting point. The findings will, hopefully, provide sufficient insight to encourage further development and refinement of methods for investigating victimization in settings like Pakistan.

Data were analyzed through successively more complex statistics. Descriptive statistics summarized distributions of variables. Pearson's product-moment correlation was calculated for all interval measures and used to cull variables. Crosstabulations with gamma, an ordinal measure of association (γ) and Chi-square (X^2), a measure of dispersion, were calculated for the zero-order cross-tabulations between categorized independent and dependent variables (Costner 1965). Crosstabs were specified holding gender and stratification measures constant, examining how each was associated with poverty and social problems. Multivariate techniques were not used because of limitations imposed by the small number of crimes reported.

DATA ANALYSES AND FINDINGS

Sample households closely approximated the population distribution in size and composition, validating assumptions that the sample was random. No significant differences across either independent or dependent variables were found among villages, further indicating that sampling was unbiased. Zero-order correlations were calculated among all indicators of independent and dependent variables. Landownership, savings, and class were selected for specification because they were relatively independent and had higher correlations than other measures, including the dependency ratio, per capita income, and education of respondent. The following correlations were significant at the .001 level, although few were high enough to merit further examination. The precise measure of poverty made a difference in less than 3 percent of the cases in comparison to alternative measures. Of the 96 households with land, 5 had less than minimal food intake. Because per capita income and landownership were only moderately correlated (r = .25), many households with low incomes may have avoided the spectre of starvation by owning land.

Socio-Demographic Characteristics

The sample included slightly more women (86 = 54%) than men (74 = 46%). Respondents were systematically requested to be the male or female head of the household before the interview. No women refused to be interviewed. The total number of persons in the households was 1156. Household size ranged from 3 to 16 members, with a mean of seven (7.23). The sample dependency ratio was 50, and ranged from 0 to 100 among sample families. Dependency ratio was strongly correlated with per capita income (r = .53), indicating that the larger the family, the greater the income.

Economic measures indicated that the sample was similar to the region. Land-ownership ranged from 40 percent landless, to 52 percent smaller landowners (up to 12.5 acres) and 8 percent larger landowners (over 12.5 acres). Monthly household incomes ranged from no income, reported by 13 (8%) respondents to 54,500 Pakistani rupees (Rs), which was double the next highest household income ($1 US = 40 Rs at the time of the survey). Median monthly income was 633 Rs, approximately $192 US, per year. Most (84%) respondents reported some income from off-farm employment. Several households (12%) received income from family members living abroad. Such remittances provided essentially the entire income for 10 households.

Most (53%) respondents were illiterate. Their median education was less than four years. Women respondents (72%) were particular illiterate. Only 11 (13%) women had more than 5 years of education. Because household is the analytic unit, the most highly educated person in the household is an alternative measure of education level. Using that measure, 4 percent had no education. The respective percentages among the most educated household member who had less than 6 years, between 6 and 10 years, and over 10 years of education were 16%, 51%, and 33%, respectively. Median education was 7 years.

Fifty-one percent of male household heads were farmers. Among other occupational categories, only laborers (16%) and unemployed (12%) composed more than 10 percent of the male sample. All other categories accounted for only one-fifth (21%) of the male occupations. Few (20%) women respondents were employed outside the home.

Correlations among the indicators of independent variables broadly demonstrated the reciprocal influences of both cultural and economic variables. Women respondents were much less educated ($r = -.42$) and less likely to be farmers ($r = -.37$) than men. Their households were slightly less likely to have savings ($r = -.14$). Except for lower education and being housewives, female respondents had socio and demographic characteristics very similar to males. Age of respondents was weakly associated with occupation and savings. Older respondents were slightly less likely to be farmers ($r = -.13$) or to have savings ($r = -.19$). Economic and social status measures covaried highly and significantly, indicating that they were measuring an underlying dimension of relative advantage.

Social Problems, Crime, and Victimization

Respondents reported 28 specific types of social problems facing their households. Seventeen percent reported no problems. The three most frequently mentioned of these "most serious" problem—poverty (14%), inflation (13%), and unemployment (13%)—attested the importance of economic difficulties in rural Pakistan. Variables distinguishing problems with opportunity structure, environment, and crime were generated by categorizing open-ended responses describing the most important problem that family of the respondent was experiencing.

Table 1.   Frequencies of Problems Considered to be One of
the Three Most Important Facing 160 Households in Rural Punjab*

	Considered to be One of the Three Most Serious	
Type of Problem	Yes (100%)	No
Lack of Opportunities	93 (58.1%)	67 (41.9%)
Environment	22 (13.8%)	138 (86.2%)
Crime	11 (6.9%)	149 (93.1%)
Other Problems	6 (3.8%)	154 (96.2%)
No Problems	18 (17.4%)	

Note: Based on the survey question,
*"What are the three most important problems facing your household?"

Table 2.   Victimes of Past Crimes: Respondents and Family Members
During the Past 1 and 5 Years in 160 Rural Pakistan Households

	1 Year				Past 5 Years			
	Respondents		Family Members		Respondents		Family Members	
Variables	Frequency	Percent	Frequency	Percent	Frequency	Percent	Frequency	Percent
None	149	93.1	1151	99.6	143	89.4	1142	98.8
Animal theft	7	4.4	2	.17	11	6.9	4	.34
Unlawful entry	—	—	1	.08	1	.6	1	.08
Robbery—unarmed	—	—	—	—	1	.6	1	.08
Robbery—armed	1	.6	—	—	1	.6	1	.08
Extortion/black-mail	3	1.9	—	—	3	1.9	1	.08
Abduction, Kidnapping	—	—	1	.08	—	—	1	.08
Murder	—	—	1	.08	—	—	4	.34
Total	160	100.0	1156	100.0	160	100.0	1156	100.0

Opportunity problems (58%) included income, employment, marriage expenses, and education. Opportunity problems were much more frequent that environmental (14%) or crime (7%) problems, which included civil and other legal disputes (see Table 1).

Crime was specified to be considerably less problematic for most households than the most serious problem facing their family. When asked to compare crime to the most serious problem specified by the respondents, crime was given a mean Likert score of 3.2 (1 = no problem and 5 = most serious problem). More respondents did not perceive crime to be a problem (16%) than perceived it to be as serious as the most important problem faced by their family (11%). Whether measured categorically (7%) or comparatively (11%), crime was regarded as an important problem by a small minority of respondents.

Victimization responses are summarized in Table 2. Among 160 respondents, almost none had experienced crime during the last year (93.1%) or the past five years (89.4%). Eleven (6.9%) respondents reported being victims of crime during the past year. Seventeen (10.6%) had been victims during the previous five years. Five crimes were reported for other household members during the past year (.4%), and 12 household members had been victims during the past five years (1.2%).

The figures in Table 2 convert to the percentages of victimization reported in Table 3. The estimated numbers of victims were, respectively, 106/1,000 respondents, 312/1,000 households, and 31/1,000 household members during the past five years in rural Pakistan. Respondents were much more likely to report themselves as victims than to report other household members.

The most commonly reported victimizations, accounting for about two-thirds (64%) of the crimes against respondents and four-tenths (40%) of the crimes against other household members during the past year, involved theft of livestock. Excluding this, the overall frequency of crime would have dropped by more than one-half. The remaining crimes tended to be extremely serious by Western standards. Blackmail/extortion and murder were the second and third most frequent crimes. About one-fourth of respondents who were victims during the past year, had been blackmailed or extorted. Four murders had been committed against household members in the past five years. These figures were much higher than those reported in most industrial societies for the same categories of crimes. Conversely, crimes typical to industrial societies, such as unlawful entry with intent to steal, robbery, and sexual assault were rarely reported in rural Pakistan. The number of murders was too few to allow precise generalization although they are consistent over a five-year period. However, the corresponding murder and blackmail/extortion rate would be 8/1,000, many times higher than in Western nations. Other types of property crime were relatively rare, and no sexual crimes were even reported.

Crime, as a problem reported by respondents, was not highly correlated with self-reported problems of other types. Only the correlation between victimization of the head of household during the past year and reporting environmental problems as serious ($r = .14$) exceeded .10. Indicators of crime, however, were interrelated. Believing that crime was a serious problem, as an open-ended response, was moderately associated with responses that crime was the most serious problem ($r = .24$), along with victimization among respondents during the past year ($r = .14$), and victimization of other household members during the past year ($r = .13$), the past five years ($r = .23$) and in total ($r = .32$). Reporting crime as the most serious problem facing the family showed even higher correlations with victimization of other household members during the past twelve months ($r = .23$), five year ($r = .32$), and in total ($r = .39$). Although crime was described as the most serious problem for only 11 households, those families were likely to have recently suffered from it. Victimization of household members was a stronger discriminative indicator than was victimization of the respondent, although respon-

Table 3.   Victims per 1,000 Households, Respondents, and
Persons in Rural Pakistani Households, 1992-1996

	Pakistan
Households (N = 160)	*160*
Break and Enter	31/000
Attempted Break and Enter	—
Total Break and Enter	31/000
Animal theft	(281)/000
Total households	312/000
Persons (respondents) (N = 160)	
Robbery (and Extortion)	106/000
Assault	—
Sex Assault (and Abduction)	—
Total	106/000
Persons (total in households) (N = 1156)	
Robbery (and Extortion)	19/000
Assault (and Murder)	8/000
Sex Assault (and Abduction)	4/000
Total	31/000

Notes: Estimates for victims are five times the 1996 violations; for households they are five times the combined
victim and household 1996 violations. When there are five-year reports, but no 1996 violations, the
estimates is of the combined victim and household five-year reports.

dents were at much higher risk than other household members. That is, when household members had been victimized, that increased the perception that crime was a problem even more than when respondents had been victimized.

Qualitative Association Between Stratification and Dependent Variables

The questions of whether social stratification, in general, and poverty, in particular, were associated with reporting social problems, crime and victimization were central to this research. Table 4 summarizes how relative advantage was associated with perceiving crime as an important problem and with having been a victim during the past year. Lower status respondents were more likely to have been victims during the prior year ($\gamma = .36$, X^2 ns). Conversely, higher status respondents more frequently although insignificantly, perceived crime as the most serious problem ($\gamma = -.22$, X^2 ns). Only 6 percent of lower caste respondents believed crime was the most important problem facing their family, one-half the figure (12%) for upper castes. Although statistically insignificant, caste was more associated with victimization than were landownership, savings, income, or gender.

The findings regarding landownership, household savings, and gender were analogous to caste. More large landowners (30%) believed that crime was the most serious problem facing their households ($\gamma = -.27$, $X^2 = .03$) than landless (6%) or

Table 4. Caste, Perception of Crime Problems, and Victimization Against Respondents During the Past 12 Months

	Crime is Most Important[*]		Victim in Household Last Year	
	Agree	Disagree	Yes	No
Caste	$\gamma = -.22$	$x^2 = $ NS	$\gamma = -.36$	$x^2 = $ NS
Land (acres) owned	$\gamma = -.27$	$x^2 = .03$	$\gamma = -.06$	$x^2 = $ NS
Household savings	$\gamma = .20$	$x^2 = $ NS	$\gamma = .18$	$x^2 = $ NS
Total income	$\gamma = -.26$	$x^2 = $ NS	$\gamma = .21$	$x^2 = $ N
Gender	$\gamma = .22$	$x^2 = $ NS	$\gamma = .05$	$x^2 = $ NS

Note: [*]The same 11 respondents who listed crime was one of the "three most important problems facing your household" also reported that "crime is serious as the most serious problems facing your family."

small landowners (4%), although there was no difference in their having been victims ($\gamma = -.06$, $x^2 = $ ns). Consistently, women and respondents with lower incomes were a little more likely, although insignificantly, to perceive crime as important. These findings will be specified in more detail in the following section. Similarly, neither women ($\gamma = .22$, $x^2 = $ ns) nor households without savings ($\gamma = .20$, $x^2 = $ ns) regarded crime as more important than men or households with savings.

Perceptions about the seriousness of crime did not vary significantly with social status and economic position, although some differences were apparent. For example, among the 18 respondents who said crime was equivalent to their most serious problem, 11 reported that they had no savings and were in the lower castes. Nevertheless, the statistical associations between economic and status indicators were weakly and insignificantly related. Although landownership was moderately associated, *no independent variables were strongly and significantly associated with experiencing crime, defining crime as the most important family problem, or ranking it as a serious problem.*

Landownership, caste, gender, and having household savings were all strongly and significantly associated with the perception that a lack of opportunity was the most serious problem facing their households. Land holding also was inversely related to believing that lack of opportunities was the most serious problem. Even so, the data are bi-modal. The largest landowners and the landless were more likely to be concerned about opportunities. Households without savings were much more likely ($\gamma = .47$, $x^2 = .001$) to report opportunity problems (see Table 5 for a detailed numeric description). Caste was strongly associated ($\gamma = .37$, $x^2 = .02$) with perceiving opportunity problems. Caste was also moderately associated with someone in the household having been a victim during the past year ($\gamma = .36$, $x^2 = $ ns). Opportunity structure thus emerged as the most serious differentiating measure of social disadvantage, far greater than the concern with crime.

Table 5. Caste, Gender, Household Savings, Landownership, and
the Belief that Opportunity is the Most Serious Problem

	Opportunity is the Most Serious Problem		
	Agree	Disagree	Total
Caste ($\gamma = .37\ X^2 = .02$)			
Low	40	14	54
	(74.1%)	(25.9%)	(34.0%)
Medium	41	39	80
	(51.3%)	(48.8%)	(50.0%)
High	12	13	25
	(48.0%)	(52.0%)	(15.7%)
Landowners ($\gamma = .36\ X^2 = .001$)			
None	49	15	64
	(76.6%)	(23.4%)	(40.3%)
.25-5 acres	23	30	53
	(43.4%)	(56.6%)	(33.3%)
5-12.5 acres	14	18	32
	(43.8%)	(56.3%)	(20.1%)
12.5+ acres	7	3	10
	(70.0%)	(30.0%)	(6.3%)
Gender ($\gamma = -.77\ X^2 = .002$)			
Men	33	40	
	(45.2%)	(54.8%)	
Women	60	26	86
	(69.8%)	(30.0%)	(54.1%)
Savings ($\gamma = -.47\ X^2 = .001$)			
Yes	32	40	72
	(44.4%)	(55.6%)	(45.3%)
No	61	26	87
	(70.0%)	(29.9%)	(54.7%)
Total	93	66	159
	(58.5%)	(41.5%)	(100.0%)

Gender and Social Problems

Men and women respondents differed little with regard to experiences or perceptions related to crime. Responding to the question, "Were you a victim of
crime during the past twelve months?" few men (4/74 = 5%) or women ($N = 7/86$
= 8%) had been victim to crime during the last year. Women were slightly and
insignificantly more likely to have been victims than men ($\gamma = -.22$, $X^2 = 0.46$
[ns]). Very few men or women perceived crime to be a serious or important problem facing their families. Gender-based violations common in the West, particularly sexual assault and spouse abuse, were occasionally reported in newspapers.
None were reported by a respondent. Colleagues had maintained from the outset
of the research that most crimes probably were not reported to the police. Men's

testimony is given higher priority in Pakistan, making reporting often fruitless and hazardous for women victims. Reported sexual attacks often conclude with murder, presumably to prevent identifying the assailant. What might have ended as rape in the West, may eventuate as murder in Pakistan. To further complicate matters, women may be selected as victims in retaliations to family and feudal feuds.

These qualifications explain why sex-based crimes might be underreported and how they may be associated with other types of crimes. However, sexual assaults may be less frequent in Pakistan than in the West. The value-placed on protecting and isolating women probably reduces their vulnerability to sexual assault, but increases the danger when it occurs. Frequencies of such acts, and of the differences between the actual assaults and their reported frequencies, are among the most opaque of the dark figures of crime. Decades have been required to unravel these knotty questions in industrial societies. Answers may come even slower in the traditional gendered division of labor in rural Pakistan.

Stratification, Gender, and Opportunity Problems

The most unequivocal differences associated with social disadvantage and social problems were between gender and lack of opportunities. Women were

Table 6. Gender and Perception of Opportunity Problems, Controlling for Landownership, and Household Savings

| | "Opportunity Problems are Most Serious" | | | | | |
| | Landless | | | Landowners | | |
	Agree	Disagree	Total	Agree	Disagree	Total
Men	15	34	49	18	26	44
	(30.0%)	(69.4%)	(81.7%)	(40.9%)	(59.1%)	(48.4%)
Women	8	3	11	30	17	47
	(72.7%)	(27.3%)	(18.3%)	(63.8%)	(36.2%)	(51.6%)
Total	23	37	60	48	43	91
	(38.3%)	(61.7%)	(100.0%)	(52.7%)	(47.3%)	(100.0%)
	$\gamma = -.71\ X^2 = .009$			$\gamma = -.44\ X^2 = .03$		
	Households With Savings			Households Without Savings		
	Agree	Disagree	Total	Agree	Disagree	Total
Men	14	18	32	19	42	61
	(43.8%)	(56.3%)	(47.1%)	(31.1%)	(68.9%)	(73.5%)
Women	23	13	36	15	7	22
	(63.9%)	(36.1%)	(52.9%)	(68.2%)	(31.8%)	(26.5%)
Total	37	31	68	34	49	83
	(54.4%)	(45.6%)	(100.0%)	(41.0%)	(59.0%)	(100.0%)
	$\gamma = -.39\ X^2 = .9$			$\gamma = -.65\ X^2 = .002$		

significantly more likely than men to report that an absence of opportunities was the most important set of problems facing their families ($\gamma = .77$, $X^2 = .002$). Two measures of stratification, savings and landownerships, were examined. Table 6 indicates than women were much more likely than men to believe that an absence of opportunities was the primary problem facing their families, whether their families had savings, owned land, or not. Women were more concerned than men about opportunity problems in households with savings ($\gamma = -.39$, $X^2 = 09$), and even more concerned in households without savings ($\gamma = -.65$, $X^2 = .002$). Women from families that owned land, shared a similar sentiment with women from landless families. Women with land ($\gamma = -.44$, $X^2 = .03$) and, especially, without land ($\gamma = -.71$, $X^2 = .009$) both agreed significantly more often than did men, that lack of opportunity was the most serious problem facing their families.

Having discovered that women were more concerned with an absence of opportunity problems than were men, the final question was whether women's level of advantage affected how they perceived the problem. Did the "haves," women from households with land and savings, differ from those from disadvantaged households, the "have nots." Table 7 indicates that poverty strongly influenced how women responded according to the economic disadvantages endured by their households. Women from households without land ($\gamma = .78$, $X^2 = .001$) and without savings ($\gamma = .64$, $X^2 = .002$) were much more likely than women from more materially secure households to believe that the most critical problem facing their families had to do with limited opportunities.

SUMMARY

This analysis suffers from difficulties of both *epistomological* and *methodological relativism* (Beirne and Messerschmidt 1995) that are almost inevitable in exploratory research in the developing world. The small sample is sufficient to measure associations within the sample, but not for statistically representing the

Table 7.   Perception of Opportunity Problems among Women from Households With or Without Land and Savings

Opportunity Problems	Land		Savings		
	Women With Land	Women Without Land	Women With Savings	Women Without Savings	Total
Yes	26	34	18	42	60
	(61%)	(92%)	(58%)	(86.7%)	(75%)
No	17	3	13	7	20
	(39%)	(8%)	(42%)	(14.1%)	(25%)
Total	43	37	31	49	80
	(54%)	(46%)	(39%)	(61%)	(100.0%)
	$\gamma = .78$, $X^2 = .001$		$\gamma = .64$ $X^2 = .002$		

larger population. It is limited to a single observation in time. Criticisms made about comparative international victimization surveys in developed countries apply to this project to some unknowable degree. Despite the methodological morass of such research, there are interesting and important findings. The high reporting of extremely serious crime, such as murder, extortion, and kidnapping validates the value of the study. Contrary to the expectations of our Pakistani colleagues, some victims of crime told of their experiences, although many have remained silent. Certainly their recollections beyond one year are suspect, except for the most serious crimes. With the possible exception of animal theft, reported crimes were hardly trivial offenses that led to some criticism about self-reported victimization (Elliott and Ageton 1980). Equally important, the variations in response patterns within the sample provide valuable information regarding the incidence and perceptions about crime, poverty, and other social problems among the advantaged and disadvantaged, men and women.

Discrepancies in number of crimes reported to some extent supported contention by project reviewers that respondents would not report victimizations, particularly of family members. The roughly five-fold greater number of crimes reported by 160 respondents for themselves than for the 996 other household members indicates that crimes against household members were grossly underreported. Nevertheless, household heads would be expected to be more vulnerable to crime than the dependent and highly protected majority of family members. The approximate doubling of the number of crimes reported over the five-year period in comparisons to the previous 12 months indicated that there also was underreporting over the longer time span.

The implications of the findings must be understood within the context of the rural Pakistani community. Although poverty in the Punjab study area is extensive and intense, it may be less of a problem than in most of Pakistan. Despite considerable variation in social stratification, incomes in rural Pakistan are among the lowest in the world. Although the focus of this research has been upon disadvantage and social problems, even middle class people in Pakistan are poor by international standards. Many have low incomes, no savings, and own little or no land. Many depend on someone outside the household for much of their income. Many, especially the women, are illiterate.

The types and amounts of crime in Pakistan can be understood in terms of its social structures. Rural Pakistan is Gemeinschaft. Approximately 80 percent of the population is rural and agrarian. Traditional economic and religious values and norms are largely intact. The home is sacrosanct and helps to reduce the risk of theft. As a practical matter, the nature of protection conforms to Cohen and Felson's (1979) parlance of a "routine activities approach." Someone is almost always at home because of quasi-cloistered large families. The extended family is relatively immobile because of the large number of members, the local nature of agricultural work, and the allocation of women's roles to activities in the home. Family structure is central to the village structure. Near proximity of neighbors and high density of acquaintanceship (Freudenberg and Jones 1986) increase the likelihood of detecting thieves as well as deterring unlawful entry. Assaults, sexual or not, were usually deliberate and conscious gestures of power exchanges within the structures of family and community. Assailants were likely to be recognized local residents who were part of a primary group in opposition to a group with which the victim was member. Although these feuds were likely to be justified on religious, political, or economic grounds, they were inextricably entangled with caste, family, and community affiliations. In rural Pakistan social structures other than social class, especially family and caste, seemed more pertinent for explaining crime and victimization. Violent crimes and extortion/blackmail were comparatively frequent. Concern with crime, however, was relatively low. The moderate concern may indicate that only a small segment of the population experienced serious crime, making their level of risk extremely high. Crime was the most serious problem to many who had recently suffered it. Some of the wealthy, who had more possessions to lose, were more afraid of losing them. For most others, whether poor or prosperous, crime was not a serious problem or issue. Another possible explanation for the moderate concern about crime is that, however serious a problem it was, crime paled in comparison to the problems associated with low opportunities.

Pakistan clearly lies toward the traditional end of the modernization continuum. Following world values terminology, residents were primarily concerned with scarcity rather than security. Nevertheless, the wealthier respondents were more similar to findings from the First World. They disproportionately were worried about crime although they were no more likely to be victims. However, the women and the poor, especially poor women, believed that the major problem they faced was a lack of opportunities. They were especially concerned with scarcity values. This finding is important because it demonstrates a level of differentiation by status and gender in this relatively traditional country.

The "dark figure" of crime is obviously lurking behind these data. As is typical for such unknown figures, the amount and sources of discrepancies between actual crime and the amount that was acknowledged is difficult to know. Serious violations, such as assault, kidnapping, and murder may correspond more closely to the actual number of incidents, because those crimes also were likely to be reported to police. The high incidences of murder and blackmail were intriguing, especially because most types of thefts were comparatively rare. The nature of victimization implies that intense personal entanglements were occurring within the extended family and community. While victimization that was acknowledged did occur, it is quite likely that actual victimization was much higher. Moreover, patterns of reporting victimization might be influenced by social and demographic characteristics that were not evident in this analysis. Future analyses of victimization and social problems should consider that possibility.

CONCLUSION

This research was initiated as a general exploratory investigation of rural victimization. As the data unfolded, it increasingly became an analysis of institutional implications of social control among the poor and, especially, among women. The primary initial theoretical concerns were with how community structure affected being a victim and perceiving social problems. The first concern was investigated by discovering what kinds of crimes occurred, with what frequency, and how important crime was in comparison to other social problems in conjunction with community structure. The second concern was explored by examining how being disinfranchised, that is, poor and a woman, affects being a victim and perceiving social problems, including crime.

The answers to the first questions were clear and straightforward. Village Gemeinschaft enormously increased the likelihood of some types of crime. If property was stolen, it usually was either of unattended animals living outside the home or in confrontation with a robber, usually outside the home. Confrontations within and between families and castes were likely to be intense because of Gemeinschaft. Disagreements and differences led to confrontations with extreme intimidation and violence. Animal theft deserves comment. Farm animals were ubiquitous, kept at almost every rural home. Small animals can be quickly snatched and eaten, leaving little suspicious evidence. However, neighbors often had accurate suppositions about where their animals had disappeared. One informant told how she walked into to an untrustworthy neighbors' house, as soon as she noticed two chickens were missing. She chastised her neighbor, who was butchering the birds, tucked them under her arm, and went home. The context, the crime and the solution all occurred within the close, intimate, personal, familiar, face-to-face context of community.

Answers to the second were much more complex and enlightening. The realization came to the author that the importance of the research pertained to substantive issues of gender and to the orientation of feminist theory more than had been anticipated at the outset of the project. The following comments attempt to integrate theoretical issues that had initiated the research into the emerging corpus of feminist theory. Victimization and crime are not simply described through modern functional or conflict orientations. Structural adaptations to the complex of quasi-feudalistic Islamic community only partially reflect class structure. Following conflict theory, opportunity is linked to advantage, whether through wealth or gender. From a functional perspective, both advantaged and disadvantaged struggle to perpetuate the structures of which they are a part. Amoral familism is an appropriate concept for describing the simultaneous operation of conflict and maintaining social order in rural Pakistan. The traditional societal concern about having enough, about scarcity, superseded concerns about personal and social safety, that is about the modern meaning of security. Perpetuation of a system of relative advantage is evident throughout the society. Whether the system is perpetuated through domination by the advantaged is arguable in a traditional community with widespread scarcity, because essentially no one, rich or poor, contributes to a civil commonwealth.

Idiosyncrasies in the social structure influenced the perceptions and reporting of social problems and victimization. Economic difficulties were clearly considered to be the most important problems facing most households. By any objective measures, the economic position of the lowest 15 or 20 percent, frequently low status, wageless and landless, made them among the poorest of the international poor. Nevertheless, their perceptions of problems were determined by cultural definitions as well as by objective circumstances. Moreover, economic dimensions frequently were mentioned in conjunction with other institutional difficulties, such as the marriage of daughters and familial disputes.

The identification of economic factors as the primary sources of social problems indicated that the rural traditional village was indeed rational and materialistic. Both poorer and wealthier families regarded lack of economic opportunities as their most serious problems, although poorer respondents were significantly more likely to feel pressured by economic problems. Advantaged and disadvantaged had accepted the prevailing metaphor that economic problems were most important. Accepting the validity of the economic metaphor deflected the possible importance of other types of problems. However problematic the economy of the family unit, it was one important problem among many. Moreover, economic problems were likely to be effects of underlying causal factors, such as corruption or the costs of weddings for several daughters. In other words, focusing on opportunities may have detracted from potential solutions to problems that were fundamentally social and cultural.

The findings that criminal victimization was very weakly associated with social and economic status is noteworthy. Although "have nots" were the victims of poverty, they were scarcely more likely to be victims of crime. Advantaged households were more likely to believe that crime was a serious problem in their lives. Those with possessions felt more vulnerable to crime, but were no more vulnerable to it. Those with something had more to worry about losing than those with almost nothing. The theoretical implication that crime and victimization were not associated with social class was that conflict between the classes did not appear to cause crime, Certainly, the absence of crimes typical in the rural First World, such as vandalism and assault, indicates that crime in the rural Third World may have distinct patterns, following different causal forces.

An absence of opportunities is closely linked to poverty, landownership, and high fertility. The economic implication of smaller acreages per family is that production, hence profit, is being reduced at a time when the world economy increasingly excludes them from entering the global economic system. The local economic consequences for the communities are of declining services and availability of goods. The entrenched nature of poverty within the social structure offers little reason for optimism about rapidly and markedly reducing poverty.

Few adjustments for reducing that, if conditions permit, many households seek opportunities and increase their standards of living (Jobes, Stinner, and Wardwell 1992). Migrating to locate work and choosing to have smaller families are both common responses individuals have made to improve their personal circumstances. These human capital decisions are being exercised in Pakistan, although fertility and poverty remain very high.

The poorest citizens have severely limited choices for improving their own well-being. A litany of opportunities instituted through an honest and efficient political-economic structure is often cited as the foundation for widespread increases in standard of living. Universal literacy brought about through primary education will increase the quality of the work force. Development of transportation and communication infrastructures will increase the efficiency and profit of production and trade. Reliable and equitable institutions and policies for governance and trade will increase international exchange and profit. Accomplishing such developments to reduce poverty and to improve the overall well-being of the great mass of citizens, however, has been beyond the capacity of Pakistan. Ironically, these accomplishments may also be accompanied by more crime, if the experience of prosperous Western countries provides a template.

A tragic irony has become apparent through the current distribution of agricultural land. Land once carried the promise of productivity and independence. As indicated by the propensity of the landless to be especially troubled by their lack of opportunities, this promise is to some extent still being fulfilled. The landless poor are truly destitute. Increasingly, however, land is becoming a millstone around the necks of poor small land holders. The land provides little more food than is required for subsistence, but shackles owners from being able to move freely to more profitable and dependable ways of life. A small piece of land is the most valuable asset many small farmers have, perhaps just enough to hold them in continual poverty. Eventually, farmers are forced to secure off-farm employment in order to survive. Most are appropriately afraid to take the risk of giving up their small acreage. The social implications of the smaller land holdings for the next few decades are even more varied than are the economic implications. Most directly there is a growing spectre of insufficient food and other agricultural resources for the rapidly expanding population. Out-migration, which already is high, becomes essential to generate income and to reduce the strain on already stretched social and environmental resources.

Landownership also has implications for gender. Many married women tacitly own land through inheritance. In fact, land which women would inherit is passed to the family of the husband as part of the dowry. This tight linkage between the woman and the land that is in effect traded with her, simultaneously creates a tension and a bind between the families. Some of the consequences are similar to what might be expected from a liberal and individualized perspective common in Western nations. The woman and her family are acutely aware of her worth, the property that her family has paid her husband to marry her. She and they also are aware that the land, that once was theirs now is in the husband's control. The women feel deeply obligated to stay to protect the exchange. Some feel disenfranchized as they see "their" property taken from the control of their family.

However, it is essential to *not* arrive solely at such conclusions that might be valid in the West, where cultural notions of personal independence reign supreme. In Pakistan, women speak with considerable pride that their parents could afford to arrange a marriage through exchange of property (whether land or other wealth). Daughters of wealthy families openly brag of their exchange value. In contrast, the poor women are further deprived of status and power. The common obligation felt by both rich and poor women is to make the marriage work. The alternative to any but the most undesirable marriage is worse. However, women from more privileged backgrounds enjoy the knowledge that their family of procreation is behind them, looking after them because they care about them, and more crassly, because they care about the investment the family has made for them. Less privileged women suffer from more than living lives with work and financial hardship. As most poor realize, they suffer because they know that their personal status and worth have been cast by inequity. Their realization is simply demonstrated in their responses about social problems.

The conscious awareness of their disadvantages among the poor, the landless, and women may be a powerful initiator of change. Because these groups are aware of their disadvantages, the foundations for change may be in place (Friedman 1992). That is the optimistic way of considering the equation for resolving the differences between aspirations and opportunities. The pessimistic interpretation is that the structure of disadvantage is so entrenched that changing it will be slow and difficult, if indeed it happens at all.

Much of the support and strength of rural Pakistan rests in traditional informal institutions extended to family, caste and village. The cohesive context of community provides relatively dependable and trustworthy support. Family and community offer a haven in the broader inequitable and corrupt social system. The social integration and cohesion present in traditional informal institutions also can be liabilities, impediments to escape from poverty, and its associated problems. The intense interdependence within extended families benefits the fortunate few whose pooled labor and assets contribute to advantaged status. In this environment of dwindling resources, such sharing leads to a perpetuation of poverty.

Classic structural explanations, such as conflict and functional theories, are not sufficient to explain the differences in responses between men and women observed in this research. Classic structural theories fail to address the clear substantive concerns with issues of inequity, which are so evident on the agenda of women. Edwards (1990) maintains that there is no single female criminology nor feminist legal studies. She maintains, however, that diverse theorists in the feminist tradition continually discover social and legal vulnerability among women. In her summary of the most extreme acts against women, she declares, "feminists have drawn attention to not only the abuse of substantive law relating to rape in marriage and violence against women, but also to the lack of enforcement of existing law and, in those instances where law is applied, to the trivial sentences meted out by a largely aging, male judiciary." The findings from this study suggest that subtle and entrenched structures form the foundations in which differential experiences of men and women lead to differential perceptions of inequity and associated problems. The analysis of how the roles of women (and men) are maintained becomes a feminist theoretical question, whatever the structural foundations, functional or conflict, may be. Gelsthorpe and Morris (1990) maintain that feminist criminology exposes cases of victimization among women, exposes institutional sexism, and identifies alternative modes of social control. By their definitions, this study falls both substantively and theoretically into feminist criminology.

The problems of social disadvantage are ages old. Globally, the sheer numbers of poor people are increasing because of their disproportionately high fertility and of their concentration in the periphery. Direct problems of poverty—poor diet, inadequate housing and medical care, to name only a few—are only one aspect of being poor. Indirect consequences, such as poor education, place some of them at further disadvantage. Together, these problems multiply the disadvantages passed on to subsequent generations, through limited educational and occupational opportunities, and the inability to pay for dowries for daughters. These collective problems of the poor are especially concentrated among the most vulnerable of the poor. They also are clearly more recognized by the most disadvantaged, the women and the poor. If neo-Malthusian social scientists are correct, the immediate future for the developing world may be even bleaker than the recent past, as populations soar and resources dwindle (Coombs 1990).

ACKNOWLEDGMENTS

The author gratefully acknowledges the support provided by the World Bank for this project through a twinning agreement between the University of Agriculture Faisalabad (UAF) and the University of New England (UNE). Special appreciation is given to interviewers and data processors on the project, all of whom were either academic professionals or postgraduate students at UAF. They were: Salman Asfar, Muhammad Asif Aziz, Rehman Qadir Khan, Shahida Rani, Saif-Ur-Rehman, Lubna Riaz, Muhammad Saif, Abul Saboor, and Saman Zubair. The survey also was made possible by the administrative support and encouragement of Madame Kishwar Ijaz, Mr. Chaudhry Mohhammed Aslam, and Dr. Bashier Ahmad. Appreciation also is noted for the patience shown by the Clairborne-Ortenberg Foundation while this work was being done. This research was a joint effort shared with Brian Davidson, Department of Agriculture Economics (UNE).

REFERENCES

Agarwal, B. 1994. *A Field of One's Own.* Cambridge: Cambridge University Press.
Agger, B. 1989. *Fast Capitalism: A Critical Theory of Significance.* Urbana: University of Illinois.

Ahmad, M. 1993. *Choice of a Norm of Poverty Threshold and Extent of Poverty in Pakistan.* Islamabad: Ministry of Finance.

Allen, J. 1989. "Men, Crime and Criminology: Recasting the Questions." *International Journal of the Sociology of Law* 17(1): 19-39.

Ali, M.S. 1995. "Poverty Assesment: Pakistan's Case." *Pakistan Development Review* 34(1): 43-54.

Alfano, S.S., and A.W. Magill. 1976. "Vandalism and Outdoor Recreation," U.S.D.A. Forest Service Gen. Tech. Report RSW-17, Berkeley, CA.

Archer, D., and R. Gartner. 1984. *Violence and Crime in Cross-National Perspective.* New Haven, CT: Yale University Press.

Australian Bureau of Statistics. 1994. *Crime and Safety.* Canberra: Australian Government Printing Office.

Banfield, E.C. 1958. *The Moral Basis of a Backward Society.* Glencoe, IL: Free Press.

Becker, G. 1981. *A Treatise on the Family.* Cambridge, MA: Harvard University Press.

Beirne, P., and J. Messerschmidt. 1995. "Comparitive Criminology." Pp. 563-602 in *Criminology,* 2nd ed. Fort Worth, TX: Harcourt Brace.

Belyea, M.J., and M.T. Zingraff. 1988. "Fear of Crime and Residential Location." *Rural Sociology* 53(3): 473-486.

Berik, G. 1996. "Understanding the Gender System in Turkey: Fieldwork Dilemmas of Conformity and Intervention." Pp. 56-71 in *Feminist Dilemmas in Fieldwork,* edited by D.L. Wolf. Boulder, CO: Westview.

Bhaskar, V., and A. Glyn, eds. 1995. *The North the South and the Environment.* Tokyo: United Nations University Press.

Biderman, A.D., and J.P. Lynch. 1991. *Understanding Crime Incidence Statistics.* New York: Springer-Verlag.

Blumberg, R.L. 1984. "A General Theory of Gender Stratifiation." Pp. 23-101 in *Sociological Theory,* edited by R. Collins. San Francisco: Jossey-Bass.

Brown, A. 1986. *Modern Political Philosophy: Theories of the Just Society.* Harmondsworth, UK: Penguin.

Buttel, F., and H. Newby, eds. 1980. *The Rural Sociology of the Advanced Societies.* Montclair, NJ: Allanheld, Osmun.

Carlen, P. 1988. *Women and Poverty.* Milton Keynes: Open University Press.

Chafetz, J.S. 1990. *Gender Equity: An Integrated Theory of Stability and Change.* Newbury Park, CA: Sage.

Chase-Dunn, C.K. 1989. *Global Formulation.* New York: Basil Blackwell.

Chodorow, N. 1978. *The Reproduction of Mothering.* Berkeley: University of California Press.

Cleland, C.L. 1990. "Crime and Vandalism on Forms in Tennesse," SP-90-01, Institute of Agriculture, University of Tennessee, Knoxville, TN.

Clinard, M.B. 1944. "Rural Criminal Offenders." *American Journal of Sociology* 50(1): 38-45.

Cohen, L.E., and M. Felson. 1979. "Social Change and Crime Rate Trends: A Routine Activity Approach." *American Sociological Review* 44(3): 588-608.

Coleman, C., and J. Moynihan. 1996. *Understanding Crime Data: Haunted by the Dark Figure.* Buckingham: Open University Press.

Cook, R. 1994. "Women's International Human Rights Law: The Way Forward." Pp. 1-36 in *Human Right's of Women: National and International Perspectives,* edited by R. Cook. Philadelphia: University of Pennsylvania.

Cook, T.D., and D.T. Campbell. 1979. *Experimentation: Design and Analysis Issues for Field Settings.* Chicago: Rand-Mcnally.

Coombs, H.C. 1990. *The Return of Scarcity.* Sydney: Cambridge University Press.

Costner, H.L. 1965. "Criteria for Measures of Association." *American Sociological Review* 50(3): 341-353.

Dreze, J., and M. Saran. 1995. "Primary Education and Economic Development in China and India: Overview and Two Case Studies." Pp. 182-241 in *Choice, Welfare and Development*. Oxford: Clarendon.

Duncan, O.D., and L.F. Schnore. 1959. "Cultural, Behavioral, and Ecological Perspectives in the Study of Social Organization." *American Journal of Sociology* 65(1): 132-146.

Durkheim, E. 1947. *The Division of Labor in Society*, trans. by G. Simpson. Glencoe, IL: Free Press.

Edwards, S. 1990. "Violence Against Women: Feminism and the Law." Pp. 145-159 in *Feminst Perspectives in Criminology*, edited by L. Gelsthorpe and A. Morris. Milton Keynes: Open University Press.

Elias, N. 1994. *The Civilising Process*, one vol. ed. Oxford: Basil Blackwell.

Elliot, D.S., and S.S. Ageton. 1980. "Reconciling Race and Class Differences in Self-Reported and Official Estimates of Delinquency." *American Sociological Review* 21(1): 95-110.

Engels, F. 1948. *The Origin of the Family, Private Proverty and the State*. Moscow: Progress.

England, P., and B.S. Kilbourne. 1990. "Feminist Critique of the Separative Model of Self Implications for Rational Choice Theory." *Rationality and Society* 2(2): 156-171.

Friedman, J. 1992. *Empowerment: The Politics of Alternative Development*. Oxford: Basil Blackwell.

Freudenberg, W.R., and R.E. Jones. 1986. "The Density of Acquaintanceship: An Overlooked Variable in Community Research." *American Journal of Sociology* 92(1): 27-63.

Gelsthorpe, L, and A. Morris. 1990. "Introduction: Transforming and Trangressing Criminology." Pp. 1-10 in *Feminist Perspectives in Criminology*, edited by L. Gelsthorpe and A. Morris. Milton Reynes: Open University Press.

Gottfredson, M.r., and T. Hirschi. 1990. *A General Theory of Crime*. Palo Alto, CA: Stanford University Press.

Government of Pakistan. 1995. *Economic Survey 1994-95*. Islamabad: Finance Division.

_____. 1996. *Agricultural Statistics of Pakistan 1994-95*. Islamabad: Ministry of Food, Agriculture and Livestock.

Gunew, S., and A. Yeatman. 1993. "Feminism and the Politics of Irreducible Differences: Multiculturalism Ethnicity Race." Pp. i-xxii in *Feminism and the Politics of Difference*, edited by S. Gunew and A. Yeatman. Sydney: Allen and Unwin.

Hagan, J. 1989. *Structural Criminology*. New Brunswick, NJ: Rutgers University Press.

Harries, I.D. 1971. "The Geography of American Crime." *Journal of Geography* 70(2): 204-213.

Hindelang, M.J. 1979. "Sex Differences in Criminal Activity." *Social Problems* 27(2): 143-156.

Hossain, S. 1994. "Women's Rights and Personal Laws in South Asia." Pp. 456-494 in *Human Right's of Women: National and International Perspectives*, edited by R. Cook. Philadelphia: University of Pennsylvania.

Huntington, S.P. 1996. *The Clash of Civilizations and the Remaking of World Order*. New York: Simon and Schuster.

Inglehart, R. 1990. *Culture Shift in Advanced Countries*. Princeton, NJ: Princeton University Press.

_____. 1997. *Modernization and Postmodernization*. Princeton, NJ: Princeton University Press.

Jacobsen, J. 1994. *The Economics of Gender*. New York: Blackwell.

Jamieson, K.M., and T.J. Flanagan, eds. 1989. *Source Book of Criminal Justice Statistics—1988*. Washington, DC: U.S. Department of Justice, Bureau of Justice Statistics, USGPO.

Jobes, P.C., W.F. Stinner, and J.M. Wardwell, eds. 1992. *Community Society and Migration*. Lanham, MD: University Press of America.

Johnson, M. 1993. "Functionalism and Feminism: Is Estrangement Necessary?" Pp. 115-130 in *Theory on Gender: Feminism on Theory*, edited by P. England. New York: Aldine de Gruyter.

Kowalski, G.S., and D. Duffield. 1990. "The Impact of the Rural Population Component on Homicide Rates in the United States: A Country-Level Analysis." *Rural Sociology* 55(1): 76-90.

Lewis, O. 1961. *The Children of Sanchez*. New York: Random House.

Manis, J.G., and B.N. Metzer. 1994. "Chance in Human Affairs." *Sociological Theory* 12(1): 45-56.

Marx, K., and F. Engels. 1947. *The German Ideology*. New York: International Publishers.

McMichael, P. 1996. "Globalization: Myths and Realities." *Rural Sociology* 61(1): 25-55.

Mies, M. 1986. *Patriarchy and Accumulation on a World-Scale.* London: Zed.

Miller, G., and J.A. Holstein. 1993. *Constructionist Controversies: Issues in Social Problems Theory.* Hawthorne, NY: Aldine de Gruyter.

Nelson, B.J., and N. Chowdhury, eds. 1994. *Women and Politics World Wide.* New Haven, CT: Yale University Press.

Newman, W.L. 1997. *Social Research Methods: Qualitative and Quantitative Approaches.* Boston: Allyn and Bacon.

Nowak, S. 1989. "Comparative Studies and Social Theory." Pp. 34-56 in *Cross National Research in Sociology,* edited by M.L. Kohn. Newbury Park, CA: Sage.

Patai, D. 1991. "US. Academics and Third World Women—Is Research Possible?" Pp. 137-153 in *Women Words: The Feminist Practice of Oral History,* edited by S.B. Glueck and D. Patai. New York: Routledge.

Quinney, R. 1977. *Class, State and Crime.* New York: Longman.

Redfield, R. 1955. *The Little Community.* Chicago: University of Chicago Press.

Reiss, A.J., and M. Tonry. 1986. *Communities and Crime.* Chicago: University of Chicago Press.

Scovill, J.G. 1991. "Introduction." Pp. 1-19 in *Status Influences in Third World Labor Markets: Caste, Gender, and Custom,* edited by J.G. Scoville. New York: Walter de Gruyter.

Sen, A.K. 1992. *Inequality Reexamined.* Oxford: Clarendon.

Smart, C. 1976. *Women, Crime and Criminology: A Feminist Critique.* London: Routledge and Kegan Paul.

Smith, D. 1994. *Geography and Social Justice.* Oxford: Blackwell.

Schrag, C. 1971. *Crime and Justice: American Style.* Rockville, MD: National Institute of Mental Health.

Summer, C. 1982. *Crime, Justice and Underdevelopment.* London: Heinemann.

Summers, G. 1991. "Minorities in Rural Society." *Rural Sociology* 56(2): 177-188.

Taylor, I. 1983. *Crime, Capitalism and Community: Three Essays in Socialist Criminology.* Toronto: Butterworths.

Toennies, F. 1957. *Community and Society,* trans. by C.P. Loomis. East Lansing: Michigan State University Press.

Travis, G., S. Egger, B. O'Toole, D. Brown, R. Hogg, and J. Stubbs. 1995. "The International Crime Surveys: Some Methodological Concerns." *Current Issues in Criminal Justice* 6(3): 346-361.

UNICEF. (1995). *The Progress of Nations.* Paris: UNICEF.

United Nations. 1995. *Ninth United Nations Congress on the Prevention of Crime and the Treatment of Offenders, Cairo, 1995.* New York: United Nations.

van Dijk, J.J., and P.J. Mayhew. 1993. *Criminal Victimization in the Industrialized World: Key Findings of the 1989 and 1992 International Crime Surveys.* Ministry of Justice: The Netherlands.

Vold, G.B., T.J. Bernard, and J.B. Snipes. 1998. *Theoretical Criminology,* 3rd ed. New York: Oxford.

Wallerstein, I. 1975. *World Inequality.* Montreal: Black Rose Books.

Ward, K.B. 1988. "Women in the Global Economy." *Women and Work: An Annual Review* 3(1): 17-48.

_____. 1993. "Reconceptualizing World System Theory to Include Women." Pp. 43-68 in *Theory on Gender/Feminism on Theory,* edited by P. England. Hawthorne, NY: Aldine de Gruyter.

Weber, M. 1958. *The Protestant Ethic and the Spirit of Protestantism,* trans. by T. Parsons. New York: Scribner's.

White, J.B. 1994. *Money Makes Us Relatives: Women's labor in Urban Turkey.* Austin, TX: University of Texas Press.

Wolf, D. 1993. "Introduction: Feminist Dilemmas in Field Work." *Frontiers* 13(1): 1-7.

Zetterberg, H.L. 1986. *On Theory and Verification in Sociology,* 3rd ed. New York: Bedminster Press.

URBAN EXPLOSION AND ETHNIC CONFLICTS IN INDIA:

DOES POVERTY MATTER?

Raj S. Gandhi

ABSTRACT

Although the community studies tradition has started incorporating the studies of communal conflict and urban violence, they assume an increasing significance as the rapid urbanization of underdeveloped countries exacerbate the extremes of ethnic violence under the conditions of rural-urban migration. As the members of ethnic divisions, the urban poor experience high unemployment, inadequate diet, and unsanitary living, deprived of the basic necessities of life: food, clothing, and shelter. A large majority of them live in squatter settlements without sewer system, drinking water, and electricity. Three case studies of Indian cities—Bombay, Ahmedabad, and Surat—show that the urban situation has become explosive. The government's manipulation of ethnic identities and the promotion of state capitalism linking Indian cities to a world system does not help the situation of the poor, but creates the communal polarization as the less powerful make a choice at the local level.

Research in Community Sociology, Volume 9, pages 123-140.
Copyright © 1999 by JAI Press Inc.
All rights of reproduction in any form reserved.
ISBN: 0-7623-0498-7

Although an overview of the most recent research in community studies (Chekki 1998) reveals much beyond the issues of community cohesion and urban identity, urban neighborhood and urban networks, the urban community studies tradition has been constrained to incorporate the issues of tensions between city and community, and street gangs and urban ethnic communities. The most challenging areas of further analysis and social research are community contradictions and communal conflicts, urban riots and communal violence, communal killings and urban anomie.

The accommodation of the issues of urban ethnic conflicts and communal killings, terrorism and urban violence assume special significance in view of the emergence of a general perspective of urban expansion in the Third World, and the considerations of urban development in the context of a world system (Gilbert and Gugler 1993). Ongoing theoretical developments suggest that community research is moving beyond the treatment of a Third World city as a separate case, especially in view of the acceleration of the state of urban growth and change in the Third World, as the Third World urban patterns take on global dimensions (Flanagan 1993). Moreover, the issues of violence, terrorism, conflicts, and killings in the Third World cities, accompanied with their rate of growth, expansion, and the patterns of change should be considered in relation to the problems of urbanization and underdevelopment, which incorporate the predicament of the urban poor and the deprived members of the cities as they are rapidly drawn into the worldwide currents of industrialization, internationalization, and globalization.

Yet, the Third World cities could be considered country by country for the critical social analysis of the main communities and the dominant conflicts within them as the major social transformation is occurring under globalization. The cities of India are a case in point. It will be futile to consider them to be the mere replications of the "earlier stages" of the economically advanced economies. Nor are their disruptions and violent conflicts "very similar" to the latter, as there are important historical, political, social, and economic differences underlying urban growth and change in India. Additionally, the enormous differences in the population sizes and densities of Indian cities exhibit lingering effects of colonialism. Although the latter introduced international control and the majority of Indian cities are clearly exhibiting connections with world economy if not outright integration, their economic and ecological structures are somewhat different and show significant variations as their styles of industrialization differ. Although outwardly modern technology has imposed certain obvious similarities in the forms of Indian cities, and their patterns of production and consumption have an international dimension, the poor of those cities have continued to eat and dress in the same traditional way. There are more than ten million people living in each of the cities of Bombay, Calcutta, and Delhi. Of these, a substantial proportion (about 40%) of the growth of urban population is due to the migration of people from rural to urban areas. The majority of migrants are young adults in their peak reproductive years; and as they are searching for employment, they have immediate impact on the urban employment market. Age has many correlates. The urban studies have proven that "the higher the median age of a group, the higher its income; the lower the median age, the higher the unemployment rate and the higher crime rate" (Wilson 1996, p. 193).

URBAN EXPLOSION, UNDERDEVELOPMENT AND URBAN POVERTY

Unimpressively and mildly labeled as "urban India," India's urban explosion in its 3,245 cities and towns strikes as the most dramatic phenomenon as the millennium is drawing to a close. India's massive size of urban population is the second largest in the world. Perhaps never in India's history has there been such a striking surge in its urbanization. Because the total urban population of India (based or the 1991 census; see Government of India 1992) accounts for only 215,771,612 (25.73%) of the total Indian population, it deceptively appears to be lower than 74.27 percent of its rural population (622,812,376). But when we compare it with the increase from about 53 million in 1951 to about 78.94 million in 1961, and 215 million in 1991, it indeed deserves the label "urban explosion."

Not only do the spiraling urban millions now account for more than one-fourth of the country's people, but every year an estimated five million people leave behind the unproductive parched lands of rural areas and head for the distant glare of urban lights in search of livelihood. It is estimated that India's million plus metropolises have grown from 12 to 23. Bombay and Calcutta have already become megalopolises with a population of 12 million and 13 million each. But Delhi is not far behind. Its population was 1.4 million in 1951, reaching 10 million in 1991. One cannot fail to notice the increasing concentration of urban population in the comparatively larger cities. In 1991, 65.2 percent of the total urban population was reported to be living in cities with over 100,000 population, while at the beginning of the century, the relative share of large cities was only 26 percent of the total population.

Instead of becoming "engines of development," Indian cities are heading for a shocking disorder. The endless stream of migrants pour into subhuman squatter settlements (*bastis, jhopdis,* and *chawls*) turning metropolises into giant slums. One-third of the urban population lives in ramshackle huts with gunny sacks as doors and pavements for toilets. Another one-half of the populace is squeezed into one-room tenements or live in monotonous rows of multistoried flats. With no efforts to scatter the migrants into smaller towns, the big cities keep bloating up. Most metropolises have been growing at a disturbing average of 4 to 7 percent annually—twice the nation's rate of population growth. In Calcutta, 2,000 migrants flow in every day. In Bombay, 25,000 a month. Together, the 12 Indian metropolises now account for one-fourth of the total urban population. Mathur (1994) raises the issue of natural increase versus rural-to-urban migration as the principal determinant of urban population growth, and finds that the former may be more important than the latter in the long run. But when a 60 percent natural increase is compared with about 40 percent rural-to-urban migration, the "urban explosion" of Indian cities is still striking. Furthermore, comparing the level of urbanization in 1961, about 17.91 percent to about 25.73 percent in 1991, the urban explosion explains the situation much better. Moreover, the National Commission on Urbanization (Government of India 1988) expressed a grave concern that the poverty and deprivation in Indian urban areas are widespread. But there are many dimensions of poverty such as low average consumption and wages, inadequate nutritional intake (leading to vulnerability to various diseases), and low literacy rate. Furthermore, there is a high correlation between the dimensions of poverty and the dimensions of what has been identified as underdevelopment: "the indicators of underdevelopment include high infant mortality rates, low life expectancy, limited access to health care, low levels of literacy and limited years of schooling, and insufficient diet" (Flanagan 1993, p. 111). Hence, Flanagan insists that the more recent theoretical developments which includes world system theory, makes a strong case for drawing the analysis of the rapid urbanization of underdeveloped areas, urban growth, and change into the mainstream urban sociology as the scope of urban analysis takes on global dimensions. We now turn to the consequence of rapid urbanization of Indian cities.

The Economic Consequences

It is true that much like the populations of other Third World cities, Indian cities also suffer from high rates of unemployment and underemployment. However, on a positive side, it has been argued that, "although the proportion of the urban work force in relation to the rural work force is small, over 65 percent of the total manufacturing employment, 64.7 percent of employment in trade, commerce, and financial services, and 68 percent of transport sector employment are concentrated in urban areas" (Mathur 1994, p. 54). But, Mathur quickly checks his optimism with reference to the report of the National Commission on Urbanization (1988) which shows the widespread poverty and deprivation, the most brutal and inhuman living conditions with large sections of the citizens (almost one-half in Bombay and Delhi) living in squatter settlements.

The Planning Commission emphasized the severity of urban problems in India associated with urban poverty, deprivation, and urban slums. About 20.1 percent or 41.7 million persons of the total urban population of India live under the conditions of absolute poverty to the degree that they are unable to consume at least 2,100 calories per day. According to one report (Hashim 1989), about 69.87 percent of poor urban households could not have enough income for the per capita consumption expenditure. Moreover, the vast gap between the per capita consumption expenditures of urban poor versus urban nonpoor households is alleged to be the major source of tensions in urban areas. Mathur (1994, p. 56) further contends that "the gap between the availability and demand for shelter, infrastructure, and services have widened over the years. By 1985, nearly 47 million people in urban areas (21.7 percent) had no access to safe water supplied, 124 million (71.6%) were reported to be without any form of basic sanitation, and another 49 million (35.2 percent) of the population over 5 years of age, without schooling. These figures may also be an underestimate, since the existence of service does not necessarily imply that it is quantitatively and qualitatively adequate." Add to this Flanagan's (1993, pp. 110-111) contention that there is a close correlation between the issues of Third World urbanization and underdevelopment, the latter being a part of the major concern for economic underdevelopment, as the city at times is interpreted as the physical and spatial expression of economic arrangement and conditions. Even if we take into account Mathur's optimistic note that from 37 percent Net Domestic Product in urban India (which increased to 41 percent in 1980-81) and thus in an urban area an average worker produces over three times the Net Domestic Product as a rural worker, there seems to be little doubt that the large segment of urban population especially the blue-collar, within a given city (e.g., Bombay or Ahmedabad) would suffer from unfavorable consequences of economic policy, and only marginal participation in an expanding economic mainstream with likelihood of any significant improvement in life chances.

The Structural Consequences

Coming to the central focus of our topic, it should be further noted that the differences in life chances that result from differential access to the benefits of economic growth may be qualified by the relative stratificational positions of various ethnic communities, the relative socioeconomic status of a particular ethnic community, its degree of access to the people in power, and the relative degree of literacy of the members of ethnic communities. The division of Indian cities into ethnic communities, which cuts across castes and social classes, is an important social fact. These divisions at once unite and divide the members of ethnic communities. They cooperate and come into conflict as the occasion arises. This particular problem of ethnic divisions and ethnic conflict is further explored in this paper, limiting our analysis to the Hindu-Muslim conflicts in the rapidly growing cities (in terms of the rate of urban growth) in India. Moreover, the paper would intentionally focus on three major cities, namely Bombay, Surat, and Ahmedabad, which witnessed the most violent conflicts in the 1990s, resulting in mass violence, killings, atrocities, serious injuries, and the disruption of the daily lives of the people living in those cities.

CONFLICT AND COHESION

A note on conflict and cohesion between ethnic communities will not be out of place here. Sociologists of communities will be greatly benefited if research material is subjected to the conceptual interpretations based on theories of conflict. However, for the task at hand, the use of such a concept here and the analysis of the case studies of conflicts in three aforementioned cities could be adequate. A word of theoretical caution is also appropriate. Both conflict and cohesion are two extremes of theoretical poles. They exist in relative degree in every society. A given social order is a temporary reconciliation of the two extremes. Communal life is disrupted when the temporary reconciliation is disturbed. A minimal degree of consensus is required to make social life in a community possible. An extreme degree of violent conflict jeopardizing the lives of so many individuals in the communities may tilt the balance toward disorder, or even a mild degree of anomie. However, this should not obscure our sociological insight that the dynamics of conflict and cohesion is an essential ingredient of every organized community; its dialectics is an important aspect of sociological understanding. People unite in order to fight, and they fight in order to unite. An ethnic community, when engaged in a violent conflict with the members of a rival ethnic community, may experience solidarity, while at the same time, disrupting the solidarity of a rival community. The latter, when mobilized against what it defines as its rival or enemy community may go through a similar experience. This dialectical process is the essence of community life. Despite the extremes of violence between two communities, and in spite of the importance of other concepts and variables, the sociological imagination related to the dialectical process should not be obscured. Needless to mention that conflicts (even violent ones) perform social and social-psychological functions. Moreover, conflicts may be due to a variety of reasons such as demographic, ecological, economic, cultural, political, historical, religious, and social, none of which should be underemphasized.

THE IMPORTANCE OF URBAN FACTOR

Hindu-Muslim riots are not a new phenomenon in India. There is a long history of hostility between these two major ethnic communities. The seven hundred years of Muslim rule in pre-British India, the discontent of Muslims in British India, the role of colonialism and the partition of one country in two nations—India and Pakistan—and in its aftermath the mass violence in two communities resulting in the loss of lives, limbs, and properties, are only the major highlights. The postindependent, postcolonial India of 1947 inherited the problems of a newly emergent nation-state, including the major problem of reconciliation of two aforementioned communities. It was Indian government's intention to solve the problem through the constitutional policy of secularization. The policy failed because of the continual discontent of the Muslim minority on the one hand, and the fear and the contention of the Hindu majority that the Muslims are disloyal on the other hand. Added to this is the perennial problem of Kashmir (the northern most part of India where the borders of two nations meet)—the presence of Islamic Pakistan next door asserting Islamic fundamentalism and the display of the growing strength of Hindu fundamentalism in India in more recent times. Even while the constitutional policy was being implemented, both communities were experiencing the communalization of politics. It spread rapidly in the first two and one-half decades following India's independence, and in the last two and one-half decades there has been an increasing politicization of communalism itself. The violent conflicts between the two communities have erupted from time to time, accelerated in the 1980s, and continued with increased intensity in the 1990s.

The explanations of the communal conflicts in terms of historical, ideological, cultural, economic, and stratificational differences (or in terms of class divisions) are not uncommon (Chandra 1987, 1989; Thursby 1975; Joshi 1980). Still more common explanations in terms of sociocultural and religious differences as the different symbol-markers (Jeffery and Jeffery 1994) have been utilized by the members of Hindu and Muslim communities as well as social scientists for explaining conflicts. However, they neither explain the reasons for the sharp increase in conflicts in more recent times nor do they explain the greater increase in the frequency and intensity of communal conflicts in an urban situation, taking into account the role of urban factor as such.

There is a long debate about what really constitutes urban. From the days of Durkheim's ([1893] 1933) insistence on the concomitant variations of variables (such as the large size, high density, and the increase in the "dynamic density" of populations which can effect transition from rural to urban), to Wirth's ([1927] 1938) classic statement in "Urbanism as a Way of Life" (which shows logical deductions concerning ecology, social organization and social psychology from three interrelated variables such as urban size, density, and heterogeneity), the issue has been subjected to intensive analysis and research, qualifying many of the assumptions and deductions made by Wirth. A thorough review of it is unnecessary here. However, it gave rise to the studies of a variety of urban phenomena from the city street gangs to urban ethnic communities, highlighting the typical city-community tension problem. It further brought into focus the studies of ethnic neighborhoods, ethnic solidarity, and ethnic cohesiveness (Gans [1962]; 1982; Fischer 1975, 1984; Portes 1981; Wong 1987; Kwong 1987). It also brought to light the studies of the disturbances and conflict in South Central Los Angeles in the 1990s (Moore 1991; Bing 1991) and the demonstration of Simmel's ([1908] 1955) hypothesis that the conflict between groups produced solidarity within groups. While all such theoretical observations and empirical research are useful in isolating urban factor for the analysis of Hindu-Muslim conflicts in Indian cities, it should also take into account the most current trend of linking the major Third World cities with the world system. This brings into focus the major issues in Third World urbanization and underdevelopment, including the issues of urban poverty, deprivation, lack of shelter and adequate diet, extremely low income, unemployment, underemployment, inhuman and brutal conditions in which slum-dwellers live; and the slums that lack sanitation, health care, hygiene, clean water, and electricity. These factors are as important in the analysis of ethnic conflicts in Indian cities as the recognition of the historical significance of colonial exploitation, the creation of port cities for that purpose, the destruction of indigenous cities of India, and their linking with the international marketplace within the global context.

THE CASE STUDIES OF CONFLICTS IN THREE INDIAN CITIES: BOMBAY, AHMEDABAD, AND SURAT

The divide between two ethnic communities—the Hindus and the Muslims—which continue to survive, coexist and cooperatively live together, was never as apparent in urban India as in Bombay in 1992. This big Indian city, now reported to be the world's third most expensive city to live in, and lived in by so many of India's richest multimillionaires and billionaires, also provides the richest soil for communal frenzy to build on poverty.

The spark for igniting communal fire was provided by an event that could have been ordinarily by-passed by this bustling metropolis; but the "squatter population" of the cities of India, estimated to be some 30 million in various cities, is densely concentrated in Bombay. In that city about one-third of its population is estimated to be living in slums where human excreta float around in clogged open drains, rats and rag-pickers scurry around in reeking open garbage piles, and the festering sore of urban poverty is visible in over-crowded buses, chaotic roads, lengthening water queues and clogged drain pipes that spew out filth. The naked display of wealth by a few in the midst of appalling misery heightens communal tensions, because in this city the Hindus happen to be in majority and they are usually better-off than the minority of Muslims who live in poverty.

The communal fire was ignited by an incident on December 6, 1992 as the report came that the militant Hindus destroyed a sixteenth-century mosque in the northern town of Ayodhya, the birthplace of Lord Rama. The Hindus had claimed that the mosque was built over an ancient temple of Lord Rama. The day after, India's cities were swept by bloody rioting and explosive violence. In the communal frenzy that gripped the country in the aftermath, almost 95 percent of the 1,500 victims died in urban areas. One and one-half months after the demolition of mosque, Ahmedabad, Bombay, and Surat, the main cities of Western India, were the worst affected by the riots. The cities continued to be consumed by barbaric savagery—people being made into human torches, women gang raped, and parents killed in front of their children. No city, in fact, seemed to be immune to the communal virus: Baroda, Banglore, Bhadrak, Bhopal, Bijnor, Calcutta, Delhi,

Hyderabad, Meerut, Mysore, Sharanpur, and Sikandrabad, to name a few more. Nowhere was the destruction of property, the number of dead and injured greater than in the cities of Bombay, Ahmedabad, and Surat. Hence we will subject them to detailed analysis in the description that follows.

Mumbai: What Happened to the Beautiful City of Bombay?

In the early 1920s the British gave the title Bombay the Beautiful to the city which then grew rapidly as an industrial and commercial hub of western India. Now more than 12 million strong, Bombay (now renamed Mumbai) has grown into a megalopolis with the constant influx of people from various parts of the country. More than one-half of its population lives in slums in the most miserable conditions. These slums have mixed populations of various regions, religions, and castes. The slums are mainly controlled by slum-lords and they have mutually supportive relationships with the police and the government authorities. Additionally, the ever-rising rate of unemployment boosts crimes in these slums. Moreover, Bombay's underworld is ever-expanding and there are gang rivalries, with the gangs often divided along communal lines. The gangsters have their own political connections, even with different factions of the ruling party, and hence, the differential access to the people in power and different positions of power.

Dharavi area of Bombay is well known as the biggest slum in Asia. People from different castes and communities live in it. Dharavi is also a den of criminals and slum-lords. One can understand how explosive the situation can become once it gets out of hand; and it did get out of hand after the demolition of Babri Masjid (a mosque alleged to be built by the Muslim emperor Babar). On December 6, 1992 some Hindus took out a victory procession (in honor of the demolition of a mosque) with 500 persons. On December 7, stoning began early in the morning by both sides. The Muslims alleged that a mob of about 100 people led by the local corporator attacked Muslim houses and about 56 houses were looted and burned. During this confrontation both communities, Hindu and Muslim, were totally polarized along communal lines, irrespective of their regional origin.

In Social Nagar part of Dharavi, Muslims are in a majority. Yet on December 9, 1992, a Hindu mob set fire to 56 huts, 46 of which belonged to Muslims. When the police came, they opened fire killing six Muslims; 18 persons were injured, of whom one was a Hindu. In the vicinity of Social Nagar, two Hindu temples were damaged. Although Muslims set ablaze about 50 houses of Hindus, the Hindus (in different incidents) burned down 100 Muslim houses. The killings and burning were accompanied by arson and looting. In all, in Dharavi, about 42 persons were killed, of whom 40 died at the hands of the police and two in mob violence. Of those who were killed by police, 30 were Muslims and 10 Hindus.

Mindless violence started spreading to the suburbs of this megalopolis. The eastern suburb of Govandi has one of the largest slums with a considerable Muslim population. When Muslims reacted to the demolition of Babri Masjid by damaging some Hindu temples, the police went on a rampage and made the Muslims their special target. According to the police report, in all 58 persons died in the Govandi area. However, according to the Govandi Relief Committee, 92 persons were killed and 210 injured, including women and children; almost all were Muslims.

The communal killings also took place in other suburbs of Bombay such as Jogeshwari, Malad, Bandra East, Mahim, Kurla, and Ghatkopar. The total number of deaths admitted by the police sources was 202, of which 137 were killed by police. In a fact-finding report (Agnes 1993) of Behrampada, a slum area with a predominantly Muslim population in Bandra (east) in Bombay (the area branded as a den of Muslim fundamentalists), the total number of dead reported were 22 Muslims and 12 Hindus, while there were 58 injured Muslims and 26 injured Hindus, respectively. Bombay is under very strict police control since 1993. But the most recent (1998) acts of terrorism in Bombay raise the suspicion of a communal element in it. Bombay is witnessing the rise of urban terrorism (alleged to have a "Muslim" element in it) and Hindu fundamentalism as never before.

Because of the rise of Hindu fundamentalism and the political parties supporting it, the propaganda among Hindus stated that the lack of opportunities and high unemployment among the Hindu youth are due to the government policy of the "appeasement" of Muslims. Swelling their numbers was the phenomenon that seemed to be happening in most metropolises: there was a much larger migration of Muslim poor into the city in the past two decades than before. Furthermore, with the outbreak of communal violence in cities becoming more frequent, it has driven people of each community into areas where they dominate. It is now causing a dangerous divide of cities into Hindu and Muslim areas. Although the natural segregation existed in Indian cities along religious and ethnic lines in the past, it is now becoming even more pronounced as Muslims are rushing to the city ghettoes because of the outbreak of riots in Bombay and Ahmedabad. This is even more clear in the case of Ahmedabad as we now turn to it.

The Communal Growth of Urban Ahmedabad

The crown city of Gujarat, Ahmedabad, is caught in the fast pace of urbanization in India. The city's population growth rate during 1981-1991 was 23.31 percent. There are 4.8 million people living in Ahmedabad. The festering sore of urban poverty has spread to Ahmedabad. In Ahmedabad, the army of migrants squatted on the eastern part, the city's pride, once proclaimed as the green belt, but now covered in thick black, surrounded by a row of ramshackle huts. About 20.3 percent of all Ahmedabadis are classified as "slum-dwellers."

In the past, Ahmedabadis made their city a throbbing center of commerce and industry where the flourishing textile trade caused Ahmedabad to be called the Manchester of India. Its population gradually swelled, making it one of the biggest cities in the country. The Hindu and Muslim communities traded and prospered together, but now a razor sharp wedge exists between them.

Communal disturbances are not new in Ahmedabad. In fact, one of the worst communal carnages after Independence (1947) hit the city in 1969 and killed over 1,000 people in just three days. After the 1960s, the rapid urban decay of Ahmedabad has joined hands with that of Bombay. In a survey of homes without power, tap water, and toilets (as a percent of total population in major cities), *India Today* (1989) reported that while 22.4 percent of people in Bombay were living without electricity, Ahmedabad had 24.2 percent living without electricity supply. The difference is striking when the relative size of the cities is compared. The similar figures of lack of tap water supply were: Bombay, 41.7 percent and Ahmedabad, 33.1 percent. While 26.6 percent of the people of Bombay did not have basic toilet facilities for their private use, in a comparatively smaller city of Ahmedabad the figure was almost the same: 26.1 percent despite its population now being one-third of Bombay. Needless to mention that a major proportion of such people live in squatter settlements where people are denied the basic facilities of life. The comparative figures for the increase in the number of crimes in those two cities are even more striking. In Bombay, while the reported serious crimes almost doubled in two decades: 1961—19,379 and 1981—35,263, respectively; in Ahmedabad they more than tripled: 1961—3,436 and 1981—10,502.

The tensions between Muslims (about 15% of the city's total population) and Hindus had been festering since the riots of 1969 and they exploded when Muslims, infuriated by the sacrilege at Ayodhya (1992), went onto the streets to protest. Finding that the police were using considerable force against them, they felt even more indignant. The feeling was that the police did not even use a stick when Hindus demolished the mosque but were shooting Muslims when they protested against the destruction. The day after the Ayodhya event, in Ahmedabad, 28 of the 37 Muslims who died were killed by police bullets. The administration lurked in the shadows, showing no will to stop the carnage. Five days after it began, the army had to be called in.

Complicating the communal factor is the caste factor in Gujarat. The Patels (a caste of landowners) are a rising caste since the early nineteenth century. Socially and economically they are upwardly mobile, and more often than not make use of religion to fulfill their mobility orientations. In their rivalry with the caste of the Kshatriyas (martial or warrior caste) they become militant. In claiming their status of the Kshatriyas, the militancy is also used against Muslims. The dynamics of development in the urban areas of Gujarat have favored the Patels, many of whom have been landlords and landowners. Since the 1960s, the Patels have used every available avenue to occupy positions of power and privilege and continued their hegemony with other castes and ethnic communities. In the contest for political power, whenever the Patels are left out, they use caste or communal card to dislodge the power structure. While there is a rivalry for power between the Kshatriyas (the Rajputs) and the Patels, the latter have also claimed the Kshatriya ancestry in the game of power and continued to downplay the role of Muslim minority. This is one of the reasons why Ahmedabad has become communally more sensitive and communal violence has become endemic.

Gujarat also has a relatively good record of economic development and the big cities, like Ahmedabad and Surat (both in Gujarat), have greater urban industrial growth than the other parts of India. But this growth is not without a price, and it is accompanied with the growth of a large number of criminals and antisocial elements. There is a total prohibition on the sale of alcohol in the state of Gujarat. The powerful gangs, some controlled by Muslims and some by Hindus, engage in bootlegging and rivalries for selling illegal alcohol, often leading to serious communal clashes. In this case, crime is not only politicized but also communalized. In this game, there is both the communalization politics and the politicization of communalism. Additionally, all the bootleggers have close links with the ministers and the municipal councilors of their choice. On July 2, 1992, the Hindu procession of Lord Jagannath sent the communal tensions soaring in the Dariapur locality of Ahmedabad. The latter, along with Kalupur, Shahpur, Bapunagar, and Nagoriwad are considered to be "communally sensitive" areas. Some of these areas are Muslim-dominated and they are also within what is known as the "walled city" of Ahmedabad.

Because of increasing communal violence in Ahmedabad, the demographic face of the city is changing forever in a manner that can only deepen the divide between the two communities. The Muslims are forced to live in the congested walled city. The remaining Hindus are migrating out to suburbs while the Muslims from Hindu areas are moving into the walled city. The implication of this division of the city into Hindu and Muslim pockets is already making itself felt in trade, business, and everyday life. Because troubles break out spontaneously in almost all areas of the walled city, it is believed to be totally controlled by bootleggers, many of whom are also gun-runners. Because they have political and police patronage, this classic connection is hard to break. The orgy of communal killings in 1986 and in 1992-1993 have made the residents of Ahmed Shah's city (Ahmedabad) feel that the urban social fabric has been, perhaps, irreparably damaged by prolonged communal strife. But with the help of police control and the heavy handed actions of the city authorities, serious attempts have been made most recently (1997-1998) for cleaning the city and mending the relations.

The Growth and Decay of the "Golden City" of Surat

When the news of the death of the Muslim mafia don Alamzeb Pathan, in an encounter with the Surat police, reached Ahmedabad, the Muslim establishments in Kalupur, Dariapur, and Gomtipur observed mourning by closing down for a day. He was popular among the Muslims of Ahmedabad because he financed communal elements and supplied them with arms. This shows a close communal network between the two cities of Gujarat: Ahmedabad and Surat.

Surat has a population of 1.5 million of whom nearly 84 percent is Hindu. Surat has witnessed the fastest pace of urbanization in India during the last three decades. The city's population growth was 92.63 percent during 1961-1971, the highest in the country. During 1981-1991 its growth was 62.80 percent, next only to the rapidly industrializing city of Bangalore in the south. Surat's main working population was 39.66 per cent in 1981, but slightly declined to 38.70 percent in 1991. Surat became famous as the world's leading center for small diamond cutting. But the diamond cutting has seen a continuous slump in the last three years, and the illiterate Kanbi-Patel immigrants, from outside Surat who mainly worked in that business, have experienced unemployment and discontent. Moreover, the male-female ratio in Surat, (only 839 females to 1,000 males) is lower compared to all of India men-women ratio of 930 females to 1,000 males. This brings out the scope for the rise of lumpen elements and the availability of a large number of men without family encumbrances to get involved in urban conflicts. Moreover, the city's rapid industrial growth attracted waves of labor immigration from the back areas of northern (U.P.), southern (Maharashtra, Andhra), and eastern (Oriya) areas of India. The migrants are largely industrial workers living in some 300 slum pockets. Although industries in silk, art silk, textiles, and diamonds are in the hands of the Gujaratis, Punjabis have a small part of the textile industry in their hands. Muslims are largely concentrated in the Rander area, west of the river Tapi of Surat; the immigrant Muslims live largely in slums scattered on the periphery of Surat and its industrial pockets.

In the hands of such immigrant people, there is an easy flow of illegal earnings from smuggling and bootlegging activities, while the "black money" is generated by the thriving textile and processing industries, the diamond business, and the underhand deals in licenses for art-silk. The powerful urban pull of Surat, which soon resulted in the mushrooming of slums, also gave rise to land-grabbing, sky-rocketing prices of land, and the illegal construction by builders, some of whom went from rags to riches within a short period of a decade to become the city's *nouveau riché* (an upstart elite). The city's unprecedented boom for some three decades also saw the networking of local dons and slum-lords with known boot-leggers from outside who, finding themselves hotly pursued elsewhere, sought refuge in Surat. The induction of mafias, the flow of arms, and the unstable nature of business such as diamond-cutting all yielded a rich crop of lumpen elements, leading to a considerable degree of anomie or "normlessness."

The power and patronage structures and the economic interest groups were taken over by the new class of entrepreneurs, the *nouveau riché* and the mafias, who along with de-classed lumpen elements and the underclass of migrant labor brought with them their own political subculture. They hardly had any stake in the system and no interest in the city's traditional pattern of life. The new power elite had hardly any imagination or capacity to comprehend the municipal and planning complications of urbanization and development at such a fast pace. Political considerations of winning over voter groups also made them lose their will to enforce whatever urban development policies were formulated regarding widening of roads, construction of buildings, or land-use patterns. Even the minimum need of augmenting the city's coercive forces, like the police, was not paid heed to.

Although having no history of recurring riots, as soon as the news of the demolition of Babri Masjid spread (December 6, 1992), Surat, like other cities, became tense. A Muslim mafia don having underworld connections gave a call for strike. Near Chowk Bazar area, four shops belonging to the Hindu majority community were set ablaze. The Shanitinath Dyeing Mill was also damaged by the minority Muslim community. This invited well-organized retaliation from the majority community. With a call "to destroy Muslims," a mob of nearly 2,000 people came equipped with swords, knives, iron rods, acid bulbs, bottles, and stones. They first looted 50 houses belonging to the Muslims and then set them on fire. They also killed some 15 Muslims and threw their bodies nearby or burned them. The manner in which the large-scale looting, burning, and killings took place shows that they were preplanned. The kinds of weapons they used, the free use of gasoline they made in spite of the closure of the gas stations—all indicate that the violence was well organized.

The worst incident took place in Vijay Nagar No. 2. A 12-foot high wall of bamboo was erected to prevent the Muslims from running away and floodlights were installed to watch the movement of people in the area. A mob of about 800 people well-armed with choppers, iron bars, and swords came on the night of December 7, 1992. The mob set some 250 houses of Muslims on fire after looting them. They killed around 70 Muslims on the night of December 8. The mob raped 13 to 16 women and each woman was raped by 4 to 10 persons. After the rape, these women were brought out and made to walk through the floodlit area.

Thus the well-famed golden city of Surt saw brutality which even a city with a chronic history of riots such as Ahmedabad has not seen. The recent riots left some 185 dead, thousands injured, hundreds of houses looted and burned, females raped, and the scenes of burning people alive and raping have been video-filmed by rioters. The horror stories told by victims show the depth of decadence and dehumanization and level of communalization that the city has witnessed.

Surat's 25,000 power looms producing goods worth Rs.250 million per day remained closed during the period of curfew; some 400,000 workers in the power loom factories lost Rs.20 million a day in wages. Some 200,000 migrant laborers left the city—a sort of reverse migration. Some 17,000 took refuge in the city's relief camps, most of them Muslims. The majority of those killed were also Muslims. Moreover, the riots exposed a mafia-lumpen police network existing in the city. The 1992 communal carnage reveals (*India Today* 1992) that while the immediate provocation was the Ayodhya incident, the answer must be sought in the city's rapidly changing socioeconomic environment. Since 1993, attempts have been made by the city authorities to lure back the laborers, rejuvenate the ailing industries, and clean up the city. But the memories of the 1992 communal clashes linger on in the minds of both communities (Sheth 1993).

CONCLUSION

Three case studies substantiate our hypothesis that the urban situation in India, especially in its large cities, showing a faster rate of urban growth is more susceptible to urban riots, manifested more clearly in 1992 Hindu-Muslim conflicts in Bombay, Ahmedabad, and Surat. From the analysis of what happened in those three cities, it is obvious that the concepts "conflicts" or "riots" are milder terms perhaps expected to be value-neutral. But "value-neutrality" apart, it is clear that those are violent conflicts, bloody conflicts involving not only arson, robbery, looting, and destruction of property, but killing, torturing, and maiming of thousands of men and children, including the open raping of women, inflicting indescribable suffering on the members of both ethnic communities. In addition to the conflicts having an urban element, it also shows that the conflicts and killings have deep historical roots which provoke intense psychopathological reactions in the minds of the members of two communities, a factor that needs a deeper analysis.

By the same token, it would be a mistake to assume that the conflicts do not take place in small towns or rural areas. The most recent conflicts (in the 1990s), however, have occurred with greater frequency and higher intensity in the rapidly expanding cities of India, clearly indicating the role of the urban situation, the situation which is described as "confusing and equivocal" because of the paradox of the concentration of greater growth, skills, employment, and wealth on the one hand, but on the other hand, "the most brutal and inhumane living conditions, with large numbers of citizens living in squatter and high health-risk settlements" (Mathur 1994, p. 57). But, precisely this paradox itself is an important characteristic of urban situation as those who have closely scrutinized the classic statements of Wirth ([1927] 1938) and Simmel ([1905] 1950) would testify.

As per the 1991 census of India, the Muslims constituted the minority: 12.12 percent of the total population compared to the majority of 82 percent Hindus. This minority status of Muslims is also found in many larger cities of India, resulting in their residential segregation. But the segregation is further reinforced by their religious beliefs and practices. Their rate of fertility in general is higher but their rate of literacy is lower. Muslim women are even more segregated than Hindu women, and traditionally Muslims practiced their typical occupations although in big cities they are now found in a variety of different occupations, jobs and professions. But over all, they are found to be in a less advantaged position, having on average, less per capita income and expenditure than Hindus, although there are significant variations from city to city. However, they are set apart from Hindus and they also define the situation in the same way. This drives a wedge in their relationship with Hindus, despite the obvious cooperation and coexistence of both communities in daily life.

The Mughals, the practitioners of Islam and the supporters of Muslims, had ruled over India for several centuries before the advent of the British. The British (as a colonial power) destroyed many of the indigenous towns and cities, discouraged the indigenous industries (many of which were owned and practiced by the Muslims), and Muslims in general, showed a greater resistance to change ushered in by westernization, industrialization, and colonial-style capitalism. All these historical memories persist and are manifest in inequalities between two communities. They are rationalized in the name of religion, expressed in ecological segregation, symbolized in their places of worship, and manifested in terms of their acts of loyalty to their communities. What is of greater importance is the destruction of preindustrial cities and the establishment of colonial port cities like Bombay and Calcutta, which gradually expanded like London or New York. The growth of cities was generally unplanned and when the British left, overexploited and divided India was left in the state of underdevelopment, which has a direct bearing on its urbanization and its growing cities have higher unemployment, inadequate shelters, slums, lack of health care, disease, and poverty. Slums and squatter settlements are therefore, a typical feature of large and expanding cities of India. Fewer people living in slums have regular employment, resulting in the casualization of the labor and constraining the work force to engage in illegal means to earn their livelihood. Poverty and deprivation are further evident in high infant and child mortality rates. "According to recent estimates, the infant mortality rate in urban areas is 61 per 1000 live births, and the child mortality rate is estimated at 23 per 1000 child population. In the slum and low-income settlements, the infant and child mortality rates are reported to be often as high as in the rural areas" (Mathur 1994, p. 57).

The large cities of India today are linked with the international marketplace, the world system in a global context. For example, any decrease in demand for small polished diamonds or silk and artificial silk textiles will affect the employment situation in Surat. Similarly, stock market fluctuations in New York, London, or Tokyo would directly affect the economy of Bombay. Not only are underdevelopment and Third World urbanization are interconnected but, the populations of Third World cities are at a disadvantage within the single web of economic expansion, competition, and change that links the world regions together. Cities have been the main "power containers" in the process of industrialization. They "mediate between locality and wider regional processes" (Giddens 1989, p. 281). Within this context, the focus is not only on the forces of globalization but on the city level as well where the powerful and less powerful face choices about how to live today and plan for tomorrow in the midst of uneven economic development— the kind of "developmentalism" promoted by the capitalist state which manipulates the ethnic and communal identities of the rich and the poor in Indian cities. Cities in a developing country such as India, their rapid industrialization, urbanization, and the advocacy of capitalism with built-in unjust power structures which do not solve the problems of the urban poor, experience increasing communal polarization and explosive situations.

REFERENCES

Agnes, F. 1993. "Two Riots and After: A Fact-Finding Report on Bandra (East)." *Economic and Political Weekly.* XXVII: 265-68.

Bing, L. 1991. *Do or Die.* New York: Harper Collins.

Chandra, B. 1987. *Communalism in Modern India.* New Delhi: Vikas Publishing House.

_____. 1989. *India's Struggle for Independence: 1857-1957.* Delhi: Penguin Books.

Chekki, D.A., ed. 1998. "Profiles of American Community Issues and Patterns of Development." Pp. 3-12 in *Research in Community Sociology.* Stamford, CT: JAI Press.

Durkheim, E. [1893] 1933. *The Division of Labor in Society,* trans. and edited by G. Simpson. New York: Free Press.

Fischer, C.S. 1975. "Toward a Subcultural Theory of Urbanism." *American Journal of Sociology* 80: 1319-1341.

_____. 1984. *The Urban Experience,* 2nd ed. New York: Harcourt Brace, Jovanovich.

Flanagan, W.G. 1993. *Contemporary Urban Sociology.* New York: Cambridge University Press.

Gans, H.J. [1962] 1982. *The Urban Villagers,* updated and expanded ed. New York: Free Press.

Giddens, A. 1989. "A Reply to My Critics." Pp. 249-310 in *Social Theory of Modern Societies: Anthony Giddens and His Critics,* edited by D. Held and J. B. Thompson. New York: Cambridge University Press.

Gilbert, A., and J. Gugler. 1993. *Cities, Poverty and Development: Urbanization in the Third World.* New York: Oxford University Press.

Government of India. 1988. *Report of the National Commission on Urbanization.* New Delhi: Manager of Publications.

_____. 1992. *Census of India, 1991. Provisional Population Totals.* New Delhi: Registrar General of India.

Hashim, S.R. 1989. "Monitoring Poverty—The India Experience." Unpublished paper.

India Today. 1989. "Communalism: Dangerous Dimensions". October: 14-22.

_____. 1992. "Bloody Aftermath." December, pp. 40-43.

Jeffery, R., and P.M. Jeffery. 1994. "The Bijnor Riots, October 1990: Collapse of Mythical Special Relationship?" *Economic and Political Weekly* XXVII: 538-551.

Joshi, P.C. 1980. "The Economic Background of Communalism in India—A Model of Analysis." Pp. 35-51 in *Essays in Modern History,* edited by B.R. Nanda. Delhi: Oxford University Press.

Kwong, P. 1987. *The New Chinatown.* New York: Hill & Wang.

Mathur, O.P. 1994. "Responding to the Urban Challenge: A Research Agenda for India and Nepal." Pp. 49-100 in *Urban Research in the Developing World: Asia,* edited by R. Stren. Toronto: University of Toronto Press.

Moore, J.W. 1991. *Going Down to the Barrio: Homeboys and Homegirls in Change.* Philadelphia: Temple University Press.

Portes, A. 1981. "Modes of Structural Incorporation and Present Theories of Immigration." Pp. 279-297 in *Global Trends in Migration,* edited by M.M. Kritz, C.B. Kealy, and S.M. Tomasi. Staten Island, NY: CMS Press.

Sheth P. 1993. "Surat Riots—I: Degeneration of a City." *Economic and Political Weekly* XXVII: 151-152.

Simmel, G. [1905] 1950. "The Metropolis and Mental Life." Pp. 409-424 in *The Sociology of Georg Simmel,* edited by K.H. Wolff. New York: Free Press.

_____. [1908] 1955. *Conflict and the Web of Group Affiliations,* trans. by K.H. Wolff and R. Bendix. New York: Free Press.

Thursby, G.R. 1975. *Hindu-Muslim Relations in India.* Leiden: E.J. Brill.

Wilson, W.J. 1996. "The Truly Disadvantaged: The Hidden Agenda." Pp. 191-215 in *Urban Theory,* edited by S. Fainstein and S. Campbell. Cambridge: Blackwell Publishers.

Wirth, L. [1927] 1938. "Urbanism as a Way of Life." *American Journal of Sociology* 4: 1-24.
Wong, B. 1987. "The Chinese: New Immigrants in New York's Chinatown." Pp. 243-271 in *New Immigrants in New York,* edited by N. Foner. New York: Columbia University Press.

POVERTY AMIDST PLENTY:
HOW DO CANADIAN CITIES COPE
WITH RISING POVERTY?

Dan A. Chekki

ABSTRACT

In recent years, the number of poor in Canadian cities has been dramatically increasing. The poverty rate for families, especially for single-parent mothers, has remained at an unacceptably high level, thereby rendering more than a million children in poverty. The number of families suffering from long-term unemployment has risen. Educated young people have trouble finding work. It is getting harder for many poor people to work their way out of poverty. The number of people using food banks has doubled, and the number of communities with food banks has tripled. The government spending cuts on social programs raise the prospect of ever increasing rates of poverty for the next century. This paper attempts to examine the policies aimed at, and services provided by, different levels of government, nongovernmental organizations, the private sector, and community groups. The author evaluates different models of poverty alleviation programs, and argues in favor of the self-help model of reducing poverty.

Research in Community Sociology, Volume 9, pages 141-152.
Copyright © 1999 by JAI Press Inc.
All rights of reproduction in any form reserved.
ISBN: 0-7623-0498-7

INTRODUCTION

According to the United Nations' quality of life indicators, Canada is still the best country in which to live and one of the richest countries in the world. But Canada apparently has a major problem with poverty. "Poverty in Canada exists in a social system where government bails out and gives massive subsidies to big businesses, creates tax loopholes for the wealthy, grants tax holidays and other incentives to foreign investors, yet it claims to cherish the ideals of equality and freedom" (Allahar and Côté 1998).

Socialists and ecologists have argued that the survival and persistence of poverty in the era of the modern welfare state and of ascendant capitalist democracy is no accident; and that capitalism not only creates poverty but it also needs poverty to sustain its internal dynamic (Dean 1998). The United Nations Committee on Economic, Social and Cultural Rights issued a report (1998) denouncing Canada's treatment of the poor, single mothers, and aboriginal people. It highlighted "crisis" levels of homelessness, skyrocketing usage of food banks, cuts in welfare rates, and inadequate funding for battered women's shelters.

The gap between the rich and the poor has been increasing during the past three decades. In 1973, the richest 10 percent of families (with children under 18) earned 21 percent more than the poorest 10 percent of Canadian families. By 1996, the richest 10 percent of families made 314 times more than the poorest 10 percent of Canadian families.

Between 1981 and 1996, the earned incomes of the poorest 20 percent of households with dependent children was cut in half, from $12,000 to $6,000. The bottom half of the Canadian population holds less than 6 percent of the country's net wealth. The top 10 percent holds 51.3 percent of the nation's wealth. Since 1995, the top 100 corporate chief executive officers have seen their total income rise by over 100 percent. Meanwhile, the average wage for the rest of Canadians has failed to keep pace with inflation.

The purpose of this paper is to delineate the extent and patterns of poverty in Canadian cities, and to examine how these cities cope with the problems of increasing poverty, unemployment, housing shortage, and homelessness. Our primary focus will be on policies and programs designed by the government, nongovernmental organizations (NGOs), and community groups to alleviate poverty. The social safety net model and the charity model of poverty alleviation programs are examined. The community-based self-employment/self-help model, however, seems to be an effective strategy in reducing poverty.

THE EXTENT OF POVERTY

The number of poor Canadians in 1995 was higher (5.1 million) than it was during the last two recessions since the early 1980s (National Council of Welfare 1997).

The poverty rate hit a 17-year high of 17.6 percent and the child poverty rate jumped to 20.9 percent in 1996 (National Council of Welfare 1998b). This is a disturbing story of poverty despite a growing economy and a declining unemployment rate. The poverty rate for all (non-elderly) families increased, thereby contributing to a rising poverty rate for children (1.5 million). There was a continuing decline in poverty among seniors from 1980 to 1995 (33.6% to 16.9%). However, the poverty rate for seniors increased to 18.9 percent in 1996, an increase of 2 percent from the previous year.

Single-parent mothers and single people (more women than men) living outside families were most likely to be poor. Single-parent mothers under age 25, with children under age 7, who did not graduate from high school had a very high (82+ %) poverty rate. Also, unattached youth under the age of 25 had a high (64.7%) rate of poverty. Statistics Canada estimated that the cost of bringing all poor people out of poverty in 1995 would have been $16.3 billion, while the value of goods and services produced was $776 billion. What is disconcerting is the fact that poverty rates continued to rise even as the economy continued to recover from the previous recession. The number of "working poor" Canadians has grown in recent years, and there has been a freeze or decline in the income support provided by government welfare programs.

The National Council of Welfare (1998a) report, "Profiles of Welfare: Myths and Realities," made some important observations: (1) there is no such thing as a "typical" welfare case; (2) welfare is a vital support for children as well as adults, and (3) welfare has become a long-term source of income for a surprisingly large number of Canadians who are old as well as young, able-bodied and disabled, well educated and poorly educated. People on welfare also differ in their reasons for assistance, family types and sizes, housing arrangements, length of time on welfare, and outside sources of income. The estimated one and one-half million welfare cases (1997) represented almost three million children, women, and men, or about 10% of Canada's population, and 54% of the welfare cases had been on welfare continuously for 25 months or more.

The federal and provincial governments and private sector have been unable to create more job opportunities despite increasing corporate profits and declining government deficits. Political leaders, the corporate elite, and social policy analysts have to develop new policy options to deal with the problem of long-term dependency on welfare. By international standards, the quality of life in Canadian cities ranks as one of the highest. Four Canadian cities are recognized as the most livable among the top 12 worldwide. However, poverty has been rising in Canada's urban centers. Urban life in Canada, despite affluence, includes people on welfare, the homeless, food banks, and unemployment.

URBAN POVERTY

Poverty is increasingly an urban phenomenon. In 1994 (CCSD), 7 out of every 10 poor families in Canada lived in an urban center with a population of 100,000 or greater, while 56 percent lived in cities with a population of 500,000 or more. From 1973 to 1994 there has been an increase in the number of poor families in large urban centers (Chekki 1995). Today, families in cities are at a much greater risk of poverty than those living in rural communities.

Poverty rates vary among cities (Lockhead and Shillington 1996). For example, the poverty rate in Montreal is 2-1/2 times greater than in Oshawa. The two largest cities—Toronto and Montreal—have rates of 15 and 22 percent respectively. Poverty rates in urban Quebec are high compared with other cities in Canada, because four of the seven Canadian cities with the highest poverty rates are in Quebec. Windsor and Oshawa, both dependent on the automobile industry, have widely divergent poverty rates. These variations in the poverty rates of different cities need an explanation in terms of sociodemographic and economic factors, such as the number of single-parent families, the aboriginal/minority population, the unemployment rate, and the influence of the industrial and occupational composition of the workforce.

Canada has the second highest (next to the United States) rate of child poverty in the developed world. The child poverty has continued to rise during the 1990s, and in 1996, 1.5 million children were living in poverty, suffering from poor health and lower levels of educational attainment. One in four children under age 12 lived in low-income families in 1994. In 1992, 42.3 percent of single people and 16.2 percent of families in Manitoba lived below the poverty line, and Manitoba has the second highest rate of child poverty in Canada (National Council of Welfare 1998b). In 1996, 72,000 children in the province of Manitoba lived below the poverty line, 9,000 more than the estimated number in 1995.

The poverty rate among two-parent families with a single earner increased from 15 percent in 1973 to 25 percent in 1993. In contrast, the poverty rate for families with two or more earners was 6.5 percent in 1993. However, if we compare data for the four urban centers with the highest poverty rates to the four with the lowest rates, there is little variation in the proportion of two-parent families with two or more income earners. For example, Edmonton and Oshawa have the same population of dual-earning two-parent families, yet their respective poverty rates vary strikingly. Of the approximately 10,000 poor two-parent families in Calgary in 1990, one-half had at least two earners in the family.

Among large cities (500,000 or more), there is a strong correlation between the rate of unemployment and the rate of poverty among working-age individuals. The relationship is weaker but still evident for medium-sized cities, although there remain some important exceptions. Although the rate of unemployment in an urban community is closely related to its level of poverty, more research is needed to better understand why some cities with high unemployment rates have relatively low rates of poverty.

While poverty rates among seniors have declined since the early 1980s, the rate for seniors living as "unattached individuals" (those living alone or with nonrelatives) remains high. There is a considerable variation in poverty rates for seniors in urban centers: highest in Winnipeg, Montreal, and Quebec City, and lowest in Saskatoon, Regina and Oshawa.

Studies by the Canadian Mental Health Association and the Manitoba Centre for Health Policy and Evaluation have found that poor people are three times more likely than rich people to develop a psychotic disorder. Among adult urban residents, people in treatment for mental health disorders are disproportionately concentrated in neighborhoods with low to average household incomes. In 1993, inner-city residents in Winnipeg received hospital and physician services valued at an estimated average of $943 annually per patient.

In 1996, 26.8 percent of women with children using food banks in Toronto reported experiencing severe food deprivation and suffered from hunger. While the food assistance that food banks provide undoubtedly helps poor families, it does not prevent them from going hungry. A recent (Lichter 1997) review of poverty among children in the United States observed that since the "war on poverty" in the 1960s, there are roughly as many poor children today as before, that the rate of child poverty is now at a 30–year high, and that the income gap between rich and poor children is greater than at any other time in recent memory. The Canadian Human Rights Commission (1998) considered poverty as a serious breach of equality rights and urged the federal government to review the Human Rights Act and include provisions to protect people from discrimination based on income, and also to make sure that poor people in Canada get equality of treatment.

POVERTY ALLEVIATION PROGRAMS

Poor people are concentrated in the inner-city neighborhoods of Winnipeg. There is the formal system to deal with poverty through the welfare system, Child and Family Services, the police and justice system, employment programs, parenting programs, and soup kitchens and food banks. However, increasingly, there is a mean spiritedness about these formal systems. Under the recent (1998) federal and provincial government agreement, Ottawa is directing $850 million toward poor Canadian families for child benefit, positive parenting programs, early childhood nutrition initiatives, child care, and so forth. However, it is too early to review the impact of these programs.

There is another set of programs that have been growing in Winnipeg during the past few years. These programs are generally more informal and offer personal connections for poor people, helping them use the strengths within themselves and those around them to begin moving ahead. They help people deal with the problem of poverty—unemployment, abuse, neglect, drinking—rather than simply living with the problem.

For example, the Andrews Street Family Centre in the north end of Winnipeg serves as a welcoming place for anyone who walks in the door. It houses a kids drop-in, a food bank, a community store, a kitchen, a food-buying club, parenting programs, and a clothing depot. All of the staff are local people. The Broadway Community Centre is a coalition of 65 different programs which include rebuilding a colony of houses, providing home buying courses, and running Aboriginal Headstart nurseries; and single moms strengthen one another through mutual sharing, credit circles that provide women with a line of credit and mutual help in establishing a business, counselling programs, women who have been through the cycle of abuse helping other women, and many more.

What these programs have in common is that they are community-based, and they focus upon building personal strengths and providing people with opportunities, not just handouts. Unlike the formal systems, these programs speak to people's strengths, not their weaknesses. They build up people, rather than systems and infrastructures.

There is inner city decay, poverty, urban sprawl, and a crumbling infrastructure. Community workers indicate that building housing is relatively easy, but it is building a community that is hard. Through dozens of similar small programs throughout Winnipeg's inner city, hundreds of significant changes in poor people's lives are taking place.

Canada's rich are getting richer, while its poor get poorer. According to Statistics Canada, incomes of the wealthiest families increased 1.8 percent in 1996 over 1995. The poorest 20 percent of families saw their incomes drop by 3 percent, with cuts attributed partly to lower Employment Insurance payments. (The EI fund has more than a $15 billion surplus.) In 1996, an estimated 5.3 million people lived in poor families which included an estimated 1.5 million children. Children in female single-parent families were five times more likely to live in a low-income situation than those in two-parent families. The National Council of Welfare (1997), an anti-poverty organization, has called for standard welfare rates across the country to prevent provinces from arbitrarily cutting social assistance payments.

Many seniors are spending up to one-quarter of their incomes on prescription brand-name drugs, which are very expensive compared to generic versions, so seniors are demanding a roll back in patent protection for brand-name drugs so that lower-cost generic versions can come to market sooner.

Food banks now risk becoming a permanent fixture in Canadian cities in a way they were never intended. They were supposed to be a short-term, emergency response to an acute crisis, not a major social service for a substantial proportion as they now are. The number of people using food banks has doubled across Canada, and the number of communities with food banks has tripled. The number of households using food banks in Manitoba jumped to 5,024 in 1997 from 712 in

1991. In Winnipeg, 35,000 people are food bank users, of whom 41 percent are children. The number of people using Winnipeg's largest food bank (Winnipeg Harvest) rose by nearly 70 percent during 1998. Welfare rates in Ontario and Alberta have been cut as a result of a reduction in government expenditures. There is a great need to create more jobs, to reinstate national standards on welfare, to provide better child care, to provide housing for low-income groups, and to provide a shorter work-week and job sharing.

Schellenberg and Ross (1997) have observed that it is getting harder for Canadians to work their way out of poverty, and that more than one-half a million Canadian families relied on public income support to keep them above the poverty line in 1994. Without government social assistance, the number of poor Canadian families would have jumped by 56 percent in 1994. The average "market poor" family, defined as a family headed by adults who are fit to work and want to work but may not necessarily have a job, would have been poorer by $5,700 without government programs. The incidence of "market poverty" has remained almost constant. In 1994, 450,000 families were market poor although one adult in the family had worked the entire year. Another 100,000 families were poor although both adults worked all year.

The estimated number of homeless in Canada is well over 100,000, and in 1990 the coalition of social service agencies in Toronto estimated that 10,000 or more young people (ages 16-24) were homeless in Toronto (O'Reilly-Fleming 1993). In the late 1980s, Montreal was reported to have a homeless population numbering in the thousands; 5,000 women alone were reported to be homeless. Reports in the daily press and electronic media from Vancouver to Halifax confirm the growing size and diversity of the homeless population in Canadian cities. The federal and provincial governments have, in recent years, reduced funding to low cost housing, thereby exacerbating the problem of homelessness.

Some previous studies (Bahr 1973; Wallace 1968) indicated that many, if not most, of the homeless were itinerant men and deinstitutionalized mental patients. In recent years, however, the steady increase in homelessness is mainly among women and children. A Report of the Mayors (1999) estimated that there are more than 30,000 homeless people in Toronto. Project Warmth in Toronto has been distributing thousands of sleeping bags to the growing number of homeless people. Because all existing shelters are filled to capacity, Toronto's city council is trying to organize emergency shelters in armories, and mobile homes in parks, along with in any existing vacant buildings. In cities across the country, many groups (Wood 1999) are struggling with limited resources to respond in creative ways to the expanding epidemic of homelessness.

There are 37,000 people on the Toronto Social Housing Connections waiting list who are in need of affordable housing. There are estimates that from 40,000 to 80,000 people are considered "precariously housed." That is, they currently live in overcrowded or substandard housing without sufficient income to pay the rent. The homeless poor are one of the fastest growing populations in Toronto, where the provincial government has cancelled social housing programs, eliminated rent controls, and reduced welfare payments by 21 percent in order to provide $5 billion a year worth of tax cuts to the upper- and middle-income people. There seems to be a close link between poverty, homelessness, and government policies.

The United Nations Committee on Economic, Social and Cultural Rights (1998) is gravely concerned that a wealthy country such as Canada has allowed the problem of homelessness and inadequate housing to grow to such proportions that the mayors of Canada's 10 largest cities have declared homelessness a national disaster. The mayors' conference emphasized the need for low income housing to be treated as a "national emergency," called for national standards for welfare, a reform of the Employment Insurance program, and more funding from the federal and provincial levels of government to combat poverty—especially among women and children.

Unless the three levels of government tackle the problems of lack of employment opportunities, poverty, and shortage of housing, homelessness in Canadian cities will continue to increase rather than decline. Municipal governments, in partnership with the private sector and nonprofit and volunteer/charitable organizations, should take an active role in providing low-cost housing to the working and nonworking poor. The National Anti-Poverty Organization, the Assembly of First Nations, Native Friendship Centres, the Fred Victor Mission in Toronto, Habitat for Humanity, and similar organizations have made a modest effort to deal with the problem of housing for low-income families.

Cities such as Toronto, Vancouver, Regina, and Winnipeg have a separate city department of housing entrusted with the task of responding to the urban housing needs of disadvantaged groups. However, the efforts of city governments in providing low-cost housing, thus far, have barely met the growing need.

The federal government has withdrawn (since 1992) its assistance to cooperative and nonprofit housing. In the meantime, economic inequalities and inner-city problems have worsened. In response, in Winnipeg for instance, several neighborhood-based community organizations have emerged to tackle the need for housing for low-income residents. The Assiniboine Credit Union has provided financing for the acquisition and renovation of houses for the working poor and welfare recipients. The neighborhood revitalization initiatives are focused on providing long-term affordable housing for inner-city residents. Community land trusts and new housing co-ops are emerging. Community groups are buying dilapidated houses and fixing them up to create better neighborhoods.

Liberation theology pursued by church organizations helps the poor to organize themselves for social action and change. A study (Kehler 1998) of four churches in the inner-city neighborhoods of Winnipeg revealed how the church creates community, and a sense of belonging, for the poor by involving them as volunteers in food banks, shelters, child care centers, support groups for single teen moms, and also by providing help in finding jobs, counselling and friendship.

Although these charitable organizations are not able to solve the problem of poverty, they seem to empower the poor to gain access to resources such as food, housing, social networks, counselling, and spiritual support.

The Assiniboine Credit Union, unlike chartered banks, has taken the lead in providing loans to nonprofit corporations, small business, lending-circles, and micro-enterprises. Technical assistance and "partnership advertising" has been supporting employment initiatives by people with disabilities along with community-based businesses such as workers' food cooperatives, community day care centers, and other nonprofit social service organizations.

In the United States, the United Kingdom and elsewhere, poverty rates have generally trended upward in recent decades, rising faster among children than any other age group (Jensen 1998). Ten million children in America do not have basic health care (Wellstone 1997). The changing family structure in the industrialized north, leading toward single-parent families, has played a role in the rise in child poverty (Cornia and Danziger 1997). Children in poor households are twice as likely to have low scores on school tests as children from families with greater economic resources. Child poverty has very real consequences in terms of higher mortality, aggressiveness, substance abuse, decreased mental health, and increased illness. Even with government assistance, many children in Canada are poor. In 1994, one in five children lived in poor families. In other words, children from low-income families are at a significant social, physical, and emotional risk.

In most Canadian cities, poverty is concentrated in inner-city neighborhoods. For example, in Winnipeg seven inner-city neighboorhoods suffer the highest levels of social and economic deprivation and contain (1991) 23 percent of the welfare recipients. About 67 percent of these households contain individuals dependent on welfare, compared to 9 percent in the rest of Winnipeg. Fifty-seven percent of inner-city households live below the poverty line; 60 percent depend on welfare or employment insurance, as do 75 percent of aboriginal single parents.

As part of a tri-level government initiative (Winnipeg Development Agreement), a preventive child and family services program, community-based solutions for children and families living in poverty, and innovative early intervention approaches with respect to prenatal nutrition, early childhood development, young adolescents, and aboriginal mothers are being undertaken in the inner-city neighborhoods of Winnipeg. The Housing program provides assistance to nonprofit organizations to acquire, renovate or build shelters for high-risk groups such as victims of family violence, homeless youth, disabled persons, and aboriginals. Job training and access, and employment equity programs are intended to develop skills and provide employment opportunities for aboriginal people, women, people with disabilities, and visible minorities. The neighborhood improvement program supports the revitalization of older, predominantly residential, low-income declining neighborhoods. The aim is to improve the quality of living for residents by addressing basic human needs of the poor.

The city government of Winnipeg provides financial assistance and employment programming for employable people who are unemployed or underemployed and destitute, while the provincial government assists sole-support parents and people with long-term disabilities. This two-tier social assistance system is now under review, aiming to develop a single-tier system by setting minimum welfare rates and standardizing eligibility criteria, policies, and procedures.

The federal and provincial governments cover about 80 percent of the costs of the municipal welfare programs for the poor. The city of Winnipeg has faced a consistent unemployment rate of between 8 and 10 percent for several years. Changes and cuts to the Employment Insurance program have resulted in an increase in the Winnipeg Social Service caseloads to an average of 17,000 monthly. All major Canadian cities have experienced similar problems as a result of the economic recession, technological advances, a restructuring of the labor market, and reductions to other income support programs. Most of the job loss in Winnipeg has occurred in unskilled and semi-skilled occupations, while much of the limited labor market growth has occurred in highly technical, high-skilled jobs which are beyond the current capabilities of most of the people on social assistance. Over the past 15 years, Winnipeg's share of social assistance costs has risen from $4.3 million to over $20.4 million, a six-fold increase in the number of people on welfare.

SEED Winnipeg Inc. is a nonprofit charitable organization. Its aim is to combat poverty, assist in the renewal of inner–city neighborhoods, assist low-income individuals and groups to become financially self-supporting, and to establish viable economic enterprises. It has entered into partnerships with a diverse community organizations and governments, and has taken the initiative in undertaking the training, counselling, and financing of various community economic enterprises and self-employment programs for the disabled, newcomers to Canada, women, and aboriginal groups. In 1996, SEED Winnipeg placed over 300 welfare recipients into permanent full-time work. In the same year, the city government of Winnipeg reported that more than 3,500 welfare recipients moved off welfare and into the workforce as a result of "Employment 96," a project matching recipients and available jobs.

CONCLUSION

The National Council of Welfare (1998c) urges the federal government to redouble its commitment to fighting child poverty in all forms, and recommends that all low–income families receive and keep the full Canadian Child Tax Benefit, and that it should be fully indexed to increases in the cost of living. Furthermore, it is emphasized that part of the solution to poverty lies in better wages for parents. That would arise from job creation, higher minimum wages, and better labor standards.

Canada's family policies and programs reduce family poverty less effectively than the European programs (Baker 1995). The federal and provincial governments in Canada, despite promises to eliminate child poverty and reduce family poverty, have failed to reallocate resources, reform taxation, and revise social legislation. How much inequality do Canadians think is fair or just? How much inequality of opportunity should Canada tolerate? It is beyond the scope of this paper to address these questions (Ross 1998), albeit crucial, from the standpoint of ideology and public policy aimed at reducing inequality.

For many decades, the social safety net model and the charity model have been influential in assisting the poor to survive. These models are nothing more than band-aid solutions, making poor people depend on handouts, and these strategies have neither solved nor reduced the problem of poverty. On the contrary, poverty has been increasing despite economic growth and affluence. Unless there are major structural changes in our social institutions, ideologies and policies, it is unlikely that poverty will diminish in Canadian cities. In the meanwhile, the community-based self-employment/self-help model appears to be making significant changes in the lives of thousands of low-income people in Canadian cities.

REFERENCES

Allahar, A.L., and J.E. Côté. 1998. *Richer and Poorer: The Structure of Inequality in Canada.* Toronto: Lorimer.

Baker, M. 1995. *Canadian Family Policies: Cross-National Comparisons.* Toronto: University of Toronto Press.

Bahr, H.M. 1973. *Skid Row: An Introduction to Disaffiliation.* New York: Oxford University Press.

Canadian Council on Social Development (CCSD). 1994. *The Canadian Fact Book on Poverty.* Ottawa: Author.

Canadian Human Rights Commission. 1998. *Annual Report 1997.* Ottawa: Minister of Public Works and Government Services Canada.

Chekki, D.A., ed. 1995. "Inequality and Poverty in Canadian Cities: Ideology and Policy-Programs." Pp. 249-270 in *Research in Community Sociology,* Vol. 5.

Cornia, G.A., and S. Danziger. 1997. *Child Poverty and Deprivation in the Industrialized Countries, 1945-1995.* Oxford: Clarendon Press.

Dean, H., and M. Melrose. 1998. *Poverty, Riches and Social Citizenship.* London: Macmillan.

Jensen, L. 1998. "Child Poverty in Comparative Perspective." *Crop Newsletter* 5(February): 1.

Kehler, T.F. 1998. "The Church and the Poor: A Community Development Approach." Unpublished paper, University of Winnipeg.

Lichter, D.T. 1997. "Poverty and Inequality Among Children." *Annual Review of Sociology* 23: 121-145.

Lockhead, C., and R. Shillington. 1996. *A Statistical Profile of Urban Poverty.* Ottawa: Canadian Council on Social Development.

National Council of Welfare. 1997. *Poverty Profile 1995.* Ottawa: Supply and Services Canada.

_____. 1998a. *Profiles of Welfare: Myths and Realities.* Ottawa: Public Works and Government Services Canada.

_____. 1998b. *Poverty Profile 1996.* Ottawa: Public Works and Government Services Canada.

_____. 1998c. *Child Benefits: Kids are Still Hungry.* Ottawa Public Works and Government Services Canada.

O'Reilly-Fleming, T. 1993. *Down and Out in Canada: Homeless Canadians*. Toronto: Canadian Scholars' Press.

Report of the Mayors. 1999. *Homelessness Action Task Force: Taking Responsibility for Homelessness, An Action Plan for Toronto*. Toronto: City of Toronto.

Ross, D.P. 1998. "Rethinking Child Poverty." *Perception* 22: 1.

Schellenberg, G., and D.P. Ross. 1997. *Left Poor by the Market: A Look at Family Poverty and Earnings*. Ottawa: Canadian Council on Social Development.

United Nations. 1998. *Report of the Committee on Economic, Social and Cultural Rights*. New York: United Nations.

Wallace, S.E. 1968. *Skid Row as a Way of Life*. New York: Harper Torchbooks.

Wellstone, P. 1997. "If Poverty is the Question..." *The Nation* (April 14).

Wood, C. 1999. "Small Solutions." *Macleans*. 112(10).

PART III

NEW PATTERNS OF WORK AND
COMMUNITY QUALITY OF LIFE

FORWARD TO THE PAST?
HOME-BASED WORK AND THE MEANING, USE, AND DESIGN OF RESIDENTIAL SPACE

William Michelson, Karin Palm Lindén, and
Tomas Wikström

ABSTRACT

This paper integrates the meaning, use, and design of residential space in an examination of home-based work. It relies on representative time-use data from Sweden
(1990-1991) and Canada (1992) which are used both to identify two different types
of home-based workers (extensive and intensive) and to compare their everyday
behaviors with those of conventional workers along lines suggested by previous literature. Complementary qualitative data from an original study of 22 teleworkers in
Sweden sheds additional light on everyday behavior while also detailing diverse
ways in which they deal with their homes. Both types of data show that gender further specifies ways that people experience home-based work and its associated
behaviors and space use. While confirming certain unique patterns of behavior and
ideal types of space use among home-based workers, this analysis nonetheless
concludes that their complex contexts do not lead to simple or monolithic outcomes.

Research in Community Sociology, Volume 9, pages 155-184.
Copyright © 1999 by JAI Press Inc.
All rights of reproduction in any form reserved.
ISBN: 0-7623-0498-7

INTRODUCTION

Recent history presents a scenario of technological innovations enabling the reorganization of human life, from the micro situation of individuals trading the quill for the word processor to the macro world economic order. The speed and number of such innovations accelerates. Ogburn (1964) long ago coined the concept of *cultural lag*, denoting the phenomenon in which people's adaptation to the implications of innovations necessarily follows their use, often by many years.

The target of this paper is *home-based work*, a person's regular paid employment, carried out partly or full-time at home. Another related term, *teleworking,* means that people use information technology such as telephones, fax machines, and computers with modems for work. Still another, *telecommuting,* means replacing to some extent travel to work by telecommunication. In this paper, however, the three terms—home-based work, teleworking, and telecommuting—are used according to context.

The 1990's have seen a surge of renewed interest in working at home, made possible in large part by developments in electronic telecommunications devices and the marketing campaigns of their manufacturers. Sizable percentages of households in many countries own one or more computers, and many of these households are connected to the Internet. Home offices increasingly include such other devices as copiers, fax machines, scanners, and elaborate telephone systems. What is less well known and documented is how many people have decentralized their workplace to home, to what extent these people carry out their main work in these home locations, and what implications such changes have had for individual behavior, for family dynamics, and for the contexts of everyday behavior, ranging from the home to the larger community and society. This paper focuses on explicitly bringing together the meaning, use, and design of residential space in conjunction with telecommuting.

Home as a Place for Paid Work

Home as a place for work is not a new phenomenon. Industrialism was preceded by the unity of working and dwelling in peasant society. However, in Western industrial society the division between employment, on the one hand, and dwelling and leisure on the other, has characterized everyday life of large groups of the population: "Telecommuting emerges in a world where home and work is constructed as spatially separate, dichotomous, and gendered realms of social life" (Aitken and Carroll 1996).

Studies of home-based work in general have produced important knowledge that to some extent is relevant for the field of teleworking. Paid work in the home is portrayed by two British researchers as an anomaly: "Homeworking constitutes a physical, interactional, and personal disruption to hopefulness" (Bulos and Chaker 1995). According to their analysis, home-based work constitutes a problematic intrusion in a sphere characterized by conceptions of nonwork. Other researchers mean that the view of home-based work as new and foreign to home is based upon a false, male picture of the home as the antithesis of the world of work. For women, even the modern home is a place for work—unpaid domestic work (Ahrentzen 1992). The owner-occupied house also comprises a number of tasks traditionally carried out as unpaid work by men: care, maintenance, repairs, and renovation. However, apart from those domestic tasks of women and men, in most dwelling environments, employed work in the home constitutes a deviation from a dominating pattern of relations between home and work. Thus, the introduction of paid work in the home (with or without the use of telecommunication) is often described as problematic.

Several researchers stress the complexity of problems related to the home becoming a place for paid work (Ahrentzen 1992; Gurstein 1995). Feelings of social isolation and entrapment are problems for some home-based workers. Others feel invaded by clients or business partners. Home-based workers, especially women, may not be respected in their professional roles, but become identified by others with the domestic work nature of home (Ahrentzen 1992). Has the fact that work life has entered the private sphere affected the ways home is experienced by the women and men of our study? Does home-based work undermine the role of the dwelling as a place of rest, recreation, and family life? Alternatively, does the proximity between activities of working and dwelling—between parents and children, between spouses, between neighbors—rather give opportunities for an enriched everyday life?

Hypothesized Behavioral Dynamics of Home-based Employment

Within the home, daily routines are made up from an array of specific behaviors, carried out by the respective members of the household. Behaviors required and/or chosen may reflect a number of personal and family characteristics such as age, life-cycle stage, lifestyle, gender, and employment. In turn, the behaviors of household members, whatever their derivation, interact with one another and with the physical parameters of the household unit, with varying degrees of perceived success.

Including employment within the behavioral array at home is thought to have implications for everyday life. A growing number of studies provides hypotheses as to the dynamics of home-based employment (Ahrentzen 1987; Christensen, 1988; Brown 1994; Conference on Homeworking 1994; Spittje 1994; Gurstein 1995; Heck Owen, and Rowe 1995; Huws 1996; Hochschild 1997; Huws and Gunnarsson 1997; Orser and Foster 1992; Sturesson 1997; Winter, Puspitawati, Heck, and Stafford 1993).

A very important factor in behavioral dynamics is *travel*. It appears logical that those working at home will save time otherwise allocated to commuting. Taking this situation very simplistically suggests that the average homeworker will have an hour or more per day more than the conventional worker to use for other activities. Some suggest that the time thus saved will be allocated to recreational purposes, or to sleep, or to time spent with other family members, or to activities in the local community, or combinations of such behaviors. Such tradeoffs of commuting time for other nearby activities are viewed as ecologically positive. On the other hand, there is no a priori reason why time released from commuting cannot be reallocated to travel for other purposes—and not necessarily in the local community—or for more work. It is also not precluded that home-based workers will make work-related trips to clients, suppliers, other specialists, and/or to head offices. The hypothesis of time available from foregone commuting is very much an empirical question to be tested from sufficient, representative data sources.

A second behavioral dynamic focuses on *isolation*. Given the demands of paid employment, it is hypothesized that those who do it at home will be alone while working. This may lead to more time during the day spent alone. But is this isolation? One may or may not be isolated from work mates. But in a multi-person household, being at home for work may in the scope of the entire day lead to more contact with other household members. Spouses, for example, may spend more time together if one or both work at home. The pattern of the day in terms of contact and isolation is important to learn. As is the nature of household space in which contact and isolation occur.

Another dynamic focuses on the *presence of children* in particular. Work outside the home generally precludes simultaneous responsiveness to children, whether as direct care or availability in the event of need. An early motive by women for home-based work was to enhance the possibilities for such responsiveness. Although it is often hard to combine the tasks of paid employment with those of child care, it is at least theoretically possible to enable a *pattern* that involves both as needed during the 24-hour day. Furthermore, it is even more realistic to consider that home-based work may assist parents to be available for acute access to their children, as well as to be in the same location as children for more hours in the day. The same logic suggests that home-based workers may carry out more domestic activities, given their immediate access to their home context. Relationships between parents, children, and work activities raise further questions about the nature and allocation of household space.

Designing for Home-based Work

The introduction of employed work in the home implies the encounter between two worlds separated during industrialization—the worlds of dwelling and working. Understanding home-based workers' use of home space from an architectural point of view means understanding home as a process, as an interplay of individuals' dreams, needs, and actions. The spatiality of dwelling is not static, nor is it limited to relations between spatial elements. It is continuously created in the flow of everyday activities by which a group of people interacts to appropriate built space, to make it a home. This makes the dwelling a complex issue of design, whether it is a new or already existing building. How is the use of the different rooms in the home affected? What negotiations, compromises, and priorities have to be made when the home is adapted to new demands? How do men and women, singles and couples with children establish their work spaces? How do they use the rest of the dwelling when working at home?

Not only do home and paid work stand for different values in life—reproduction and achievement—they also correspond to different aesthetic values. When going into the details of furniture and technological equipment, how can the dilemma of conflicting aesthetic preferences be solved?

METHODOLOGY

Getting adequate and representative data with which to examine the various phenomena surrounding home-based work, and which at the same time are both subjectively and contextually sensitive, is a daunting task. One difficulty is finding respondents and/or situations that reflect home-based work as found in contemporary societies. This work situation at present still applies to only a relatively small percentage of the population. Identifying these people for study is not assisted by universalistic directories or registers. For this reason, much of the extant literature utilizes case studies or surveys of people working for companies known to foster home-based work. A second difficulty comes from our perceived need to benefit from survey data of large numbers of home-based workers, while at the same time generating sensitive information about people's motivations and plans, as well as knowledge of the physical parameters of their homes. For this reason, we used a multi-method approach.

Time-use Analysis

To optimize breadth in our analysis, we turned to a secondary analysis of time-use data, gathered from representative national surveys in Sweden and Canada. In a time-use survey, respondents enumerate the activities they performed on a particular day in chronological order, including the times each activity started and finished, where activities took place, what other person or persons may have been present, and, as an option, some evaluative aspect of the activity. Time-use data can be used to identify, among other things, where a person carries out regular paid employment, as well as how much time in the day is devoted to a job at home or at an external workplace. Thus, a national time-use file can provide information on approximately how many and which persons perform home-based work on a random day as well as what their behavior patterns and physical and social contexts are like on those days. This can be compared to those found to work nearly exclusively in conventional work settings on the day in question. Such a data set does not typically provide extensive information on other aspects of interest, such as details on the actual nature of work they do or on what they do on other days. But it does identify a larger and more representative array of home-based workers than do most other approaches.[1] Clearly, not all the persons selected as home-based workers necessarily use computers and other products of the new information technology. They represent a variety of employment situations.

The Swedish data were collected by Sweden's Central Statistical Bureau during 1990-1991.[2] A working sample of 1,261 respondents was gleaned by selecting employed respondents whose first day's time-use protocols pertained to a weekday in which they devoted some time to their main job. The Canadian data were collected by Statistics Canada in 1992 as part of that year's General Social Survey (number 7).[3] On the same logic as was used with the Swedish sample, a working sample of 3,117 was drawn. The two time-use surveys are largely similar, although some differences remain which had to be reconciled in specific comparative analyses.

In-depth Study

The Swedish coauthors, both architects, conducted a complementary study within Sweden that focused on qualitative information in greater depth (cf. Wikström, Palm Lindèn, and Michelson 1998). The empirical research was based on in-depth interviews with 22 Swedish men and women, and on their own diaries from a typical working day.

Snowball sampling was used to identify subjects through different channels: innovative companies, planning agencies, experts, researchers, and our own contacts. The intention was to cover a wide range of teleworking situations regarding dwelling, household, surroundings, distance to work, portion of work-time at home, type of work, employed or freelancer, and gender.

The interviews, involving conversations on previously determined themes, were conducted in the homes of the respondents. The recorded interviews were typed and processed, using software for qualitative data analysis (NUD*IST). The dwelling was documented by drawings, photographs, and sketches. These documents were very valuable when understanding the contexts of individual teleworkers. At the visit, a time-budget protocol was handed out, to be filled in on a typical workday at home. Fifteen respondents completed the diary.

Sample Characteristics

The identification of home-based workers in the time-use surveys was based on the criterion that they were found to spend at least one hour on the day studied doing their principal paid employment at home. Overtime work or homework was not counted, eliminating some peripheral candidates for home-based work. The one-hour threshhold is certainly minimal as a criterion for inclusion. However, our analyses found that if a person spent at least one hour doing his or her main paid work at home, the odds were that much more time would be devoted to it; those spending less than one hour this way were found to do little or none. Qualifying on this minimalistic basis were 6.7 percent of the Swedish sample (82 persons) and 12.6 percent of the Canadian sample (392 persons). The Canadian figure falls squarely within the Canadian estimates of 5-23 percent by Orser and Foster (1992).

Because this selection process had such simple criteria, further attention was paid to differences between "high" home-based workers (4+ hours) and "low" (1 or more hours but less than 4). Two different styles of home-based work were identified. The low home-based workers are what has been called multisite workers (Huws 1996), dividing their time between home (a mean of 40% of work time) and external workplaces (60%); this group is, therefore, conceptualized as *extensive* home-based workers. The high group was found to do most of their work (85%) at home, although some still outside; this group will now be called *intensive*. The analysis in this paper will examine the extent that intensive home-based workers exceed extensive home-based workers in the degree that they evince hypothesized behavioral outcomes. An alternative is that these are qualitatively different versions of home-based work. Additionally, the null hypothesis is that there is no significant difference in the daily lives of conventional workers and the two categories of home-based workers.

In the in-depth study of Swedish teleworkers, the amount of time spent working at home varied from one-half to one day a week to almost all the time. All in all, a little less than one-half of them seemed to exemplify the category of intensive home-based work mentioned above. Thus the majority, working 2 days or less than that at home, come under the extensive group. The 20 households visited included two couples where both adults were teleworking. Eleven of them were women, and the same number were men. Although the participation of respondents of both sexes was intended, the even distribution of women and men was a coincidence. Six women but only one man worked part time. Two women and two men were freelancers or self-employed.

The respondents of the in-depth study represent a relatively well-situated group. Most of them had independent jobs requiring qualifications, and also a certain freedom to choose whether and to what extent to work at home. Employed work had a great positive value for most of them. Their tasks were often independent and involved both cooperation and individual work. In spite of these apparent similarities regarding positions and working conditions, the dwelling situations and the spatial solutions, as well as the motives for working at home, were strikingly diverse.

RESULTS AND CONCLUSIONS

The Day of the Home-based Worker: Behavior

Work Location Categories and Behavior

Table 1 shows the significance levels of relationships from the time-use data sets between the work location categories and specific behaviors.[4] Although the Canadian data show more significant differences by work location categories, the raw data show remarkably similar trends in the Swedish data. In both cases, the intensive-extensive distinction is shown to account for considerable differences in daily timeuse.

Travel (of all kinds during the day), the first of the activities for which hypotheses were made, shows statistical significance in both the Canadian and Swedish samples. However, the absolute amount of difference in daily travel time between conventional workers and telecommuters is relatively small. It is not a matter of all or nothing. This gives little time to redistribute to leisure and community-based activities. In fact, the extensive home-based workers travel as much as the conventional workers, while the intensive group travels about one-third less. But even then, the intensive group does not reallocate this time to leisure or sleep. Greater understanding of the nuances of travel behavior emerges from the in-depth study shown later.

Both Canadian and Swedish home-based workers do spend more daily time alone, as hypothesized. However, they also spend more time than the conventional workers with members of their nuclear family; the intensive workers, not surprisingly, spend the most time with family members. However, whatever tradeoffs enter the behavioral dynamic do not lead to greater daily contact with friends and neighbors. In Table 1, this is indicated by the time spent in other persons' homes.

Consistent with the hypotheses, domestic activity (which for this purpose includes child care), is greater among the home-based workers, particularly the extensive home-based workers. The extensive home-based workers are also distinguished by the fact that they put in the least daily time at work, less than the conventional workers and much less than the intensive home-based workers. As well, their travel time is spent more in automobiles than the conventional workers, offering meager support for the ecological argument for at least one brand of home-based work.

The intensive home-based workers, as noted, spend the most time working and with other family members. Not surprisingly, they also spend the most time at home. They spend the least time in external workplaces, in travel time, and in shopping. They appear to support most of the hypotheses about the impacts of homeworking without being extremely isolated.

Table 1. Summary of Analyses of Variance in the Relationships of Different Workplace Locations to Minutes per Day Devoted to Selected Activities, Locations, and Persons Present, Canada (1992) and Sweden (1990-1991)

| | Canada | | | | | Sweden | | | | |
| | Means | | | | | Means | | | | |
	Conventional	Extensive	Intensive	$F =$	Sig.	Conventional	Extensive	Intensive	$F =$	Sig.
Activities										
Travel	78	76	44	21.970	.000	66	66	44	3.742	.024
Main job	450	413	512	19.506	.000	449	434	481	1.315	N.S.
Domestic	67	86	70	6.301	.002	65	79	76	1.477	N.S.
Child care	23	28	19	1.241	N.S.	21	16	19	0.347	N.S.
Media	118	126	116	0.696	N.S.	80	72	71	0.712	N.S.
Personal care	560	570	573	2.014	N.S.	468	470	483	0.600	N.S.
Shopping	26	37	19	5.818	.003	14	15	14	0.053	N.S.
Location										
At home	763	930	1226	467.024	.000	753	919	1185	92.534	.000
External workplace	478	310	79	439.002	.000	491	323	117	124.477	.000
Other person's home	26	15	23	2.265	N.S.	27	15	8	1.248	N.S.
Persons Present										
Alone	280	384	492	77.967	.000	451	549	501	2.894	.056
Family	189	227	254	11.733	.000	262	299	322	1.570	N.S.
$N =$	2725	250	142			1179	49	33		

163

An analysis of episodes of work during the day (Michelson 1999a), shows that the *pattern* of daily activity differs between the conventional workers and the home-based workers, extensive and intensive alike. Workers of all categories start work episodes at different times in the morning in a rough normal curve. They do the same in the afternoon. However, only the home-based workers show a third, minor curve for episodes of work through the evening, as foothills to the two mountains denoting weekday starts to work episodes. Home-based workers have more episodes of work throughout the day, and intersperse what they do to a finer degree.

Thus, although home-based workers do not differ in thoroughgoing, dramatic ways from conventional workers in their everyday behavior, there are differences in the amount of time spent in certain expected behaviors and situations. These differences become sharper and even more logical when a distinction is made between two styles of home-based work, extensive and intensive. Nonetheless, the differences are not greater than they are because a major dynamic factor, commuting time, does not involve such great differences between home-based workers per se and conventional workers to account for major differences in a number of other specific behaviors with the time lost or saved while commuting or staying home.

Gender and Behavior

As we noted earlier, everyday behavior is a potential function of many aspects of life. Many of the usual explanatory factors were examined to see if home-based workers are a significantly different lot in sociodemographic and socioeconomic terms. It appears that they are not.

Nevertheless, because gender has been shown to impact everyday behavior strongly (cf. Michelson 1985), we analyzed it further in this context despite the fact that the ratio of 57 men to 43 women participating in the labor force on the day of the time-use survey applies almost exactly to both the conventional workers and the two categories of home-based workers. While differences between the work location categories cannot be ascribed to different gender ratios, it is possible that the mean durations of time describing participation in particular activities attributed to the work location categories are arbitrary combinations of different male-female behavior durations and patterns.

Looking at time devoted in the day to specific behaviors according to gender, as in Table 2, brings out a number of statistically significant differences. Indeed, more types of behavior vary significantly by gender than by workplace location, although some vary significantly by both factors. The Swedish sample shows *many* more significant relationships by gender than by workplace location, resembling the Canadian picture even more closely than before.

Women spend significantly more time than men in both countries at home, with family, doing domestic activities and child care, personal care (including sleep),

Table 2. Summary of Analyses of Variance in the Relationship of Gender to Minutes per Day Devoted to Selected Activities, Locations, and Persons Present, Canada (1992) and Sweden (1990-1991)

	Canada				Sweden			
	Means				Means			
	Men	Women	F =	Sig.	Men	Women	F =	Sig.
Activities								
Travel	77	76	.196	N.S.	66	64	.528	N.S.
Main job	481	413	163.826	.000	483	404	124.56	.000
Domestic	45	96	318.215	.000	36	105	461.895	.000
Child care	16	32	70.768	.000	16	28	22.823	.000
Media	129	106	37.640	.000	88	69	23.555	.000
Personal care	548	577	59.756	.000	457	483	36.310	.000
Shopping	19	35	62.993	.000	11	18	27.167	.000
Location								
At home	764	837	89.549	.000	719	838	106.445	.000
External workplace	474	412	78.871	.000	511	427	84.969	.000
Other person's home	26	24	.319	N.S.	29	22	2.203	N.S.
Persons Present								
Alone	313	280	15.598	.000	476	428	7.895	.005
Family	181	213	22.137	.000	246	289	9.967	.002
N =	1707	1410			716	545		

and shopping than do men. These differences reflect long-standing gender roles from the past, regardless of other changes in their roles and in society.

Men in both nations spend significantly more time in their principal paid employment, at an external workplace, tuned into media, and alone. Although media access is not a traditional gender role, differences in participation derive from one spouse having less time to do this as a function of greater devotion of time to domestic and child-care activities.

Interaction between Work Location, Gender, and Behavior

It remains to assess the extent that the combination of categories of work location and gender makes a difference in itself, that is, an interaction effect. Two-way analyses of variance were carried out, with work location and gender as the independent variables and time devoted to specific behaviors as the dependent variable. As summarized in Table 3, significant interaction effects were confined to the Canadian sample, insofar as there were more work location effects with which to start. The Swedish sample does show many instances of an independent gender effect in the 2-way analysis of variance (e.g., hours of work, $F = 18.366$, sig. $= .000$; domestic work, $F = 92.755$, sig. $= .000$; child care, $F = 4.327$, sig. = .038; media, $F = 5.578$, sig. = .018; shopping, $F = 8.335$, sig. = .004; at home, $F = 10.864$, sig. = .001; at an external workplace, $F = 11.378$, $p = .001$; and alone, $F = 6.444$, sig. = .011). But the impact of *combinations* of workplace location and gender on behavior was greater among Canadian respondents than among those in Sweden.

What cannot be seen in Table 3 with regard to these relationships is what shape the interaction takes among the Canadian respondents (and, in the same direction, among the Swedes). As we know already from Table 2, men are likely to spend more time than women doing their principle paid job and in an external workplace, while women outdo men regarding domestic activity, shopping, and time with family members. What the data show when the sex differences are broken down by workplace location (cf. Michelson 1999a) is that the consistently greatest gender difference is among the extensive home-based workers. The least gender difference in aggregate is among the conventional workers. Gender equality *declines* with home-based work, particularly extensive home-based work.

Flexibility

Let us turn to our *in-depth study* for perspectives and results that complement the time-use analyses. One advantage of teleworking is said to be flexibility: the

Table 3. Summary of the Interaction between Different Workplace Locations and Gender from 2-way Analyses of Variance Regarding the Minutes per Day Devoted to Selected Activities, Locations, and Persons Present, Canada (1992) and Sweden (1990-1991)

	Canada		Sweden	
	$F =$	Significance	$F =$	Significance
Activities				
Travel	2.247	N.S.	1.693	N.S.
Main job	4.913	.007	1.756	N.S.
Domestic	10.841	.000	2.710	N.S.
Child care	1.397	N.S.	0.102	N.S.
Media	1.554	N.S.	1.242	N.S.
Personal care	1.895	N.S.	0.775	N.S.
Shopping	6.871	.001	0.533	N.S.
Location				
At home	1.565	N.S.	0.903	N.S.
External workplace	6.395	.002	1.743	N.S.
Other person's home	0.598	N.S.	0.003	N.S.
Persons Present				
Alone	1.597	N.S.	1.350	N.S.
Family	4.059	.017	0.547	N.S.
$N =$	1261		3117	

spatial flexibility to "work where you want" and the temporal flexibility of working when you like. The in-depth study confirms the time-use conclusions cited that flexibility might be an advantage of home-based work. The diaries told us that the deviations from ordinary working hours during the day primarily were taking breaks more often, taking time off in the afternoon and compensating this by working at night.

However, this flexibility had its limits. Most home-based workers felt that they had to be available for colleagues and clients during working hours. Another important reason for conforming to normal office hours is that they coincide with the rest of the family being away from home. The motive of not being disturbed explains the eagerness of many of the interviewed persons to start working as soon as the home was empty. For employees and freelancers alike, time-use depended on the requirements of others. Employed teleworkers, both men and women, claimed to have difficulties breaking the routines of the office:

> Still I feel that being available is important. I'm not busy all the time with people wanting to get in touch with me, but it feels important that they can reach me if something happens or if they need something from me.

This young man, working in a telecommunications company, saw the fact that "the others have normal working hours" as one important reason to keep office hours when working at home.

The demand of being available stressed some teleworkers more at home than in the office. In the regular workplace, it is all right to linger outside one's own office and thus be hard to reach. The insistence on being available on the telephone or through e-mail becomes an "electronic leash." Those who lived close to their regular place of work sometimes felt reluctant about taking time off in the middle of the day to do errands in town. They did not want to risk being seen during work hours, although free disposal of working time was officially granted.

Some of these problems concerning the pressure of being available are explained by the fact that many employees working at home feel that they have to prove that they are efficient. For many of them, the work ethic is a question of presence at the workplace during office hours (whether at home or in the office) rather than of results. Nevertheless, neither work ethic nor regular office hours prevented the employed teleworkers from *long workdays*. Several of them told about periods with a heavy workload and much overtime work. Some of them also felt that they had to prove to colleagues and employers that they were more efficient when working at home. Others often feel the pressure to finish a task by working overtime. Teleworkers typically reported *working in the evenings or on weekends*.

Freelancers also have to adjust to the working hours of their clients and customers. Choosing freely when to work and when to take time off was not possible for them. Controlling their work hours seems harder for freelancers, as their results are more directly related to their success and income. The fear of missing interesting and gainful options makes it important to be able to be reached. As none of them had an international clientele, this first meant being available during normal working hours.

The relative temporal flexibility was beneficial in a way that strengthened the tendency to work late: taking a few hours to work at night to deal with work tasks that worried them was easy for the home-based workers. One of the freelancers said: "It gives more freedom, freedom to work all the time!" Obviously there was flexibility, although not necessarily always in a positive sense.

Merging and Separation

Home-based work implies *regionalization* (Giddens 1984) of activities going on in the same place and often at the same time. Regionalization here means establishing a "region" in time space for certain activities by conducting them in a context of other activities, thus sustaining this region. When separating work and leisure, spatial and temporal boundaries are used for organizing everyday life, with a certain time and place for each type of activity. Merging allows a more flexible situation, where work activities are carried out between other doings and where the location and timetable of employed work may change according to the dynamics of work and family life. Thus, the temporality of home-based work is clearly related to the use of space and to patterns of actions involved in starting, conducting, and finishing work.

Domestic Duties

> It's all right for me to run the washing machine while I'm working. Pushing a button is no household work. I push a lot of buttons during the day. Since there is a lot of brain work in what I do, solving problems... If I sit on a sofa or hang up the laundry in my solitude, and simultaneously do some thinking, it works just as well for me, I think and solve problems all the same... If I hang up the laundry at the same time, it's even as though doing something practical with my hands helps me to arrive at a solution faster than if I stay put.

All home-based workers have in common that their work is carried out in an environment that already constitutes a workplace, a place for the "invisible" domestic work. The advertising campaigns of computer corporations tell us that merging work and leisure is advantageous—without mentioning domestic work. According to North American research, however, home as a context for employed work may be problematic for both women and men. A woman's employed work at home is often depreciated by people in her environment (e.g., Ahrentzen 1992). It is associated with the low-status domestic doings that she is expected to carry out while managing her paid work. Men working at home have to struggle with their professional identities, home being a place of femininity and intimacy (Aitken and Carroll 1996). Thus, home and domestic activities do not represent a neutral background for paid work. Rather, home is a place saturated with meaning and characterized by tasks waiting to be carried out.

Most of the teleworkers interviewed in the in-depth study experienced the opportunity of merging domestic chores and paid work as an advantage. A few of them, however, told about a tension between the worlds of work and home, a blurring of boundaries that became problematic. Regardless of gender, the vast majority of the teleworkers told about carrying out household tasks during their working day. Such tasks served as relaxing breaks or as ways of getting inspiration. These results coincide with those of other researchers. The sharing of space for domestic and paid work activities is said to promote sharing of family roles, for example, husbands taking on more domestic duties (Ahrentzen 1990). Nonetheless, some respondents endeavored to keep the worlds of employed work and home separated. Thus, the conceptual distinction between merging and separation as patterns of regionalization was reflected in the empirical examples. Time-use results suggest that perhaps more separation occurs than merging for male home-based workers, with the opposite among women (Michelson 1999b).

Family Life

For the wife of a freelancing engineer it was easy to see the advantages of teleworking: If only her husband had started looking after the children years ago, when the children had to be looked after! In those days, her husband was away from home most of the time, often working late at night. It would have been a relief just having him nearby, being able to support her when things were getting out of hand.

In the in-depth study, this example of traditional role relations in a family is contrasted by others with a more egalitarian pattern. The study covers a whole range of family situations, from one-person households to couples with three or more children representing different stages in the life cycle. The fact that the home-based worker is present in the home makes it possible for her or him to become involved in family activities, but also calls for solutions that allow paid work to be conducted without disruptions. The physical proximity between activities of paid work and family life makes the (spatio-temporal) regionalization of each activity crucial.

On the one hand, the presence of a working parent or spouse in the home raises expectations of social intercourse or other family involvement. On the other hand, ongoing leisure activities in the home might disturb the home-based worker, not only because of the noise, but because the sounds represent people busy in other activities, for example, enjoying themselves, not having to work. Everyday situations where two or more activities occur simultaneously in the same space implicate a complex interplay between people involved. The managing of boundaries

(Ahrentzen 1990) can be seen as an aspect of the regionalization of daily life, the appropriation of time and space in a delicate interplay through which people are included in activities or kept outside. To draw up the boundaries between working and spending time with spouses and children is not an easy task for the interviewees. Rather, this is a matter of day-to-day negotiations.

Behavior in relation to family involvement did not differ very much between female and male teleworkers of the in-depth study. Both women and men took the opportunity to be flexible and spend time with their children. Both women and men faced problems of letting work take time from being with their partners. Two or three of the women, though, had accepted combining paid work in the home with a traditional role, being mainly responsible for home and children. For the younger men, working at home seemed compatible with taking a greater interest in domestic life and child care.

The children seemed to gain from having a teleworking parent at home, by not having to hurry in the morning just because the parents have to leave for work or by finding somebody at home when returning from school. The spouses seemed to be the losers. The evenings and nights were often occupied by work, to compensate for having spent time with the children earlier in the day or just being ambitious.

With the workplace so close to family activities, one would expect the home-based workers to have problems of concentration, not being able to resist the involvement in family life. However, the most difficult problem was rather the opposite, the lure to spend leisure time solving tasks of employed work. Some teleworkers mentioned having the world of work so easily accessible as hard to manage. One of them felt that he was confusing home and work, and others had a general feeling of working too much or using work as an easy way out when feeling bored. In this perspective of family involvement, home may sometimes be the perfect workplace—and in others the worst place of work possible.

Travel

The in-depth interviews of a small number of teleworkers did not explicitly address effects on traveling patterns. However, as the change in travel often was involved in the motives for working at home, the question was discussed.

The teleworkers' reports about their travel gave different pictures with respect to the goals and purposes for their trips. When describing work travel, there are not only trips to and from work but also *travel associated with work*. For some teleworkers, task-oriented mobility went with the job. Consultants, some of whom have to travel far and often between remote places, are dependent on their cars. "It's impossible for me to use public transportation, just look at the equipment I need!" one woman exclaimed. Yet, for local business within the town she sometimes took her bike. A graphic designer described how some traveling, like delivering sketches or finished products, had diminished with the use of telematics.

However, to talk with a customer, he said, you have to meet him face to face. Now these trips have increased, as he often goes to the customer's place instead of meeting at the office.

Regarding *work trips*, an important motive to work at home for many respondents of the in-depth study was to avoid the daily traveling to and from an office. "It was so stupid to spend all that time on travel, I felt so idiotic" is a typical reply. Some teleworkers still have to visit their office regularly. Short trips in small towns are often by foot or by bike, while those who live in the suburbs of a city mostly have to go 10 kilometers or more by car or subway.

Teleworkers living in the city area appreciated the option of choosing when to travel to be able to avoid the rush hour. To work an hour or two at home before leaving for the office is very efficient, a young man said, and you get rid of the rush. However, he did not use public transportation. The temporal flexibility of his teleworking made it possible for him to go by car instead of taking the subway.

Teleworkers living in the countryside have the longest trips, sometimes 50 km or more. Living far from the main office means having to organize work more efficiently. By gathering all meetings on certain days, her husband avoids extra travels, one woman living in the archipelago explained. Another man, who was in charge of the office of an organization in the big city, definitely changed his traveling pattern when starting teleworking from the island of Gotland. Nowadays his car trips go either to the airport or to the local post office, he explained. Another respondent living and working on the same island goes by car to the harbor to spend some hours on the ferry, working during the crossing. These examples seem to confirm results of other research, that telecommuting may lead to more long-distance traveling as people choose to live further from the employer's premises (Engström and Johanson 1995).

When it came to *shopping trips* and travels concerning personal errands, some interviewees said that those had often become more structured now than before. For some families with children, it is not where you work as much as where your children's day nursery lies that decides where and when you do your errands. "We have the day-nursery's schedule to think of, and often adapt our purchases to that." One woman explained that her needs for just going around in town faded after having worked at home for some time. *Transporting children and other family members* is another type of travel. Most families with children know that much transportation is needed for their different activities. The teleworkers' traveling was also influenced by family members' needs, especially when living far from town. One man, who worked most of his time at home, told that he was "almost a taxi driver" for his wife when she needed a drive to town. The same was described by parents of teenagers living in the rural areas.

A common hypothesis is that, when you work at home, the need of *leisure time travel* will increase (Engström and Johanson 1995). This thought is supported by some of our respondents: "Yes, I can feel that although I work just a small time at home, I would like to move a little," one man confessed. Those, however, who did much traveling as a part of their work, did not go out during their spare time just for the pleasure of "getting out."

After all that has been said about the importance of telecommuting for reducing travel, it was paradoxical to note to what extent the teleworkers of the in-depth study depended on cars for transportation. Virtues of teleworking, like temporal and spatial flexibility, seem to harmonize with the benefits of the private car. In this respect, the in-depth study seems to confirm the results of the time-use analysis, that home-based work does not lead to significantly less travel. In some respects, the opposite seems just as likely.

The Use of Dwelling Space for Home-based Work

In ads for teleworking equipment, two ways of picturing the work situation dominate. The first type shows a man working all alone. In one of the ads, for a telephone company, you can see him sitting in a small greenhouse with just enough space for himself, absorbed by his work. The second type is a kind of family portrait around the teleworker: a woman in the middle, sitting by her computer in the living room or outside in the garden, surrounded by her children. Of course, both types of images give false impressions of the reality of working at home. Nevertheless, in an exaggerated way, they still reflect the extremes of regionalization of employed work in the home, by merging it with domestic life or separating it from those activities. They also associate these extremes with gender, with different assumed ideals for men and women.

Integration and Seclusion

To characterize the use of *physical delimitations*, we will employ the terms integration and seclusion, basing our observations on the results of the in-depth study. The managing of boundaries between regions for paid work and home life basically implies opening or closing connections between places within the dwelling. Where seclusion primarily implies the use of physical demarcations like walls, doors and distance, integration emphasizes other ways of demarcating employment work activities: the use of social and temporal boundaries. However, if we understand the spatiality of dwelling not in a mechanical way, but as a process of mutually creating lived space, seclusion and integration clearly involve all aspects of managing boundaries. The closed door of the home office does more than block the view and diminish noise from outside. It is also a (social) symbol of not wanting to be disturbed, and its opening and closing may be related to a temporal pattern. To define the variations in location and integration/seclusion of the workplace we have used the following "degrees of seclusion": (1) no permanent work space, (2) permanent work space in a room also used for other activities

(bedrooms, living rooms, etc.), (3) workroom used as a thoroughfare or with open connection to the rest of the dwelling, (4) separate workroom within the

Table 4. Variations in Location and Integration/Seclusion of the Workplace

Case Number	Standards of Space[*]	Type of Workplace	Workroom Area m^2	Degree of Seclusion
Women				
(01)	+	separate room	11	4
(02w)	+	living room	40	2
(07w)	+	mobile	—	1
(08)	−	bedroom	12	2
(10)	+	part of kitchen/mobile	8	2
(11)	+	separate room	10	4
(15)	+	separate room	14	4
(17)	−	living room	20	2
(19)	−	mobile	—	1
(20)	−	passageway	10	3
(21)	+	separate room	7	4
Average				2.6
Men				
(02m)	+	living room	40	2
(03)	=	separate room	12	4
(04)	+	separate room	8	4
(05)	+	room in basement	24	3
(06)	=	separate room	12	4
(07m)	+	separate building	16	5
(09)	+	separate room in basement	18	5
(12)	+	separate rooms in basement	23	5
(13)	+	living room	20	2
(14)	=	passageway	15	3
(16)	+	separate room	12	4
Average				3.7

Note: [*]Standards of space: + more than one extra room in dwelling beyond dwelling needs; = one extra room; − no extra room (for exclusive use as a workroom).

dwelling, and (5) separate workroom in a separate part of the dwelling or in its close vicinity.

As noted in Table 4, most households have one or more spare rooms beyond customary Swedish standards available for paid work activities. The ones that have too few rooms according to our criteria (marked with −), had chosen to conduct their work in bedrooms, thoroughfare rooms, or living rooms, or they moved their workplace around according to the activities of the rest of the family. Most households with sufficient space for a separate workroom (marked with = or +) employed this option. Two home-based workers, however, with more than enough rooms (marked with +), preferred to move around instead of having a separate workroom. Of the four households that just have room enough for an extra workroom (marked with =), only two had arranged one. The others had chosen solutions such as a workplace in a passageway or in the living room.

Workplaces for Men and Women

The locations of the work space differed to some extent between men and women. Women's workrooms were also often more spatially integrated in the dwelling than those of the men. Many men conducted their work in a room secluded from home activities, in basements or even in a separate building, whereas the women with the most secluded work space used a spare bedroom for their work. Seven men but only four women had separate home offices. None of the men had chosen to work without a regular work space, while three of the women more or less deliberately refrained from establishing a permanent space for employment work in the home. The average degrees of seclusion of women and men respectively underline this difference, the men's mean seclusion being higher than the women's. Thus, the different solutions illustrated by the commercial advertising mentioned earlier—men placed in isolation, women in the middle of the family—might have some correspondence to reality. (Similar patterns of female space use are described by Hytter 1994.) When using separate rooms, women had smaller rooms than men.

Public and Private Regions of Home

Home-based work might, for some professions, mean having to open one's home for outsiders—clients or customers. This raises the question of spatial integration or seclusion in relation to interaction with "strangers," visitors of the professional world. A woman consultant related:

> Usually when I meet with clients at home we enter through the main entrance, take the stairs up and close all other rooms, and there (in the central hall) I have a type of conference room or meeting-room.

If there is not the opportunity to make demarcations by simply closing doors, clients or colleagues visiting the home make it necessary to keep certain areas "less homely"—to tidy up and keep personal belongings out of sight, to give areas that are visible by visitors a more formal appearance. This situation, however, was not common in the in-depth study. Most of the respondents preferred meeting at the offices of the employer or clients.

Mediated interaction (using telephone or even video-conferencing) seems to be just as involved in the use of the dwelling for teleworking as are encounters face-to-face. Even when teleworkers had separate workrooms, talking on the telephone was a work activity that had implications for home life. Sometimes the stereo or the television had to be turned off and children told to be quiet. Obviously, business conversation on the telephone put restrictions on a relaxed and spontaneous family life. It was no accident that a teleworking lawyer had his home office in a detached building, thus being able to have conversations with clients without being disturbed or interfering with family activities. Apart from (in a physical sense) bringing clients into the home, it seems that telephone calls or conferences, of all types of paid work activities, put the strongest demands on seclusion.

Patterns of Space Use

Four metaphors represent separate patterns of space use. We created them from the results of the in-depth study. They do not refer to physical space only, but to the typical procedures by which space is taken into use when conducting employed work, that is, activities and time are dimensions involved. Thus, these patterns do not simply constitute ways of responding to the physical properties of the dwelling, but individual attitudes and procedures for coping with the full context of home-based work.

Working in *a place in the sun* means being mobile within the dwelling, looking for "the best place," for instance where there is peace and quiet for the moment or where the sun shines at that time of day. This appeared to be a "female" solution, as far as only women among our respondents had chosen it. *Hiding in the corner*, having a workplace in a corner of the living room or bedroom means the close integration of professional life in the home, also having to adjust work-times to family routines. Working *at the hub of events* implies the use of a central place, having to adapt the work situation to the rest of the family or setting the rules, thus letting professional work dominate. *In splendid isolation* means having a separate office, for example, in the basement or in a spare bedroom. This seemed to be a typical "male" solution, as the most secluded and also the largest workrooms of our study belonged to men.

Where *integrative spatial solutions* mean making efficient use of home space, a pattern of regionalization employing the periods in daytime when many homes are deserted by their inhabitants, the *seclusion of the workspace* puts higher demands on sufficient space and physical delimitations, but makes employed work activities less dependent on home life.

Space and Furniture for Work

Whatever has been said above about the dynamics of dwelling, the in-depth study showed that sufficient space is still a prerequisite for carrying out information-related work at home, whether or not in a separate workroom. Although documents are produced electronically, paper still is used to a large extent. The hard-drive of the computer must often be supplemented by a bookshelf. The amount and measures of workplace furniture and equipment imply demands of sufficient space. The one-person bedroom is often considered too small for working most of the time at home. Ergonomic office furniture was seldom used by the respondents, partly because of lack of space, and partly because they conflicted with the atmosphere of the home. The teleworkers demanded a design of furniture and equipment that harmonized with the ambience of the home. When furnishing the workspace, they learned that regular office furniture would interfere with the aesthetics of home. Thus, the furnishing of workspaces largely reflected the ways employed to regionalise paid work in the home. Office-like furniture and equipment predominated where the workplace was spatially secluded, whereas more home-like furnishing characterized workplaces spatially integrated in the home. Thus, regular desk chairs and other furniture, suitable for a good work environment from an ergonomic point of view, were mostly found in separate workrooms.

Being Close but not Disturbed

Working at home also implies *the presence of other people and their activities.* One feature that makes working at home attractive is that normally one is disturbed neither by colleagues nor family members during daytime. But in the afternoon, the home-based worker is confronted, for example, with children coming home from school or smaller children that have to be collected at the day-care center. Furthermore, as many home-based workers tend to work in the evenings, there are other family activities that have to be dealt with. Working professionally at home presupposes continuously adjusting to family life and domestic chores and "negotiating" the boundaries of its regionalization. The physical demarcations of the separate workroom might be helpful in this process, but the seclusion is never complete. Thus, seclusion does not represent the ultimate solution. Under circumstances of a very intense home life, not even a separate workroom may be sufficient to allow people to fulfill demanding work at home. The strength of the integrative approach is that paid work is dealt with as one activity among others carried out in the home. An important motive for working at home is to be part of an environment that is different from that of the regular workplace.

In the home-based work situation, there is an obvious contradiction between needing not to be disturbed and wanting to be close to home life. Thus, rather than primarily striving for strictly secluded work spaces in the home, the design of dwellings for home-based workers should reflect the interplay of integration and seclusion, allowing the activity of paid work to become merged on some occasions and separated on others.

Home-based Work and the Meaning of Home

People often find it difficult to express what home means to them. Home can be seen as primarily a matter of *practical consciousness* (Giddens 1984). Although it is continuously involved and transformed in our actions, it largely belongs to the realm of tacit knowledge. However, there are situations in life that force us again to reflect upon what has become a matter of unreflected routines. The introduction of paid work in the home may be one such situation that makes evident for people their expectations about home itself:

> I feel at home here when I work, although at the same time work pervades home, but that doesn't necessarily have to be negative. We have a society where it is separated— working life and home life (...) it is two different worlds, but sometimes this unity might be something positive. Because in a way this division of the day in eight hours of work, eight hours of sleep and eight hours of eating, cleaning, etc. makes you live by the clock and that's a bit unnatural. When working at home, it's not like that, it all becomes more of a whole.

Home-based work means letting one's home become a place for employed work. On one hand, this implies the opportunity of making home a place for all aspects and activities of life, in the way (we wish to believe) dwelling in traditional societies constituted a totality of life. Just like the man quoted above, some people find the temporal and spatial order of society artificial. On the other hand, there is a risk of losing parts of the autonomy of home in relation to the demands of public life and work life.

One would think that the quite different ways of life of the teleworkers also would give way to different conceptions of home. However, the manifold meanings attributed to home shown by previous research (Després 1991; Dovey 1985; Lawrence 1987; Wikström 1994) are confirmed by the in-depth study. When asked, women and men alike appeared to view home as a place where one feels comfortable and at ease. Home is "a place where one can go and be just the way one wants to be. Curl up. One feels at home. One feels cozy." It is the base of the family, the center of life, to which one always returns. The fact that home had become the place where part of paid work was carried out did not essentially change these emotions.

Many of the men *described home in contrast to work*. It is a place where one can relax and be private. Thus, home was described as the opposite to work although their teleworking made it a place for work. The women stressed the importance of living in an environment that they have formed and of which they are in charge. It is their order, their taste and personality that prevail. There were only a few hints of meanings of home related to a place of creative activity and work. A few of the women used metaphors related to active places where a lot of people come and go, where people are busy doing things they like: a center, a workshop, a base camp, a place created by people together. Both women and men stressed autonomy, safety, rest, and control, although home now had become a place for employed work. Home in most cases seemed to represent qualities that are not found in the world of work. With this view of home, one would expect employed work in the home to be experienced as more problematic than what is suggested in our interviews: as an intrusion. The teleworkers' pictures of home did not seem to be compatible with carrying out employed work in the home.

When not explicitly asking the interviewees about home, however, another picture emerged. Some of the respondents obviously had conceptions of home which *included occupational work*, either based on childhood experience or developed later. The merging of home and paid work was not foreign to them but rather something for which to strive. Others wanted to see work as separate from home, by allowing a demarcated foreign territory within the home. Work activities and the spaces and signs of work were thoroughly kept apart from home life. In both cases, however, there was an element of viewing home as an ideal work environment for certain work tasks. The very qualities that made work appear as a foreign strain, were utilized when conducting those tasks; feeling more relaxed and having the opportunity of working at one's own pace were qualities considered to contribute to work performance.

None of the respondents of our study considered the fact that their homes now contained a workplace to be a disadvantage for the home or to diminish the sense of home. Our suspicion that the work space would be experienced as an intrusion to home, reminding about obligations waiting to be carried out, was not openly corroborated by the interviewed teleworkers themselves. However, there were signs of *teleworking being disruptive*. Examples illustrating the problem of letting work take over described by Gurstein (1991) and others that can be attributed to the proximity and the lack of distinct boundaries between recreative space and work space. However, most of the teleworkers seemed to regard the workplace as something that *improved the home*. One explanation might be that the Swedish respondents represent a rather privileged group (as mentioned above), many of them with relatively spacious dwellings and given the choice whether and to what extent to work at home. Having succeeded in combining the two roles of home as a dwelling for the family and as a workplace, they felt at ease with their situation as teleworkers.

DISCUSSION

Information Technology and Sociocultural Patterns

Earlier predictions of the development of telecommuting have been shown completely wrong. In the 1970s, some qualified spokesmen believed that all American workers were going to be teleworkers in 1990. Today there is a better insight into the social and cultural contexts involved in this development. But even today, the development of information technology is portrayed in the mass media as the most important factor in the increase of teleworking. It is, however, worth considering that the ordinary telephone, perhaps even today the most important tool for teleworking, has been available for more than one hundred years (Benedikt 1991). Thus, paying attention to the sociocultural prerequisites for the introduction of new technology is important. The results of our studies of the home as a context of home-based work offer some clues to the cultural lag mentioned earlier. Complex social and cultural patterns are involved when teleworking is introduced in a society where the worlds of home and work are "constructed as spatially separate, dichotomous, and gendered realms of social life" (Aitken and Carroll 1996). Thus, the development of teleworking is not only a question of technology. In many respects, the division of society between the world of employed work and the world of home has probably never been stronger. Desirable or not, the development toward more widespread teleworking will be a slow process.

In the same vein, one can question whether technological change will remain a one-way process toward decentralization. At first, mainframe computers centralized computer work. Then the personal computor led in the opposite direction. What would have to happen to take away the incentive for decentralized work? The answer might well lie outside pure technology but rather how it is managed in society. For example, some current trends toward marginalization of the work situation of many home-based workers may bring in its wake countermovements to the restoration of career situations physically located in centralized workplaces—forward to the past?

The time-use data suggest that even though home-based work has not as yet revolutionized daily life, some differences have emerged in the amount of time devoted to specific behaviors and the pattern which is formed in the course of the day. Depending on the strategy taken toward home-based work, working at home is associated with putting more time into a job, being flexible to do more at home and spend more time with other family members, and having time to work alone. These are often desired objectives, and these data suggest they are being fulfilled. Saving travel time occurs more when people specialize their work at home, but home-based work does not sui generis appear to decrease travel time sufficiently to justify claims of significant ecological savings or tradeoffs of time to lifestyles which involve greater recreation or local community participation. Indeed, those home-based workers who travel the most are doing so by automobile, the antithesis of green objectives.

Whither Gender Roles?

A major open question is whether the findings reflecting interaction between gender and workplace location reflect volition or tradition. The data show clearly that home-based work (and one variant of it in particular) is related to an increase in gender differences in the direction of roles from earlier in the century. Can it be that the persons involved still cherish these gender roles and utilize home-based work as a tool to enable the restoration of these roles back to their everyday routines? Do men and women alike enjoy their ability to return to the gender roles of yesterday through home-based work? The data reported do not in and of themselves answer these questions (or point to the alternative, that it is possible for gender roles to return even if not desired). Work in progress examines this matter in greater depth (Michelson 1998, 1999b).

Aitken and Carroll (1996) review several research reports suggesting that the motives for telecommuting differ between men and women (among others Gottlieb 1988; Gurstein 1991; Wajcman and Probert 1988). While women often emphazise family and children, men talk about becoming more efficient carrying out their work and escaping the control of the workplace. For many men, home represents a refuge from the "face-to-face-authority" of the workplace. Others experience that teleworking offers better control over their lives.

The Swedish in-depth study provides some clarification for this quandary. When asked about their motives for working at home, one-half of *both men and women* mentioned *concern for the family*. In the Swedish context the differences between men and women appear to be less important compared with differences in the family and work situations of individuals. With one exception, all households that expressed this concern had children, either small children or children going to school. One of the women said, for instance, that she personally was skeptical of the idea of bringing work home, but the motive to stay home for the children's sake was more important.

The respondents that gave *other motives for teleworking* than family had grown up children or none at all. Independent of gender, they saw the same advantages. They wanted to avoid daily traveling to work, being able to work without being disturbed, and the opportunity to choose what time to work. These other motives were not primarily related to home itself, but rather to society's spatial and temporal order, where home and work basically are kept apart by, for instance, the separate allocation of dwelling areas and workplaces and the subdivision of the day in work-time and leisure. The fact that many dwellings are empty in the day-time, making them ideal places for undisturbed work, is a consequence of this. For the respondents that gave other motives, home-based work seemed to offer an extra degree of freedom by saving traveling time, being able to concentrate on one task at a time, and working at one's own pace. This freedom, however, was not spent on home and leisure but to increase work performance.

Finding Room for Home-based Work

Home-based work means using a limited space for simultaneous activities belonging both to the professional world and to the world of home and family. This makes it necessary to develop routines for the use of home space—which includes the managing of boundaries between employed work and home life, also in a temporal and social sense. Teleworking is mostly an activity that had to be fitted into an already existing dwelling situation. The existing home must then be taken as a precondition. However, this appears to be in perpetual change: The homes of the teleworkers are highly dynamic contexts, their capacity for employed work activities fluctuating with the ever-changing lifecycle of the family.

The choice of space and the location of the workplace in the dwelling are closely related to the amount of space available for paid work, as just one of many activities demanding space. Obviously, the nature of work carried out affects the type and amount of space needed. But choices are also made for other reasons. Apparent strategies in choosing the place to work are either to arrange a secluded workroom, or to integrate work in space used for other activities. Where seclusion primarily means the use of physical demarcations, integration means using social and temporal boundaries.

The choice of home space for teleworking cannot be made exclusively from the point of view of work. Even the secluded separate workrooms were often considered as integrate parts of the dwellings. The worktable sometimes also has to be used for other activities than paid work. The computer workplace is viewed as an asset by other members of the family, sometimes also for people living in the vicinity who get to use the computer facilities. The multifunctional work space may require more space than the specialized office workroom, and its location within the dwelling must be chosen considering spatial connections to family rooms.

The four types of space use (a place in the sun, at the hub of events, hiding in the corner, and in splendid isolation) illustrate the intricate ways in which spatial solutions and, thus, housing design is intertwined with family life and domestic activities. Home-based work may be organized in many ways. The best solution possible is the one that is well adapted to the conditions involved. Teleworking is an activity that has to be negotiated in relation to other activities occurring in the home.

Designing for home-based work means becoming involved in all the changes that affect people's lives and living in contemporary society. There is no ultimate housing design. What designs of dwellings allow for the complexity of living in which teleworking occurs? How can existing dwellings be employed or remodelled the best way? These are some of many questions that might be addressed by architects and social scientists working in tandem.

Forward to the Past?

In the day-to-day life of a family, home is the place where daily activities of individual family members start and end. During the day the individuals spread out geographically to many other places: school, the day-care center, work, and so forth. The space of daily life is polycentric, characterized by movements between significant places (Waldenfels 1985). In contrast to the typical double-working household of modern, Western society, the teleworking family regains some of the qualities of traditional culture, where dwelling meant living and working at the same place, a context of simple, concentric space.

Nevertheless, as we have seen above, bringing employed work home does not imply reestablishing a traditional, place-bound life-mode. According to Donna

Haraway, writing about the conditions for women in the late twentieth century, modern life implies not only dealing with tensions between the dual worlds of work and home. It presupposes moving through and managing a number of contexts (or spaces) involved in day-to-day life and implied in each other: home, market, paid workplace, state, school, clinic-hospital, and church (Haraway 1991, p. 170).

Thus, living means taking part in and being affected by contexts that all differ from each other, each with its own conditions, and—temporally and spatially— joining those fragments together into everyday life. The type of tensions experienced by home-based workers when trying to combine employed work and domestic life are typical for today's Western society. Thus home-based work as a part of everyday life means something completely different from work in traditional, place-bound life.

ACKNOWLEDGMENTS

This is a revision of a paper presented to the World Congress of the International Sociological Association, August 26-31, 1998, Montreal, Canada. This paper was facilitated by research grants from the Swedish Council for Building Research, the Swedish Transport and Communications Research Board, and the Social Sciences and Humanities Research Council of Canada. We also acknowledge research grants from the Swedish Council for Planning and Coordination of Research and travel grants from the University of Lund. We appreciate helpful suggestions from anonymous peer reviewers.

NOTES

1.   The identification of home-based workers through answers to the time-use protocol was validated successfully by comparison to a survey question in another analysis (Michelson 1999b).

2.   The availability of the data was facilitated by Klas Rydenstam, in connection with a study analyzing multinational time-use files with nontradional analytic methods, in collaboration with Andrew Harvey, Clarke Wilson, and Jonathan Gershuny, under a grant from the Social Sciences and Humanities Research Council of Canada.

3.   These data were made available by the Data Library within Robarts Library at the University of Toronto, whose personnel were extremely helpful. For further specification, see Statistics Canada (1993).

4.   Activities are selected for Table 1 in terms of their relevance to the hypotheses presented earlier in the paper, as well as the availability of similar codes for them in both the Canadian and Swedish surveys.

REFERENCES

Ahrentzen, S. 1987. *Blurring Boundaries: Social Spatial Consequences of Working at Home.* Milwaukee: Center for Architecture and Urban Planning Research, University of Wisconsin, Milwaukee.

———. 1990. "Managing Conflict by Managing Boundaries: How Professional Homeworkers Cope with Multiple Roles at Home." *Environment and Behavior* 22: 723-752.

———. 1992. "Home as a Workplace in the Lives of Women." In *Place Attachment*, edited by I. Altman and S. Low. New York: Plenum Press.

Aitken, S., & M. Carroll. 1996. "Man's Place in the Home: Telecommuting, Identity and Urban Space." Internet 1997-05-02: www.ncgia.ucsb.edu/conf/BALTIMORE/authors/aitken/paper.html

Benedikt, M. 1991. *Cyberspace: First Steps.* Cambridge, MA: MIT Press.

Brown, D. 1994. "Working at Home: Too Much of a Good Thing?" *Executive Female* (Jan./Feb), p. 76.

Bulos, M., & W. Chaker. 1995. "Sustaining a Sense of Home and Personal Identity." In *The Home: Interpretations, Meanings and Environments*, edited by D. Benjamin and D. Stea. Aldershot: Avebury.

Christensen, K. 1988. *Women and Home-based Work.* New York: Holt.

Conference on Homeworking. 1994. *From the Double Day to the Endless Day.* Ottawa: Canadian Centre for Policy Alternatives.

Després, C. 1991. "The Meaning of Home: Literature Review and Directions for Future Research and Theoretical Development." *Journal of Architectural and Planning Research* 8(2).

Dovey, K. 1985. "Home and Homelessness." Pp. 33–64 in *Home Environments*, edited by I. Altman and C. Werner. New York: Plenum Press.

Engström, M., & R. Johanson. 1995. *IT-utveckling och verksamheters organisation—mer, mindre eller annat resande? [(The Development of Information Technology and the Organization of Firms—More, Less or Varying?)].* Nordplan Meddelande 1995:5. Stockholm.

Giddens, A. 1984. *The Constitution of Society.* Cambridge: Polity Press.

Gottlieb, N. 1988. "Women and Men Working at Home: Environmental Experiences." Pp. 149-164 in *EDRA 19 Proceedings*, edited by D. Lawrence. Washington, DC: Environmental Design Research Association.

Gurstein, P. 1991. "Working at Home and Living at Home: Emerging Scenarios." *Journal of Architectural and Planning Research* 8: 164-180.

———. 1995. Planning for Telework and Home-Based Employment: A Canadian Survey on Integrating Work into Residential Environments. Vancouver: Canada Mortgage and Housing Corporation.

Haraway, D.J. 1991. *Simians, Cyborgs, and Woman. The Reincarnation of Nature.* New York: Routledge.

Heck, R., A. Owen, and B. Rowe. 1995. *Home-based Employment and Family Life.* Westport, CT: Auburn House.

Hochschild, A.R. 1997. *The Time Bind: When Work Becomes Home and Home Becomes Work.* New York: Holt.

Huws, U. 1996. *Teleworking: An Overview of the Research.* London: Analytica Social and Economic Research Ltd.

Huws, U., and E. Gunnarsson, eds. 1997. *Virtually Free?* Stockholm: NUTEK.

Hytter, K. 1994. *Datorn på Köksbordet [(The Computer on the Kitchen Table)].* Lund: University of Lund, Department of Sociology.

Lawrence, R. 1987. "What Makes a House a Home?" *Environment and Behavior* 19: 154-168.

Michelson, W. 1985. *From Sun to Sun.* Totowa, NJ: Rowman & Allanheld.

———. 1998. "Home-based Work: What Does Time-Use Indicate?" Presented to Thematic Group on Time-Use Studies, World Congress of the International Sociological Association, Montreal, July 27.

———. 1999a, in press. "Home-based Employment and Quality of Life: A Time-use Analysis." In *Quality of Life Theory and Research*, edited by E. Diener. New York: Kluwer/Plenum.

_____. 1999b, in press. "Time Pressure and Human Agency in Home-based Employment." *Society and Leisure*.

Ogburn, W. 1964. *On Culture and Social Change*. Chicago: University of Chicago Press.

Orser, B., and M. Foster. 1992. *Home Enterprise: Canadians and Home-based Work*. National Home-based Business Project Committee.

Spittje, H. 1994. "Effects of the Tele/homeworking on Travel Behaviour." Paper presented to the XIII World Congress of Sociology, Bielefeld, Germany.

Statistics Canada. 1993. *The 1992 General Social Survey—Cycle 7: Time Use. Public Use Microdata File Documentation and Users Guide*. Ottawa: Statistics Canada.

Sturesson, L. 1997. "Telework—Symbol of the Information Society?" Pp. 79-90 in *Virtually Free?*, edited by E. Gunnarsson and U. Huws. Stockholm: NUTEK.

Wajcman, J., and B. Probert. 1988. "New Technology Outwork." In *Technology and the Labour Process*, edited by E. Willis. Sydney: Allen and Unwin.

Waldenfels, B. 1985. *In den Netzen der Lebenswelt (In the Web of Everyday Life)*. Frankfurt am Main: Suhrkamp.

Wikström, T. 1994. *Mellan Hemmet och Världen [(Between Home and the World)]*. Stockholm/Stehag: Symposion.

Wikström, T., K.P. Lindén, and W. Michelson. 1998. *Hub of Events or Splendid Isolation*. KFB-Meddelande 1998:3. Stockhom: KFB.

Winter, M., H. Puspitawati, R. Heck, and K. Stafford. 1993. "Time-management Strategies Used by Households with Home-based Work." *Journal of Family and Economic Issues* 14: 69-92.

WORKING AND LIVING IN THE
QUALITY-OF-LIFE DISTRICT

Leonard Nevarez

ABSTRACT

In information-economy sectors like software and motion picture/television production, the centrality of human talent gives elite workers the labor market power to negotiate where they will live and work. One consequence is the quality-of-life district, an industrial space where the chief locational assets are community amenities that elite workers value. Quality-of-life districts are created through a sequence of labor market contingencies, as elite workers migrate out of industrial regions subjected to rising costs of living, urban blight, or other sources of labor reproduction crises. Alongside a minimum level of industrial infrastructure, communities which become quality of life districts contain specific lifestyle niches that fit the subjective demands of elite workers at particular life stages. After the quality-of-life district and its variable dimensions are theorized, the paper describes sociopolitical contradictions that communities, which confront the quality-of-life district phenomenon, may experience.

Research in Community Sociology, Volume 9, pages 185-215.
Copyright © 1999 by JAI Press Inc.
ISBN: 0-7623-0498-7

The software engineers at Alias Wavefront have it pretty good.

It's not just the handsome salaries, flexible hours and casual, footwear-optional dress code—perks like that are now all but standard in the industry.

These engineers, who develop special-effects software for the film industry, enjoy something far more unique: a physical setting that puts even the loveliest parts of Silicon Valley to shame.

For some, the commute to work is an eight-minute downhill bike ride from a hillside canyon home; for others, it's a roller blade trip on quiet, tree-lined streets. No traffic. No smog.

Many spend their lunch breaks surfing, windsurfing or jogging on a beach that's just two blocks away. Or they can grab a bite in a thriving, yet uncrowded, down-town area, with its plethora of cafes, restaurants, shops, bars and movie theaters.

Welcome to Santa Barbara, Southern California's newest high-tech mecca.
                                                            —Helft (1997, p. D1)

In this paper, I explore how the centrality of human talent in information-econ-omy sectors like software and motion picture/television production produces new spatial forms of industry and, consequently, community. *Quality-of-life districts*, I contend, result when the labor market power of highly skilled workers valorizes community amenities that, in turn, influence decisions of workers and firms as to where they will locate. My aim here is to describe and theorize this new model of industrial-community space. I do not show the geographical extent of the quality-of-life district in the United States, nor conclusively determine the factors for its appearance, although I hope to persuade readers of its prevalence beyond the examples cited here.

The quality-of-life district case studies in this paper come from Southern Cali-fornia: Santa Barbara and San Luis Obispo, two mid-to-small coastal cities known by many for their high quality of life (which I define below). I also observe com-parable phenomena at a hybrid quality-of-life/industrial district: Santa Monica, a city within the Los Angeles metropolis. The data come from over 80 interviews with information economy business leaders, traditional industry business leaders, and community representatives, as well as fieldwork and secondary data gather-ing conducted in the research sites. I supplement these data with news articles and other secondary data regarding the information economy in other places besides the research sites.

The paper is organized as follows. First, I describe how the geography of the information economy offers precedents for the quality-of-life district. Next, I describe how elite workers increasingly determine the location of production through their labor market power; I illustrate this with an extended scenario from the software industry. I then examine comparable processes of location and pro-duction in the motion picture-television industry. Next, I elaborate a theoretical model to explain the formation and variation of quality-of-life districts. I conclude with a brief discussion of political contradictions and limits of the quality-of-life district model.

GEOGRAPHICAL PRECEDENTS IN
THE INFORMATION ECONOMY

The quality-of-life district manifests the geographical arrangement of the information economy and, specifically, the power to decide where corporate branches locate. During the Cold War defense economy, the genesis of the contemporary information economy, high-tech regions resulted from command-and-control modes of corporate governance in which corporate executives articulated and imposed upon employees *firm-level* agendas of organization, profit-making, and so on. Regarding the question of location, large high-tech firms chose to locate in places near defense contracting sources, pools of skilled engineering and manufacturing labor, and military bases (Scott 1993). With certain exceptions (for example, Motorola in Phoenix; see Glasmeier 1988), these early high-tech firms tended to locate near one another and in this manner created the original high-tech districts. For example, the contemporary high-tech cluster in Boston/Route 128 region rests upon an older industrial center of automobile and electronic manufacturing; while the region lost most of its traditional manufacturing industries, Raytheon (originally a refrigerator manufacturer) and other early high-tech pioneers thrived from Cold War defense contracts and set the basis for the region's contemporary high-tech cluster (Rosegrant and Lampe 1992). Corporations integrated production within themselves and encouraged secretive corporate cultures which, it should be noted, obscured to many observers the *regional* concentration of production networks (Saxenian 1994).

In the customary exception to this clustering tendency, early high-tech firms often located research and development (R&D), the most knowledge-intensive stage of production, in sites far away from their own corporate divisions and other production activities in general. In keeping with conventional wisdom that a pleasant environment enhances knowledge workers' creativity, many R&D parks were located in pastoral settings at nonurban "innovation centers" (such as Columbus, Ohio; Boulder, Colorado; and Salt Lake City, Utah) where residential and workplace amenities are paramount (Malecki 1980).[1] Still, the decision to disperse R&D resided with the firm; despite its different geography, the traditional innovation center continued to reflect command-and-control corporate organization.

The organizational and locational dynamics of contemporary high-tech industries, such as software and computer design, differ dramatically from the command-and-control mode described above. As research on the "new industrial geography" has shown, production that was formerly internalized within a few firms has largely been externalized onto a network of specialized firms that occupy a common region, such that *industrial districts* are now the most accurate unit of analysis to describe industries.[2] Industrial districts attract pools of specialized assets (labor, suppliers, customers, support services). Markets willing, a self-sustaining "critical mass" is eventually achieved in which firms benefit from external economies (Scott 1995, 1996; Storper and Walker 1989).

However, as increasing demand for space in high-tech regions pushes real estate costs higher, spatial constraints force firms in these places to reassess their need to stay put. Generally, firms reorganize and relocate production according to the particular "value-added" level of various activities and the human skill levels which they require. For example, local networks of communication and learning are most important to knowledge-intensive activities and small batch manufacturing; consequently, firms tend to retain these in industrial districts even where real estate prices and labor wages run high. By contrast, traditional cost factors (such as wage rates and real estate) most constrain the bottom line in routine activities like standardized (large-batch) manufacturing; as a result, firms tend to disperse these to peripheral regions where, ceteris perebus, the costs of spatial distance match the benefits of low cost factors. Important conditions for this centralization/deconcentration dynamic are the technological and organizational capacities to "compress time and space," such as reduced shipping costs or the digitalization of services into forms that can be transmitted across phone lines (see Dicken 1992, pp. 103-110).

Typically, in this new industrial geography, high-tech regions concentrate the most innovative activities; activities of a cross-industry nature (e.g., legal services) cluster in their own industry centers, while more routine activities disperse to pockets of less specialized labor. The result is a spatially dispersed production network. For example, a software design firm might house its headquarters/R&D functions in Silicon Valley, obtain legal and accounting services in New York, subcontract for routine coding in Pittsburgh, and manufacture its final products (for example, CD-ROMs) in East Asia. Still, *firm-level* criteria, such as innovators' need for spatial proximity or the wage levels of skilled labor, are what give coherence to places in the new industrial geography.

High-tech Industry in the Research Sites

The history of high-tech industry in the research sites in large part conforms to the new industrial geography models described above. To begin with, defense spending spurred development of the greater Los Angeles "technopolis" in the Cold War era. Large aerospace manufacturers internalized much of the region's high-tech industrial base, and Santa Monica (1990 population: 86,905) comprised an important node. In the 1920s, the city was still a quiet, "Main Street" community with no highway connection to downtown Los Angeles when it became home to the Douglas Aircraft Company, one of the first aircraft assemblers in the region. Douglas Aircraft thus made Santa Monica an important center for the command-and-control high-tech economy, as did other aerospace manufacturers in neighboring communities (in Los Angeles' Westside and San Fernando Valley areas; see Scott 1993). In the 1950s, the locally-based Rand Corporation, one of the premiere Cold War-era think-tanks in the United States, spun off the Systems Development Corporation, a for-profit software company with 800 employees (later bought by Honeywell and incorporated into Unisys). By so doing, Rand helped create the current software district along Santa Monica and elsewhere in Los Angeles' Westside, a region that some locals now call "Silicon Bay." With the 1966 connection to United States Interstate 10, Santa Monica joined Los Angeles' freeway system; population growth and urban development soon transformed the city and the rest of the Westside into integrated metropolitan settings. Still, its coastal location and relative lack of development kept Santa Monica and adjacent coastal communities (e.g., Malibu, Pacific Palisades, Venice) among the most desirable places for many Angelenos to live.

Santa Barbara (1990 population: 85,571), despite its distance (about 60-90 miles) from the Los Angeles technopolis, was incorporated as a center for R&D starting in the late 1940s, when city leaders successfully lobbied the state legislature to convert a nearby Navy base into a University of California campus (UCSB). Importantly, some dozen miles of coast, agriculture, and undeveloped land separate Los Angeles from Santa Barbara and its satellite communities (Goleta, Montecito, Carpinteria) and have long enhanced the city's reputation as an exclusive getaway for Los Angeles elites. Along these lines, Raytheon chose Santa Barbara over rival sites to locate an R&D facility in 1955, according to one official, for its environmental and cultural amenities (Van de Kamp 1996). Several other defense electronics firms followed Raytheon's lead, and thereby initiated the city's status as an innovation center nestled in an attractive coastal setting (see Malecki 1980, p. 230). In large part because of its defense research milieu, UCSB was selected in the late 1960s as the third site of the NARPA-Net, the military precursor to the contemporary Internet; the campus' host laboratory in turn spun off dozens of software and telecommunications firms, many of which remain in Santa Barbara in corporate name or executive personnel.

Finally, San Luis Obispo (1990 population: 41,958) reflects the geographical limits of traditional high-tech agglomeration. The most isolated and rural of the three research sites, the city lies some 90 miles north of Santa Barbara and is roughly equidistant from Los Angeles and San Francisco. It is home to a state polytechnic university (California Polytechnic University of San Luis Obispo, or "Cal Poly") that has important ties to regional agricultural businesses. Otherwise, the city had little connection to California's early high-tech geography. A nuclear power plant constituted San Luis Obispo's only remotely "high-tech" industry until 1978, when a Hewlett-Packard employee visited the city for the first time and selected it as the site for his new computer engineering firm.

The Role of Elite Workers

The dispersion of high-tech production, which I have described to this point as the new industrial geography, is fairly well understood. This paper does not challenge its central tenets but instead amends its conceptualization to account for new spatial forms which it cannot satisfactorily explain. These forms, I believe, stem from two consequences of human talent's primacy in the information economy.

First, many high-tech companies regard the scarcity of highly skilled intellectual and managerial labor as a fundamental obstacle in firm growth, as illustrated by industry lobbying in 1998 to boost U.S. immigration of foreign informational workers (see Pear 1998). Accordingly, many firms base their strategic goals around recruiting the best talent; the primary question a software firm faces is "who are the immediate people that you can grab that are really interested in this with the money you've got," as a software CEO told me. Second, the occupational and status distinctions that traditionally distinguish firm executives from their informational employees have increasingly blurred. As an example, a nonexecutive software designer can work at one firm, become a director on a second firm's executive board, consult for a third, then leave the first to start up a fourth firm. This fluidity of human talent parallels the mercurial structure that information economy firms can adopt. For instance, a software firm can design a successful product, license or sell it to a second firm, then reorganize as a new third firm to design a separate product. Thus, the locus of industrial power—that is, the ability to organize production networks—has in large part shifted from the firm to *elite workers*: executives who govern firms, to be sure, but also would-be entrepreneurs, project-based freelance workers, and other employees with skills that the labor market values highly.

An important consequence of the centrality of human talent in the information economy is that elite workers have a high degree of labor market bargaining power vis-à-vis current and potential employers (that is, hiring firms or scheming entrepreneurs). This power has inflated wage levels and encouraged firms to offer new incentives (for example, equity options) in order to recruit the best available employees. A less recognized corollary of elite workers' labor market power is that firms may also negotiate the location of production—that is, where elite workers will work and live. When attracting scarce talent is an employer's strategic goal, then sought-after employees' locational preferences may inform the firm's locational strategy. More generally, the fluidity of human talent that entrepreneurial activity epitomizes points to a larger conclusion: *locational power has increasingly shifted from firms to elite workers*.

What spatial consequences result from this shift in locational power? Although they have traditionally concentrated in industrial districts with the best employment opportunities, elite workers are also understood to be "very sophisticated consumers of place" (Knight 1989, p. 237; see also Kotkin 1998b) who rank places with a perceived high *quality of life* favorably among their locational preferences. Generally, quality of life refers to desirable attributes of domestic residence and community; among elite workers in the informational economy, it embodies the lifestyle tastes of a particularly professional class. For example, in one survey, engineers gave their top locational considerations: housing affordability and availability, desirable climate (warm, coastal, dry, mountainous), quality of primary and secondary schools, recreational opportunities, job opportunities for spouse, community attitudes, cultural opportunities, and taxes and municipal services (Ady 1986, p. 81). As this partial inventory suggests, quality of life is, at first glance, not an "industrial" criterion for location. However, the diffusion of industrial power to elite workers with their own lifestyle interests, I hope to show, means that in some cases quality of life become a de facto industrial criterion.

LEAVING SILICON VALLEY

From elite workers' power to determine the location of production emerges a new spatial form: the quality-of-life district, which I define as production sites where the chief locational assets are community amenities that elite workers value. To a certain extent, the older command-and-control logic of corporate governance has helped to build quality-of-life districts, as when large firms regard satisfying their elite workers' quality-of-life demands as a worthwhile investment in firm productivity and consequently establish satellite branches in places where those demands are fulfilled. However, my interviews with executives from small- to mid-sized firms indicate that, especially where the software industry is concerned, quality-of-life districts more commonly emerge via the labor market and start-up activity. Thus, I give special attention to how elite workers exercise their labor market power to arrive in the quality-of-life district. Below, I illustrate this dynamic as an *experiential process* by following an elite worker—with the skills, say, to design important innovations in business utilities software—through the software labor market. Through the following scenario, composed from accounts of real firms and workers, I highlight the sequence of labor market contingencies which lead to the quality-of-life district.[3]

The quality-of-life district originates with the attraction that bona fide industrial districts exert on elite workers. Fresh out of one of the best computer science college departments in the United States, our elite worker must make a personal decision which occasions the first of several contingencies: Does she wish to be paid the top market wages for her skills? If so, the labor market will compel her to move to a software district like Silicon Valley, the current capitol of the software industry. If not, she may wander into another field of work that will probably not lead her to Silicon Valley. As thousands of software workers answer this question affirmatively, a talent-pull process is reiterated repeatedly, and Silicon Valley develops a competitive employment base that further reinforces the process. In other words, with a critical mass of employers, Silicon Valley offers a career "safety net" (or what regional economists call a localization economy) that entices engineers, programmers, and managers to find work in Silicon Valley. As a software CEO told me, "people up there [in Silicon Valley] are used to being able to go right down the road and find another job in five minutes if something happens to their company."

However, the critical mass of firms and workers that concentrates in bona fide industrial districts may produce unforeseen spatial consequences. Silicon Valley's development, for example, has occurred through poor regional planning that over the years has increased infrastructural/environmental strain for the region and the cost of living for residents (Saxenian 1984; Belser 1970). As Silicon Valley residents well know, local housing has grown scarce and costly, resulting in residential sprawl and long traffic commutes. Rapid employee turnover within firms prevents many workers from organizing car pools or using mass transit for long (if at all). Regional freeways, schools, and services are often stressed beyond capacity; one software CEO told me, "it bums me out when I'm in Mountain View that I can't drive 20 minutes and go to a restaurant where I can get a table and have lunch in an hour and be done and back at my office."

While Silicon Valley's spatial strain threatens the social reproduction of local labor at all levels, its impact on elite labor poses the greatest potential crisis for the region's industry (see Hof and Hamm 1997). Consequently, minor yet discernible *talent-push* pressures build up that, at the level of lived experience, occasion the second analytical contingency: Do employees, like our software developer, find that the personal costs of living in Silicon Valley outweigh the career benefits? Elite workers may decide to leave Silicon Valley and become quality-of-life migrants. Some firms manage this potential labor crisis by dispersing their human talent to new locations where they perceive the quality-of-life balance to be better. Alternately, entrepreneurial employees may seize the moment to start up their own firm in such locations.

There are at least two components to this talent-push contingency. The first is the career profile of likely Silicon Valley emigrants; the personal security to leave Silicon Valley will likely be strongest for elite workers who can reasonably expect to find work elsewhere or to have the industry follow them. Second, the decision to leave Silicon Valley has a psychological basis in personal quality-of-life preferences (see Hayes 1989). Quality of life is highly subjective, and what appeals to some people goes unnoticed by others; or, as a software CEO told me, "I work with a lot of high-tech people who think quality of life is a Mountain Dew [soft drink] and [an office] window to the outside world."

Quality-of-Life Migrants

Should our software developer decide to leave Silicon Valley for personal reasons, she faces another decision: Where will she go? The choice of migratory destination represents yet another contingency based on the content of personal lifestyle preferences, which may vary according to particular life stage. For example, many residents feel the burdens that Silicon Valley place on domestic life (e.g., schools, shopping), but these may be less tolerable for workers with families. Alternately, the disappearance of wilderness and other natural amenities saddens many, but single and/or younger workers most likely to make time for regular outdoor recreation may consider this an important "push" factor out of Silicon Valley. Workers in a dual-income household will have to consider spousal career opportunities which may or may not be in software, compelling a decision to move to places with other industries besides software. For our software developer and others, particular lifestyle preferences make likely particular locational choices.

Workers who cannot start up their own firm or otherwise expect the industry to follow them will have to find work at an existing firm. For this reason, I first address how firm executives, entrepreneurs, and freelance workers select a migratory destination and, subsequently, provide employment for other workers (like our software developer) making the same decision. Along the particular factors described in the preceding paragraph, these pioneer quality of life migrants will choose their destination among the places that enable their particular lifestyle preference. A Santa Barbara software CEO's remarks are illustrative: "Moving here was not a big deal; we pretty well could have moved anywhere we wanted to. We chose Santa Barbara for environmental factors: proximity to the ocean, lifestyle, that sort of thing."

For pioneer migrants, another contingency is whether the desired destination has a minimum of infrastructure: high-speed telecommunications capacity, proximity to airports with Silicon Valley connections, and perhaps university computer science or engineering departments that provide collaborative opportunities or entry-level labor. In many cases, the Internet enables the dispersal of Internet-based production (web design, content providers) and some software development activities out of Silicon Valley, albeit with qualifications.[4] As one journalistic account describes:

> If there is any promising sign for would-be entrepreneurs outside the valley, it is that the Internet is reducing the importance of geography in the high-tech world, said Esther Dyson, a Silicon Valley veteran who in recent years has helped entrepreneurs in Eastern Europe find funding and markets for their ideas.
>
> "I just funded a company based in Prague that's doing Java development tools," Dyson said. "I don't think they're under any big disadvantage. You can create a presence over the Internet."
>
> Still, she said, "it can't replace going out to lunch in Silicon Valley. And at some point you're going to have to travel there" (Miller 1998, p. A26).

Absent such technological infrastructure, a host of places that otherwise meet an executive's lifestyle preferences may be poorly suited for firm location. If these factors are present, individual entrepreneurs and executives can then relocate an entire company (if they are authorized to make that decision, e.g., as head of a privately owned firm); they may be recruited by an existing remote firm; or, most infrequently, they move first and then start up a new company.[5]

Once in place, these pioneers must recruit highly prized talent in development, marketing, and management (as well as workers with more routine or entry-level skills), and so these firms create a "pull" for quality-of-life migrants at the elite worker levels, such as our ideal typical software developer. Through repeated iteration, the selective migration by more firms and more workers produces an industrial quality-of-life district, whose coherence lies in the subjective affinity between worker lifestyle preferences and place amenities.

LIFESTYLE NICHES

So far my analysis has described the conditions needed for quality-of-life migrants to leave high-tech districts. What particularities of place enable some communities to attract industry as quality-of-life districts? My research sites suggest that quality-of-life migrants select a destination in large part based on their self-perceived fit with a community's particular lifestyle niche.

Santa Monica

Let us return to our imaginary software developer who so far has decided not to live and work in Silicon Valley. She decides instead to find a job in Southern California because she prefers temperate weather and beaches. She is contacted by a business recruiter from a large Santa Monica firm and accepts his offer to visit the company, which is located in a well-scrubbed office park right next to a movie studio. After the recruiter's presentation, she is impressed with the company's prominence (e.g., it publishes one of the top 10 best-selling business utilities programs for Windows) and its competitive job offer. However, she is leery of living in the Los Angeles region, knowing of its reputation for smog, traffic, and crime. On a sight-seeing drive, the company's recruiter attempts to reassure her by pointing out Santa Monica's demographic composition (she is subconsciously put at ease by the other white, professional faces she sees driving around in sport utility vehicles), a vast array of stores and restaurants, pedestrian-friendly neighborhoods and parks, and the city's ineffable "community feel."

Our software developer decides to take the job in Santa Monica, only to find that the limited housing available within the city limits provides less space per dollar than in neighboring communities. If she is single or married with no children, she may find a condominium in adjacent communities like Culver City or Marina Del Rey, where her initial disappointment at the absence of Santa Monica's amenities gradually fades away as she grows accustomed to commuting by car to work and the beach. If she has children, the cost of living may compel her to move to the San Fernando Valley, where she finds a "suitable" single-family dwelling (four bedrooms, two-car garage) and "good schools" (the realtor assures her how well funded the local grade schools are). Her daily commute to Santa Monica is on average one hour each way (via the gridlocked 405 Freeway); after little more than a year of working in Santa Monica, she quits the firm for a job at a rival company's development branch deeper into the Valley.

For software firms in Santa Monica, locational assets are often conventionally agglomerative, because the city lies within the Silicon Bay software district, the entertainment industry's business service cluster, and growing pockets of "new media" firms that feed off these. Yet given a choice of employers across the Los Angeles region, Santa Monica's pull on elite workers is heavily lifestyle-oriented. The weather and beach figure largely in most informants' accounts of Santa Monica's allure. A software CEO emphasizes the cultural, recreational, and consumer amenities: "It's sunny, there's an ocean, and the lifestyle is freer and easier, more open to younger people than a lot of places you can think of." The organizer of a local software business group cites the city's ineffable community feel: "The beach, that it's its own community—that it *is* a community. There's nothing else in Southern California that really is a community, except maybe Carlsbad [near San Diego] and a couple of towns along the coast."

As our hypothetical software developer illustrates, whether these amenities successfully lure a software worker who has already decided to forego Silicon Valley and work in Los Angeles is contingent partly on personal taste (e.g., she prefers urban living) but heavily dependent on life stage. For employees of the marrying-childbearing age, Santa Monica's local amenities are frequently outweighed by what they perceive as the costs of living in an urban setting: the comparatively high cost of housing in many neighborhoods, density, infrastructural strain, and crime. Notes the CEO of a large software firm headquartered in Santa Monica:

> The problem comes up around the age of 30, which you can see as engineers get married and have families. West Los Angeles is expensive, dense, and some may feel it's too urban for the kids. Then where do you go? They may move out to Agoura [in the San Fernando Valley] or wherever, and that's a huge commute, and the company can feel it. We lose people frequently, although a lot less than we used to in difficult times. Workers would commute here from Agoura, then they would find a start-up there and go work there.

Those with families who live in Santa Monica either feel especially comfortable living in apartments or can afford the high costs for even modest-sized housing. For Santa Monica's information economy, one result is that firms often orient their hiring strategies toward younger workers who will appreciate (or at least tolerate) the city's urban lifestyle. Small firms that cannot pay highly competitive wages are especially limited to a young workforce; as these firms grow and seek experienced managerial talent, this may constitute a disincentive to remain in

Santa Monica. Separately, in many Santa Monica software firms, employees do not always (or even mostly) live within the city. Quality-of-life factors, then, are not confined to Santa Monica city limits; locals work, live, and play within a commutable constellation of neighborhoods.

Santa Barbara

Instead of the preceding scenario, let us say our software developer instead rejects the Santa Monica job. Earlier, she was also contacted by a Carpinteria firm recruiter—who quickly informed her that "Carpinteria is basically Santa Barbara!" (In fact, it is five miles west of Santa Barbara.) Researching on the World Wide Web, she learns that the firm may have some staying power (it plans an initial public offering on NASDAQ for next year), and she is surprised to find over 100 local software firms, several of which she knows, listed on a regional business organization's website. Deciding to give the firm a look, she rents a car from Los Angeles to Carpinteria and is enchanted by her drive through the undeveloped coastal stretch before Santa Barbara. After a persuasive presentation at the company, the recruiter takes her around Santa Barbara, where she is delighted by the city's exclusive ambiance, Spanish architecture, and stores and restaurants (not as many as in Santa Monica, but similarly upscale). She also notes how this place is less dense, has a slower pace, and seems safer than Santa Monica (which, she notes in retrospect, did not seem all that different from the rest of Los Angeles); she is also encouraged to find roller-bladers along the beach.

Our software developer decides to take the job. If she is single, she likely moves into a Victorian house or new condominium development near Santa Barbara's beachfront. If she has children, she discovers that Santa Barbara's high cost of living (roughly similar to Santa Monica's) precludes her from buying the large house she was hoping for, while Carpinteria's cost of living is more affordable but its schools are "unacceptable," due to the town's largely working-class and minority population. Instead, she buys a new house in Goleta (on the opposite side of Santa Barbara from Carpinteria), commutes 20 miles each way in 25 minutes, and goes to the beach less than once a month.

As this scenario suggests, the quality-of-life attraction of Santa Barbara is even more fundamental to its information economy, because its distance from Los Angeles puts the city at a disadvantage for firms needing close geographic proximity.[6] Informants repeatedly raise the importance of executives' lifestyle preferences to explain why firms are located in Santa Barbara.[7] A software CEO of a Carpinteria firm describes the locational needs of recent software migrants:

> For these companies, making a lot of money is their primary objective, and this enables them to move to Santa Barbara. [I have heard in the last 5-6 years about CEOs] just wanting to live in Santa Barbara, so they move their businesses here. They've been successful enough that they can do that.

A Santa Barbara software executive claims:

> When I talk to Santa Barbara-based entrepreneurs, I think virtually all of them have made a decision that they want to be in a place with a high quality of life for their family. Basically they make the decision for their family, and then subsequent to that, they say, "Gee whiz, if it appeals to me on this level, it will probably appeal to employees on this level."

Additionally, the perceived lack of crime compared to Los Angeles is another important asset, particularly for companies where employees work during nontraditional hours at all times of the day. Otherwise, notes a software executive, "You don't get people who just drop in and work and feel this real freedom in and out of the workplace if you were in a high crime area. People would leave before it gets dark if they were afraid they would get mugged going to their car."

Quality-of-life factors also include recreational and cultural opportunities, which are plentiful and do not require traveling to Los Angeles; as a software executive notes, Santa Barbara "is fun, it has great weather, it has access to recreation, you can walk all over downtown." The city's small size is another factor: "People like to feel they make a difference, and that's easier in small communities." Furthermore, as these descriptions indicate, Santa Barbara's quality of life is least implicitly constructed as the opposite of Los Angeles and its perceived urban ills.[8]

As with Santa Monica, Santa Barbara's cost of living is lower than Silicon Valley's, yet still sufficiently high that it may pose a barrier in retaining some employees with families who are used to affording larger homes outside of Southern California on a high-tech salary (or salaries). One software executive argues this cost-of-living squeeze is felt most acutely by start-up companies:

> In starting to grow the company, we would fly people here, and the recruiting would begin, because you fly them into the airport, and it was a beautiful place. And we had all the problems of a start-up. You can't really pay people a lot of money, and they're wanting to come here and bring their families, so they look at the housing prices and all these different type of issues. And that was kind of tough, so we ended up going for younger people who didn't have this type of overhead.

As in Santa Monica, then, Santa Barbara software firms often orient their workforce around young employees. Because experienced managers frequently fit the over-30/with-family profile, potential hires are often discouraged by the modest career safety net offered by Santa Barbara's software cluster. In a company's favor, however, is the "reliability wage" (see Roobeek 1987) that the area's quality of life provides; as one software CEO describes,

> The reality is, being in Santa Barbara is an advantage to us because if we recruit people here, and they love the lifestyle, which virtually everybody here does, they don't want

to leave. And in the high-tech business, if you understand the high-tech business, there's a shortage of help. In Silicon Valley, everybody's a free agent. Free agency is the order of the day, which means people walk into your office—let's say somebody's making $70,000 a year—and says, "I just got offered $85,000 and $5,000 in stock options to move to another company; match it or I'm out of here." I don't have that kind of stuff going on here.

San Luis Obispo

Finally, let us say our software developer foregoes the Santa Monica and Santa Barbara scenarios altogether. Perhaps she finds the Southern California lifestyle too pretentious or superficial; maybe she simply has not found the right job yet. At any rate, earlier she arranged a "fall-back" visit to a few Silicon Valley firms. She drives her rented car up to Santa Clara via California's 101 freeway, reflecting along the way on the relative importance of lifestyle versus career; after all, she spends an average of 10 hours a workday in front of a computer screen. On the journey north, she admires the beauty of the land just north of what she considers "Southern California," where vast ranches and undeveloped hillsides replace coastlines. Some 100 miles out of Santa Barbara, she gets off the freeway for a cappuccino in San Luis Obispo and drives through a downtown that resembles the pedestrian village of Santa Barbara and Santa Monica, only even less populated and with its quaint, Depression-era architecture largely intact. Parking in a 3-story lot just off a main downtown corridor, she stops at a bookstore and is surprised to find a wide (if not thick) selection of prestige literature she associates with college towns and large cities. Stopping at a street-side coffeeshop, she overhears two men in their 20s talking about Linux programming. She asks them what they do; one is a student at Cal Poly, while the other graduated from that university and now works for an 8-person technology development company that subcontracts for another firm in town. Somewhat surprised, our software developer tells them she is in on her way to Silicon Valley but is interested in learning more about San Luis Obispo. The graduate gives her the phone number for his boss ("He answers his own calls?!" she laughs), who in turn refers her to another company. An hour later she is in the modest office of a CEO who is impressed with her credentials and informs her he is selling this company but starting up another one locally and is definitely interested in hiring her.

Three days later (after several offers in Silicon Valley), she is back in San Luis Obispo being driven around town by the CEO, who shows her the local farmer's market, beaches, Spanish mission, and lack of traffic. He points out the college students, most of whom end up not wanting to leave because "they love the place." Sensing that our software developer is sold on San Luis Obispo, the CEO offers her the job, at about 20 percent less pay than the positions she was just offered in Silicon Valley. (The CEO quickly reiterates how much lower the cost of living is here.) Thinking she may be crazy, our software developer accepts the job. If she is single, she may grow bored with the small town isolation and eventually leave. If she has children, she is delighted to find a spacious house nearby with an ocean view and a well-funded school system.

As this scenario illustrates, San Luis Obispo has little urban glitz or exclusive ambiance to offer quality-of-life migrants. Instead, local boosters make a more common but widely appealing pitch for their city, boasting it combines the cultural sophistication of a major university with a small town flavor in a relatively undeveloped coastal setting and relatively low housing costs. Local software executives attest that San Luis Obispo provides a "stress-free," nonurban milieu for knowledge-creators. With its lower cost of living (than Santa Monica, Santa Barbara, or Silicon Valley) and rural ambiance, San Luis Obispo permits uncommon opportunities for quality-of-life migrants: proximity to a scenic coastline and beaches, the chance to own vast tracts of undeveloped land for ranching or natural communion, access to horse stables and other rural forms of recreation, a "western" milieu in which to wear cowboy boots or drive big trucks. Less population, a healthy tax base,[9] and higher than average education levels have produced local grade schools with high standards and significant parental involvement. Many informants rank highly the cultural sophistication that comes with a fairly large university. ("The population is say 40,000 people, yet it has the culture of about a 200,000 population center, and that's largely because of Cal Poly," says one software executive.) Finally, almost everyone who has lived in major cities—which accounts for most of the area's residents, as many claim—points out the area's safety standards and lack of crime; for some, its relative class and ethnic homogeneity is an implicit bonus.

These local amenities make San Luis Obispo an appealing place for many technology workers to raise families, thereby filling a lifestyle niche that contrasts with the generally young/single orientation (at least for employee recruitment) of Santa Monica and Santa Barbara. The small town/family appeal is particularly important when local firms try to recruit senior management, the workforce segment most in shortage within the local labor pool, from Silicon Valley and elsewhere. Occasionally, the appeal succeeds, as one executive illustrated:

> As far as telecommunications policy people in the United States, I can hold my own with any of them; I'm not the best or anything, but I definitely know what's going on. [My firm's parent company] would love to have me in Vancouver, but I wrote it into my contract that I can't be moved to an office more than 25 miles away. If I didn't have that in my contract, I guarantee you that I would have been moved. I mean, I wouldn't have moved; I would have just resigned. With the people who live here, a lot of us, it's here or nothing. I wouldn't even consider moving.

With a substantial number of Cal Poly engineering students that want to stay in town after graduation (itself a quality-of-life indicator, for many), San Luis Obispo provides lower-level workers that make up a large part of many firms' workforces. A software CEO claims there are only two reasons why residents (including technology workers) live in San Luis Obispo: "They either decided they wanted to get out [of major cities], or they didn't want to leave [San Luis Obispo]." To be sure, San Luis Obispo's lifestyle niche is the most common, and its software industry the least developed, of the three research sites, with the result that the city's quality-of-life appeal has not produced dramatic software migration—at least not visibly. Nevertheless, quality of life comprises the predominant account for why existing software firms originally located to San Luis Obispo, and many claim it plays a large role in outside recruitment from employees. Even more so than the other research sites, quality of life functions as an important reliability wage; workers from Silicon Valley and elsewhere are frequently willing to take a wage cut in order to find a job locally, as several local CEOs claimed.

COMPARABLE PROCESSES IN THE MOTION PICTURE/TELEVISION INDUSTRY

Does the geography of motion pictures and television production also reveal quality-of-life-based forces? In many ways, the motion picture/television industry is well suited to compare with software. It depends largely on the creation of ideas (screenwriting, directing, design, etc.) and innovations; the recent boom in computer animation has increased the role of technical innovation and has introduced industrial and personnel overlaps with high-tech. Human talent has an organizational fluidity comparable to high-tech; a film director can run an independent production company, manage a postproduction studio, and simultaneously contract for a separate studio.

The Role of Region in Motion Picture and Television Production

The geographical centrality of industrial districts remains strong in motion picture/television production. The 1950s federal regulations forced studios and networks to spin off facilities, production companies, and crew into decentralized production networks. Alongside talent agents and independent "deal-makers," these independent firms and workers create externalized production networks that make locating in entertainment districts like Los Angeles and Hollywood extremely compelling for individual firms and workers. Additionally, the constraints imposed by large-scale collaborations between firms and workers (freelance creative talent and technical staff) in capital-intensive facilities further reduce the geographical mobility of motion picture and television production; production schedules entail face-to-face interaction that tend to shorten the radius within which most contracting firms can be located. Thus, despite the fact that the industry increasingly films "on location" around the world, thanks to the development of increasingly light and more mobile technology, geographical centrality still exerts a powerful pull on all other aspects of production (Christopherson and Storper 1986; Storper and Christopherson 1985). In this regard, Santa Monica hosts a substantial share of the Los Angeles region's motion picture/television production companies, postproduction facilities, and (to a lesser extent) studio headquarters. Moreover, the city's Westside environs are within commutable distance (roughly 15 miles) from entertainment offices and studios in Hollywood (legally, the City of Los Angeles), the historic center of the entertainment sector.

However, Santa Monica did not always host local motion picture/television industry or, for that matter, other business service industries (legal, architecture, etc.). As a Santa Monica bank president recalled, "Years ago it was tough to bring businesses out here, because [Santa Monica] was so far away" from metropolitan business districts. Motion picture/television industry only began appearing in the 1980s, when many major film studios moved out of Hollywood proper to the Westside and other metropolitan "edge cities." Hollywood's then-falling property values and symptoms of urban blight prompted "A-list" entertainment firms to leave entertainment's historic center in the 1980s; a recessionary real estate crash in the early 1990s widened the window of opportunity for more firms to follow. As with high-tech, relocation decisions first originated at the firm level. With their vast spatial requirements, production facilities and entertainment corporations tended to move to areas like the Westside which offered suitable amounts of undeveloped space. MGM's 1993 relocation from nearby Culver City to Santa Monica (into the custom-built MGM Plaza) exemplified this first wave of Hollywood émigrés. According to an MGM executive, the studio sought the vast acreage that only sites in Santa Monica and Century City could provide. Secondarily, MGM was looking for a campus-like environment for its corporate offices, and it was discouraged by the "urban feel and congestion" of Century City.

My data, however, suggest that quality-of-life concerns also motivated the flight of motion picture/television production out of Hollywood. First, because Santa Monica falls within commutable distance to the Hollywood district, we cannot rule out the primacy of traditional agglomerative factors in explaining the relocation of production to the city and the surrounding Los Angeles Westside. Overlaying these agglomerative incentives for relocation were widespread employee concerns about Hollywood's crime and urban decay, which for many heightened the appeal of comparatively white and affluent areas like the Westside. Thus, by the time the metropolitan real estate market recovered in the mid-1990s, much of Hollywood's historic industry had shifted to the Westside, bringing with it traditional agglomerative forces. It is also worth noting anecdotal evidence that suggests the Westside was for many the chosen home for many entertainment workers long before it became the place where the industry worked. One example raised repeatedly in my fieldwork is *Titanic* film director Jim Cameron, who located his special effects firm in Venice and his production company in West Hollywood because he lives in the Westside. Currently, the new DreamWorks SKG entertainment conglomerate is preparing to construct its first studio in the Westside community of Marina Del Rey, which boasts an undeveloped space (specifically, a wetlands) that can be built up to the latest high-tech specifications, as well as proximity to the studio principals' homes. Thus, as with software, Santa Monica represents a mixed-case of quality-of-life district/traditional agglomeration.

Quality-of-Life Forces

Santa Barbara illustrates purer forms of quality-of-life pull-factors in motion picture/television production because, in contrast to corporate migrations to Santa Monica, elite workers represent most of the relocation activity to Santa Barbara. Numerous actors and executives have made the area their second home, while (closer to my production emphasis) many screenwriters and independent producers work out of their Santa Barbara residences. More recently, these elite workers have begun to bring production firms to the city, although the wave is still quite modest. The city now houses a postproduction facility (owned by a major film director, who also lives and works here) where major motion pictures are edited, mixed, and digitally altered. Hollywood moguls Tom Pollock and Ivan Reitman have received approval to build a second facility in neighboring Carpinteria, right next to a prominent software firm's coastal headquarters. Additionally, local software firms have recently produced special effects and digital tools for Hollywood science fiction and horror films.

As I learned in interviews, the reasons why elite entertainment workers live in Santa Barbara are straightforwardly related to the local quality of life. Importantly, these workers represent a range of motion picture and television activities broader than rentals and coordinators that help Hollywood firms shoot "on location," the most mobile of entertainment production activities (Christopherson and Storper 1986). Now, they include important components of preproduction (e.g., screenwriting) and postproduction (postproduction facilities, digital effects) as well. However, Santa Barbara firms still face geographic constraints which preclude them from a greater range of projects. In postproduction, informants told me that three- to six-month projects like motion pictures allow digital effects producers, mixing/editing facilities, and other postproduction contractors to be located within a day's drive to a studio or other site of project coordination—thus, as far away from the Los Angeles metropolis as Santa Barbara. Two- to four-week projects like commercials, however, require more rapid face-to-face interaction; when firms and workers work on several projects simultaneously (five projects is not unusual) or use specialized capital-intensive equipment (like Technicolor laboratories), their interaction will be shorter and more frequent. Thus, shorter projects discourage firms and workers from locating too far in the outskirts of Los Angeles, much less outside the metropolis in Santa Barbara; this reinforces the territorial concentration of production activities and networks in the entertainment sector. Finally, by virtue of being outside the entertainment district, Santa Barbara lacks the small production and development companies whose daily transactions make Los Angeles the industry's "hiring hall."

THEORIZING THE QUALITY-OF-LIFE DISTRICT

Although data on its appearance elsewhere are largely anecdotal, the quality-of-life district is certainly not limited to the research sites. The western United States includes several high-tech quality-of-life districts with community amenities comparable to Santa Barbara or San Luis Obispo, such as Boulder, Colorado; Corvallis, Oregon; and Provo, Utah. Similarly, the Microsoft Corporation's history in Seattle suggests that lifestyle-based location decisions have produced bona fide industrial districts.[10] Importantly, natural and middle-class domestic amenities do not exhaust the range of qualities of life that elite workers seek, as the northern expansion of Silicon Valley into the San Francisco/Oakland Bay Area illustrates. For example, San Francisco's SOMA (South of Market Avenue) multimedia district provides a lifestyle popular among bohemian "urban pioneers" (Zukin 1989), while workers seeking an affordable cost of living motivate the Bay Area's metropolitan sprawl into the suburbs of Alameda County.

How should the quality-of-life district be understood theoretically? This spatial form reflects both continuity with and departure from the traditional ways that knowledge-based industries conventionally organize themselves in space. On the one hand, corporations in high-tech and traditional industries have long included noneconomic factors like residential and lifestyle amenities in their decisions to relocate company divisions or headquarters, as idyllic suburbs like White Plains, New York show. In the last 10-15 years, Los Angeles film studios and corporate headquarters from other industries moved to the Westside of Los Angeles, in part for its ample undeveloped land (where numerous corporate offices now lay) but also for its demographic distinction from ethnically diverse, older, and "blighted" sites of corporate headquarters such as downtown Los Angeles and Hollywood proper (Kotkin 1998a). Santa Barbara has also benefited from corporate migration out of metropolitan centers, particularly with the relocation of the Tenet Healthcare Corporation's headquarters in 1996. These corporate migrations represent traditional exercises of corporate command-and-control over location. While rank-and-file employees may have some say in choosing new corporate sites, locational decision making ultimately flows down from the highest corporate levels.

On the other hand, the quality-of-life districts illustrated here reflect a locational dynamic that departs from command-and-control decisions. In the quality-of-life district, locational decision-making power ultimately flows not from corporate headquarters or (to give it a human face) corporate executives but from the producers themselves. Elite workers vote with their feet as to where they are going to live; as long as information economy firms focus strategically on recruiting the most talented workers, these firms move or stay put based on decisions made by the labor market, not corporate headquarters. Of course, elite labor market flows usually feed existing high-tech districts where "critical mass" often originates out of conventional corporate-level decisions. However, this conventional labor flow should not obscure how labor market contingencies can also create new centers of industry based on elite workers' personal location preferences.

Regulating the Crisis of Labor Reproduction

Regulation theory offers a useful conceptual vocabulary to theorize the quality-of-life district. This body of literature explains how particular forms of capital accumulation result not from inevitable laws of capitalist production but from historical resolutions (or "regulations") of accumulation crises by other social spheres (see Lipietz 1987; Aglietta 1979). The quality-of-life district is one facet of the spatial logic that results from talent-push pressures out of knowledge-intensive industrial districts like Silicon Valley. As capital accumulates and production grows in an industrial district without sustainable development planning, private costs are externalized to local governments and local residents in the form of infrastructural and environmental strain. All residents who live in or would move to the region thus experience a *crisis of labor reproduction* through higher costs of living, greater congestion, perceived urban blight, and so forth. For information economy firms, quality of life frames the talent-push pressures which elite workers experience from this crisis.

Regulation theory holds that crises of accumulation are met with attempts at social regulation, which helps explain the locational decisions of some firms to amenity-rich sites. In an industrial region already prone to endemic employee turnover, firms may find it more effective to stabilize their human assets not by collectively addressing the roots of the problem (unchecked private accumulation) but by individually dispersing key employees and production processes to localities where residential and workplace amenities are seen to be more favorable. Companies reap considerable benefits from moving activities and employees to quality-of-life districts: employee stability in general, and in some cases externalized lifestyle wages that permit lower wage levels. Yet even more, the labor market increasingly performs this regulation function. For one, the fluidity of intellectual talent in the information economy suggests that some corporate-level relocation decisions—for instance, by privately owned "boutique" firms and start-ups—should be reconceptualized as originating from elite workers who happen to hold executive roles. Furthermore, elite workers in quality-of-life districts represent potential entrepreneurs, consultants, and contractors who could form new companies in their new communities (a common sequence of events for several start-up companies I studied). Thus, employee turnover/corporate relocation in Silicon Valley and software industry growth in quality-of-life

districts are in fact two poles of the same regulated flow of labor; in the vocabulary of regulation theory, they comprise a single *spatial structure of regulation*
(Feldman 1997, p. 31).

Further Characteristics of the Quality-of-Life District

Having theorized the forces that create quality-of-life districts, I now elaborate
additional characteristics which the case studies and other data suggest.

Quality of Life Forces Need Not Be the Primary Locational Asset

Elite workers' locational preferences do not always determine location exclusively, as they appear to do in Santa Barbara and San Luis Obispo. In a bona fide
high-tech district, quality of life can be a secondary factor that narrows workers'
choice of employment preferences to particular communities within a larger
industrial region. As software and motion picture/television informants in Santa
Monica indicate, firms can take advantage of sites which combine a quality of life
appeal with more conventional benefits of industrial concentration. In this regard,
Santa Monica resembles many other "edge cities" of the Los Angeles region, and
it cannot be completely characterized by the spatial structure of regulation that
disperses firms and elite workers to Santa Barbara or San Luis Obispo. Nevertheless, quality-of-life preferences may constitute a lower-order criterion that, for
example, narrows the range of communities *within* an industrial district to which
firms and workers will consider locating.

Quality of Life Districts Need Not Contain Locally Integrated
Production Networks

To generalize broadly, in the command-and-control economy, the only levels
that were typically located outside of bona fide industrial districts were R&D and
corporate headquarters. Now, thanks to the advent of space- and time-compressing technologies like the Internet, far more nonmaterial activities, from R&D to
customer order processing, can in principle be performed outside of industrial districts. Whether these activities are *in fact* dispersed outside of Silicon Valley or
other industrial districts is a separate question which need not concern us now
(although I suspect most will remain concentrated in traditional centers). Elite
labor market power and entrepreneurial activity (which also reflects elite labor
market power) reside in workers through a broad range of production levels,
which will be reflected among the firms in a quality-of-life district.[11]

However, the same capacity that permits certain firms, elite workers, and production activities to be uprooted also diminishes the likelihood that quality-of-
life districts contain locally integrated production networks. At least in their origins, the only industrial coherence to quality-of-life districts is elite workers'

shared migration experience and not firms' proximity to specialized pools of labor, contractors, customers, and other assets characteristic of bona fide industrial districts. Indeed, the capacity to forego proximity to such specialized pools is exactly what makes quality-of-life districts possible in the first place. Over time, as a critical mass of like firms grows, then locally self-sufficient production networks may emerge (much to the pride of local high-tech boosters, no doubt). How this happens is another question altogether, and one better explained by the new industrial geography.

Spatial Distance from Bona Fide Industrial Regions Varies Across Sectors

Despite the proliferation of space- and time-compressing innovations, information economy sectors vary in the frequency and kinds of exchanges within production networks. In turn, these appear to limit how far production activities can be dispersed from industrial regions, as the comparison between software and motion picture/television production illustrates. As a motion picture director living and working in Santa Barbara told me:

> I think as long as people are interested in working with people—actors, directors, and writers—they sort of need to smell each other. With Internet stuff, you're just designing stuff that's coming up Xs and 0s, and it's not important, other than just having people give you feedback on whether it's working or not. A writer can go off and write anywhere, but maybe he needs to be in the middle of New York to get the right feeling, or he or she should be in the middle of the country to get the right feeling.

In entertainment, postproduction activities (e.g., special effects, editing) for long-term projects like motion pictures require less frequent consultation with directors, producers, and studios than do the same activities for short-term projects like commercials. Firms that specialize in short-term projects may also oversee several projects simultaneously, which also increases the need for consultation with directors, producers, and studios. These suggest that only one-at-a-time, long-term postproduction activities are likely to be located out of entertainment districts, and even then the ease of traveling back into Hollywood or New York becomes a paramount factor. The contrast between different kinds of preproduction activities is even starker; screenwriters can be virtually self-sufficient in their business and, therefore, take long blocks of time away from their colleagues, while producers, who are on the phone or in meetings almost all of the time, can hardly afford to be far from "the action." Furthermore, the *quality* of business interaction also varies between sector and may also affect the remoteness of quality-of-life districts (Boden and Molotch 1994). For software production and Internet business, telecommunications is a native technology, and therefore firms in these industries may have different expectations regarding virtual communication than do motion picture and television directors.

CONTRADICTIONS AND LIMITS

Given their export basis, software and entertainment sectors are usually thought to be like traditional industries (and unlike growth coalition industries) in their structural independence from local resources. This assumption is warranted only if we confine our observations to traditional indicators of local dependence: reliance on local labor and infrastructure, relationships with local decision makers, and so on (see Cox and Mair 1988). Yet my research interviews indicate that high-tech and entertainment firms locate to Santa Monica, Santa Barbara, and San Luis Obispo, at least in part, to capture an important yet frequently overlooked local resource for the production of symbolic goods and services: the local quality of life. Community quality of life, in short, is the glue which in many ways binds these otherwise footloose firms to the research sites.

My theorization awaits further elaboration and modification by future research. Therefore, instead of a bold restatement, I conclude this paper by identifying several contradictions and limits to the quality-of-life district. These highlight the political tensions and unanticipated outcomes that communities transformed by quality-of-life district dynamics may experience.

Forging the Quality-of-Life Agenda

As the epigraph opening this paper illustrates, journalistic accounts of software and entertainment industry growth in Santa Barbara and San Luis Obispo may not analyze quality-of-life-based development in the conceptual detail offered here, but they more or less effectively describe the nature of the quality-of-life district's pull on elite workers and therefore industry. What many industry observers and participants often fail to recognize, however, is that this new industrial space also has a local history. Wilderness and beaches, small-town ambiance, and other local amenities often reflect the fruits of political struggles of community activists against local growth coalitions. Santa Monica, for example, has long held a reputation as Southern California's most progressive city, thanks to the tenant's right coalition known as Santa Monicans for Renters Rights, which made its first political impact on city politics in 1978. With real estate and development a major part of the city's traditional economy, landlord-tenant conflicts quickly escalated to enmesh growth coalition industries and homeowners and dominate local politics in the 1980s (Capek and Gilderbloom 1992; Clavel 1986). Over those years, local progressives successfully mobilized to place on the political agenda many issues of city life—homelessness, open space preservation, pollution, public art, child care—that never get raised in many other cities. In an important break from traditional municipal acquiescence to development interests, the city levied developers with unprecedented fiscal exactions to fund city programs (Warner, Molotch, and Lategola 1992; Capek and Gilderbloom 1992).

Santa Barbara's spatial form reflects an environmentalist politics in which community activists oppose developers and urban growth. Slow growth sentiments date back at least to 1920s civic leaders who consciously envisioned the city's Spanish Mission architecture, village atmosphere, and surrounding wilderness as a distinction of Santa Barbara's superiority to bustling Los Angeles (Molotch and Freudenburg 1996; Starr 1990). While virtually all of Santa Barbara protested after the 1968 oil spill, UCSB students would extend radicalism to burning a local bank in 1970. Currently, the university population (faculty and staff as well as students), informational workers (including government employees), and the leisure population (retirees and the independently wealthy) have tended to back liberal politicians and environmental organizations that advocate slow growth and controlled resource consumption, much to the dismay of conservative business leaders. Tourism has legitimated quality-of-life concerns both minute (like architectural styles) and vast (air quality, offshore oil drilling, and so on) that frustrate developers and conventional industries alike. The resulting coalition has at times splintered, pitting environmentalists against more moderate slow-growth voters on issues like importing water supplies (Nevarez 1996), but has otherwise produced a stable, liberal electorate that backs governmental intervention on behalf of environmental protection and community preservation.

The most isolated and rural of the three research sites, San Luis Obispo is guided by a bipartisan electorate which opposes uncontrolled growth and industrial risk. Surrounded by mountains and large ranch estates, the city retains a small-town atmosphere that has been defended by residents against the local growth coalition since at least the 1950s (McKeen 1988). This initial progressive constituency was amplified in the 1960s by dramatic growth at the Cal Poly campus, from which came important liberal political leaders (mayors, planning commissioners, etc.). Local politics received an environmentalist texture starting in the 1970s, when activists from across the nation descended upon San Luis Obispo to protest energy utility PG&E's Diablo Canyon nuclear power plant (Epstein 1991). The university, government, and PG&E continue to constitute major players in the local economy as the largest employers and, in PG&E's case, the biggest taxpayer by far in the county. Currently, San Luis Obispo's growth comes from retirees and others who discovered the city on the highway journey between northern and southern California, or perhaps by traveling to nearby tourist destinations like Hearst's Castle or the beach towns of Morro Bay and Pismo Beach. An important demographic presence,[12] the newcomers give tremendous political weight to slow growth sentiments, despite their bipartisan character.

An irony felt keenly by many long-time residents in quality-of-life districts is that the local quality of life did not *just happen*, yet many quality-of-life migrants do not know how it emerged. Consequently, the growing information economy puts an unexpected twist on local politics in the research sites, because software and entertainment companies appear largely as unexpected newcomers to both community activists and the older growth coalitions. To the surprise of many growth advocates, the new industries have grown locally because elite workers value the amenities preserved by earlier slow-growth, pro-environment efforts. In some cases, liberal environmental activists have cited the need to protect the local information economy as justification for *opposing* unwanted projects like coastal oil facilities and beach-front hotel expansion. As my interviews with business and community representatives indicate, however, solid relationships between new information economy elites and either local progressives or the older business community are far less concrete than the quality-of-life connection that elite workers establish with their feet.

In the absence of such durable relationships, local politics are currently shaped by an ambiguous quality-of-life agenda, the trajectory of which remains unclear. Perhaps the most far-reaching event that I observed occurred in Santa Barbara. Following skirmishes over proposed high-tech campuses on scenic agricultural land outside of urban limit lines, local software industry groups and environmentalists began collaborating on land-use issues affecting the spatial form that high-tech growth will take. Environmentalists endorsed land-use planning principles to facilitate high-tech growth, such as giving land-use priority to new high-tech projects over low-value commercial development and supporting industrial and commercial densities at higher levels than local growth control ordinances permit. In return, high-tech business organizations expressed commitment to preserve the anti-sprawl intent of local growth controls by respecting urban limit lines; a few industry leaders even contributed re-election funds to Santa Barbara's liberal mayor to defeat her more traditionally "pro-business" opponent. The needs of local liberals to fund their electoral campaigns and non-profits helps explain such locally unprecedented business-environmental alliances, but so does liberals' desire to cultivate strategic allies against their traditional pro-growth adversaries. As a Santa Barbara environmentalist organizer told me: "[T]he environmental community is now faced with the good problem of saying, "High-tech growth does seem to be growing here, now how do we get behind it?" Because no one wants to be seen as saying no to everything." In turn, business-favored liberals face strong pressures to endorse the information-economy sectors' growth.

Economic Development and the Stratification of Places

If the local growth coalitions did not foresee how quality of life could drive high-tech growth in my research sites, the fault is not theirs alone, because the quality-of-life district defies the usual American practices of economic development. Conventionally, cities and regions compete for capital investment by offering tax incentives and other public subsidies in the hopes of luring businesses and industries away from other places. While auto malls and "big box" discount retailers are perhaps the most familiar product of this competition, many localities pin their hopes on attracting information industries that promise higher than average wages and "clean" industrial output. Whether local residents have the training or municipalities, the infrastructure for such industries are seldom raised questions. Instead, localities usually subsidize speculative schemes like economic development organizations, science parks, and office complexes in the hope of recruiting industries where there are none as of yet. Fearful of falling behind, other localities usually follow suit and subsidize similar enterprises for the same reasons. The end result is that localities join a "race to the bottom" in which each subsidy further levels the economic playing field while increasing localities' fiscal vulnerability.

The quality-of-life districts described in this paper may offer a persuasive critique of this race to the bottom, even as they paradoxically raise the stakes of the race. Information-economy firms have come to the research sites not for the attributes that are common to many places (i.e., public subsidies for capital accumulation, which none of the research sites offer) but for the attributes which *distinguish* them from many places, namely, their quality of life (see also Harvey 1989, pp. 293-294). These places succeed by appealing to the appropriate unit of analysis in the information economy: elite workers, not firms. Elite workers bring domestic concerns (as, of course, do all other residents) that, in amenity-rich places like the research sites, are best addressed by preserving the community status quo. As opposed to threatening open spaces, municipal funds, and service infrastructure with office parks and other questionable enterprises, these localities protect urban amenities and maintain a community status quo that benefits resident and newcomer elite workers, and all other residents as well. In short, if quality-of-life districts offer any lesson for economic development policy, it may be: "If it isn't broke, don't fix it."

By attracting industries that pay high wages, protect environmental and urban amenities, and appease residents, quality-of-life districts accumulate the place-based goods that improve individual, collective, and regional fates. In so doing, quality-of-life districts enhance their comparative advantage in the stratification of places (Logan 1978) vis-à-vis other places that unsuccessfully gamble local assets on economic development. This outcome is ironic, given that localities have traditionally sacrificed urban quality of life in their competition for economic advantage. Yet this reflects the new foundation of production and profit in the information economy: human talent and, specifically, elite workers. To be sure, more conventional industrial economies still thrive; although their forms of production are largely factor-based and tend toward routinization, mechanization, and dispersion to the global periphery, the geographical centers of these older economies still retain their prominence in the stratification of places. Yet the global importance of talent-based industries suggests that quality of life may become a serious factor through which places prosper economically.

Limits to the Quality-of-Life District

Are there limits to the dynamics that sustain the quality-of-life district? I conclude this paper by suggesting two. First, not all residents are equal in the quality-of-life district. Information-economy growth in these new industrial spaces may reduce community diversity by selectively attracting elite workers who fit the most apparent quality-of-life niches. Armed with high education, better than average wages, and the sensibilities of sophisticated cultural consumers, software and entertainment workers help homogenize these places' demographic and cultural constitutions. Long-time residents whom I interviewed attested to intangible yet significant shifts in their communities' feel; for example, sport utility vehicles increasingly crowd their streets, while once-quaint stores and restaurants now calculatedly orient themselves to the new class. In some neighborhoods, information-economy growth triggers gentrification, because elite workers can afford higher rents in growth-conscious communities with slow-growing housing stocks. In both posh office complexes and renovated industrial warehouses, software and entertainment companies outbid local businesses for commercial space. Because most information-economy work requires advanced education, it provides few job opportunities for working-class residents.[13]

A second limit to the quality-of-life district lies in the delicate balance between quality of life and industry. As I have shown, in their pure form, quality-of-life districts attract information-economy firms not because of their agglomerative economies but because of their domestic and community amenities. Yet the spatial regulation of labor which these new industrial spaces reflect is dynamic and not necessarily sustainable over time. For example, according to the popular wisdom of many Southern Californians, Santa Monica, Santa Barbara, and San Luis Obispo can be characterized at different stages within a single growth sequence; as a Santa Barbara software organizer told me:

> If you take Santa Monica, Santa Barbara, and San Luis Obispo, you're going to find in fact that Santa Barbara is between Santa Monica and San Luis Obispo, not just physically but also in this whole process. I think you're going to end up with San Luis Obispo being the place essentially where people who perhaps long for the old Santa Barbara will end up going to San Luis Obispo, and people who feel they don't want to go quite as far as Santa Monica has gone will be in Santa Barbara.

Some fear that the push for a "critical mass" of information-economy firms that some local industry representatives seek also stresses a community infrastructure. If what starts out as piecemeal agglomeration proceeds unabated over time, this cycle of industrial development could eventually jeopardize a locality's quality-of-life amenities. Many business informants seem aware of this delicate balance and insist their growth would not jeopardize it, as one high-tech CEO told me:

We need some breathing room so if an opportunity comes, we can respond quick enough so that we can get that share of business. But we're not here just to make Santa Barbara grow. We're here because this is a nice place to live, it's a good place to attract intelligent, hard-working people, and we want to stay here.

It remains to be seen if existing land-use policies can lock in critical aspects of the local quality of life or, by contrast, allow high-tech growth to repeat the history of Silicon Valley's development.

ACKNOWLEDGMENTS

The author would like to thank Harvey Molotch, Richard Appelbaum, Mitchell Duneier, and Richard Flacks for their helpful comments.

NOTES

1.   The traditional dispersal of R&D away from corporate divisions, however, does not invalidate the largest pattern whereby cities have traditionally contained the bulk of separable knowledge-intensive activities like R&D as well as more familiar production processes. This is because knowledge workers' locational preferences have long coincided with the industrial concentration of knowledge-intensive activities in metropolitan areas. Among the reasons for this, in-demand employees quite frequently already reside in the urban agglomerations where industrial districts usually emerge, while entry-level employees are both available elsewhere and mobile (Angel 1989; Malecki 1987). Additionally, with their "potential for sophisticated leisure and consumption" (Castells 1988, p. 60) and spousal career opportunities, major cities often satisfy both workers' lifestyle preferences and firm's locational needs.

2.   Useful overviews of high technology's spatial organization include Storper and Walker (1989), Malecki (1991), and Castells (1989, 1996). Representative works on the new industrial geography for software production include Saxenian (1994) and Markusen (1996). Storper and Christopherson (1985; Christopherson and Storper 1986; Christopherson 1996) describe the geography of entertainment production.

3.   Here I borrow Howard Becker's methodological "trick" (in turn borrowed from Everett C. Hughes) of describing deterministic processes as a series of contingencies (Becker 1998, pp. 28-35).

4.   Conversely, the Internet also facilitates geographical concentration of certain activity. Notably, producer services like law firms, accounting, and marketing tend to agglomerate in global cities, even as the Internet makes possible their increasing distance from business clients (Schoonmaker 1996; Sassen 1996).

5.   Research on other industries suggests that entrepreneurs rarely migrate to start their own companies and instead start them in situ (Molotch, Woolley, and Jori 1998, p. 145; Reynolds 1989, p. 8). This pattern held true for software entrepreneurs in my research sample, although the case of Oddworld Inhabitants, a San Luis Obispo video game publisher, provides at least one exception. The circumstances of its San Luis Obispo location appear unusual. The firm's primary investor was simultaneously funding another local company and attached one condition to his Oddworld offer. He wanted to show clients his companies on business tours up the coast of California. That meant "we needed to take a look at San Luis Obispo," a place which Oddworld's cofounder had previously only known as "a sign on the road," yet which they now acknowledge met their quality-of-life needs (personal field notes; see also Utterman and DeMaria 1998).

6.   While not within easy daily commuting distanced of Los Angeles, too much should not be made of Santa Barbara's 60-90 mile distance from the larger metropolitan area. Several software executives highly value how the city is still a "stone's throw from Hollywood."

7.   Executives need not relocate their entire firm to Santa Barbara to live there. Instead, many executives (from Los Angeles or further) buy second homes in secluded local neighborhoods like Montecito or Hollister Ranch, as well as exclusive communities outside the South Coast, like Santa Ynez. More generally, Santa Barbara has long been a popular weekend destination for Los Angeles residents.

8.   Firms and boosters in other Southern California high-tech regions emphasize their quality-of-life contrasts to Los Angeles as well. A human resources spokesperson for a San Diego firm says recruiters there refrain from associating their region's high-tech growth to Los Angeles, because the latter invokes "earthquakes and guns, which is a drawback. They would worry that it would taint what we are pushing, which is the quality of life here" (quoted in Kaplan 1998, p. D12).

9.   San Luis Obispo Country's tax base is sustained largely by PG&E's nuclear power plant, which generated 15 times more property tax revenue in 1995 than the next-highest paying property owner.

10.   Microsoft founders Bill Gates and Paul Allen started the company in Albuquerque, New Mexico, but relocated it to Seattle, Washington, in 1979 because they wanted to live in their home state; their locational decision was not affected by venture-capital financing or regional economic development programs (Haug 1991, p. 880). In subsequent years, the corporation has attracted vast pools of labor, suppliers, and contractors by virtue of its sheer industrial dominance, thereby short-circuiting a more gradual path of industrial district formation.

11.   There may be a limit to this process. Rapid growth increased the division of labor within several firms I studied; consequently, many moved routine production and service out of quality-of-life districts to more cost-factor conscious sites within the United States and overseas to countries like Ireland, Scotland, and Brazil.

12.   Retirees constitute over 25 percent of all residents in neighboring communities like Pismo Beach.

13.   Ethnic and racial homogenization is not absolute, because many of these elite workers bring demand for domestic and other service work which (in the research sites) Latino workers predominantly fill (see Mollenkopt and Castells 1991). However, these lower-income workers often can only afford to live in communities outside the quality-of-life district.

REFERENCES

Ady, R.M. 1986. "Criteria Used for Facility Location Selection." Pp. 72-84 in *Financing Economic Development in the 1980s,* edited by N. Walzer and D. Chicoine. New York: Praeger.

Aglietta, M. 1979. *A Theory of Capitalist Regulation: The U.S. Experience.* London: New Left Books.

Angel, D.P. 1989. "The Labor Market for Engineers in the U.S. Semiconductor Industry." *Economic Geography* 65: 99-112.

Becker, H.S. 1998. *Tricks of the Trade: How to Think about your Research While You're Doing it.* Chicago: University of Chicago Press.

Belser, K. 1970. "The Making of Slurban America." *Cry California* 5(4): 1-18.

Boden, D., and H.L. Molotch. 1994. "The Compulsion of Proximity." Pp. 257-286 in *NowHere: Space, Time and Modernity,* edited by R. Friedland and D. Boden. Berkeley: University of California Press.

Capek, S.M., and J.I. Gilderbloom. 1992. *Community versus Commodity: Tenants and the American City.* Albany: State University of New York.

Castells, M. 1988. "The New Industrial Space: Information-Technology Manufacturing and Spatial Structure in the United States." Pp. 43-99 in *American's New Market Geography,* edited by G. Sternlieb and J.W. Hughes. New Brunswick, NJ: Center for Urban Policy Research.

_____. 1989. *The Informational City: Information Technology, Economic Restructuring and the Urban-Regional Process.* Oxford: Blackwell.

_____. 1996. *The Rise of the Network Society.* Cambridge, MA: Blackwell.

Christopherson, S. 1996. "Flexibility and Adaptation in Industrial Relations: The Exceptional Case of the U.S. Media Entertainment Industries." Pp. 86-112 in *Under the Stars: Essays on Labor Relations in Arts and Entertainment,* edited by L.S. Gray and R.L. Seeber. Ithaca, NY: ILR Press/Cornell.

Christopherson, S., and M. Storper. 1986. "The City as Studio; The World as Back Lot: The Impact of Vertical Disintegration on the Location of the Motion Picture Industry." *Environment and Planning D: Society and Space* 4: 305-320.

Clavel, P. 1986. *The Progressive City: Planning and Participation, 1969-1984.* New Brunswick, NJ: Rutgers.

Cox, K.R., and A. Mair. 1988. "Locality and Community in the Politics of Local Economic Development." *Annals of the Association of American Geographers* 78(2): 307-325.

Dicken, P. 1992. *Global Shift: The Internationalization of Economic Activity,* 2nd ed. New York: Guilford Press.

Epstein, B. 1991. *Political Protest and Cultural Revolution: Nonviolent Direct Action in the 1970s and 1980s.* Berkeley: University of California Press.

Feldman, M.M.A. 1997. "Spatial Structures of Regulation and Urban Regimes." Pp. 30-50 in *Reconstructing Urban Regime Theory: Regulating Urban Politics in a Global Economy,* edited by M. Lauria. Thousand Oaks, CA: Sage.

Glasmeier, A. 1988. "Factors Governing the Development of High Tech Industry Agglomerations: A Tale of Three Cities." *Regional Studies* 22(4): 287-301.

Harvey, D. 1989. *The Condition of Postmodernity: An Enquiry into the Origins of Cultural Change.* Cambridge, MA: Blackwell.

Haug, P. 1991. "Regional Formation of High-Technology Service Industries: The Software Industry in Washington State." *Environment and Planning A* 23(6): 869-884.

Hayes, D. 1989. *Behind the Silicon Curtain: The Seduction of Work in a Lonely Era.* Boston: South End Press.

Helft, M. 1997. "Sun, Sand, and Silicon." *Los Angeles Times,* January 20, pp. D1, D5.

Hof, R., and S. Hamm. 1997. "Too Much of a Good Thing?" *Business Week,* August 25, pp. 134-135.

Kaplan, K. 1998. "Tech Coast: Entrepreneurs and Officials Seek to Ride an Innovation Wave to Rival that of Silicon Valley." *Los Angeles Times,* March 9, pp. D1, D12.

Knight, R.V. 1989. "City Development and Urbanization: Building the Knowledge Based City." Pp. 223-242 in *Cities in a Global Society,* edited by R.V. Knight and G. Gappert. Newbury Park, CA: Sage.

Kotkin, J. 1998a. "The Dream Suburb Eating L.A." *Los Angeles Times,* March 22, pp. M1, M6.

_____. 1998b. "Business Leadership in the New Economy: Southern California at a Crossroad." La Jolla Institute Report, in collaboration with Pepperdine Institute for Public Policy and the Center for Continuing Study of the California Economy.

Lipietz, A. 1987. *Mirages and Miracles: The Crisis of Global Fordism,* trans. by D. Macey. London: Verso.

Logan, J.R. 1978. "Growth, Politics, and the Stratification of Places." *American Journal of Sociology* 84(2): 404-416.

Malecki, E.J. 1980. "Corporate Organization of R and D and the Location of Technological Activities." *Regional Studies* 14: 219-234.

_____. 1987. "The R&D Location Decision of the Firm and "Creative" Regions—A Survey." *Technovation* 6: 205-222.

_____. 1991. *Technology and Economic Development: The Dynamics of Local, Regional, and National Change.* New York: Longman Scientific & Technica John Wiley & Sons.

Markusen, A. 1996. "Sticky Places in Slippery Space: A Typology of Industrial District." *Economic Geography* 72(2): 294-314.

McKeen, R. 1988. *Parade Along the Creek: Memories of Growing Up with San Luis Obispo.* San Luis Obispo, CA: Rose McKeen.

Miller, G. 1998. "Pretenders to Silicon Valley's Throne." *Los Angeles Times*, March 8, pp. A1, A26.

Mollenkopf, J., and M. Castells, eds. 1991. *Dual City: Restructuring New York*. New York: Russel Sage Foundation.

Molotch, H., and W. Freudenburg. 1996. *Santa Barbara County: Two Paths*. OCS Study MMS 96-0036 under Contract No. 14-35-001-30663. Camarillo, CA: US Minerals Management Service, Pacific Region.

Molotch, H., J. Woolley, and T. Jori. 1998. "Growing Firms in Declining Fields: Unanticipated Impacts of Oil Development." *Society and Natural Resources* 11: 137-156.

Nevarez, L. 1996. "Just Wait Until There's a Drought: Mediating Environmental Crises for Urban Growth." *Antipode* 28(3): 246-272.

Pear, R. 1998. "Accord Would Increase Cap on Visas for Skilled Workers." *New York Times*, July 25, p. A7.

Reynolds, P. 1989. "New Firms: Enhancing their Growth." *Economic Development Commentary* 13(2): 4-11.

Roobeek, A. 1987. "The Crisis of Fordism and the Rise of a New Technological Paradigm." *Futures* 19(2): 129-154.

Rosegrant, S., and D.R. Lampe. 1992. *Route 128: Lessons from Boston's High-Tech Community*. New York: Basic Books.

Sassen, S. 1996. "States and the New Geography of Power." Paper presented at the annual meeting of the American Sociological Association, August 16-20, New York.

Saxenian, A. 1984. "The Urban Contradictions of Silicon Valley: Regional Growth and the Restructuring of the Semiconductor Industry." Pp. 163-197 in *Sunbelt Snowbelt: Urban Development and Regional Restructuring*, edited by L. Sawers and W.K. Tabb. New York: Oxford University Press.

_____. 1994. *Regional Networks: Industrial Adaptation in Silicon Valley and Route 128*. Cambridge: Harvard University Press.

Schoonmaker, S. 1996. "Annihilating Space with Time: Digital Trade, Services, and Capitalist Development." Paper presented at the annual meeting of the American Sociological Association, August 16-20, New York.

Scott, A.J. 1993. *Technopolis: High-Technology Industry and Regional Development in Southern California*. Berkeley: University of California.

_____. 1995. "The Geographic Foundations of Industrial Performance."' *Competition & Change* 1(1): 51-66.

_____. 1996. "Regional Motors of the Global Economy." *Futures* 28(5): 391-411.

Starr, K. 1990. *Material Dreams: Southern California Through the 1920s*. New York: Oxford University Press.

Storper, M., and S. Christopherson. 1985. *The Changing Organization and Location of the Motion Picture Industry: Interregional Shifts in the United States*. Los Angeles: UCLA Graduate School of Architecture and Urban Planning.

Storper, M., and R. Walker. 1989. *The Capitalist Imperative: Territory, Technology, and Industrial Growth*. Oxford: Blackwell.

Utterman, A., and R. DeMaria. 1998. "It's an Odd, Odd, Odd, Odd World: How Oddworld Created a Formula-Defying Hit Game." *Interactivity* 4(3): 46-52.

Van de Kamp, M. 1996. "Local Defense Industry Pioneer Dies." *Santa Barbara News-Press*, June 29, pp. A1, A18.

Warner, K., H. Molotch, with A. Lategola. 1992. *Growth Control: Inner Workings and External Effects*. Berkeley: California Policy Seminar, University of California.

Zukin, S. 1989. *Loft Living: Culture and Capital in Urban Change*, 2nd ed. New Brunswick, NJ: Rutgers University Press.

PART IV

RESIDENTIAL COMMUNITY OF SENIOR CITIZENS

IDENTIFYING THE ELEMENTS
OF COMMUNITY CHARACTER:
A CASE STUDY OF COMMUNITY DIMENSIONALITY
IN OLD AGE RESIDENTIAL AREAS

Ivan J. Townshend and Wayne K.D. Davies

ABSTRACT

The systematic study of the differences between social areas or place communities within cities has been handicapped by the fragmentation of work into several different traditions of analysis. A review of these traditions shows that they have produced a great deal of knowledge on the differentiation of places but there is a need to integrate the various approaches and to define and empirically measure the separate dimensions or elements of community variation. A total of 54 individual indicators of variation dealing with the local interactions of residents, as well as their perception, attitudes, and feelings toward their community areas were derived from a questionnaire survey in old-age areas in Calgary (Alberta, Canada). A multivariate analysis of the data revealed the presence of 17 different dimensions of variation, accounting for almost 70 percent of the variance in the data set, each of which can be regarded as part of the multidimensional character of social areas in cities in the behavioral and cognitive-affective domains.

Research in Community Sociology, Volume 9, pages 219-251.
Copyright © 1999 by JAI Press Inc.
All rights of reproduction in any form reserved.
ISBN: 0-7623-0498-7

INTRODUCTION

Cities have often been described as mosaics of social worlds because they are composed of a large number of areas of different character, making the urban experience endlessly fascinating. Some may argue that the individuality of places is so unique that only subjective descriptions of area, based on intuitive insights into their distinctiveness, can capture their essential character—an approach that has gained new impetus with postmodern ideas. But those who seek to develop a body of systematic literature on the ways that areas differ from one another in a social context have adopted very different approaches. Just as psychologists like Spearman (1904) have been able to isolate different features of intelligence and human personalities—described as the elements or separate dimensions of variation—so some students of social areas have tried to isolate and measure the various sources of variation in cities that in combination produce territorial communities of different character. Unfortunately, most of this urban literature deals with only part of the rich variety of features that account for the differentiation of distinctive areas of the city—whether through the census variable approach of factorial ecology; the extent of neighboring; the study of images, or the degree of symbolism of areas, and so forth. A systematic integration of these partial perspectives may not be immediately forthcoming. In fact the author of a well-known book on neighborhoods and communities (Keller 1968, 1988) was pessimistic of past progress in the development of a systematic literature: "despite the hundreds and even thousands of existing community studies we do not have even the rudiments for a comprehensive classification—no Periodic table, no Leontieff chart. The legacy of past studies thus lies fallow" (Keller 1988, p. 177). Many students of place communities would argue that such systematization is impossible. This paper takes the opposite view by arguing that it is possible to identify and measure the range of features that account for the differentiation of intra-urban space and the creation of areas or territorial communities of different character. Indeed, contrary to Keller's viewpoint, there has been considerable progress in this approach. However, there is still, conceptually, a need to unpack the various sources of differentiation that are embedded in the concept of community—considered in a territorial not a relational context—to provide more empirical evidence of the differentiation of the composite elements. These are the goals of this study, which is divided into four sections: a brief review of the various traditions in the conceptualization or measurement of social areas or place communities in cities; the data and techniques used in the case study; the results derived; and a brief conclusion. These objectives mean that the study does not deal with the social-structural and individual forces that lie behind community differences— part of the so-called structuration approach of Giddens (1984).

TRADITIONS IN THE STUDY OF URBAN SOCIAL DIFFERENTIATION

More than a century has passed since Booth's (1897) investigations into the life and labor of the people of London that pioneered the social survey tradition and left us a legacy of detailed case studies of the various areas of London, detailed maps of the variation of poverty, and the conditions under which people laboured. But Booth also provided a quantitative measurement of the extent of social differentiation in London by combining a set of census indicators to define a single index of what he call the "social condition" of areas (Booth 1893). It can be argued that this quantitative approach provided the beginnings of comparative and systematic work on the social variation of urban areas. Yet, unfortunately for the coherent development of the field, this contribution was almost forgotten in subsequent work. Instead, the systematic study of the variation of social areas in cities has been developed through very different traditions, frequently associated with students from different disciplines—often with minimum contact between them—who have stressed different parts of the multidimensional reality of the urban social mosaic.

One of the best known of these traditions is represented by continued efforts to refine the measurement of urban social variation using census variables, as seen in the 3-axis model of Shevky and Bell (1955) in which urbanization or family status and ethnicity needed to be added to the social rank axis—the latter in many ways mirroring Booth's index of social condition. The adoption of factorial methods confirmed the importance of these axes as dimensions of social variation (Berry 1971; Murdie 1969). But subsequent work, using far wider data sets, has shown that there are far more axes of differentiation involved in Western cities than was previously thought (Davies 1984; Davies and Murdie 1991), while other workers have focused on defining the variations in areal types (Weiss 1988). A major limitation of these approaches is that most of the work has been based on census variables, meaning that only the social variety of census areas has been dealt with. Behavioral and attitudinal variations have been ignored in this approach, ensuring that the factorial ecology approach only deals with part of the complexity and character of intra-urban social variation.

A less quantitative and more conceptual and theoretical tradition can be seen in studies initiated by the Chicago School of Human Ecology in the 1920s. One of the key objectives of these researchers was to identify and analyze the so-called "natural areas" or distinctive community areas of the city. Case studies of particular areas and distinctive groups were combined with the use of concepts developed in plant ecology to interpret the spatial variations of cities. But pioneers in this tradition also sought to uncover the distinctive features that define variations in place-based communities. For example, Park (1925, p. 7) recognized the importance of proximity and neighborly contact, local interests, and associations that bred local sentiment and local government, while Keller (1968, p. 87) pointed to the importance of local area boundaries. Additional breakthroughs in understanding the variety of features involved in territorial community definition were provided by workers in allied areas. One of the best known was Hillery's (1955) attempt to summarize the variety of common features in the definition of territorial communities under the headings of "area, common ties, and social interaction." These early ecological studies were followed by two very different approaches, which can be summarized as the behavioral and the social psychological.

In the case of the behavioral approach the emphasis was on the interaction of people in subareas in cities. Many studies were designed to show the breakdown of local area connectivity, and with it a decrease in the importance of local residential areas in people's lives due to the decline of the friction of distance. The declining importance of local community areas as containers of behavioral interactions led to the ideas of "community without propinquity" (Webber 1964)—the demonstration that associations between people take place over larger areas thus liberating community from spatial or local area dependence (Wellman and Leighton 1979); and more recently, the recognition of the virtual community (Rheingold 1993). However, other studies also pointed to the continued importance of intra-urban community. Students of ethnic areas, gangs, and spatially immobile groups such as the elderly, showed the vital importance of local areas for these groups, indicating that local communities based on common associations with place still existed, while other researchers showed that neighboring could still play and important role (Bulmer 1986; Unger and Wandersman 1985) in urban social life. While there are still many studies of the importance of local area interaction to the creation of distinctive social areas, much of the interest in local resident interaction has been subsumed in the more general study of social networks (Wellman and Berkowitz 1988)—an analytically advanced and methodologically sophisticated approach that stresses the importance of social ties that extend beyond the immediacy of local community areas.

Although the origins of the social psychological approach to community study can be found in Park's (1925) work, Firey's (1947) demonstration of the importance of symbolism as well as sentiment in differentiating places and Lynch's (1960) work on images sparked off major interest in the importance of people's psychological attachment to places. But it was Suttles' (1972) demonstration that communities were "socially constructed," not "given," that led to the crystallization of a new approach to the study of social areas and the identification of place communities. This meant that communities were not simply a "bundle of features and interactions" derived from the social character or behavior of the residents. Instead, much of the differentiation of these territorial entities were constructed by the perceptions, feelings, and attitudes of people, both from within and from outside the area. Moreover, these areas were not fixed or spatially determined entities—they varied in size and shape because they were differentially perceived by various groups. In addition it was recognized that just as people had varied commitment to their local area—in Janowitz's (1967) words, they were "communities of limited liability"—so people identified with what Hunter (1974) described as a "hierarchy of symbolic communities" of different scales, from blocks to local communities to sectors of the city, or even to the city itself and beyond. These changes led students of community to argue that there are three crucial categories or sources of variation in the multidimensional nature of communities: the ecological and sustenance community, the social interactional and institutional community, and the social psychological and cultural community (Hunter 1974; Hunter and Riger 1986).

Even more rigorous conceptual and analytical advances in the study of social areas and communities were produced by exponents of a new field called community psychology. Although the authors of a major review argued that the initial work in the study of "sense of community" added to knowledge in the field, they criticized these contributions as "lacking a coherently articulated conceptual perspective focused on sense of community [because] none of the measures used in the studies were developed directly from a definition of sense of community" (McMillan and Chavis 1986, p. 8). They proceeded to rectify this situation by identifying four major elements as being crucial to the concept: fulfillment of needs, membership, influence over group activities, and shared connections; although their discussion of many of these elements makes it clear that each of these categories has a series of sub-elements. In a parallel work, Unger and Wandersman (1985) attempted a similar task in the context of neighboring. Rather than restricting the idea to the traditional interaction features related to social support and social networks, they showed how neighboring needed to incorporate psychological issues—moving it into the realm of spatial or cognitive identification and into the affective domain of feelings and attitudes about places. Within each of these four categories their review identified a series of separate components of differentiation, although it must be emphasized that there is overlap between the elements that were proposed as comprising "neighboring" and "sense of community." Subsequent analytical work in the field has attempted to refine and measure these two important concepts. They have been treated either as single entities (Plas and Lewis 1996; Skjaeveland et al. 1996) or in combination, such as Weenig, Schmidt, and Middens' (1990) use of several variables to measure features of community differentiation called "sense of community" and "neighboring," as well as their role in defining a fourfold typology of communities in Dutch cities. Although this literature has produced some of the most comprehensive studies of community variation it is rarely linked with studies of the area or ecological approaches, although Coulton, Korbin, and Su (1996) have tried to measure the distinctive environmental features of place to define the neighborhood context of these behavioral and cognitive-affective approaches.

A fifth approach to the study of community differences can be seen in the more applied work of the architects and planners of residential areas. Their efforts to create distinctive residential areas in the city—either on the grounds of aesthetics, health, or quality of life, or because they wished to obtain a competitive advantage in the sale of houses in these areas—go back to the origin of cities. But the modern attempt to develop distinctive areas can be traced back to the Garden City movement and subsequently to Perry's (1929) attempt to codify the basic principles upon which residential communities should be built. Here the objective was not only to provide basic services to these areas, but, given the greater anonymity of life in suburban areas, to encourage greater integration between the residents of these communities. Although subsequent modification and additions to Perry's list of desired features—especially the addition of cul-de-sacs and networks of walkways to community nodes—did not usher in a new phase of community integration, they provided more livable if rather sterile communities because of their almost exclusive residential character. Moreover, the problems caused by the aging of areas, the provision of new shopping centers outside the area, and increasing mobility that led people to spend more time outside their neighborhood areas, led to criticisms of the neighborhood unit concept. Nevertheless, many of the principles still dominate the development of contemporary planned residential units. In addition, it is worth remembering that planners, since time immemorial, have been attempting to influence behavior by their designs, while Lynch's (1960) seminal work on perception was designed to show how areas had different imagability so as to guide future development. In the last 20 years, a series of much more explicit design features linked to behavioral and attitudinal features have been applied to the construction of new residential areas and to new towns, incorporating, for example, the pattern language ideas of Alexander, Ishikawa, and Silverstein (1977).

All of these traditions have contributed to our understanding of the differentiation of social or residential areas within cities—that is, intra-urban place-communities. As well, there are increasing signs of cross-fertilization of the ideas and their application to the creation of the built environment. Plas and Lewis (1996), for example, have recently demonstrated the utility of McMillan and Chavis's (1986) sense of community ideas in the context of the planned town of Seaside. Nevertheless, the systematic study of place-communities or social areas in cities has been fragmented by the focus on the analyses of sets of different community features and by the discipline- or tradition-specific emphases described above. These problems led to arguments for the integration of the field and the development of a conceptual model or classificatory schema designed to summarize the variety of elements of differentiation isolated in the various traditions discussed above (Davies 1992, 1995; Davies and Herbert 1993). The classification, summarized in the first column of Table 1, extended the contributions of many people, proposing that the multidimensional character of place-communities could be categorized in terms of three broad categories or domains of the elements involved in community variation: *Areal or Environmental Content, Behavior or Interaction,* and *Conceptual Identity*—the latter being separated into *Cognitive* and *Affective* subdomains. All of the elements, whether features or attitudes, have to be set in both the *Dynamic* or temporal contexts; and can apply at various ecological or geographical *scales*.

In each of the three main domains (Areal Content, Behavior/Interaction, Conceptual Identity) a series of individual dimensions or sources of variation were proposed. When combined, they account for, or at least provide a preliminary checklist, of the ways that local or place-communities may be seen to differ. Some, such as the factorial ecology dimensions that summarize social variety in the Areal Content domain, or the symbolic and sentiment dimensions in the Affective domain described above, are well known. Others, especially those in the Cognitive and Affective domains, need to be more carefully isolated in both conceptual terms and through empirical confirmation in order that different labels are not given to the same concept. In addition, it is necessary to relate the ideas contained in the conceptual schema (Davies and Herbert 1993, p. 36; see also Table 1, 1st col.) to the local culture and to the forces in the surrounding society that cause these variations to occur.

An obvious issue surrounding the empirical testing of the conceptual schema summarized in Table 1 (1st col.) is that in toto it may be too comprehensive for any *single* empirical study because it attempts to capture a full array of physical, social, behavioral, cognitive, and attitudinal dimensions of variation in the communities of cities. In addition, it deals with changes in these dimensions through time and their manifestation at different resolutions or spatial scales. Empirical verification of the utility and composition of such a conceptual model will involve studies that deal with parts of the schema and then systematically attempt to integrate the elements, their relationship to one another, their presence or their absence in some communities, and indeed their variation through space and time. Yet in a simple and approachable way, the framework also provides a means for researchers to hold one domain (or dimensions within one domain) relatively constant and examine the dimensional variation in the other domains. For example, the framework could be used to determine the number of different community dimensions in the Behavioral and Conceptual Identity domains by looking at areas of a specific age, socioeconomic, or family status type, or those that contain relatively similar design morphologies and physical environments. Likewise, holding all but the Dynamic domain constant could provide insight into the variation in community dimensionality through time for all other domains. Alternately, one could hold all but the Scale domain constant in order to investigate geographical scale effects—that is, the intra-urban scales at which particular dimensions of community may be maximized, at what scale they appear or disappear, and in what way and in what combinations they relate to each other for different spatial geometries. It is not difficult to imagine the implications of the latter for urban design initiatives. Therefore, the conceptual schema summarized in Table 1 has the potential to furnish students of community with a more comprehensive and much needed conceptual and analytical device from which to understand the bases of community differentiation.

Table 1. Variables Used to Index Postulated Domains and Dimensions

Postulated
Dimensions Variable Codes and Titles   Description of Variables

Postulated Domains: A, B, CP, CA
A: Areal Content (not used)
A1: Size/Distance; A2: Environment; A3: Facilities/Stores, etc.; A4: Morphology; A5: Social Variety—Factorial Ecology Dimensions
B: Behavior (Interactions)

Postulated Dimensions	Variable Codes and Titles		Description of Variables
B1	Facility use	V1	Maximum facility use	Max. frequency of use of any one community-based facility in a month
		V2	Known facilities	Total no. of facilities (shops, etc.) known in area
		V3	Facility use score	Total weighted usage of all facilities used in area
B2	Informal interaction	V4	Neighbor recognition	No. of 20 nearest neighbors recognize on the street
	Non-intimate	V5	Neighbor conversations	No. of 20 nearest neighbors regularly converse with
		V6	Neighbor first name	No. of 20 nearest neighbors known by first name
		V7	Neighbor visits	No. of 20 nearest neighbors visited in home: monthly
	Intimate	V8	Neighbor close friends	No. of 20 nearest neighbors considered to be close friends.
		V9	Neighbor confidant	No. of 20 nearest neighbors able to discuss intimate problems with
		V10	Friendship clustering	Percentage of all friends living within 3 or 4 blocks
		V11	New local friends	No. of block neighbors who have become close friends
B3	Mutual informal cooperation	V12	Borrowing	Frequency of borrowing from neighbors in the past month
		V13	Home visits	Frequency of neighbors visiting in house in the past month
		V14	Information aid	Frequency of requesting information/advice from neighbors in the past month
		V15	Physical aid	Frequency of asking neighbors for physical help in the past month
B4	Organizations	V16	Organizations number	Membership in local voluntary organizations: number of organizations
		V17	Organization dedication	Degree of involvement in organizations
B5	Political participation	V18	Local political orientation	Propensity to vote in community association and civic elections
		V19	Outside voting	Propensity to vote in provincial and federal elections

(continued)

Table 1 (Continued)

Postulated Dimensions	*Variable Codes and Titles*		*Description of Variables*
B6	Supportive milleu	V20 Govt. agency support	Extent of support of local government agencies for the needs of the community
		V21 Organization support	Extent of support by organizations/agencies in the city for the local community
B7	*Economic or capital flows (not used)*		
CP: Conceptual Identity, Perception and Cognition			
CP1	*Place identity*	(not used)	
CP2	Cognitive mapping	V22 Mappability	Perceived ability to map main 4 or 5 streets in community area
		V23 Street naming	Perceived ability to name the main 4 or 5 streets in community area
		V24 Transit stops	Perceived ability to locate nearest transit stop on a map
		V25 Convenience location	Perceived ability to locate nearest convenience store on a map
CP3	People identity	V26 People similarity	Perceived similarity of age, appearance, wealth, and behavior of 20 nearest neighbors
		V27 Age similarity	Perceived age similarity of 20 nearest neighbors
		V28 Ethnic similarity	Perceived ethnic similarity of 20 nearest neighbors
		V29 Appearance similarity	Perceived similarity in dress/style of 20 nearest neighbors
CP4	*Symbolic communication*	(not used)	
CA: Conceptual Identity, Affective (Attitudes and Motivation)			
CA1	Place symbolism	V30 Financial symbolism	Degree to which residence in area signifies financial success
		V31 Status symbolism	Degree to which residence in area signifies status enhancement
CA2	Sentiment and attachment	V32 Age symbolism	Degree to which community area signifies age homogeneity
		V55 Rootedness	Degree of attachment to area (variable dropped from analysis—see text)
CA3	Evaluation	V33 Relative satisfaction	Relative satisfaction with present community compared to others lived in
		V34 Relative desirability	Relative desirability of present community compared to others lived in
CA4	Nuisances— place appearance	V35 Local nuisances	Degree of nuisances occurring within community area
		V36 Extra-local nuisances	Degree of annoyances from outside which impinge on the community
CA5	Safety and security	V37 Night safety	Perceived safety in the community after dark

(continued)

Table 1   (Continued)

Postulated Dimensions	Variable Codes and Titles		Description of Variables
		V38 General safety	Perceived safety/security of the local community area
		V39 Personal fear	Perceived fear of personal safety if alone in the community
		V40 Property fear	Perceived fear of break-and-enter or property vandalism
CA6	Empowerment	V41 Personal power	Personal power/influence in opposing unwanted development in the area
		V42 Informal collective power	Perceived power by neighbors uniting in opposition to unwanted development
		V43 Formal collective power	Perceived power by collective action in opposing unwanted development
CA7	Place appearance	V44 Appearance rating	Rating of tidiness/maintenance of the community area
CA8	Latent involvement/ participation	V46 Latent aid	Expected willingness of neighbours to collect mail and check house if away
		V47 Non-obligatory aid	Perception that neighbor participation is obligatory
		V48 N'hood latent participation	Degree to which residents are perceived to be always willing to help
CA9	Aesthetics	V45 Relative beauty	Rating of "beauty" of present community area compared to others in the city
CA10	Common values	V49 Life agreement	Perceived commonality with neighbors about what is important in life
		V50 Moral similarity	Perceived commonality with neighbors of social and moral behavior
		V51 Non-offensive lifestyles	Perception that some neighbors exhibit offensive lifestyles
CA11	Empathy and belonging	V52 Belonging	Feeling that respondents truly "belong" in the community area
		V53 Sense of community	Extent to which the neighborhood provides a sense of community
		V54 Cohesion	Index of Cohesion (average of 5 indicators: belonging, sense of community, feeling at home, loyalty to others, fellowship)

Recognizing the need for an incremental approach to testing the conceptual schema, this study focuses on the extent to which the dimensions of variation proposed in the Behavioral and Conceptual Identity domains can be empirically recognized as separate and distinctive sources of variation. This is achieved by means of a case study of old-age residential areas within the city of Calgary (Canada). For the purposes of this analysis, we have heuristically operationalized "old-age residential areas" based on relative age concentration criteria. These areas are those census tracts with higher than metropolitan average concentrations of individuals aged 55 or older but *simultaneously* lower than metropolitan average concentrations of individuals of two other major age groupings.[1] These types of areas are not unique to Calgary—120 such areas were identified within the Canadian metropolitan system in 1991, and they exist in 80 percent of Canada's 25 metropolitan areas.[2] In absolute terms the number of areas with age concentration profiles as defined above range from 23 in Toronto to one in St. John's. In relative terms they range from 1.2 percent of tracts in St. Catharines-Niagara to 7.5 percent of tracts in Edmonton, although on average they comprise 3.9 percent of the metropolitan area census tracts.

Despite the age concentration that sets these areas apart from other urban neighborhoods, these areas should not be interpreted as geriatric ghettoes because they do typically exhibit a range of social characteristics that make them similar to the average Canadian neighborhood in many respects. The areas are generally similar to the national neighborhood profile in terms of Areal Content features such as socioeconomic status, ethnic status, housing attributes, and income levels and occupational profiles. However, the age profile means that higher proportions of retired or semiretired individuals can be expected in these areas. In the broader Canadian metropolitan context, the major differences in Areal Content features are associated with what others (Davies and Murdie 1991) have termed Early-Late Family attributes, Family and Age attributes, Movers, and a Young Adult social dimension, although it is primarily age and family status features that differentiate these residential areas.[3] These neighborhoods generally have high concentrations of completed families (empty-nesters), high concentrations of early and late middle-aged individuals, older children if any remain at home, and few young adults aged 20 to 24 years. In 1991 the areas had a relative paucity of large households and young families. Given these features, it is not surprising that the areas may be experiencing greater household turnovers with marginally higher than average proportions of local or intra-urban movers. This means the areas are aging inner-city or inner-suburban postwar neighborhoods. As Moore and Rosenberg (1997) have pointed out, the social attributes and community character of such areas is expected to increasingly ripple through Canadian urban social space with the structural aging of the population.

These aggregate similarities and differences at a national scale should not obscure the fact that there may be important city-specific differences in the degree to which the old-age areas are similar or different to the city or metropolitan-wide profile of neighborhoods. There is an obvious need to explore the relevance of the conceptual model summarized in Table 1 for all different types of social areas—whether identified at a national urban system scale or at a metropolitan scale. However, the decision to focus this empirical study on old-age areas was justified on a number of grounds. Community researchers and practitioners have long argued that community, in the sense of place-based community, may be more important for some social groups than others. The elderly, for example, may not only become more spatially constrained as a natural aging process, but in-situ aging may have created strong attachments to place (Campbell et al. 1976; Rowles 1978; Herbert and Peace 1980). In addition, it is increasingly recognized that demographic structural change has given rise to elders who may now be characterized as being in their "third age." This has produced a renewed societal and individual search for both community and self-identity—a feature that may increasingly rely on a rediscovery of "attachment to place community" (Laslett 1987,1991).

The growth in the development of age-exclusive retirement villages within metropolitan areas in the past few decades attests to the potential importance of rediscovering Behavioral and Conceptual Identity features of community within otherwise homogeneous (Areal Content) areas (Gober 1985; Heintz 1976; Seiler 1986; Stallman and Jones 1995). A content analysis of metropolitan newspapers in Alberta[4] indicates that these developments began in the early 1980s, and by 1993 approximately 48 and 67 retirement or age-restrictive villages had been developed in Calgary and Edmonton, respectively. Advertising brochures and slogans for these developments typically include not only demographic forecasts but statements about age-peer living, exclusivity, value commonality, well-being, friendship ties, and the maximization of self-fulfillment within segregated maintenance-free residential environments. This suggests that many of the behavioral and affective elements of place-community are being deliberately commodified and target-marketed to specific segments of a differentiated aging population. This age group may increasingly be searching for a sense of community in the urban environment—even though the majority of seniors will continue to age in-situ within established residential areas (Moore and Rosenberg 1997).

Given the large number of very different social area characteristics in even one city, it is unlikely that any single area or areas within a single city will contain all possible sources of community variation identified in Table 1. However, the inner suburban tracts of Canadian cities such as Calgary—those that contain many in their third age who have aged in-situ—may therefore be key areas with well-established social networks, friendship patterns, neighboring contacts, established community-based membership patterns, established cognitive patterns of community, and long established socio-emotional or affective attachments to place. In short, it may be expected that many of the dimensions of community summarized in Table 1 should be found in such areas.

It must be emphasized that the study is not designed to compare different areas but to measure and expose the extent to which the various dimensions or elements in Table 1 can be identified as distinctive dimensions of place-based community. If they can be confirmed, then the study provides evidence of the utility of the provisional classification of place-community elements identified in Table 1. This initial classification may well require modification as more evidence becomes available from studies of community dimensions found in different areas, times, or scales.

STUDY AREAS, DATA, AND TECHNIQUES

The utility of the summary conceptual schema, or the degree to which the proposed elements of community can be empirically recognized, is investigated through a case study in Calgary, Alberta, within areas that we have defined above as old-age neighborhoods. Calgary is a young and affluent city with over three-quarter of a million people. With a median age of 31.6 years and median household income levels of $44,417 at the last published census in 1991, Calgary ranked fourth among all census metropolitan areas (CMAs) in Canada on both the above age and income indicators (Statistics Canada 1992, 1993). Although it has low proportions in the elderly age groups (only 14.9% are over 55 years old and 7.8% over 65 years old) it is one of the most age-segregated CMAs in Canada at the census tract or neighborhood scale (Okraku 1987). Based on the 1991 data, there were 11 census tracts (the census equivalent of intra-urban community areas) with location quotients (LQ) over 2.0 for the population aged 55 or older, but simultaneously having LQs less than 1.0 for two other major groups of younger population. These areas, defined here as old-age residential areas, therefore, had twice the concentration of over 55 population as the metropolitan area as a whole, but also had below average concentrations for two other major age segments of younger population. In short, they were well-established inner-city or older suburban areas, and most contained predominantly single family residences built during the 1950s and 1960s. Based on objective census indicators the areas were significantly different to the remainder of Calgary's neighborhoods with the same kinds of features described for the national pattern (i.e., the differences are primarily associated with family structure, age structure, residential mobility, and one indicator of socioeconomic status was also different). For example, these tracts had few young children, smaller households, fewer two-parent families, and few young adults. They also had higher incidences of old age and late middle-age individuals, low female participation in the labor force, and relatively large numbers of completed or empty-nester families. With the exception of only one of the areas, these tracts are relatively stable—they had lower incidences of residential mobility, and had very little new housing development in the past decade. Taken together, the 11 areas were generally middle income with a median household income of $48,200, slightly above the Calgary average, and contained relatively few individuals employed in blue-collar occupations. In essence, the areas were close to being typical of other Calgary community areas, with the exception of high concentrations of old-age residents, and corresponding family structures of completed or empty-nester families.

In the interest of initially testing the schema with those in the areas who were likely to have developed extensive place-based behavioral and conceptual identity community elements (i.e., those that have aged in-situ), this study was restricted to residents with more than 20 years of residence at the same address. The sample of old-age residents, ideally defined as aged 55 or older, but operationally identified by a household member with more than 20 years of adult residence in the same place in one of the old-age residential areas, was identified by a systematic comparison on one-third of the households in the 1974 and 1994 telephone and reverse city directories for the areas. This yielded a total of 751 matching households from the 2,544 addresses compared, from which 380 completed a self-administered survey questionnaire.[5]

The survey instrument, consisting of almost 200 separate items and organized into six sections,[6] was designed around three major sets of questions. One dealt with basic residential history, demographic, and household characteristics— issues described in Table 1 as Areal Content. A second set measured attributes that should be associated with dimensions in the Behavioral, Cognitive, and Affective domains. The third, unrelated to this study, attempted to explore variations in individual perceptions of aging, psychological well-being, and individual self-fulfillment within the context of aging, retirement, and place-communities. The second component of the questionnaire provided the basic information for this study. Individual items or sets of items were developed in an attempt to tap into potentially distinctive dimensions of community that may fall within the Behavioral or Conceptual Identity domains of place-community that are identified in Table 1. Where possible, questionnaire items were conceptually based upon, or modified from, previous community studies. For example, within the context of the Behavioral domain, items measuring *facility use* drew on previous work in the field (Connerly 1985); *informal interaction* or neighboring items were based on the work of Weenig et al. (1990), Unger and Wandersman (1985), Rosow (1967), and Woolever (1992); and *intimate informal interaction* items were derived in part from concepts proposed by Lowenthal and Haven (1981), Shea et al. (1988), Lopata (1981), and Fried (1986). Constructs that measured *mutual informal cooperation*, sometimes identified as sub-elements of neighboring, were derived from studies by Unger and Wandersman (1985), O'Brien et al. (1989), and Weenig et al. (1990). Measures of *organization involvement* were developed from ideas proposed by Unger and Wandersman (1982), Wandersman (1981), Streib et al. (1985), McMillan and Chavis (1986), Logan and Rabrenovic (1990), and Davies and Townshend (1994). The concept of *political participation* included a number of scales of participation, from the local or neighborhood context to the federal context, although this can also be linked to issues of local autonomy and power (Streib et al. 1985). Additional items within this domain were an attempt to identify the degree to which there was a perceived *supportive milieu* (Gottlieb 1978; Hunter and Straggenborg 1986; Davidson 1979).

Within the context of what may be distinctive Cognitive dimensions of community, features of two major dimensions were identified: *cognitive mapping* (Unger and Wandersman 1985; Sarason 1974; Golant 1986); as well as *people identity* or familiarity on age-related as well as nonage attributes (McMillan and Chavis 1986; Unger and Wandersman 1985).

Questionnaire items that attempted to tap into the Affective structure of community were based on previously defined ideas such as: *status symbolism* (Ginsberg 1985; Coleman and Neugarten 1972; Hunter 1974); subjectively-based community or housing *evaluations of desirability factors* (Hunt and Ross 1990; Guest and Lee 1983; Unger and Wandersman 1982); perceived *externality or nuisance factors* (Chavis and Wandersman 1990; Logan and Rabrenovic 1990); the degree of community *safety and security* (Golant 1980); and issues of local resident collective *empowerment* or collective efficacy (Heller 1989). Other questionnaire items designed to tap into features of this domain were based on ideas normally associated with "sense of community." However, this concept can be broken down into separate ideas such as: a sense of *belonging* or *empathy* with neighbors, a sense of *rootedness* in place, and *common values* with neighbors (Weenig et al. 1990; Unger and Wandersman 1982, 1985; McMillan and Chavis 1986; Riger and Lavrakas 1981; Sarason 1974; Buckner 1988).

Table 1 identifies 54 variables, derived from either single or composite items in the survey instrument, that were potential indicators or surrogate measures of the features that may be associated with the dimensions or proposed separate sources of variation identified in the Behavioral and Conceptual Identity domains. The analysis did not include any potential Areal Content dimensions because it focused on age-segregated areas—one of the classic factorial ecology dimensions—and was carried out within one city within relatively homogeneous residential areas. Unfortunately not all of the dimensions of community differentiation proposed in the first column of Table 1 could be adequately examined. Adequate indicators were not available to measure either the Economic or Capital flows into or out of the residential areas, or a Symbolic Communication dimension—such as might be seen by the presence of territorial markers or by the deliberate addition of symbols identifying some group presence. Table 1 also shows that there were problems associated with the measurement of three other expected dimensions, which restricted the degree of fit of the empirical analysis to the proposed model. In the Cognitive domain it was taken for granted that Place Identity, as defined by a distinctive community name, was known to these long-time residents for two reasons. First, Calgary's residential areas are divided up into a series of named community areas that are confirmed by the city authorities (Davies and Townshend 1994), and second, the study was restricted to a small number of areas and to long-time residents, not to external observers. The length and complexity of the questionnaire also meant that only limited attention could be paid to the possible dimensions of Place Appearance and Aesthetics. These sources of differentiation are likely to be weak in the type of area studied here, given the architectural homogeneity and relative affluence of these essentially middle-income areas. In addition, questions that attempted to measure the familiar Sentiment dimension, usually measured by the "attachment to the area" or "degree of rootedness" of the population, had virtually identical ratings from the respondents, providing almost no variance or differentiating ability on these measures. Hence, these questions were dropped from the analysis, which meant that the study lost the ability to recognize separate *Sentiment* and *Attachment to Area* dimensions. Despite these operational problems, the study was able to provide measurements that should determine the extent to which a large number of separate dimensions of variation across both the Behavioral and Conceptual Identity domains were present in the old-age areas being sampled.

As far as possible the indicators were measured in five or six category scales to ensure consistency of measurement, although a few had to use four categories because of the nature of the data dealt with. In order to prevent overemphasis on a limited number of dimensions, between two and four indicators were used to index each particular axis or proposed dimension. Exceptions were the Place Appearance and Aesthetics dimensions, which have already been commented on. Rank-order correlation coefficients were calculated between each pair of variables and subjected to a principal axes factor analysis using the Component model, followed by direct oblimin rotation to a simple structure. The chosen solution was a 17-factor model, accounting for 69.7 percent of the variance. This model was only chosen after scrutinizing a range of different solutions, and was based on a variety of technical procedures to determine the most appropriate solution—such as the scree test, communality tipping points, inter-factor correlations, as well as the factor interpretation. At 17 axes all the factors had variance explanations greater than 1.0, all communalities were over 0.5, and there were no highly correlated axes—features which would have implied under- or over-factoring. The dimensions were also tested for technique-dependency and were not found to be a product of the statistical techniques chosen. Tests showed that almost identical interpretations of the dimensions reported here were obtained when a number of different technical decisions were taken. For example, using varimax rotation in place of oblique rotation, using Pearson product moment correlations in place of Spearman rank correlations, replacing the principal axes technique with PRINCALS (principal components analysis with alternating least squares)—a procedure that can use mixed mode data and can derive factors where the variables are related in non-linear ways (de Leeuw 1984; Gifi 1991)—or by allowing those indicators that could be measured at the interval scale to use this more detailed metric, all yielded similar interpretations. The stability of the dimensional structure was also investigated for alternate case-to-variable ratios, first by adding data for similar-profiled individuals residing in age-exclusive retirement communities (respondents not included in this study), and also by exploring the structure of subsets of the 380 respondents. These tests confirmed that the aggregate structure for the sample was stable, that the results from the alternative tests meant that the dimensional structure reported here could not be considered to be the consequence of the particular techniques adopted, and showed that the data set had a strong and inherently linear structure.

RESULTS

Characteristics of the Sample

The sampling strategy was relatively successful in identifying older residents aged 55 and older who had resided in the same community for 20 or more years. Of the 380 respondents (51% response rate), 41 percent were male and 59 percent female—closely paralleling the gender ratio for seniors in Canada (Norland 1994). The median age of respondents was 66 years, and 88 percent were over the age of 55. In terms of marital status and household size, the sample reflected the census-based profile of these areas. The majority (73%) were married, although 16 percent were widowed and 6 percent were divorced. Only 4 percent claimed single marital status. The majority also resided in small households (16% resided in single-person households and another 62% resided in two-person households).

The household incomes of respondents was relatively high—median household incomes of $49,100 meant that the sample was slightly higher than the Canadian average household income of $46,100, although the median household incomes of those sampled was almost identical to the aggregate for the old age residential areas. Moreover, 78 percent of respondents had household income levels higher than $30,000, and 48 percent had incomes higher than $50,000. Respondents were also relatively well educated (68% had some post-secondary education, and only 14% had not completed a high school diploma). In terms of tenure, 98 percent were owner-occupiers of their homes, and 95 percent owned their homes "clear title." Retirement or semiretirement was the dominant employment status of respondents (64% were retired or semiretired, 12% stated that they were full-time homemakers, 10% were employed full time, and only 1% were unemployed). In general, therefore, the sample must be considered to be a relatively affluent group, with age, family, housing, and income characteristics affording them discretionary time and resources to potentially engage in numerous life-fulfilling and community-oriented activities.

Table 2.   Component Loadings of Dimensions

Variable Codes and Titles			Order Extracted	Component Loadings	Variable Mean[1]	Variable Potential Maximum[2]	Factor Title
Expected Dimensions (e.g., B1, B2)							
B: Behavior (Interactions)							
B1	V3	Facility use score	9	89	2.5	5	Facility use
	V1	Maximum facility use		84	6.2	8	
	V2	Known facilities		67	6.7	9	
B2a	V6	Neighbor first name	7	−96	4.1	6	Informal interaction
	V7	Neighbor visits		−96	4.1	6	(non-intimate) or
	V4	Neighbor recognition		−86	4.7	6	neighboring
	V5	Neighbor conversations		−83	4.1	6	
B2b	V10	Friendship clustering	1	72	1.9	6	Informal interaction
	V11	New local friends		66	2.3	5	(intimate) or
	V8	Neighbor close friends		59	2.2	6	intimate friendship
	V9	Neighbor confidant		54	1.6	6	
B3	V15	Physical aid	6	71	1.6	6	Mutual cooperation
	V12	Borrowing		69	1.4	5	
	V14	Information aid		68	2.1	6	
	V13	Home visits		53	2.7	6	
	V9	Neighbor confidant		35	1.6	6	
B4	V16	Organization number	10	96	2.6	7	Local formal
	V17	Organization dedication		94	2.8	6	organizations
B5	V19	Outside voting	14	−81	2.0	4	Political participation
	V18	Local political orientation		−72	2.9	4	
B6	V21	Organization support	15	80	3.5	5	Supportive milieu
	V20	Govt. agency support		69	3.4	5	
CP: Conceptual Identity, Perception, and Cognition							
CP1	V24	Transit stops	4	82	4.6	5	Cognitive mapping
	V25	Convenience location		81	4.6	5	
	V22	Mappability		74	4.5	5	
	V23	Street naming		66	3.9	5	
CP2	V28	Ethnic similarity	2	80	2.4	5	People identity
	V29	Appearance similarity		78	2.2	5	
	V27	Age similarity		74	2.6	5	
	V32	Age symbolism		66	2.5	5	
	V36	Extra-local nuisances		56	2.0	6	

(continued)

Table 2 (Continued)

Variable Codes and Titles			Order Extracted	Component Loadings	Variable Mean[1]	Variable Potential Maximum[2]	Factor Title
	V51	Non-offensive lifestyles		−31[*]	3.8	5	
CA1	V30	Financial symbolism	11	−84	3.1	5	Status symbolism
	V31	Status symbolism		−79	2.7	5	
	V45	Relative beauty		−56	2.7	4	
	V44	Appearance rating		−33	3.5	4	
CA2				Not Found (part of CA11)			Sentiment and attachment
CA3	V33	Relative satisfaction	8	−89	4.2	5	Evaluation and appraisal
	V34	Relative desirability		−87	4.3	5	
CA4	V35	Local nuisances	12	83	2.1	6	Nuisances
	V36	Extra-local nuisances		67	2.0	6	
	V44	Appearance rating		−37[*]	3.5	4	
	V40	Property fear		−42	3.1	5	
CA5	V39	Personal fear	3	81	3.9	5	Safety and security
	V38	General safety		77	4.0	5	
	V37	Night safety		76	3.5	5	
	V40	Property fear		46	3.1	5	
CA6	V42	Informal collective power	5	88	2.7	5	Empowerment
	V41	Personal power		76	2.0	5	
	V43	Formal collective power		73	3.1	5	
CA7				Not Found (part of CA4)			Place appearance
CA8	V47	Non-bibliography aid	17	71	4.1	5	Latent involvement
	V46	Latent aid		65	3.5	4	
	V48	N'hood latent participation		56	4.1	5	
CA9				Not Found (part of CA1)			Aesthetics
CA10	V50	Moral similarity	13	80	3.6	5	Common values
	V49	Life agreement		77	3.5	5	
	V51	Non-offensive lifestyles		60	3.8	5	
CA11	V53	Sense of community	16	−82	3.8	5	Empathy and belonging
	V52	Belonging		−81	4.0	5	
	V54	Cohesion		−59	4.1	5	

Notes: Total variance explanation (N = 380): 69.3 percent (17 axes).

[*]Secondary factor loading.

[1,2] Mean and maximum possible value for the variable (e.g., mean = 3.1, max = 5 indicates mean respondent score of 3.1 based on maximum possible value for the variable of 5).

Community Dimensional Structure

The advantage of multivariate procedures such as factor analysis (Davies 1984) is that the separate sources of variation in the data set will be identified by the different axes or factors that are produced from the analysis—in this case factors or dimensions that define the separate dimensions or elements of community differentiation. In addition to a summary title for each of the dimensions or axes, Table 2 shows the main factor loadings associated with each dimension—essentially an index of the importance of each variable on the factors. Table 2 also displays the average values for the individual indicators (i.e., the individual variables) in order to show the extent of association with, or attitudes to, the local community area. In general, there is a high degree of similarity between the proposed dimensions and the factorial results. This confirms the fact that a number of quite distinctive and separate characteristics can be empirically identified in the Behavioral and Conceptual Identity (Cognitive and Affective) domains of place-community.

Behavioral Dimensions

In the case of the behavioral dimensions that were proposed, the results confirm the separate presence of seven different sources of variation, with high factor loadings on 21 of the 54 variables. Two-thirds of these loadings are above 0.7, confirming the strength of the different axes, as measured by the variables. However, the size of the mean values of many of the individual indicators show that the degree of association with the local area is rather weak in most of the behavioral dimensions, even for a group of long-time or in-situ aging residents. This confirms the findings of researchers such as Connerly (1985) in other North American cities. Nevertheless, the more important finding here is the identification of separate sources of variation in the areal or place-based spatial interactions of the residents.

1.   The variables associated with *facility use* measured the extent to which commercial and social facilities located within the community area were used by the respondents. Three variables index this separate factor, which indicates that the use of local facilities, or the provision of needs, is a separate and independent source of differentiation in local place-community variation. However, the mean values of the indicator variables show low numbers of local facilities and limited use of the local facilities in these essentially residential areas. On average the respondents only identified between 5 and 9 different local facilities (see Table 2, V2), while the mean value (6.2) for the scale (1 to 8) that represents the maximum use of any single local facility (V1) represents only a frequency of three times a month (6.2/8.0) and an average of only 5-9 visits per month for the local facilities as a whole. These relatively low levels of local neighborhood facility use reflect the type of residential area being sampled, but the key finding here is that the

factorial results still confirm the separate existence of the use of local commercial and social activities as an independent source of place-community differentiation.

2. What was initially proposed as a potentially distinct dimension called Informal Interaction (B2 in Table 1), or the extent of personal social contacts, was empirically split into two quite separate dimensions on the basis of the variables used in this survey. One set of variables was associated with a dimension that can be called *Neighboring*. They relate to contacts with local residents who live in close proximity and are mainly interactions of a non-intimate type, such as the recognition of neighbors, the identification of neighbours by name, engaging in conversations with them, and perhaps visiting in their homes. Again, the mean values for the individual indicators defining this dimension show that the values are not very high. Mean values of 4.0 out of 6.0 represent the identification of 6 to 10 out of the 20 nearest neighbors, which, for long-time residents, may be considered to be quite low. The factor that indexes this kind of informal neighboring activity was distinct from one that represents *Intimate Friendship* linkages—indicating the important split between neighboring and deeper place-based friendship associations such as the the the presence of a neighbor who is a confidante. The mean values of the variables measuring the numbers of close friendships based on intimacy are very low, in the range of 1.6 to 2.3 on a scale out of 6.0. Thus only an average of two neighbors are regarded as close friends or confidantes out of the neighbor field of 20, showing that, in contrast to the non-intimate axis, friendship levels have dropped to the 10 percent level from the 25-50 percent levels identified in the non-intimate dimension. It is worth emphasizing that only neighboring and friendship interaction were explored in this study, even though it may be possible to conceptualize and measure other sources of informal social or functional interaction.

3. Another informal association is described as *Mutual Cooperation* and is indexed by the extent of aid, such as the borrowing of physical objects, or the provision of information to neighbors. The fact that this is a separate source of variation is worth emphasizing, but again Table 2 shows that all the average values are low, meaning that the frequency of association of such mutual cooperation behavior activities is at most biweekly.

4. A fourth behavioral axis, labeled as *Local Formal Organizations,* is defined primarily by those features (variables) that index memberships and participation in formal organizations in the local community area, such as community associations, special interest clubs, fraternal organizations, and so forth. Again, the presence of this distinct source of variation does not mean that there are necessarily very high levels of local participation. In fact the mean values of the indicators show that on average the respondents had memberships in less than two local organizations, and the average levels of participation in the latter is typically quite low.

5. The extent to which the respondents took part in political activity—both local (community or municipal) and extra-local (provincial or federal)—also

proved to be a separate dimension, which is labeled in Table 2 as a *Political Participation* axis. On average the respondents recorded that they "usually voted" in local elections compared to "seldom" in provincial or federal elections, thereby indexing local political commitment as an important and distinct feature of place-community.

6.   Questions that attempted to gauge the extent to which people believed that municipal and provincial government agencies supported the needs of the local area, or that supportive ties to influential community or political leaders could be easily cultivated, also proved to represent a separate dimension—labeled (Table 2) as *Supportive Milieu*. Ideally, additional variables that measure the actual provision of support or actual strength of linkage ties would provide more appropriate indicators in future studies of this kind, but the restriction of this study to the specific community areas meant that such features could not be assessed. The mean values for the variables defining the Supportive Milieu dimension show that the interviewed householders typically recorded between neutral attitudes (3.0) or agreement (4.0) with the view that government supported their community-based needs—there was certainly not strong agreement (5.0) that governments actively support all community needs.

Although each of the various dimensions described above vary in their importance it is clear that in an absolute sense these long-stay residents in older suburban areas have relatively low levels of behavioral interaction with their neighbors and the local area. This empirically confirms a large amount of previous work on suburban areas (Connerly 1985; Wellman and Leighton 1979). However, this is not the key finding of the analysis. Rather, this case study shows that there are several quite distinctive dimensions in the range of different behaviors that have been measured here. Hence it can be argued that each of these seven different behavioral dimensions, derived from the range of indicators that have been used to measure the behavior or degree of interaction in the local environment, add to our knowledge of the distinctive sources of variation that contribute to the differentiation of place-communities in cities.

Cognitive Domain

In the cognitive domain, only two potential sources of variation in these old-age communities were addressed by the data set: People Identity and Cognitive Mapping. It has already been noted that separate Place Identity and Symbolic Communication sources of variation could not be confirmed because of the restrictions of the data set used.

1.   Four indicators were used to ask residents whether they could map the location of the main streets in the area, name them, and identify the nearest transit stop and convenience store. Because all were associated with a single dimension

it was labeled *Cognitive Mapping or Knowledge*. The average scores for the individual indicators were all high—ranging from 3.9 to 4.6, close to the high end (5.0) on the scale of ease of mapping, demonstrating that the respondents felt it was easy (4.0) or very easy (5.0) to locate the named features. This strong cognitive identification of local area features is not surprising because these respondents have lived in the same community area for more than 20 years—the more important finding is that this dimension is empirically distinct.

2. Consistently high factor loadings are also found on four variables that measure the extent to which the respondents considered there was similarity or homogeneity in the specific characteristics of their 20 nearest neighbors. This perceived homogeneity–heterogeneity was apparent in terms of features such as age, physical appearance, and ethnicity, in addition to an externally symbolic association of the age of their community area. Thus, the axis can be described as *People Identity*. Again, the separation of the variables as a distinct dimension of variation did not mean that the respondents perceived their areas as having high levels of homogeneity in the characteristics of the people. The average scores ranged from 2.0 to 2.6, which indicated attitudes close to the disagreement category (2.0) on the homogeneity scale of strong disagreement (1.0) to strong agreement (5.0). Thus perceived *heterogeneity* rather than homogeneity of people, and little symbolic association with age, was the predominant finding, despite the fact that the areas had high concentrations of old-age residents. In other words, despite the ability to operationalize these areas as "old-age residential areas" on the basis of census-derived objective indicators such as age-based location quotients, in reality the local residents understand their areas to be diverse—certainly not geriatric ghettoes. In addition, the interviewed households did not consider their area to contain people with offensive behavior, as seen by the weak negative association with the extent to which it was believed that some residents had offensive or incongruent lifestyles.

Affective Domain

In the affective domain, 8 of the 11 dimensions that were proposed seemed to be clearly identified. Each of the axes identified have variables with high loadings uniquely associated with the individual vectors and there are low correlations between the factors. Thus, the age-segregated areas are distinguished by several different dimensions of variation associated with the attitudes, meanings, and feelings about these residential areas.

1. Three variables index an axis that can be regarded as identifying *Status Symbolism*—a dimension which is primarily linked to the variables that measure the degree to which residence in the area signified financial success (V30) and enhancement of status (V31). The additional presence of a medium loading for the variable measuring relative beauty (V45) and the weak loading of the variable

measuring perceived tidiness or appearance of the area (V44) indicates that the symbolic status is also linked to the relative appearance of these community areas in this case. Although "appearance rating" shows a high score (3.5/4.0), the other indicators have scores from 2.7 to 3.1 out of 5.0, which indicates mainly neutral values (3.0) rather than even agreement (4.0) with the view that the area enhances their status. Therefore, although the data show that in absolute terms these areas are not considered to possess high levels of symbolic status, the fact that the dimension is a separate source of variation in the overall complexity of community elements is important because it isolates a distinctive feature or element of place-community.

2.   Two variables have high loadings on an axis identified as *Evaluation and Appraisal* because they show the extent to which the residents have high levels of satisfaction with their residential area and its desirability. In this case the average values are high—over 4.2/5.0 on the rating scale. Therefore, in this case study the distinctiveness of the axis identifying the ability of residents to evaluate their area is also linked to high levels of satisfaction with their local environment. Additional studies in different community contexts will be required to demonstrate the potential uniqueness of this dimension of community variation when there are only weak evaluative and appraisal ratings.

3.   A distinctive factor measuring the way that people feel about the level of *Nuisances* within and outside their local area was also found, with a low inverse relationship with the appearance of the area. Table 2 shows the respondents regard the level of nuisances within the area and immediately outside the area as low (2.0), rather than very low (1.0) on the 6-point scale. The minor secondary loadings for property safety and appearance ratings show that the axis is a little more complex than the others, meaning that high levels of perceived and experienced nuisances is marginally related to concerns about property safety and to poor appearance ratings.

4.   The extent of *Safety and Security* in the area represents another distinctive source of variation among the range of feelings and attitudes. The average values of the indicators are all relatively high, in the 3.5 to 4.0 range, closer to the agreement (4.0 level) rather than strong agreement (5.0) on the typical measurement scale. It is worth noting that the average value of the property safety variable (V40) is much lower at 3.1, indicating an almost neutral view (3.0) about the safety of their houses and cars. This is most likely a reflection of the increasing apprehension about property theft in the city, even though Calgary is a city with relatively low crime rates compared to most Western cities.

5.   Table 2 shows that there is also a separate factor measuring the degree to which people believe they have the ability to prevent or control unwanted developments in their area–a dimension called *Empowerment*. The average values for the indicators are relatively low, mainly between 2.0 (some influence) and 3.0 (certainly some influence) rather than a great deal of influence (4.0) or control (5.0) over change. It is worth noting that the average values increase form the

personal power that individuals may have (2.0), to the effect of informal protest (2.7) and formal protest through their community associations (3.1). These mean values are still a long way from scores that would indicate the view that local residents can control unwanted development (5.0), even though most proposed land-use changes in Calgary are routinely passed from the city planning department to the local community association for comment.

6.   *Latent Involvement* is the title given to the set of variables that measure the extent to which residents feel that their neighbors will help them in times of need or crisis. The mean values for the individual indicators are all high, which shows that the residents agree (4.0), rather than strongly agree (5.0), that their neighbors would provide help should the need arise. It is worth stressing that this axis of differentiation is separate from the actual degree of help or contact, which was one of the behavioral sources of variation.

7.   Another distinctive axis captures the extent to which the residents believe that their neighbors share similar attitudes and non-offensive lifestyles and is labeled in Table 2 as *Common Values*. The average values for the indicators were moderate on the 1 to 5 scale, ranging from 3.5 to 3.8. Thus the respondents were closer to agreement (4.0) rather than expressing a neutral attitude (3.0) or disagreement (2.0) with the idea that the people in their area had similar values and non-offensive lifestyles. In short, they do believe there to be an underlying commonality of moral values and lifestyles among their neighbors.

8.   A sense of *Empathy or Belonging* to the community provides a further dimension of place-community in this study. This axis was defined primarily by the two high-loading variables that measured the extent of identification with the local area; although the more composite variable (V54) derived from Buckner's (1988) attempt to measure cohesion by integrating several different indices of the degree of cohesion, only showed a medium loading. Nevertheless, individually, all three indicators had high average values (3.8 to 4.0) on the 5-point response scale, meaning that respondents typically agreed (even though there was not strong agreement) that they both felt a sense of community and felt a sense of belonging to the local community—features which are partially subsumed by a sense of cohesion.

The presence of eight different factor axes derived from the variables used to measure the attitudes and feelings that the residents have about their residential area indicates the complexity of the sources of differentiation that have been described as components of the Affective Domain. Because none of these axes is highly correlated with any other, the independence of these attitudinal characteristics in providing distinctive sources of variation in the residential areas studied here must be stressed. However, it must be noted that it is very likely that an additional axis associated with Sentiment or Attachment to the area is also an important feature of the range of attitudes toward the area, but could not be adequately measured in this study because of the data problems described previously. Obviously these results depend on the set of variables that have been used in the study and other dimensions may be found if additional variables associated with different attitudes and feelings are included in future analyses. Because limited attention has been paid in this study to Place Appearance and Aesthetic dimensions, these may be obvious candidates as additional sources of variation in residential differentiation. In community areas with high levels of antisocial behavior the former axis may be quite important, unlike the type of areas studied here–peaceful and well-maintained middle-class suburbs with a stable population.

CONCLUSION

This study has shown that there are many different traditions in the study of the differentiation of social areas and place-communities within cities. All contribute to our greater understanding of the kaleidoscopic nature of intra-urban social area differentiation. However, it has been argued here that there is a need to integrate the multidimensional literature if the study of territorial communities is to be placed on a more systematic footing—an approach, of course, which may be anathema to those of a humanistic persuasion who argue for the ultimate uniqueness of social areas. Although the latter approach provides a rich source of ideas on intra-urban differentiation, it is believed that it is possible to conceptually and empirically unpack or subdivide the complex multidimensional concept we call place-community within cities into a series of distinctive elements or dimensions of differentiation. A partial test of the utility of a classification of these components revealed the presence of at least 17 different dimensions or measurable sources of variation in the behavioral, cognitive, and affective domains. Although the study was limited to one type of area, the results appear to confirm that a number of distinctive sources of differentiation lie behind the differentiation of intra-urban space. Additional studies may be required to understand the complexity of community structure in other types of social areas, although it is possible that these dimensions are common to all areas but vary in their strength. These findings add to our knowledge of local community differentiation in that they complement the dimensions found by factorial ecologists who have investigated the census-based social variety of community areas.

An important finding of this study is that despite the presence of these distinctive dimensions of community, they are not necessarily strong or indicative of very high levels of community action, cognition, or emotional attachment to place. In this case the extent of local interaction is relatively low and not all of the attitudes toward the area show strong areal identification, even though the study was limited to old-age and long-term residents in the areas analyzed. This confirms many previous studies on the character of local residential communities within Western cities, but in this case also provides a series of measurements on the distinctive sources of differentiation, identifying the features that need to be enhanced if there is a desire for greater community cohesion.

This study has empirically confirmed the separate existence of community dimensions within the context of the Behavioral and Conceptual Identity domains within a relatively homogeneous Areal Content domain. The latter limitation immediately suggests that additional questions need to be addressed by further empirical community research if the utility of a broadly based conceptual schema of community within cities is to become stable, well defined, or useful to theorists and community practitioners beyond locally specific areas. First, similar work on other *types* of social areas is required, perhaps areas that exhibit distinctive properties of family, economic, or ethnic status within the Areal Content domain, or even places with different physical and morphological design characteristics. Additional studies of this type may add to the list of differentiating features within each of the major domains identified here, thereby extending our understanding of the range and variety of community elements or dimensions that may exist. Second, there is a need for further research to deal with the quality and *relative strength* of the dimensions in different types of areas, or even how and why different combinations or suites of dimensions are present in some areas and absent in others. For example, it is probable that in some cities, or some types of community areas, the rank ordering of the importance (in terms of explained variance) of identifiable community dimensions will differ. For instance *Empathy and Belonging* or a sense of community, may be the most important dimension in one type of social area but not in others. This will help students of community to understand the array of dimensions that may exist in specific areas, how these arrays may be inconsistent, or why the elements take on different weights in particular areas.

Third, there is a need to investigate whether the dimensions can be combined into higher level macro-structures, or if, on the other hand, some types of areas reveal that the dimensions identified here need to be broken down into more detailed features. This would mean that concepts such as "sense of community" could be derived from the combination of several of the dimensions identified here, rather than treating them as independent, although still multidimensional concepts. In addition, there may well be a difference between "sense of place" and "sense of community," with the former having a larger array of elements. Similarly, further empirical work may show that some of the proposed dimensions may prove to be made up of a number of distinctive components, or may be combined or collapsed in specific types of community areas. Fourth, there is a pressing need to look at community areas in a more comprehensive fashion, to include all three domains of information, as well as *dynamic* and *scale* changes in the Areal Content, Behavioral, and Conceptual Identity domains. The dynamic or temporal factor may be particularly important, because the distinctive character of some places may arise from episodic events, such as festivals, which leave their mark on the area. In other words, there is a need to incorporate knowledge that episodic events, or even long-run changes in the population composition of a neighborhood will cause some dimensions of community to emerge or disappear, or perhaps even result in the reconfiguration of the importance of individual dimensions. Likewise, in terms of spatial scale, it may be important to investigate community structure at different spatial resolutions. Studies in this area will need to focus on how the dimensionality of community within the Areal Content, Behavior, Cognitive, and Affective domains behaves with respect to scale, and may revolve around the following kinds of questions. Do dimensions appear, disappear, or reconfigure themselves at the block front level, the micro-neighborhood scale, or the community area or census tract scale? Are there particular spatial scales at which the intensity and diversity of community structures seem to be maximized?

Fifth, in an explanatory context it seems important not only to link the measurable features of community described here with the deep-seated forces that explain the creation of these differences—from structural economic forces to the influence of human agency. In other words, does social inequality or social polarization, an increasingly important feature of Western cities (MacLachlan and Sawada 1997; Bourne 1993), give rise to different *sets* of community dimensions in different areas? Does this inequality limit the range of dimensions that exist or the types of dimensions that can be socially constructed? A related theme or area for future research is the extent to which the various dimensions may affect or influence each other. For instance, does the realization or achievement of one dimension, or an increase in its strength, spawn others? For example, it seems plausible that significantly increasing the degree to which residents use local area facilities, such as community centers, would result in changes to other dimensions—perhaps increased levels of neighboring, increased levels of attachment to place, and so on. Finally, the systematic approach to the problem of community complexity would be improved by more consistent measurement, particularly through replication and identification of the key variables that define the distinctive dimensions of variation in place-communities within cities.

Although this study poses numerous questions for future research, and indeed exposes only a minor part of the complexity of place-community within cities, the results do have practical significance that will become more pronounced as additional conceptual, theoretical, and empirical work on community begins to integrate our understanding of the multifaceted nature of communities within cities. Urban planners and designers frequently focus their efforts on only selected dimensions of the Areal Content domain—the physical or morphological attributes of communities. However, systematic attention to all of the domains of community will potentially lead to a greater understanding of what kinds of design principles, urban morphologies, or zoning practices are associated with, or enhance, other behavioral, cognitive, and affective dimensions of community in particular types of social areas. Once the understanding of these kinds of links becomes codified in a more comprehensive way, urban designers or planners will be better able to "situate" their efforts within the physical, social, and psychological domains of communities. Community practitioners, from activists to social workers, recreation service providers or health care providers, can also benefit from an integrated approach that focuses on the multidimensional character of communities and the recognition of links between dimensions. This approach provides a conceptual apparatus from which community workers can begin to identify "missing" dimensions of community in certain areas. The social construction of community may be enhanced by creating new dimensions or by filling out the suite of dimensions in particular places, or even boosting the level of facility usage at neighborhood recreation centers.

The community development industry may also benefit from this type of integrated understanding of the structure and functioning of community, although it is likely that this will also potentially lead to the commodification of community dimensions. The developers of age-exclusive retirement villages have already recognized that there is a suite of community dimensions that are highly sought after by niche markets of early retirees. These include, for example, the need for a sense of belonging, social and socioeconomic status homogeneity, age homogeneity, a sense of safety and security, freedom from nuisances and annoyances, and an environment characterized by peers with a sense of common values or moral standards. In an indirect way, these kinds of developments are drawing upon many of the dimensions of community described above, and are attempting to offer environments that will maximize the array of elements that are present. Developers typically do not treat these as separate elements—rather they are offered as a collective but important selling feature of residential communities. It is not difficult to imagine other types of developments following suit by drawing upon a more comprehensive schema of community. As a more useful framework of community dimensions and their links emerges, developers may begin to engineer not only new subdivisions, but communities that have the potential to maximize the expression of community, either by design or by social construction. Additional place-based community research on the types of questions identified above within an integrated conceptual schema—such as that proposed in Table 1—has the potential to further illuminate the multifaceted and dynamic elements of community within cities, not only for researchers, but for practitioners. As such, it may provide a solid footing from which to understand and debate the nature or "chemistry" of place-communities within cities.

NOTES

1. Major age groupings in this study are heuristically based on the four "life course" stages proposed by Laslett (1991). We have operationalized the ages as: (1) 0-24 years, (2) 25-54 years, (3) 55-84 years, and (4) 85 or more years. For the purposes of this discussion the third and fourth categories have been collapsed.

2. Old-age residential areas, as defined in the text, are found in at least one census tract in 80 percent of Canada's 25 metropolitan areas in 1991. In 1991 the exceptions were Chicoutimi-Jonquiere,

Sherbrooke, Oshawa, Windsor, and Victoria. The latter is a function of the fact that, although Victoria contains the highest percentage of people aged 55 and over, they are relatively dispersed throughout the city, not residentially segregated.

3.   All of the Canadian metropolitan census tracts were measured on 39 separate social indicator variables that parallel those used by Davies and Murdie (1991). We have based this comparison on further analysis of data used by Davies and Murdie (1996) in which we identified significant differences in mean factor scores on 11 distinctive factorial ecology dimensions for the old-age areas in comparison to all others.

4.   The *Calgary Herald* and *Edmonton Journal* newspapers were reviewed for the first Saturday of every month from 1980 to 1993 in order to identify age-based community developments. These findings were augmented by specific data from residential development corporations specializing in age-restrictive retirement villages.

5.   One neighborhood, Victoria Park (the city's lowest income area), resulted in only 6 address matches for 20-year residents and a 0 percent response rate. Results reported here are based on the remaining 10 census tracts that have been defined as old-age residential areas.

6.   The questionnaire was organized around six sections:

(1)   residence and community area (length of residence, residential histories, images of community boundaries, tenure, etc.),

(2)   life and society (well-being, life satisfaction, aging, and retirement issues),

(3)   neighborhood identity (ethnic and age similarities, satisfaction, nuisances, safety, appraisals, collective action, status symbolism, perceptions of moral similarities etc.),

(4)   neighborhood activity or behaviors (shopping patterns, facility locations, frequency of facility use, neighboring, borrowing, memberships in organizations, political activities, etc.),

(5)   demographics (gender, household size, age, marital status, education, employment, income), and

(6)   individual comments (open section for additional qualitative comments from respondents).

REFERENCES

Alexander, C., S. Ishikawa, and M. Silverstein. 1977. *A Pattern Language*. New York: Oxford University Press.

Berry, B.J.L. 1971. "The Logic and Limitations of Comparative Factorial Ecology." *Economic Geography* 4(supplement): 209-219.

Booth, C. 1893. "Life and Labour of the People of London: An Enquiry Based on the 1891 Census." *Journal of the Royal Statistical Society* 56: 557-596.

_____. 1897. *Life and Labour of the People of London*, 2nd ed., 9 vol. London: MacMillan.

Bourne, L.S. 1993. "Close Together and Worlds Apart: An Analysis of Changes in the Ecology of Income in Canadian Cities." *Urban Studies* 30(8): 1293-1317.

Buckner, J.C. 1988. "The Development of an Instrument to Measure Neighbourhood Cohesion." *American Journal of Community Psychology* 16: 771-791.

Bulmer, M. 1986. *Neighbors: The Work of Phillip Abrams*. New York: Cambridge University Press.

Campbell, A., P. Converse, and W. Rodgers. 1976. *The Quality of American Life*. New York: Russell Sage Foundation.

Chavis, D., and A. Wandersman. 1990. "Sense of Community in the Urban Environment: A Catalyst for Participation and Community Development." *American Journal of Community Psychology* 18(1): 55-81.

Coleman, R., and B. Neugarten. 1972. *Social Status in the City*. San Francisco, CA: Jossey-Bass.

Connerly, C.E. 1985. "The Community Question: An Extension of Wellman and Leighton." *Urban Affairs Quarterly* 20: 537-556.

Coulton, C.J., J.E. Korbin, and M. Su. 1996. "Measuring Neighbourhood Context for Young Children in an Urban Area." *American Journal of Community Psychology* 24: 5-32.

Davidson, L. 1979. *Political Partnerships: Neighborhood Residents and their Council Members.* Beverly Hills, CA: Sage.

Davies, W.K.D. 1984. *Factorial Ecology.* Aldershot: Gower Press.

———. 1992. "Affective Dimensions of Community Character." Unpublished paper presented to I.G.U. Commission on Urban Systems, Wayne State University, Detroit.

———. 1995. "The Power of Communities." *Acta Wasaensia* 45: 49-75.

Davies, W.K.D., and D.T. Herbert. 1993. *Communities Within Cities: An Urban Social Geography.* London: Belhaven.

Davies, W.K.D., and R.A. Murdie. 1991. "Consistency and Differential Impact in Urban Social Dimensionality," *Urban Geography* 12: 55-79.

———. 1996. "Social Differentiation of Canadian Metropolitan Areas: 1971-1991." Unpublished paper presented to the Canadian Association of Geographers annual meeting, University of Saskatchewan, May 11-16.

Davies, W.K.D., and I.J. Townshend. 1994. "How Do Community Associations Vary? The Structure of Community Associations in Calgary, Alberta." *Urban Studies* 31: 1739-1761.

de Leeuw, J. 1984. "The Gifi System of Non Linear Multivariate Analysis." *Data Analysis and Informatics* III: 415-424.

Firey, W. 1947. *Land Use in Central Boston.* Cambridge, MA: Harvard University Press.

Fried, M. 1986. "The Neighborhood in Metropolitan Life: Its Psychosocial Significance." Pp. 331-363 in *Urban Neighborhoods: Research and Policy,* edited by R.B. Taylor. New York: Praeger.

Giddens, A. 1984. *The Constitution of Society: Outline of a Theory of Structuration.* Berkely, CA: University of California Press.

Gifi, A. 1991. *Non-Linear Multivariate Analysis.* New York: John Wiley.

Ginsberg, Y. 1985. "Dimensions of Neighborhood Prestige Perceptions: Findings from Tel Aviv." *Social Science Quarterly* 66(3): 724-732.

Gober, P. 1985. "The Retirement Community as a Geographical Phenomenon: The Case of Sun City, Arizona." *Journal of Geography* 84(5): 189-198.

Golant, S.M. 1980. "Locational-Environmental Perspectives on Old-Age-Segregated Residential Areas in the United States." Pp. 257-294 in *Geography and the Urban Environment,* Vol. 3, edited by D.T. Herbert and R.J. Johnston. Chichester, England: John Wiley and Sons.

———. 1986. "Understanding the Diverse Housing Environments of the Elderly." *Environments* 18(3): 35-51.

Gottlieb, B.H. 1978. "The Development and Application of a Classification Scheme of Informal Helping Behaviors." *Canadian Journal of Behavioural Science* 10: 105-115.

Guest, A., and B. Lee. 1983. "The Social Organization of Local Areas." *Urban Affairs Quarterly* 19(2): 217-240.

Heintz, K.M. 1976. *Retirement Communities, For Adults Only.* New Brunswick, NJ: Center for Urban Policy Research, State University of New Jersey.

Heller, K. 1989. "The Return to Community." *American Journal of Community Psychology* 17(1): 1-15.

Herbert, D.T., and S.M. Peace. 1980. "The Elderly in an Urban Environment: A Case Study of Swansea." Pp. 223-255 in *Geography and the Urban Environment.* Vol. 3, edited by D.T. Herbert and R.J. Johnston. Chichester, England: John Wiley & Sons.

Hillery, G.A. 1955. "Definitions of Community." *Rural Sociology* 20: 779-791.

Hunt, M.E., and L. Ross. 1990. "Naturally Occuring Retirement Communities: A Multiattribute Examination of Desirability Factors." *Gerontologist* 30(5): 667-674.

Hunter, A. 1974. *Symbolic Communities.* Chicago: University of Chicago Press.

Hunter, A., and S. Riger. 1986. "The Meaning of Community in Community Mental Health." *Journal of Community Psychology, Special Issue: Psychological Sense of Community, I: Theory and Concepts* 14: 55-71.

Hunter, A., and S. Straggenborg. 1986. "Communities Do Act: Neighborhood Characteristics, Resource Mobilization, and Political Action by Local Community Organizations." *The Social Science Journal* 23(2): 169-190.

Janowitz, M. 1967. *The Community Press in an Urban Setting.* Chicago: University of Chicago Press.

Keller, S. 1968. *The Urban Neighbourhood: A Sociological Perspective.* New York: Random House.

_____. 1988. "The American Dream of Community: An Unfinished Agenda." *Sociological Forum* 3: 167-183.

Laslett, P. 1987. "The Emergence of the Third Age." *Ageing and Society* 7: 133-160.

_____. 1991. *A Fresh Map of Life: The Emergence of the Third Age.* London: Weidenfeld and Nicolson.

Logan, J., and G. Rabrenovic. 1990. "Neighborhood Associations: Their Issues, Their Allies, and Their Opponents." *Urban Affairs Quarterly* 26(1): 68-94.

Lopata, H. 1981. "The Meaning of Friendship in Widowhood." Pp. 368-379 in *The Life Cycle: Readings in Human Development,* edited by L.D. Steinberg. New York: Columbia University Press.

Lowenthal, M., and C. Haven. 1981. "Interaction and Adaptation: Intimacy as a Critical Variable." Pp. 359-367 in *The Life Cycle: Readings in Human Development,* edited by L.D. Steinberg. New York: Columbia University Press.

Lynch, K. 1960. *The Image of the City.* Cambridge, MA: MIT Press.

MacLachlan, I., and R. Sawada. 1997. "Measures of Income Inequality and Social Polarization in Canadian Metropolitan Areas." *Canadian-Geographer* 41(4): 377-397.

McMillan, D.W., and D.M. Chavis. 1986. "Sense of Community: A Definition and Theory." *Journal of Community Psychology* 14: 6-22.

Moore, E.G., and M.W. Rosenberg, with D. McGuinness. 1997. *Growing Old in Canada.* Scarborough, Ontario: International Thomson Publishing.

Murdie, R.A. 1969. "Factorial Ecology of Metropolitan Toronto, 1951-1961." Research Paper No.116, Department of Geography, University of Chicago.

Norland, J.A. 1994. *Profile of Canada's Seniors.* Statistics Canada, Focus on Canada Series, catalogue 96-312E.

O'Brien, D., M. McLendon, and A. Ahmed. 1989. "Neighborhood Community and Quality of Life". *Journal of the Community Development Society* 20(2): 59-71.

Okraku, I. 1987. "Age Residential Segregation in Canadian Cities." *Canadian Review of Sociology and Anthropology* 24: 431-452.

Park, R.E. 1925. *The City.* Chicago: University of Chicago Press.

Perry, C. 1929. "The Neighbourhood Unit." In *Neighborhood and Community Planning.* New York: Regional Plan of New York and Environs, Volume VII.

Plas, J.M., and S.E. Lewis. 1996. "Environmental Factors and Sense of Community in a Planned Town." *American Journal of Community Psychology* 24: 109-143.

Rheingold, H. 1993. *The Virtual Community.* Reading, MA: Addison Wesley.

Riger, S., and P. Lavrakas. 1981. "Community Ties: Patterns of Attachment and Social Interaction in Urban Neighborhoods." *American Journal of Community Psychology* 9: 55-66.

Rosow, I. 1967. *Social Integration of the Aged.* New York: Free Press.

Rowles, G. 1978. *Prisoners of Space? Exploring the Geographical Experience of Older People.* Boulder, CO: Westview Press.

Sarason, S. 1974. *The Psychological Sense of Community.* San Francisco, CA: Jossey-Bass.

Seiler, S.R. 1986. "How to Develop Retirement Communities for Profit." *Real Estate Review* 16(3): 70-75.

Shea, L., L. Thompson, and R. Blieszner. 1988. "Resources in Older Adults' Old and New Friendships." *Journal of Social and Personal Relationships* 5: 83-96.

Shevky, E., and W. Bell. 1955. *Social Area Analysis.* Stanford: Stanford University Press.

Skjaeveland, O., T. Garling, and J.G. Maeland. 1996. "A Multidimensional Measure of Neighbouring." *American Journal of Community Psychology* 24: 413-435.

Spearman, C. 1904. "General Intelligence, Objectively Determined and Measured". *American Journal of Psychology* 25: 201-293.

Stallman, J., and L. Jones. 1995. "A Typology of Retirement Places: A Community Analysis." *Journal of the Community Development Society* 26(1): 1-14.

Statistics Canada. 1992. *Profile of Census Metropolitan Areas and Census Agglomerations, Part A.* Supply and Services Canada, Census of Canada, catalogue 93-337.

_____. 1993. *Profile of Census Metropolitan Areas and Census Agglomerations, Part B.* Supply and Services Canada, Census of Canada, catalogue 93-338.

Streib, G.F., W.E. Folts, and A.J. Lagreca. 1985. "Autonomy, Power, and Decision Making in 36 Retirement Communities." *Gerontologist* 25(4): 403-409.

Suttles, G. 1972. *The Social Construction of Communities*. Chicago: University of Chicago Press.

Unger, D., and A. Wandersman. 1982. "Neighboring in an Urban Environment." *American Journal of Community Psychology* 10(5): 493-509.

_____. 1985. "The Importance of Neighbours: The Social, Cognitive and Affective Components of Neighbouring." *American Journal of Community Psychology* 13: 139-169.

Wandersman, A. 1981. "A Framework of Participation in Community Organizations." *Journal of Applied Behavioral Science* 17(1): 27-58.

Webber, M. 1964. *The Urban Place and the Non Place Urban Realm*. Pp. 79-138 in *Explorations into Urban Structure*, edited by M. Webber et al. Philadelphia, PA: University of Pennsylvania Press.

Weenig, M., T. Schmidt, and C. Midden. 1990. "Social Dimensions of Neighbourhoods and the Effectiveness of Information Programs." *Environment and Behaviour* 22: 27-54.

Weiss, M. 1988. *The Clustering of America*. New York: Harper and Row.

Wellman, B., and B. Leighton. 1979. "Networks, Neighbourhoods and Communities: Approaches to the Study of the Community Question." *Urban Affairs Quarterly* 14: 363-390.

Wellman, B., and S.D. Berkowitz. 1988. *Social Structures: A Network Approach*. Cambridge: Cambridge University Press.

Woolever, C. 1992. "A Contextual Approach to Neighborhood Attachment." *Urban Studies* 29(1): 99-116.

PART V

URBAN HOUSING AND
NEIGHBORHOOD IMPROVEMENT

HOUSING NEED, NEIGHBORHOOD IMPROVEMENT AND THE CONTRIBUTIONS OF EXPERTS IN NORTH POINT DOUGLAS, WINNIPEG, 1971–1981:

A GENDER AND 'RACE' SENSITIVE ANALYSIS

Fran Klodawsky

ABSTRACT

In this paper I step back from the many discussions about housing need per se to interrogate the connections between a particular social and political milieu, and the framing of and responses to housing need in that place. More particularly, I examine how those who claim expert knowledge, such as urban planners and social service providers, have contributed both conceptual linkages and material outcomes for those in housing need and I raise questions about whether gender and race play a role in influencing this process. This paper's specific objective is to examine the question of how housing need for poor households was identified and responded to

Research in Community Sociology, Volume 9, pages 255-283.
Copyright © 1999 by JAI Press Inc.
All rights of reproduction in any form reserved.
ISBN: 0-7623-0498-7

in the context of the Neighbourhood Improvement Program (NIP) in North Point
Douglas, Winnipeg between 1971 and 1981.

Discussions about housing need have peaked and subsided in Canada over the last
quarter century, but throughout, attempts to place this talk in the context of *how*
needs are prioritized and defined have been almost completely absent. In this paper
I want to step back from the many discussions about housing need per se (see, for
example, Ark Research Associates 1996; Roeher Institute 1990; Spector and
Klodawsky 1993; Wekerle 1993), to interrogate the connections between a particular social and political milieu, and the framing of and responses to housing need
in that place. More particularly, I wish to examine how those who claim expert
knowledge, such as urban planners and social service providers, have contributed
both conceptual linkages and material outcomes for those in housing need.

   Following Fraser (1989), I will argue that the discursive space between identifying a housing need and programmatic responses to it in a particular locale,
offers a potentially rich site of investigation. Instead of searching for the best way
of responding to a certain need, it is at least as important to appreciate the context
in which "best" and "need" come to be defined. This paper's objective is to investigate the question of how housing need for poor households was identified and
responded to in a specific time and place. Its substantive focus is the neighborhood Improvement Program (NIP) in North Point Douglas, Winnipeg (Figure 1).

   The 1973 National Housing Act (NHA) amendments, of which NIP was one
element, represented an important moment in Canada's history of federal housing programs. They introduced a series of programs that expanded the opportunities for individual municipalities and third-sector organizations to initiate
innovative nonprofit housing developments (Bacher 1993; Banting 1990; Hulchanski 1986; Klodawsky and Spector 1997). This same period was also
marked by the growth in organized efforts by women and aboriginal groups,
among others, to influence discussions about housing and urban development,
both in Winnipeg and elsewhere in Canada (Bird 1970; Croteau and Zink 1975;
Damas & Smith 1975; Griffiths 1975; Peters 1996; Stinson 1979; Vincent 1971;
Wekerle, Peterson, Morley 1981). In all these realms, 'experts' played a particular and significant role in translating the concerns of those in need into a governmental framework, some by working outside formal state structures and
others within (Rose 1996; Isin 1998). The nature of their contributions and the
impacts of choices they made are of particular interest here.

   NIP was especially significant in Manitoba and Winnipeg: the province
received more NIP funds than any other—about $24 million—and it chose to allo-
cate most of these monies to six Winnipeg neighborhoods (CMHC 1979c; Lyon
and Newman 1986). Surprisingly, however, the considerable resources represented by these funds did not lead Winnipeg to develop innovative proactive
municipal housing and neighborhood improvement initiatives. While Winnipeg

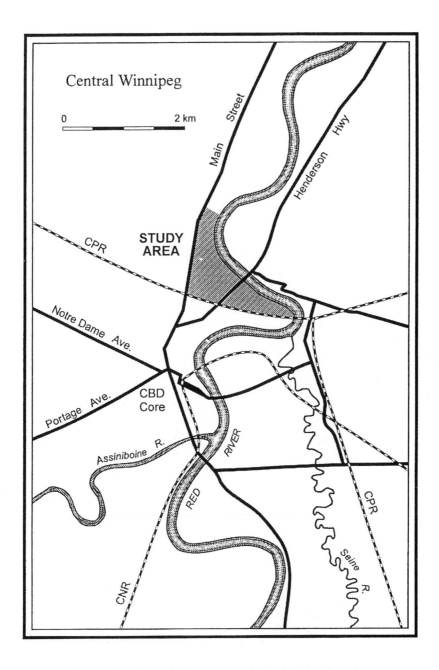

Figure 1.   Central Winnipeg and North Point Douglas

today includes a substantial stock of non-profit housing units, the main providers have been service clubs and church groups. Neither they nor the municipality have taken an assertive coordinated role of the sort that has been identified in such cities as Ottawa, Vancouver, or Toronto (Carter and McAfee 1990; Newman 1986; Pollack 1994; Radewich 1986; Ufoegbune 1993). Indeed, according to Carter and McAfee (1990), Winnipeg has been a "reactor" city in its level of support for social housing (Carter and McAfee 1990, pp. 233-234; see also, Radewich 1986). Moreover, the lack of in-depth and co-ordinated citizen involvement that helped initiate NIP has been a focus of critique in the 1990s in Winnipeg, as excerpts from three recent reports attest.

> [T]here is a lack of holistic programs which attempt to meet a number of needs as opposed to treating needs in isolation from one another. For the mental health disadvantaged, for example, there is a lack of supportive housing programs. For Natives, there is a lack of programs which take into account the spiritual development of program participants. For the single parent, there is a lack of programs which take into account the entire network of supports—housing, transportation, day care, etc.—necessary to ensure continued participation in programs (Institute of Urban Studies 1990, p. 35).

> Perhaps surprisingly, we heard from many that there were adequate dollars within the social service system, but that there is too much fragmentation and proliferation of professionals and agencies serving specialized needs. A related suggestion that we need to rethink the fundamental top down nature of the approach taken by housing and other social support agencies is seen as a major step in the right direction. Indeed, most people see the bottom up, community-based approach as the way of the future (Carter et al. 1993, p. 57).

> The Social Planning Council of Winnipeg believes that "disadvantaged" neighbourhoods can become sustainable and be stable, fulfilling and healthy places where people can live and develop their potential when:

> • Residents are empowered to identify and priorize their issues and make decisions on options and solutions, and work together to control those things that affect their health, and their lives.
> • Residents develop a sense of caring and sharing, engage in mutual support and self-help and take pride in their neighbourhood.
> • The larger community—governments, business, labour, service clubs, churches, people from other areas of Winnipeg and Manitoba—are understanding of their situation and the structural conditions affecting their lives, and are supportive and encouraging.
> • People residing in neighbourhoods and communities are committed towards creating and improving their physical and social environments and expanding community resources which enable them to mutually support one another.
> • The larger community takes an interest in these neighbourhoods towards neighbourhood stabilization and safety (Social Planning Council of Winnipeg 1995, p. 11.)[1]

An assumption in this paper is that there are insights to be gained about these current concerns through examination of debates about citizen involvement, housing need and neighborhood improvement during the period in which NIP was initiated and implemented in Winnipeg. The specific focus on North Point

Douglas is appropriate for several reasons. Traditionally, an area of low-income households with significant housing problems, during the period under investigation North Point Douglas experienced significant population change of a very specific sort. It changed from an area with a majority of poor older Eastern European and especially Ukrainian homeowners to one with a still poor, but more diverse population that included many Metis and other aboriginal peoples who were more likely to be young female single parents with children. Including an explicit focus on women's housing needs and those of aboriginal peoples has been a way of examining how experts in Winnipeg addressed the needs of social groups likely to be regarded as "other," given their own social and educational backgrounds. However, a limitation of this focus has been a lack of success in locating documents or even newspaper articles that capture the voices of community members during this period, outside the context of official government documents. Although interviews with several key community activists who had some memories of this period have informed this analysis generally, the relative silence of people living in North Point Douglas during the period under investigation is acknowledged. It has not been possible to probe in any depth the interactions between community members and the experts that spoke on their behalf, both within and outside of municipal government.

NEEDS TALK AND HOUSING

Nancy Fraser (1989) makes a persuasive argument that "needs talk" or debates about who needs what and how these needs should be fulfilled, are very important elements of political discussions in late capitalist societies. She sees these debates as consisting of chains of "in-order-to" relations that encapsulate complex sets of assumptions. Fraser's perspective is that in order to contest political claims, one first requires an understanding of how they came to be accepted and by whom. She argues that by doing so, it is possible to first, "bring into relief the contested character of needs talk" and second, to "relate this discourse model to social-structural considerations, especially to shifts in the boundaries between "political", "economic", and "domestic" or "personal" spheres of life" (1989). For example, as many feminist theorists have clearly shown, women's needs are more likely to be enclaved as nonpolitical, private, or domestic (Fraser 1989; Fraser and Gordon 1994; Pateman 1989). In housing terms, this suggests that the working conditions under which primarily female caregivers carry out their responsibilities is likely to receive far less public policy attention than are the working conditions of those in factories or offices (Rosenberg 1990).

Fraser also puts forth a notion of "runaway needs" to describe a situation in which there has been, at least temporarily, a successful challenge to assumptions about both the problem and its solution:

Where do runaway needs run to when they break out of domestic or official economic enclaves? I propose that runaway needs enter a historically specific and relatively new societal order to mark its noncoincidence with the family, the official economy and the state. As a site of contested discourse about runaway needs, 'the social' cuts across these traditional divisions. It is an area of conflict among rival interpretations of needs embedded in rival chains of in-order-to-relations (1989, p. 169).

Coupled with this notion, Fraser also conceptualizes three major kinds of needs discourses whose interactions result in a particular understanding of the "politics of needs": the oppositional, "when needs are politicized from below"; the reprivatized which "emerge in response to the first"; and the expert, "which link popular movements to the state" (p. 171). She characterizes 'oppositional' needs talk as originating in groups who do not have significant access to state or private market decision makers, in contrast to reprivatization needs talk which originates from those who have power and want to hold on to it. Expert needs talk is seen as the purview of professionals whose relation to power is indirect, and whose role is primarily one of translating oppositional needs talk into a form that does not threaten extant power relations. Fraser characterizes the spaces of expert discourses as somewhat ambiguous: while they are most likely to contribute to the coopting of politicized needs into discourses and in-order-to relations that are easily accommodated with state operations, this is not always or completely the case:

expert discourses tend to be restricted to specialized publics. Thus, they are associated with professional class formation, institution building, and social "problem solving." But in some cases...expert vocabularies and rhetorics are disseminated to a wider spectrum of educated laypersons, some of whom are participants in social movements. Moreover, social movements sometimes manage to co-opt or create critical, oppositional segments of expert discourse publics. For all these reasons, expert discourse publics sometimes acquire a certain porousness. And expert discourses become the bridge discourses linking loosely organized social movements with the social state (Fraser 1989, pp. 173-174).

Thus, Fraser proposes a theoretical shift of focus that has methodological implications. Instead of searching for the best way of responding to a certain need, she argues that it is at least as important to appreciate the context in which best and need come to be defined. Specifically, she asserts that one should ask who is putting forth a certain political claim and what is the relation of claimants to that which is "hegemonic, authorized and officially sanctioned" (1989, p. 164). In doing so, she also acknowledges that social groups are differently situated and have different possibilities to make their positions heard (p. 164).

The period of urban renewal and its aftermath provides an interesting application of Fraser's framework. The decade prior to the 1973 National Housing Act amendments was marked by a series of protests about urban renewal and the razing of low-income central area housing (often referred to as slum clearance). Residents and advocates put forth oppositional challenges to the assumption that urban renewal was an ideal means of promoting healthy environments for the poor. They also identified the quite specific redistributions of wealth from lower income homeowners to real estate interests that seemed to occur as a result (see, for example, Fraser 1972; Lorimer 1970, 1972). Property and real estate interests came under increasing scrutiny, and reprivatization discourses from a variety of sources—government, business, and some social welfare agencies—responded with statistics about the poor state of the original housing stock and good news stories about improved living conditions for movers (Carver 1975; Rose 1980). In an effort to reinscribe urban renewal discourses, the then federal Minister Paul Hellyer established a Task Force on Housing and Urban Development, which included a series of cross-Canada public meetings. This decision and its aftermath marked an important moment in what was regarded as legitimate discourse about the right to decent housing and the implications for government policy on housing (Bacher 1993; Dennis and Fish 1972; Canada Federal Task Force on Housing and Urban Development 1969).

A key question in these debates was the extent to which housing should be regarded as a commodity, provided through the private market, or a basic need for all citizens, and therefore, an area requiring government involvement. While the former arguments were closely aligned with reprivatization discourses, oppositional arguments about housing as a right received considerable popular support. Some in favor of the latter position also were able to make the case that ensuring decent housing for all required that residents—or at least their community or municipal representatives—have a significant participatory role in housing design and development. During this period, housing was no longer firmly situated in the economic sphere of life—political and personal factors also were brought into the discussion. In Fraser's framework, this was an example of a runaway need in the realm of the social.

Although many of Hellyer's most significant recommendations were not accepted by the government of the day,[2] the proposal to freeze large-scale urban renewal initiatives in favor of selective clearance and to emphasize rehabilitation and revitalization received both popular and legislative support. Between 1970 and 1972, numerous housing and urban experts became heavily involved in translating these recommendations into government programs, and the resulting amendments included provisions for community groups and municipalities to work with the federal government to renew older neighborhoods, and to build and manage social housing for families and seniors (Young 1979). A particular confluence of circumstances had encouraged the inclusion of such provisions, including: a minority Liberal government dependent on the New Democratic Party to stay in power, Hellyer's highly publicized examination of the excesses of urban renewal, the specific proposals of experts who were aligned with opposition groups,[3] and finally the relatively weak position of provincial governments in comparison to the wealthy "feds" and their interest in courting the residents of rapidly growing Canadian cities (Canadian Council on Social Development 1977; Dennis and Fish 1972; Epstein 1974; Haire 1975).

NEEDS TALK, HOUSING, AND THE LOCAL

Fraser's framework also seems to offer rich possibilities for examining the implications and impacts of contested needs discourses among social groups in particular places. Such an application would, on the one hand, challenge the assumption
that places are unidimensional in their approaches to dealing with specific issues
(such as housing policies) and on the other, would deepen an understanding of the
impacts of various groups on how existing provincial or federal government policies are taken up, revised, or rejected. In doing so, this paper contributes to the
recent geographic literature that looks critically at the possibilities for autonomous
action by localities in the face of increasing globalization of economic activity, and
more generally to the further exploration of the relations between structures and
agents (Claval 1987; Claval and Kleniewski 1990; Elander et. al. 1991; Goetz and
Clarke 1993; Goetz 1993; Keating 1991; Logan and Swanstrom 1990; Massey
1993a, 1993b; Page 1996; Peterson 1981; Teeple 1995). At this point, certain
assumptions need to be made explicit, including the choice of such key terms as
locality, social group and local state.

Locality has been a fiercely contested term, especially in the British context
(see especially, Duncan 1989; Massey 1993a). Yet, as Massey has defined it, the
term captures notions central to this analysis: *connectedness* with social relations
and institutions at a variety of scales, *processes* of interaction in both space and
time, and, *the particular* insofar as this is the result of a particular expression and
conjuncture of social relations that occur more generally (Massey 1993b). Social
group refers to a meaningful unit of analysis in the examination of human relations which may have political impacts. Following Young (1990, p. 9), social
groups "reflect ways that people identify themselves and others, which lead them
to associate with some people more than others, and to treat others as different."
Jackson (1991) takes up a notion of social group and introduces a more explicitly
spatial perspective. He argues that it is in terms of social groups that "maps of
meaning" are used to help people make sense of the world and upon which they
base their actions. Through this use of social group, it is possible to conceive of a
process of translation where broad structural factors are interpreted locally based
on past understandings of the relation between cause and effect, the relation of
one group to others, and the efficacy of each to make its positions heard at specific
conjunctures.

Quite particular implications for a conceptualization of the state, particularly
the local state, derive from the argument that social groups are likely to adopt specific discourses of needs interpretation and that a social group's ability to make its
arguments heard effectively depends on a range of socio-spatial and structural
factors. Most generally, it supports the arguments of Jessop (1990) and Elander et.
al. (1991, p. 179) who argue that "[t]he relationship between "locality" and the
central state and other parameters must always be an empirical one, temporally
and spatially conditioned" and that contributions to theory building occur through

"historical analysis of the relationship between different levels of government and society in different countries in different times." This relational view suggests that it is extremely difficult to specify in advance the outcomes of interactions between various state institutions and social groups, and thus provides an important opening for discourse analysis.

By examining the local discourses—oppositional, reprivatization, and particularly expert—about housing for the poor, it is possible to come to a greater understanding of the differential manner in which certain senior government programs were interpreted locally and why certain initiatives were favored over others. The remainder of this paper is devoted to setting the scene and then unpacking the examination of NIP in North Point Douglas in order to address this objective.

THE NEIGHBORHOOD IMPROVEMENT PROGRAM

Although programs somewhat similar to NIP had been on the books since 1964, its incorporation as part of the 1973 NHA amendments was promoted as an innovative response to the failure of urban renewal (CMHC 1979a, 1979b; Filion 1988, p. 17; Lyon and Newman 1986, pp. 2-5; Rose 1980, pp. 57-59). Not only did it discourage widespread clearance, it was also supposed to promote citizen involvement by helping to stabilize and extend the vitality of certain central area neighborhoods through funds for social (e.g., community centers) and physical (e.g., sewage system upgrading) infrastructures. NIP was supposed to work in concert with the Residential Rehabilitation Assistance Program which would provide funds for renovations to low-income homeowners and landlords of moderate rental housing in designated NIP areas (Rose 1980, pp. 59-60). The program specified that funds be allocated to:

1. improve those residential neighborhoods which show evidence of need and of potential viability,
2. improve and maintain the quality of the physical environment of the neighborhood,
3. improve the amenities of the neighborhoods,
4. increase the effect of related programs,
5. improve the neighborhoods in a manner that meets the aspirations of neighborhood residents and the community at large, and
6. deliver the program in a manner which allows decisions to be made within known funding and time limits (this objective was subsequently revised: to deliver the program in an effective manner) (Lyon and Newman 1986, p. 8).

Government policymakers and politicians concerned about signs of an economic slowdown, were anxious to avoid establishing yet another open-ended program. NIP was designed to be of limited duration. It was cost-shared with the provinces, with municipalities expected to make a monetary contribution and take the lead on implementation (Filion 1988, p. 17). Municipal councils were formally responsible for designating where NIP funds would be allocated and for interpreting the meaning of citizen participation (Lyon and Newman 1986). City planning staff usually were responsible for interpreting the program's terms of reference to council and then following through on council's interpretation of the program. Staff was expected to work closely with NIP area residents to identify funding initiatives that would adhere to the program guidelines and be acceptable to both citizens and city council. However, despite the seeming specificity of the criteria for selecting appropriate NIP neighborhoods and for the distribution of funds, the various evaluations of this program make clear that differences in execution were very substantial. Lyon and Newman's (1986, p. 22) general observations are very applicable to the particular case examined here:

> The program's limited life accentuated the differential starting base from which municipalities and neighbourhoods entered NIP, especially those unprepared or inexperienced in terms of the broader goals included in the program's rationale. Time constraints also appeared to influence the extent to which fundamental planning, resource and organizational commitments were made to facilitate NIP.

Their national perspective complements that of Filion in his comparative treatment of the use of NIP in Montreal and Toronto. For both, the important roles of municipal politicians, staff and citizens, and the administrative structures within which they worked, are emphasized. Lyon and Newman also hint at socio-structural differences in their reference to a "differential starting base" and "those unprepared or inexperienced in...the broader goals."

An objective of research reported here has been to complement these extant contributions by, on the one hand, contextualizing North Point Douglas vis-à-vis Winnipeg and urban Canada more generally, and on the other hand, unpacking various local debates about housing need, including differences among municipal politicians, staff and citizens, and especially the role of experts. This examination is not meant to suggest that the experience of NIP in Winnipeg and in North Point Douglas is in any way generalizable. Indeed, evidence exists that its impacts varied considerably, depending on the context within which it was utilized .[4]

In this regard, Ley's (1986) systematic examination of 22 Canadian cities yielded two critical insights. The first was his emphasis on the socioeconomic characteristics of households rather than on housing stock in looking at neighborhood change; the second was his conclusion about the relative importance of economic and urban amenity factors, especially in the case of cities offering office-based services. His more recent exploration of the left-liberal politics of the new cultural class in Vancouver, Montreal, and Toronto has helped to clarify the need to go beyond broad categories of class or income, in order to explore more precisely the relation between professional, defined socioeconomically, and expert in the sense discussed above (Ley 1994).

Ley (1986, p. 531) explained his earlier contribution as "providing an explanatory context for the thick description of neighbourhood case studies" and in this regard as well, his work was of direct benefit. Most specifically, it provided a rationale for selecting two variables—average employment income and percentage of the workforce in administrative and management positions—as measures of comparison. To them were added gender distinctions in the case of income and occupation and, measures of ethnic diversity and segregation by family income groups, borrowed from Hill (1975). These data were examined at the Census Metropolitan Area and census tract levels, and compared to the national average for 22 urban areas (Statistics Canada 1971a, 1971b).

Ley (1986) together with Bourne (1979, 1993a, 1993b) and Filion and Bunting (1991) also established a basis for bringing broader economic and political factors into the analysis and this too will be a focus in the next section. Together, they provide an informative foundation from which to engage in an in-depth examination of housing needs talk during the period of NIP in North Point Douglas.

CONTEXTUALIZING WINNIPEG AND NORTH POINT DOUGLAS

Considerable evidence exists that North Point Douglas was politically marginalized at the municipal level during the period under investigation (Silver 1995; Smith 1990). The purpose of this section is to provide some understanding for why this was the case. To do so requires some appreciation of Winnipeg's situation vis-à-vis the broader Canadian urban political economy of the period. Winnipeg often has been portrayed as occupying a distinctive place in Canadian urban geography, both demographically and politically (Hill 1975; Brownstone and Plunkett 1983). In comparison to those in other Canadian cities in 1971, Winnipeg's residents had lower average employment incomes and proportions in management occupations than the average for 22 Canadian cities (see Table 1). This reflected Winnipeg's history as an older industrial city in decline. As well, Winnipeg's population included greater ethnic diversity than did any other place in Canada. During this period, Winnipeg had considerable stocks of old, run down housing, but despite an overall situation of slow growth, its suburbs expanded quite rapidly in response to the considerable incentives that also were part of the 1973 NHA amendments, and this meant an increasing concentration of poorer households in the inner city (Bostrom 1984; Kiernan and Walker 1983; Ram et al. 1989; Silver 1995).

The demographic characteristics of North Point Douglas residents accentuated much of what made Winnipeg distinct from other Canadian cities in 1971 (see Table 1). Its ethnicity index was substantially above that of Winnipeg as a whole. There were many less managers among both men and women in North Point Douglas as compared to Winnipeg. Interestingly, although male employment income

Table 1. Selected Socioeconomic Characteristics, Metropolitan
Canada, Winnipeg, and North Point Douglas
(Census Tracts 35, 36), 1971

	Metropolitan Canada (22 cities)	Winnipeg	North Point Douglas
Ethnicity Index	.51	.77	.82
Average Employment Male	7,081	6,707	4,952
Average Employment Female	3,315	2,965	2,531
Managerial Administration Male	6.5%	7.0%	1.0%
Managerial Administration Femaler	2.0%	2.0%	1.0%
Segregation Index (mean segregation index of six family income groups)	.199	.234	N/A

Source: Statistics Canada (1971b) and Hill (1975).

was far below the Winnipeg average, this was not the case for women's employment incomes, probably because working-class women formed the greatest proportion of paid female workers during this period.

Winnipeg's experience of political fragmentation throughout the twentieth century also has often been noted, and connections have been made with the negative impact on poor neighborhoods in Winnipeg, such as North Point Douglas, to influence municipal policy. Before 1960, this region consisted of 12 autonomous and quite distinct municipalities, and this past has affected Winnipeg's more recent history of municipal politics. Silver, for example, has described local politics in terms of competition between neighborhoods, exacerbated by ethnic and class antagonisms which he dates from the 1919 Winnipeg General Strike (Silver 1995; Kiernan and Walker 1983).

Not surprisingly, efforts to coordinate land-use planning and transportation at a regional level also were quite difficult prior to 1960 (Axworthy and Cassidy 1974; Axworthy 1979) and in two instances, the provincial government sought resolution through the imposition of institutional reform. The first, under Duff Roblin's Conservative government of 1958-1967, involved the creation of a second tier of government or "Metro." Although some technocratic gains were made, they were insufficient for the New Democratic Government that came to power in 1969. Two years later, a new single tier government called Unicity took the place of "Metro." In order to balance Unicity's necessarily regional perspective, the new legislation included provisions for neighborhood-based Community Committees and Resident Advisory Groups (RAGs) to play a significant policy-making role.

However, although Unicity was hailed as a radical experiment to increase citizen participation at the time of its inception, observers soon realized that new structures would not change old politicians overnight (Axworthy et al. 1973; Axworthy 1980). This was especially true given Manitoba's and Winnipeg's difficult economic circumstances (Gonick 1990; Silver and Hull 1990;

Nader 1976). During the 1970s, Manitoba ranked eighth, ninth, or tenth of all provincial economies for several years (Stewart 1993, pp. 68-82). One outcome of these social and economic factors was an entrenched business-oriented council with deep ideological reservations about challenges from social democratic points of view. The received wisdom among most Winnipeg city counselors was that the city could not afford to allocate local taxes to any initiatives beyond the minimum, except with regard to the promotion of economic growth. Communities such as North Point Douglas were especially adversely affected by this orientation and their representatives were not usually successful in bringing their specific concerns to the fore (Axworthy 1980; Gereke and Reid 1992; Kiernan and Walker 1983; Lyon and Fenton 1984; Smith 1990; Walker 1979). Thus, social, political, and economic factors all help to explain the lack of a shift to a more progressive, municipal reform stance among the Winnipeg's counselors, and especially the adverse bargaining position of areas such as North Point Douglas, in contrast to the experiences in Ottawa, Toronto, or Vancouver (Lorimer and Ross 1976, p. 123).

NIP COMES TO WINNIPEG

As noted above, the city of Winnipeg had very little previous experience with the citizen participation and neighborhood-based planning approaches being promoted through NIP. In interactions among city departments, between city hall and area residents, and between neighborhoods, little was previously available in Winnipeg within which to fit or nest NIP efforts or possibilities: much had to be invented anew. Administration of the program not only required the formation of a new branch of the Department of Environmental Planning—the Neighborhood Planning Branch—but also a new bureaucratic infrastructure in order to consult with local residents and to coordinate the efforts of various departments in NIP areas.

Initially, city staff appeared quite hopeful that the combination of generous funds and program specifications would shift the department's orientation away from past efforts to those which explicitly linked physical and social planning. Staff's initial proposals to the city council are illustrative:

Physical planning is seen as a component part of the total approach to better social living. Although housing and physical development are of fundamental importance to neighbourhood improvement, other factors should be represented in planning and program form. These other factors include the following:

- employment and training
- education
- health
- social service.

Social planning is looked at from two points of view. On the one hand it is considered as "attempting to determine the social implications of physical programs". This is especially important when one considers that initial implementation will very much relate to physical development. On the other hand, social planning is considered as establishing a social development program. This refers both to community development which encourages resident participation, and to the provision of actual social facilities and services for the neighbourhood (City of Winnipeg 1974, pp. 8-9).

Using Fraser's terminology, the chains of in-order-relations implicit in their arguments were coincidentally social and physical: for neighborhood improvement to take place, there was a requirement for responding to residents' social concerns in conjunction with physical structures where suitable facilities and resources might be found. At this early stage, their views were in keeping with the perspectives of contemporary social critics whose arguments in favor of decent housing were linked to a notion of significant resident input into government decisions about their homes and neighborhoods, as well as to arguments in favor of making strong connections between social, physical and economic planning (see, for example, Dickerson et al. 1974; Powell 1972). However, by 1975, there was a clear shift away from utilizing such comprehensive frameworks to a much narrower approach, clearly focused on what could be paid for through the NIP program. More specifically, the assumption that new physical structures alone might lead, somehow, to resident and therefore, neighborhood improvement came to be emphasized as the city council indicated its unwillingness to provide any complementary resources. Subsequent reports to the city council from the Neighborhood Improvement Branch highlighted physical infrastructure improvements, with other elements relegated to the status of a wish list depending on the availability of other funding sources (City of Winnipeg 1975).

Moreover, implementation efforts were devised on a project-by-project basis, with little consideration of initiatives that would build on the social commonalities between areas. For example, although the four locales initially recommended for NIP designation were located near one another, there was little evidence of any coordinated planning efforts between them. Instead, the argument put forth was that:

Neighbourhood improvement will respond to the needs of relatively small areas (approximately 5,000 persons). Through concentrating resources in such designated areas, improvement resources will take on greater impact in effecting change (City of Winnipeg 1974, p. 6).

Here, too, there is a shift in needs talk from one which linked residents' social relations and economic needs with physical improvements, to an almost exclusive emphasis on the latter. Generally, Neighborhood Improvement Branch staff worked to first develop residents' committees and then to identify, with residents, physical improvements to the area that were of most interest to the people living there. North Point Douglas residents were not at all involved in the hiring of staff or in the planning of how the initial sector meetings would be organized. Rather, the "script," and thus the logical relations between social, economic, and physical factors, was a set one, originating with Neighborhood Branch staff and with little room for residents to change the order or emphasis:

> Initial sector meetings consist of two parts. In the first half of the meeting residents are provided with a detailed report of the nature and intent of the Neighbourhood Improvement Program. This is followed by a slide presentation characterizing the program area in general, with special emphasis on the sector in which the meeting takes place. The second half of the meeting consists of an "Action Presentation" through which residents are exposed to examples of physical changes that could improve their area. Specific issues assumed to have dramatic effect on the whole of the neighbourhood are discussed as well as specific issues within each sector. The meeting is then opened to resident comment. For the most part, individual complaints are hurled at City staff as the program is challenged over how it can relate to specific demands (City of Winnipeg 1975, p. 4).

Where links to social welfare issues were made, the solution was seen in terms of efforts external to the NIP initiative, involving the search for funds to increase social services. The possibility of shifting the nature and relations of extant programs was not entertained. Instead, staff and residents worked with other local agencies to lobby for enhanced social service funding but their success was highly dependent on whether an existing program could be tied to their efforts. Very often, their successes were temporary ones, dependent on whether the source of funding would continue to be part of the mandate of the government of the day (Bostock et. al. 1981; City of Winnipeg 1981). In the example below, sweat equity cooperatives were presented as one of many ideas originating out of a residents' subcommittee. Staff acted to link the idea with a possible funding source, but beyond this, did not seem to regard it as in any way significant. When the most likely funder withdrew support, the initiative was dropped:

> Searching for ways by which low and moderate income families could acquire their own homes, the Housing subcommittee investigated the concept of sweat equity building co-operatives. By sweat equity is meant constructing houses by a group which will act as a labour pool and will then break up to assume individual ownership. Meetings have been held with the Provincial Department of Cooperative Development in regard to this program and the possible implementation in North Point Douglas. Through this program, members of a building co-op do most of the construction and are able to take advantage of bulk purchasing of materials, thus reducing the net cost of a house.

> Staff from the Provincial Department of Co-operative Development were deployed to work with N.I.P. in implementing a sweat equity program. However, this staff support was withdrawn by the Province prior to drawing a group of potential participants together (City of Winnipeg 1981, p. 41).

Thus, as work on NIP progressed in North Point Douglas, there was a clear narrowing of what were considered legitimate connections between the physical improvements central to NIP and other, social and economic factors that might contribute to improving the neighborhood. The increasingly restrictive interpretation of the NIP program seems to have been conveyed to residents by staff in lock step with the indications that the city council would not support other, more expansive interpretations. As will be shown below, this progression has some interesting parallels with the evolution of recommendations by local research and advocacy organizations, although the remaining distinctiveness of each set of expert needs talk is equally noteworthy.

HOUSING NEEDS TALK IN WINNIPEG AND NORTH POINT DOUGLAS

Numerous reports attest to the substantial talk about housing need in North Point Douglas during this period. Between 1974 and 1981 at least five reports were produced through the Department of Environmental Planning (City of Winnipeg 1974, 1975, 1979a, 1979b, 1981) and a sixth through the Canada Mortgage and Housing Corporation (CMHC) regional office (Bostock et al. 1981). During this same period, there were publications on such topics as: core area poverty, housing, and the specific concerns of women and aboriginal peoples, through the writings of a variety of experts outside city hall (Croteau and Zink 1975; Damas & Smith Ltd., 1975; Epstein 1974; Henderson 1973; Institute of Urban Studies 1979; Social Planning Council of Winnipeg 1977). In both analysis and recommendations, these latter reports were clearly the result of efforts to combine the forces of oppositional and expert discourses in order to shift the focus of NIP to one more attuned to the broader context within which areas such as North Point Douglas were located. However, there was little direct impact: no reference was made to these analyses in any of the official NIP publications.

Comparing the discourses about housing need offers important insights into the differing explanatory frameworks initially used by two sets of experts around the same set of issues. Both problem identification, and the relative significance of appropriate responses diverged quite fundamentally at first. In the official NIP documents, the problem was clearly the negative impacts of population change:

> The long term residents in North Point Douglas over a period of years experienced the rate and degree of change in the composition of the neighbourhood. They saw changes in building use and abuse, and were quite aware of the general overall deterioration of the area.

> Although the population was declining, the social problems mounting and the physical quality of the community diminishing and regressing, there still existed a certain sense of stability and pride, particularly among the Ukrainians whose sense of home ownership was of paramount importance. (City of Winnipeg 1981, p. 9).

According to this analysis, North Point Douglas needed to improve the physical appearance of its housing, by trying to retain as many homeowners as possible, but this would be difficult given the population changes that were taking place. The traditional, largely older Eastern European immigrant residents of the area were presented as an essential aspect of North Point Douglas' future viability, while others were implicated as part of the problem.[5] Although not discussed in any detail,[6] these others were implied to be young native families, often headed by a woman. This image was (and remains to a considerable degree) an outstanding symbol of a social problem (Peters 1996; Richardson 1994). Given NIP's funding specifications and the city council's reluctance to work proactively, solutions were articulated in terms of physical improvements and on efforts to make the area look normal:

> The eight houses under construction by the Manitoba Housing and Renewal Corporation and Winnipeg School Division are almost complete. They will soon be occupied, with preference given to public housing applicants from North Point Douglas.
>
> From a design point of view the infill housing units are beautifully blended into the existing housing stock. They are not overpowering and conform to the character of the neighbourhood. We have heard many favourable comments from residents about these houses, to the point where the Infill Program is seen as an effective way of introducing public housing into older city areas. It tells people that public housing can be sensitive to the character of the community (City of Winnipeg 1975, p. 28).

The particularity of the municipal approach becomes quite evident when juxtaposed against other discussions of the period. Not only did these latter analyses pay at least some attention to the broader policy and economic, contexts; they also made some attempt to connect the social characteristics of households with appropriate remedies. In these reports, the problem was defined not as population change per se, but rather as the result of structural, economic and political circumstances which would then explain certain outcomes, such as dilapidated inner-city housing or the high levels of poverty among mother-led and aboriginal households. Recognizing the ways in which the broader economic and social contexts impinged on neighborhood improvement was articulated in several of the reports. Two of them explicitly identified the relative lack of resources to inner-city revitalization in comparison to suburban development (Epstein 1974, pp. 361-362; Croteau and Zink 1975), while a third identified the relation between housing, and intergovernmental jurisdictional disputes about who should pay for services to aboriginal peoples covered by the Indian Act (Damas & Smith Ltd., 1975).

Solutions differed as well. They were sought in terms of counteracting negative structural pressures; and two such remedies, mentioned several times, were sweat equity and the Winnipeg Housing: Improvement Project (WHIP). The idea of making direct connections between training and employment opportunities and the need for housing rehabilitation and the development of appropriately designed social housing developments, caught the interest of a variety of the experts outside city hall.[7] Their rationale was similar to those articulated in the NIP staff's first proposal to the council: the links that would be promoted between social and physical planning, and employment and housing concerns. Moreover, making such links challenged and subverted the reprivatization arguments (strongly represented on Winnipeg City Council) that housing was best regarded as a commodity. In a 1974 report of the Institute of Urban Studies on neighborhood improvement and citizen participation, fully one-half of its overall recommendations were focused on WHIP:

> The WHIP study and related evaluations point to the efficacy of a locally based, locally staffed, and locally serving rehabilitation program. The program combines a high degree of "industrial democracy," collective responsibility, and visible improvement to the immediate physical environment. It has served as a means of "gainful employment," skill upgrading, and psychological satisfaction for the participants. It has certainly repaired homes to the satisfaction of their owners.
>
> Thus, WHIP's generation of employment possibilities in low-income residential neighborhoods could well serve as a key element within an overall improvement strategy. WHIP could combine its limited repair program with a range of related functions:
>
> • assisting clients in the securing of government grants and loans;
> • performing non-profit rehabilitation work for non-profit companies;
> • "enforcing" maintenance and building standard by-laws on behalf of the city;
> • combining with the municipality to develop rent control protection for tenants in exchange for limited repair of landlords' property;
> • generating related neighbourhood employment opportunities (e.g. warehousing and non-profit distribution of building materials, staffing of "spin off" rehabilitation companies, etc.)
> • providing education and instruction on home and property maintenance;
> • providing "second opinions" for clients contemplating more extensive home projects;
> • producing new ideas regarding alterations and functions of interior spaces;
> • assisting in the planning and administering of larger scale improvement schemes (Epstein 1974, pp. 346-347).

Two 1975 studies, largely based on interviews with nonexperts, also highlighted the potential of WHIP and sweat equity initiatives for Winnipeg's low-income women and aboriginal peoples. Croteau and Zink identified housing as the concern most commonly mentioned by Winnipeg women; an expanded WHIP initiative was one of its six housing-related recommendations:

> That a widespread rehabilitation and renovation program be undertaken in the core area of Winnipeg. This is already being done on a limited scale in very deteriorated N.I.P. areas of the city under the R.R.A.P. program. Renovations could also be carried out by a housing repair company such as Winnipeg Home Improvement Program (W.H.I.P.). This company functions as a training centre for "unemployables" and requires that the home owner only pay the cost of repair materials (1975, p. 20).

From a somewhat different perspective, a 1975 feasibility study on "The Neeginan Concept" (a Native people's community in Winnipeg), also hinted at the need to consider housing together with the broader concerns of urban aboriginal peoples in Winnipeg:

> Housing itself is not a solution to the problem. Housing has been provided for other groups of poor people, in numerous urban renewal projects, and the projects have failed as experiments

in social rehabilitation. In every case the failure has been due to the fact that the schemes were never conceived of as anything more than housing—the objective was to provide decent living accommodation, and this they did… But they did not provide the essential social development and support programs necessary to help the projects survive as healthy social entities, and achieve the objectives of social and economic rehabilitation. These programs must be built into the overall scheme from the beginning. Training facilities must be provided, perhaps in sheltered workshops; leadership must be given in developing their own initiative and managerial skills. Members from this community should certainly be involved in the management of the community's affairs, and perhaps Indian policemen could be trained and assigned to this beat (Damas & Smith, 1975, p. 8).

In each of these documents, important connections were made, using a structural analysis to explain why housing was such a concern for women and aboriginal peoples in Winnipeg, and what the appropriate remedies might be. The argument was not simply a rejection of housing as a commodity. Both reports also suggested that housing could become a significant means for improving the economic circumstances and quality of life of marginalized persons, if set within an appropriate framework of decision making and control.

In general, there was a clear distinction between the perspectives adapted by experts within and outside of municipal government, especially during the first part of the period under investigation. Given the much greater overlap among experts in other jurisdictions, it is reasonable to speculate that the weak representation of urban reform perspectives in the city council was an important contributing factor.[8] However, by 1977, there is some evidence of subtle but notable shifts in problem identification and recommendations for change among experts outside city hall. Such shifts would not be surprising, because they coincide with a period in Canadian social history in which researchers have identified a general shift among the orientation and practices of community organizations from "protest" to "coproductive" relations with the state. Furthermore, these shifts have been linked to changes in how state institutions interacted with these organizations, including the terms under which funding was allocated (Hasson and Ley 1994; Hulchanski 1986; Loney 1977).

In the case of Winnipeg, there is strong evidence to suggest that these more general trends were encouraged by the developments leading up to the establishment of the first Core Area Initiative in 1981. For example, according to Stewart (1993, p. 98):

The community of Winnipeg in general, and the resident and business representatives in particular, were invited to have input into the proposed CA1 before it was signed in 1981. This is not to suggest, however, that community involvement was solicited in the development of the model's strategy or management system. Perhaps it was the complexity of the CA1 Agreement structure and the desire to have programmes in place to take advantage of this unexpected source of funding that could be used to explain the lack of community involvement in these important early states of the Initiative. Nonetheless, each level of government undertook a series of informal meetings with inner-city service agencies to solicit ideas related to potential programming. There was also substantial interest-group lobbying of the Policy Committee in attempts to secure support for various proposed capital projects.

Stewart (1993) goes on to note that the housing and neighborhood revitalization program of CA1 were especially successful, in part because it was possible to take advantage of complementary provincial and federal funding opportunities, such as RRAP in the repair of thousand of homes (p. 106; see also Pollack 1994). However, none of these initiatives explicitly promoted the notion of directly linking the employment and training of low-income individuals and the alleviation of their poor housing conditions.

Given these broader developments, it is reasonable to ask whether a subtle shift in discussions of "sweat equity" initiatives by experts outside city hall is indicative of a changing orientation, from protest to coproduction. In raising this question here, I have identified three reports in which sweat equity might reasonably have been mentioned during this latter period: *A Housing Action Plan for Winnipeg's Inner City* (Social Planning Council of Winnipeg 1977), *Housing Conditions in Winnipeg: The Identification of Problems and High Need Groups* (Stevens 1979) and *Housing: Inner City Type Older Areas* (Institute of Urban Studies 1979). While all three documents were explicit in recognizing *who* was in most need of housing help, in contrast to the NIP documents, all three shifted *away* from an emphasis on the active participation of those in need, to a focus on recommendations for state intervention incorporating a reliance on experts. For example, *A Housing Action Plan for Winnipeg's Inner City* was produced through a series of noon hour meetings by "a group of concerned individuals who live and/ or work in Winnipeg's "core area"... to try to do something about the serious housing crisis in north/central Winnipeg" (Social Planning Council of Winnipeg 1977, p. ii). Most of the 45 participants listed an affiliation with a local nongovernment organization, including: Indian-Metis Friendship Centre, Kinew Housing, YWCA, Institute of Urban Studies and various health, seniors and tenants associations, together with 3 NIP staff and one provincial Department of Health and Social Development employee. In the opening section of the paper, the argument was made that there should be explicit recognition of who was most in need of better housing:

> The target population is largely the low-income people who live in our area, including welfare recipients, single parents, the elderly, native people, the working poor and the unemployed. Any housing policy in our area should be designed around the needs of this target population. It should be pointed out that approximately 70% of the residents of this area are tenants (Social Planning Council of Winnipeg 1977, p. 2).

The subsequent documents were even more specific, and the poor housing situations of young single parents were particularly emphasized (Social Planning Council of Winnipeg 1979; Institute of Urban Studies 1979). However, their primary objective was not on discussion of structural problems per se, but rather what a housing action plan for Winnipeg's inner city might consist of, if municipal and provincial politicians and staff were willing even to take advantage of existing programs and regulations.

At one level, the shift was a response to three immediate concerns: (1) the city council's rejection of a staff proposal to establish a city housing policy and follow the lead of such cities as Toronto, Ottawa, and Vancouver (City of Winnipeg Council Minutes, October 19, 1977, pp. 2155-2156); (2) a spate of house fires resulting in injury and death and attributed to substandard housing (Social Planning Council of Winnipeg 1977); and (3) the growing realization that the City of Winnipeg's approach of responding to housing problems in isolation actually was making the situation worse:

> Tenants are caught in the squeeze between the irresponsible landlord on the one hand, who refuses to take the steps required to make his accommodation "liveable", and the City of Winnipeg administration, which has stepped up enforcement, but has done nothing to replace substandard units they know are going to have to be replaced.

The structural analysis that had informed earlier documents was used to illustrate the negative impacts of extant initiatives and to shape future efforts:

> Even if the Province and the City were to build another 3,000 units to replace the ones that are going off the market, there is no planning for recreation, green space, parks and cultural facilities (Social Planning Council of Winnipeg 1977, p. 2).

> Given what the City proposes...we question very seriously whether this policy will in any way affect the housing situation in north/central Winnipeg. It would seem that the target population will inevitably be upwardly-mobile lower middle-class or working-class couples, who acquire a City-renovated home as a starter home (7) ...analysis of the current program options indicates...the superior cost-effectiveness of rehabilitation, as opposed to new development strategies, be they undertaken by the private, public or third sector. In spite of this fact there is currently no federal, provincial, or municipal vehicle capable of facilitating a significant rehabilitation program for the inner city (Institute of Urban Studies 1979, p. 47).

However, two other, more disturbing messages in these documents were the presentation of poor residents as "victims" in need of professional guidance, and a discussion of solutions that tend to "blame the victim" in a manner similar to the NIP reports:

> In considering the housing problem of north/central Winnipeg, it must be remembered that the majority of the people we are talking about are tenants who have fixed incomes which are very low. These people are isolated, not always aware of their rights, and lack advocacy services to which they can get ready access. There is a growing sense of community, but there really is no focal point. Many of the residents of the area have trouble adjusting to city life, let alone adjusting to a forced move from one slum dwelling to another (Social Planning Council of Winnipeg 1977, p. 5).

> The inner city is experiencing population, demographic and housing market changes resulting in a severe erosion of the quality of life in some inner city type neighbourhoods, increasing

social problems linked to concentrations of disadvantaged households, and increasing locational restrictions on housing opportunities open to middle and upper income households
(Institute of Urban Studies 1979, p. ii).

These statements suggest that there may be a link between the extent to which
sweat-equity type initiatives were highlighted, and the degree to which residents
were seen as active participants in dealing with the structural barriers they faced.
Sweat equity occupied just one line of the densely written, 18-page 1977 Social
Planning Council of Winnipeg document, "The Encouragement of Sweat Equity
Programs in North/Central Winnipeg," was included in a list of "People Oriented
Housing Alternatives" which was itself the focus of just one-half page of the
entire report (p. 14). Links between housing rehabilitation and employment training were not mentioned at all in the 1979 Social Planning Council of Winnipeg
and Institute of Urban Studies reports.

CONCLUSIONS

In this paper, I have argued there are insights to be gained from a critical investigation of the variety of expert discourses on housing need during the period of NIP
in North Point Douglas, Winnipeg. I have shown how experts working for the city
of Winnipeg gradually shifted their analysis and prescriptions from those incorporating both social and physical or environmental aspects to ones much more
heavily weighted toward the latter, in line with concerns by local politicians about
incurring additional costs for the municipality. I also identified how other experts
were much more likely to maintain a connection between the social and the environmental. In the latter case, however, there also is some evidence of change, from
an orientation in which those in housing need would be an active part of the
solution to one in which they became the passive recipients of expert action.

In both cases, the broader socioeconomic context provides some clues for why
expert discourses shifted as they did, and they also illustrate Fraser's discussion
of the ways that expert discourses sometimes can be porous. In the particular
example examined here, the direction of change, especially among experts working outside of municipal government, suggests that a more self-reflective
approach toward their work might have produced a different result. Was it simply
a coincidence that the backgrounds of the experts and those they were prescribing
solutions for, were quite different? Did they reflect attitudes similar to those documented by Evelyn Peters, about aboriginal peoples not belonging in the city
(Peters 1996)? Did this difference influence the attitude that experts brought to
their analysis, especially when material circumstances also were changing,
negatively, with regard to employment opportunities?

The purpose of this analysis is not, however, to ascribe blame for the lack of
innovative responses to the challenges occasionally identified but ultimately dis-
missed during the period of the Neighborhood Improvement Program in North

Point Douglas. Its contribution, rather, is to highlight the potential significance of needs talk, its relation to how solutions are identified in a particular time and place, and how these solutions continue to have effects many years after their immediate identification.

The introduction to this paper included two sets of observations about the problems facing Winnipeg's inner-city poor in the 1990s. In both cases, the focus was not on a lack of resources but rather on a lack of willingness to incorporate the views of those for whom programs and initiatives are being devised. This paper provides one part of the explanation of why this separation has been so difficult to overcome. During the 1970s, a variety of factors conspired to shift solutions from those who were most directly affected, to a group of experts whose backgrounds were quite different from those they were prescribing solutions for. Given the wealth of knowledge that has been accumulated between that period and this one, about colonial and patriarchal orientations of Canadian state representatives, this analysis suggests that there is an important role for self-reflexivity among experts working with Winnipeg's poor.

ACKNOWLEDGMENTS

I would like to thank the following individuals for their insightful comments on earlier drafts of this paper: Aron Spector, Deborah Gorham, Valerie Preston, Vera Chouinard, and Caroline Andrew, as well as two anonymous reviewers. I also want to thank Linda Williams and Wayne Helgasen for the many insights gained about Winnipeg local politics through my interviews and other discussions with them. I acknowledge the important financial support of the Social Sciences and Humanities Research Council File #410-95-0086, as well as the invaluable research assistance of Karen Campbell.

NOTES

1. This statement is an excerpt from an ultimately successful proposal for funding to Health Canada. Health Promotion Branch, in which the Social Planning Council of Winnipeg worked with the neighborhood organizations. Andrews Street Family Center, Winnipeg Housing Coalition, and The Pas Friendship Center.

2. Hellyer's recommendations regarding municipal land banking would have been a very significant challenge to private real state interest (see discussion in Bacher 1993).

3. As Dreier and Huchanski (1994), have noted, the 1973 NHA amendments created a much more supportive climate for building viable social housing communities than was true of the American reaction to urban renewal.

4. For example, research-in-progress about the use of NIP funds in the Centretown area of Ottawa reveals a very different pattern. In this case, a modest amount of money was allocated to one particular section of Centretown and considered one aspect of a much more general endeavor to develop a neighborhood land-use plan. Moreover, other available monies also were brought into play. For example, under the terms of a provincially funded demonstration project.

A Social Co-Ordinator has been appointed in Centre Town 3 to act as a resource to the community to gain input from the social agencies serving the area and to aid in the development of a social strategy plan so that the social needs of the area can be determined (City of Ottawa 1976, p. 25).

Thus, NIP funds were allocated within a much broader context of citizen involvement in establishing an overall neighborhood vision and plan of action. Coupled with the necessary resources, both monetary and personnel, there was an ability to use a relatively small amount of money to further broaden aims and not simply to provide an additional facility (Ontario Ministry of Housing, 1981; City of Ottawa, 1974).

NIP came to Ottawa during a period in which conditions were specially favorable to incorporating a variety of funding possibilities to try out new ideas about neighborhood planning. The reform minority on council was an effective challenge to the reprivatization discourses although they too were very much in evidence, both on council and from among certain Centretown business interests (Centretown Citizen Planning Committee 1975; Leaning 1995). Resources were available to implement ambitious approaches to citizen participation and the connecting of various threads of what was seen as relevant to the planning exercise.

5.   There is some anecdotal evidence, taken from interviews by the author with Winnipeg housing activits and experts, that this was in part due to the overlap in ethnic background between city staff and residents of European background.

6.   Mention of the significant numbersof aboriginal peoples in North Point Douglas is mentioned twice over the course of all of the NIP reports for the area:

Change is taking place in North Point Douglas relative to ethnic composition. Of significance is the decline of the Ukranian population...The Indian and Metis population is also increasing, although we do not have statistics with which to determine to what extent (City of Winnipeg 1974, p. 57).

Direct contact with parents and with non-school neighborhood organizations is made by the COMMUNITY ORIENTATION WORKER. Since a proportion of children are native Canadian, a NATIVE AID is employed and special understanding and insights can be applied (City of Winnipeg 1979b, p. 4).

7.   The decision to utilize "sweat equity" as an analytic focal point was also a result of the fact that this concept was highlighted in the successful 1995 Social Planning Council of Winnipeg proposal for funding to Health Canada, Health Promotion Branch (see note 1).

8.   See the discussion of Centretown, Ottawa in note 3.

REFERENCES

Ark Research Associates. 1996. *The Housing Conditions of Aboriginal Peoples in Canada, 1991.* CMHC: Ottawa.

Artibise, A. 1977. "Divided City: The Immigrant in Winnipeg Society, 1874-1921." Pp 300-336 in *The Canadian City,* edited by G. A. Stelter and A. Artibise. Ottawa: McClelland and Stewart.

Axworthy, L. 1979, "The Politics of Urban Populism: A Decade of Reform." Pp. 282-292 in *Urban and Regional Planning in a Federal State,* edited by W. T. Perks, I. M. Robinson. New York: McGraw-Hill.

_____. 1980. "The Best Laid Plans Oft Go Astray: The Case of Winnipeg". Pp. 105-123. In *Problems of Change in Urban Government,* edited by M. O. Dickerson, S. Drabek, J. J. Woods. Waterloo: Wilfred University Press.

Axworthy, L., and J. Cassidy. 1974. "Unicity in Transition." *The Future City Report 4*. Winnipeg: Institute of Urban Studies.

Axworthy, L., M. Grant, J. Cassidy, G. Siamandas. 1973.*Meeting the Problems and Needs of Resident Advisory Groups*. Winnipeg: Institute of Urban Studies.

Bacher, J. 1993. *Keeping to the Marketplace*. Montreal: McGill-Queens.

Banting, K. 1990. "Social Housing in a Divided State". Pp. 115-163 in *Housing the Homeless and the Poor*, edited by G. Fallis, A. Murray. Toronto: University of Toronto Press.

Bird, F. 1970. *The Royal Commission on the Status of Women in Canada*. Ottawa: Information Canada.

Bostock, A., M. Farag, C, Oliver, R. Clough, and O. Crain. 1981. *An Evaluation of the Neighbourhood Improvement Program in Winnipeg*. Ottawa: Canada Mortgage and Housing Corporation.

Bostrom, H. 1984. "Government Policies and Programs Relating to People of Indian Ancestry in Manitoba." Pp 35-201 in *The Dynamics of Government Programs for Urban Indians in the Prairie Provinces*, edited R. Breton, G. Grant. Montreal: Institute for Research on Public Policy.

Bourne, L. S. 1979. "Urbanization Trends and the Federal Response." Pp. 19-38 in *Urban and Regional Planning in a Federal State*, edited by W. T. Perks, I. M. Robinson. New York: McGraw-Hill.

_____. 1993a. "Close Together and Worlds Apart: An Analysis of Changes in the Ecology of Income in Canadian Cities." *Urban Studies* 30(8): 1293-1317.

_____. 1993b. "The Demise of Gentrification? A Commentary and Prospective View." *Urban Geography* 14(1): 95-107.

Brownstone, M., & T. J. Plunkett. 1983. *Metropolitan Winnipeg: Politics and Reform of Local Government*. Berkeley: University of California Press.

Canada Federal Task Force on Housing and Urban Development. 1969. *Report of the Federal Task Force on Housing and Urban Development*. Ottawa: Information Canada.

Canada-Manitoba Bipartite Agreement for the Economic Development of Winnipeg. 1995. *Winnipeg Development Agreement*. Winnipeg.

Canada Mortgage and Housing Corporation. 1979a. "Workshop Proceedings and Summary of Recommendations." In *Evaluation of the Neighbourhood Improvement Program*. Ottawa: CMHC.

_____. 1979b. "Provincial Position Papers." In *Evaluation of the Neighbourhood Improvement Program*. Ottawa: CMHC.

_____. 1979c. "Main Report." In *Evaluation of the Neighbourhood Improvement Program*. Ottawa: CMHC.

Canadian Council on Social Development. 1977. *A Review of Canadian Social Housing Policy*. Canadian Council on Social Development: Ottawa.

Carter, T., and A. McAfee. 1990. "The Municipal Role in Housing the Homeless and Poor." Pp. 227-262 in *Housing the Homeless and the Poor*, edited by G. Fallis, A. Murray. Toronto: University of Toronto Press.

Carter, T., R. Bublick, C. McKee, and L. McFadyen. 1993. *Interaction of Social Housing and Social Safety Net Programs: A Basis for Discussion*. Ottawa: Centre for Future Studies in Housing and Living Environments, CMHC.

Carver, H. 1975. *Compassionate Landscape*. Toronto: University of Toronto Press.

Centretown Citizen Planning Committee. 1975. "The Economic Framework to Reestablish Residential Community in the Centretown Development Plan." Paper presented to Mayor Lorry Greenberg and Members of the Ottawa Planning Board, January 16, City of Ottawa Archives.

City of Ottowa. 1974. *Centretown Neighborhood Development Plan*. Ottawa: Centretown Planning Unit, Planning Department.

City of Ottawa. 1976. *Neighborhood Improvement Program Redevelopment Plan Centre Town NIP Area 3 Ottawa, Ontario*. Prepared by Department of Community Development Branch in Co-operation with the Citizens' NIP Committee, Adopted by City Council, January 19.

City of Winnipeg. 1974. Winnipeg: *NIP 74*. Department of Environmental Planning, Neighbourhood Improvement Branch.

_____. 1975. *Neighbourhood Improvement Progress Report*. Winnipeg: Department of Environmental Planning, Neighbourhood Improvement Branch.

_____. 1978. *Winnipeg Area Characterization*. Winnipeg: Department of Environmental Planning.

_____. 1979a. *Housing and Neighborhood Strategies*. Winnipeg: Department of Environmental Planning.

_____. 1979b. *N.I.P. Says Farewell to North Point Douglas*. Winnipeg: Department of Environmental Planning.

_____. 1981. *North Point Douglas: A Neighbourhood Improvement Program*. Winnipeg: Department of Environmental Planning, Neighbourhood Improvement Branch.

Claval, P. 1987. *The Progressive City*. New Brunswick, New Jersey: Rutgers University Press.

Claval, P., and N. Kleniewski. 1990. "Space for Progressive Local Policy: Examples from the United States and the United Kingdom." Pp. 199-236 in *Beyond the City Limits: Urban Policy and Economic Restructuring in Comparative Perspective*, edited by J. R. Logan, T. Swanstrom. Philadelphia: Temple University Press.

Croteau, M. J., and W. Zink. 1975. *Women's Concerns About the Quality of Life in Winnipeg*, report # 031. Winnipeg: Institute of Urban Studies.

Damas & Smith Ltd., 1975. *Neeginan: A Report on the Feasibility Study prepared for Neeginan (MB) Incorporated*. Winnipeg: Author.

Dennis, M., and S. Fish. 1972. *Programs in Search of a Policy: Low Income Housing in Canada*. Toronto: Hakkert.

Dickerson, M., S. Drabek, J. Wood. 1974. *Problems of Change in Urban Government*. Waterloo: Wilfrid Laurier University Press.

Duncan, S. 1989. "What is Locality." Pp. 221-254 in *New Models in Geography, vol. 2*, edited by R. Peet, N. Thrift. London: Unwin Hyman.

Elander, I., T. Stromberg, B. Denrmark, and B. Soderfeldt. 1991. "Locality Research and Comparative Analysis: The Case of Local Housing Policy in Sweden." *Society and Space* 23: 179-196.

Epstein, D. 1974, "Toward Neighbourhood Improvement: Policy Development and Program Recommendations." Pp. 242-96 in *Housing Innovation and Neighbourhood Improvement: Change in Winnipeg's Inner City*, edited by D. Epstein. Winnipeg: Institute of Urban Studies.

Filion, P. 1988, "The Neighbourhood Improvement Plan: Montreal and Toronto: Contrasts between a Participatory and a Centralized Approach to Urban Policy Making." *Urban History Review* 17(1): 16-28.

Filion, P., and T. Bunting. 1991. "Introduction: Perspectives on the Canadian City." Pp. 1-22 in *Canadian Cities in Transition*, edited by T. Bunting, P. Filion. Don Mills: Oxford University Press.

Fraser, G. 1972. *Fighting Back*. Toronto: Hakkert.

Fraser, N. 1989. *Unruly Practices*. Minneapolis: University of Minnesota Press.

Fraser, N., and L. Gordon. 1994. "A Geneology of Dependency: Tracing a Keyword of the U.S. Welfare State." *Signs* 19(2): 309-336.

Gereke, K., and B. Reid. 1992. "The Failure of Urban Government: The Case of Winnipeg." Pp. 123-142 in *Political Arrangements*, edited by H. Lustiger-Thaler. Montreal: Black Rose Books.

Goetz, E. G. 1993. *Shelter Burden: Local Politics and Progressive Housing Policy*. Philadelphia: Temple University Press.

Goetz, E. G., and S. E. Clarke, eds. 1993. *The New Localism: Comparative Urban Politics in a Global Era*. Newbury Park, CA: Sage.

Gonick, C. 1990. "The Manitoba Economy Since World War II." Pp. 25-48 in *The Political Economy of Manitoba*, edited by J. Silver, J. Hull. Regina: Canadian Plains Research Centre.

Griffiths, N. 1975. *Women in the Urban Environment: Report of Workshop Proceedings*. Ottawa: National Capital Commision.

Haire, C. P. 1975. *In Want of a Policy: A Survey of the Needs of Non-Profit Housing Companies and Cooperative Housing Societies.* Ottawa: Canadian Council on Social Development.

Hasson, S., and D. Ley. 1994. *Neighbourhood Organizations and the Welfare State.* Toronto: University of Toronto Press.

Henderson, D. 1973. "A Paper on Kinew Housing Incorporated." Pp. 93-122 in *The Citizen and Neighbourhood Renewal,* edited by L. Axworthy. Winnipeg: Institute of Urban Studies.

Hill, F. I. 1975. *Canadian Urban Trends.* Ottawa: Ministry of State for Urban Affairs.

Hulchanski, J. D. 1986. "Housing Subsidies in a Period of Restraint: The Canadian Experience, 1973-1984." *Research and working paper no. 16,* Institute of Urban Studies, Winnipeg.

Hull, J., and J. Silver, eds. 1990. *The Political Economy of Manitoba.* Regina: Canadian Plains Research Centre.

Institute of Urban Studies. 1979. *Housing: Inner City Type Older Areas.* Winnipeg: Winnipeg Development Plan Review.

———. 1990. "A Community Based Needs Consultation of the Inner City: Summary Report. Prepared for the Community Services and Facilities Program, Winnipeg Core Area Initiative, University of Winnipeg, Winnipeg.

Isin E. F. 1998. "Governing Toronto Without Government: Liberalism and Neolliberalism." *Studies in Political Economy,* 56(Summer): 169-191.

Jackson, P. 1991. "Mapping Meanings: A Cultural Critique of Locality Studies." *Environment and Planning A* 23: 215-228.

Jessop, B. 1990. *State Theory: Putting Capitalist States in their Place.* University Park: The Pennsylvania State University Press.

Keating, M. 1991. *Comparative Urban Politics: Power and the City in the United States, Canada, Britain and France.* Edward Elgar. Vermont: Brookfield.

Kiernan, M. J., and D. C. Walker. 1983. "Winnipeg." Pp. 222-254. In *City politics in Canada,* edited by W Magnusson, A Sanction. University of Toronto Press: Toronto.

Klodawsky, F., and A. Spector. 1997. "Renovation or Abandonment?: Canadian Social Housing at a Crossroads." Pp. 259-280 in *How Ottawa Spends 1997-1998 Seeing Red: A Liberal Report Card,* edited by G. Swimmer. Ottawa: Carleton University Press.

Leaning, J. 1995. "Centretown is for People: The Story of The Centretown Plan." Pp. 13-65 in *A Neighbourhood Plans: Creating the Community's Vision for Ottawa'sCentretown,* edited by E. R. Smythe. Ottawa: Centretown Citizens' Community Association.

Levin, E. A. 1987. "Comedy in Three Acts: Municipal Policy and District Planning in Manitoba." *Research and working Papers 31,* Institute of Urban Studies, Winnipeg.

———. 1986. "Alternative Explanations for Inner-City Gentrification: A Canadian Assessment." *Annals of the Association of American Geographers* 76(4): 521-535

Ley, D. 1994. "Gentrification and the Politics of the New Middle Class." *Society and Space* 12: 53-74.

Logan, J. R., and T. Swanstrom, eds. 1990. *Beyond the City Limits: Urban Policy and Economic Restructuring in Comparative Perspective.* Philadelphia: Temple University Press.

Loney, M. 1977. "A Political Economy of Citizen Participation." Pp. 446-472 in *The Canadian State: Political Economy and Political Power,* edited by L. Panitch. Toronto: University of Toronto Press.

Lorimer, J. 1970. *The Real World of City Politics.* Toronto: James Lorimer.

———. 1972. *Citizen's Guide to City Politics.* Toronto: James Lorimer.

Lorimer, J., and E. Ross. 1976. *The City Book: The Politics and Planning of Canada's Cities.* Toronto: James Lorimer and Company.

Lyon, D., and R. Fenton. 1984. "The Development of Downtown Winnipeg: Historical Perspectives on Decline and Revitalization." Reports 3, Institute of Urban Studies, Winnipeg.

Lyon, D., and L. H. Newman. 1986. "The Neighbourhood Improvement Program, 1973-1983: A National Review of an Intergovernmental Initiative." Research and working paper 15, Institute of Urban Studies, Winnipeg.

Massey, D. 1993a. "The Political Place of Locality Studies." Pp. 125-145 in *Space, Place and Gender,* edited by D. Massey. Minneapolis: University of Minnesota Press.

_____. 1993b. "Politics and Space/Time." Pp. 249-272 in *Space, Place and Gender,* edited by D. Massey. Minneapolis: University of Minnesota Press.

Nader, G. A. 1976. *Cities of Canada, Volume Two: Profiles of Fifteen Metropolitan Centres.* Toronto: Macmillan of Canada.

Newman, L. H. 1986. "Municipal Non-Profit Housing: Winnipeg Housing Redevelopment Corporation." Occasional Paper 13, Institute of Urban Studies, Winnipeg.

Ontario Ministry of Housing. 1981. *Neighbourhood Improvement Program: An Evaluation, Summary Report.* Toronto: Community Renewal Branch, Project Planning Branch.

Page, M. W. 1996. "Locality, Housing Production and the Local State." *Society and Space* 14: 181-201.

Partridge, J. T., and L. Axworthy. 1974. "Administration and Financing of Non-Profit Housing: The People's Committee for a Better Neighbourhood, Inc." Pp. 63-90 in *Housing Innovation and Neighbourhood Improvement: Change in Winnipeg's Inner City,* edited by D. Epstein. Winnipeg: Institute of Urban Studies.

Pateman, C. 1989. *The Disorder of Women.* Chicago: Polity Press.

Peters, E. 1996. "Aboriginal People in Urban Areas." Pp. 305-333 in *Visions of the Heart,* edited by D. Long, O Dickinson. Toronto: Harcourt Brace.

Peterson, P. E. 1981. *City Limits.* Chicago: University of Chicago Press.

Pollack, D. M. J. 1994. "The Changing Municipal Housing Role: An Examination of the City of Winnipeg's Response to Federal Funding and Program Changes to the Federal Residential Rehabilitation Assistance Program 1974-1994." Unpublished paper, University of Manitoba, Winnipeg.

Powell, A., ed. 1972. *The City: Attacking Modern Myths.* Toronto: McClelland and Stewart Limited.

Radewich, G. H. 1986. "An Examination of Municipal Non-Profit Housing Corporations in Canada with Performance Evaluations of the Toronto, Ottawa and Winnipeg Housing Corporations." Unpublished paper, University of Manitoba, Winnipeg.

Ram, B., and M. J. Norris, K. Skof. 1989. *The Inner City in Transition.* Ottawa: Minister of Supply and Services Canada.

Richardson, B. 1994. *People of Terra Nullius.* Vancouver: Douglas & McIntyre, University of Washington Press.

Roeher Institute. 1990. *Poor places; disability-related housing and support services.* Toronto: Author.

Rose, A. 1980. *Canadian Housing Policies (1935-1980).* Toronto: Butterworths.

Rose, N. 1996. "Governing 'Advanced' Liberal Democracies." *Economy and Society* 22(3): 283-299.

Rosenberg, H. 1990. "The Home is the Workplace: Hazards, Stress and Pollutants in the Household." Pp. 57-80 in *Through the Kitchen Window: The Politics of Home and Family,* edited by M. Luxton, H. Rosenberg, S. Arat-Koc. Toronto: Garamond.

Silver, J. 1995. "The Failure of Civic Reform Movements in Winnipeg Civic Elections: 1971-1992." Urban resources paper no. 6, Institute of Urban Studies, Winnipeg.

Silver, J., and J. Hull. 1990. *The Political Economy of Manitoba.* Regina: Canadian Plains Research Centre.

Smith, D. 1990. *Joe Zukin: Citizen and Socialist.* Toronto: Lorimer.

Social Planning Council of Winnipeg. 1977. *A Housing Action Plan for Winnipeg's Inner City.* Winnipeg: Social Planning Council of Winnipeg.

_____. 1995. "An Integrated Community Approach to Health Action." A proposal to Health Canada, the Health Promotion Contribution Program, Social Planning Council of Winnipeg, Winnipeg.

Spector, A., and F. Klodawsky. 1993. "The Housing Needs of Single Parent Families in Canada: A Dilemma for the 1990s." Pp. 239-251, edited by J. Hudson, B. Galaway *Single Parent Families: Perspectives on Research and Policy,* Toronto: Thompson Education.

Statistics Canada. 1971a. "Population and Housing Characteristics by Census Tracts: Ottawa-Hull." *1971 Census of Canada* (Cat. 95-715). Ottawa: Ministry of Industry, Trade and Commerce.

_____. 1971b. "Population and housing characteristics by census tracts: Winnipeg." *1971 Census of Canada* (Cat. 95-753). Ottawa: Ministry of Industry, Trade and Commerce.

Stewart, D. 1993. "The Winnipeg Core Area Initiative: A Case Study in Urban Revitalization." Unpublished paper, School of Community and Regional Planning, University of British Columbia.

Stinson, A. 1979. *Canadians Participate.* Ottawa: Centre for Welfare Studies, Carleton University.

Teeple, G. 1995. *Globalization and the Decline of Social Reform.* Toronto: Garamond.

Ufoegbune, U. T. 1993. "An Examination of the Role of the Public Sector in Inner City Housing Affordability and Revitalization: A Winnipeg Case Study." Unpublished paper, University of Manitoba, Winnipeg.

Vincent, D. B. 1971. *The Indian-Metis Urban Probe.* Winnipeg: Indian-Metis Friendship Centre and Institute of Urban Studies, University of Winnipeg.

Walker, D. 1979. *The Great Winnipeg Dream: The Re-Development of Portage and Main.* Oakville: Mosaic Press.

Wekerle, G. 1993. "Responding to Diversity: Housing Developed By and For Women." *Canadian Journal of Urban Research* 2(2): 95-114.

Wekerle, G., and R. Peterson, D. Morley, eds. 1981. *New Space for Women.* Boulder, CO: Westview.

Young, A. B. 1979. "Federal Perspectives in the Development of the Neighbourhood Improvement Program and the Residential Rehabilitation Assistance Program: 1969 to 1973." Unpublished paper, University of Manitoba, October, Winnipeg.

Young, I. M. 1990. *Justice and the Politics of Difference.* Princeton: Princeton University Press.

PART VI

SPATIAL DIMENSIONS OF
URBAN LIFE

THE HIDDEN COMMUNITY:
SPATIAL DIMENSIONS OF URBAN LIFE

A.L. Sinikka Dixon

ABSTRACT

In contrast with the community without spatial boundaries, this paper focuses on conceptual and theoretical issues of urban spatial relationships, drawing on the author's cross-cultural experiences. In frontier society, neighbors built their residences together, much like "favela" dwellers today. In a capitalist economy, money, social class, race and ethnic origins largely determine residential location and type of dwellings, but all dwellers are anchored in space through their residences which provide for the basic human need of safety and belonging. In order to make explicit the "hidden community" of cross-cultural variation, it is necessary to differentiate between community as a "physical place" and community as a "social place" much as kapungistuminen (translated "becoming city-like") and kaupunkilaistuminen (translated like a "becoming city-dweller") do: a neighborhood impingement typology is created to measure the quality of neighborhood spatial relationships. The more neighborhood-bound the residents are by their life-cycle stages, the more important the neighborhood spatial quality becomes.

Research in Community Sociology, Volume 9, pages 287-308.
Copyright © 1999 by JAI Press Inc.
All rights of reproduction in any form reserved.
ISBN: 0-7623-0498-7

INTRODUCTION

In contrast with the community without spatial boundaries, this paper focuses on conceptual and theoretical issues of urban spatial relationships, drawing on the author's cross-cultural experiences. In the historical past, communities were built from scratch, much like "illegal" urban "favelas" are today. In frontier society, neighbors built their residences together, side by side. In today's capitalist economy, money, social class, race and ethnic origins largely determine residential location and type of dwelling. Community dwellers are anchored in space through their residences which provide for the basic human need of safety and belonging. This paper takes the view that in order to make explicit the "hidden community" of cross-cultural variation, it is necessary to differentiate between community as a "physical place" and community as a "social place," much as kaupungistuminen (translated "becoming city like") and kaupunkilaistuminen (translated "becoming like a city dweller") need to be separately analyzed.

The more neighborhood bound people are by their stages in different life cycles (age/family/education/work/leisure) the more important the neighborhood spatial quality becomes. A new conceptual tool—the *residence-neighborhood impingement typology*—has been developed to clarify these spatial relationships. A more thorough understanding of the spatiotemporal involvement of the residents in their neighborhoods will clarify some of the issues relating to the presence or absence of *community* and will facilitate better urban planning.

The first part of the paper focuses on differing views on community as a theoretical concept. The second section explains the largely inductive research methods used by the author, and the final sections deal with the development of the residence-neighborhood impingement typology and suggested applications for its use.

THE NATURE OF COMMUNITY

Community is a difficult concept to deal with. It has become an "omnibus" word, embracing "a motley assortment of concepts and qualitatively different phenomena" (Hillery 1963, p. 779). Karp, Stone, and Yoels (1977, p. 63) point to three elements most consistently found in the literature as important features of community life.

1. Community is generally seen as delineated by a geographically, territorially, or spatially circumscribed area.
2. The members of a community are seen as bound together by a number of characteristics or attributes held in common (values, attitude, ethnicity, social class, and so on).
3. The members of a community are engaged in some form of sustained social interaction.

Albrow and Eade (1994) provide an extensive bibliography and cover the whole period from classic sociology to the current thrust toward redefining community as an abstract, imagined community.

Sociologically speaking, community may be described as "having certain territorial limits and as being organized in some fashion to meet human needs" (Butler 1976, p. 264). Other characteristics of what may be called communities are face-to-face associations, common way of life, common ends, means, and goals, social completeness and self-sufficiency, collection of institutions, and interdependent way of life (Butler 1976). Kennedy (1990, p. 131) quotes Hunter (1975) saying that communities have three major roles that include a functional spatial unit, meeting subsistence needs of people in the area; a unit of patterned social interactions; and a cultural-symbolic unit of collective identity. It is outside the scope of this paper to give an exhaustive list of the various uses of the community concept, but it should be mentioned that researchers have focused on complex relations of power and status (Freeman 1968; Aiken and Mott 1970). Some of the classical concepts, like *Gemeinschaft* and *Gesellschaft,* by Tönnies (1957) are still referred to, and his Gemeinschaft is equated with community, as a group implying face-to-face interaction. Karp, Stone, and Yoels (1977, p. 63) point out that there is a "tendency to see the two types of social organization (small town and city) or *Gemeinschaft* and *Gesellschaft* as opposites, as examples of what the other is not," badly obscuring elements of both.

In fact, community is a concept which is at the interface of sociology and such other disciplines as anthropology, geography, politics, and urban planning. It is the sociologists in general who have overlooked the "rich and dynamic nature of space," which is really a social product (Marouli 1995, p. 534). Ross (1955) refers to the "physical and social community" and others feel that the "term community implies something both geographic and psychologic" (Hutchinson, Rodriguez, and Hagan (1996, p. 201). Now, in the postmodern urban society, there is a tendency to see community as no longer spatially bound; primary groups appear to be more like social networks than true groups, and the focus has shifted to the network connectedness of social actors. However, all members of society are in some way spatially bound and interspatially connected, at least as a sleeping community.

Salingaros (1998, p. 54) sees the urban web as anchored at nodes of human activity whose interconnections make up the web. These nodes are: home, work, park, store, restaurant, church and so forth. Out of these different possible ways of studying the urban community, this paper focuses predominantly on the local neighborhood community as a subarea of the larger urban community. The local neighborhood is viewed as snapshots of ethnographic data in cross-cultural perspective, as seen through the eyes of the author as a participant observer in different life-cycle stages, spatially anchored in different cultural settings.

THEORETICAL ISSUES

It is through personal observations that I have come to recognize the importance of the spatial location, which is the starting point for my residence-neighborhood frame of reference. The method whereby I arrived at this frame of reference comes closest to what is called "qualitative ethnographic social research," which requires an attitude of detachment in order to be able to make culturally relative observations of self and others, and to give reliable explanations of the social processes involved (Vidich and Lyman 1998, p. 42). Even though formally not a sociologist by profession at the time, I nevertheless, at age twelve, started my collection of participant observations.[1] According to Vidich and Lyman (1998, p. 41), modern sociology's mission is to analyze and understand behavioral patterns and social processes and the attitudes and values on which individual and collective action rests. The research task requires both observations and the act of communicating the analysis of these observations to others. I have spent a lifetime asking for reasons why people do things the way they do. "Sociology and anthropology are disciplines that, born out of concern to understand the 'other,' are nevertheless also committed to an understanding of the self" (Vidich and Lyman 1998, p. 42), if we follow the tenets of symbolic interactionism. In fact, "the data gathering process can never be described in its totality because these 'tales of the field' are themselves part of an ongoing social process that in its minute-by-minute and day-to-day experience defies recapitulation" (Vidich and Lyman 1998, p. 42). Even that which is officially recorded and reported is subject to "a report written after the research has been completed" (Vidich and Lyman 1998, p. 41). Some of the observations used as illustrations of time-space relationships in this paper are based on personal experiences of daily living in a specific cultural community, formal and informal interviews, slides, video recordings, and archival or historical data.

Although ethnographic research is usually limited to a specific time frame and often one specific community, I see my life in the various cultural settings as part of an ongoing data gathering process. In this paper, I will attempt to formulate some frames of reference around which to organize these observations in retrospect. This may not follow the usual protocol, but it will help to clarify some issues with neighborhood community as the unit of analysis. The logic applied is predominantly inductive.

One of the leading figures in community sociology, Herbert J. Gans (1962, pp. x-xi), author of the classic *The Urban Villagers,* has by his own admission in writing it, "violated several canons of sociological research reporting," such as describing "as findings what are properly speaking only hypotheses," and occasionally "generalizing beyond evidence," and not fully relating his "conclusions to the work of other sociologists."

Gans (1962, p. 264), based on his "personal value judgments, observations (he) made in the West End, and the findings of other research on working- and lower-class populations," makes an explicit value judgment: "that what I have called the professional upper-middle-class subculture is more desirable than all the rest. If cultures can be compared in the abstract, without concern for the opportunities that encourage them, and the social conditions necessary for their existence, I believe that this culture provides a fuller, more diverse life, a greater range of choices of behaviour in all major spheres of life, and the ability to deal more adequately with changing conditions and with problems than do any of the other subcultures."

In contrast, my most impressionable years were spent partly in the city, partly in a rural village, and I could never make a value judgment and put either social group higher than the other. In fact, I have subsequently made the cultural transition from an outsider to an insider many times, involving change of neighborhood, community, culture, language, society and/ or country, which has put me in a situation that forced upon me "a sufficient degree of social and personal distance from prevailing norms and values to be able to analyze them objectively" (Vidich and Lyman 1998, p. 42).[2]

In order to "fit in" into the new society, it was necessary to be able to evaluate both the new culture and one's own culture from a more or less objective point of view, asking such questions as what is similar, and what is different in the two cultures. At my first cultural transition, I fit in so well and acquired the local accent of Stockholm so well that as a student worker, selling literature from door to door in Skåne (southern Sweden where the local accent has some unique guttural sounds), a gentleman asked me where I was born. Upon hearing Finland, he called me a liar, asked my accompanying fellow student where she was born and when she said Skåne, he threatened to chase us away from his doorstep at gun point! This first move from my homeland to Sweden was the most dramatic, but was at the same time the beginning of a conscious search for universals or commonalities between communities and cultures. Time and space factors seemed to be crucial in determining the quality of life in the new setting. In retrospect, I could see that the family members experienced the move in totally different ways, depending on their stage in the various life cycles: age, education, family, work, and recreation or free-time. (See the operational definitions of these various life-cycles in the Appendix).

Taking my family of origin as an example of a family in cultural transition, we can see the differential effect of a neighborhood move on the various family members. It was a career promotional move for my father who, although from Finnish speaking part of Finland[3] had gone to school in Sweden and spoke the language. The residential move was from one low impingement residence (see Table 1 for impingement typology) in Finland to a relatively low impingement one in Sweden, except that the new dwelling was shared by two families. Of our family of five, my parents were in the adult stage of age life cycle, myself a teen, my brother ready to enter elementary school, and my baby sister at home. The residence was in a suburb (Stocksund), a relatively affluent middle-class neighborhood of single-family dwellings with gardens, large enough to grow fruit trees and have a badminton court. The closest neighbor, the family downstairs, had a little boy of my sister's age, a girl in my high school class, and an older sister who went to the city to gymnasium (preparation for matriculation into university). Both fathers worked in the same office and both mothers were housewives. During the week, breakfasts and evening meals were shared by the family members, but for the rest the residence-neighborhood interface had a different meaning for all of us.

Having a daily playmate downstairs, my sister quickly adjusted into a happy, carefree childhood, speaking perfect Swedish within a matter of months. The older girl and I either walked or cycled together to school, but once there, we hardly saw each other. I experienced both prejudice and ostracism due to my language problems and Finnish heritage. My brother, on the other hand, fit into the educational life cycle better. He started elementary school there with a cohort group of other entrants into the school system. In fact, his was such a cohesive group that they had a second- or third-grade class reunion later as adults, most still living in the larger Stockholm area.

Mother had to learn the language also, but did so informally through associations with neighbors, doing the local shopping for the family, and joining the same church she had been part of in Finland (a church with international links). She was, therefore, involved in the age, family, and free-time or leisure life cycles. She, as well as my younger sister, were the most residentially bound of the family. Father took the car to work, so she became a pedestrian with the responsibility of daily care for a four-year old, which further restricted her movements to the proximate neighborhood. My father's residential involvement was dominated by his out-of-neighborhood work situation.

As time went on and the family members moved through the different life cycles and continued to shift residential locations, I could observe the important role of the residence-neighborhood interface. These observations form the background for the rationale, for creating a residence-neighborhood impingement typology.

The neighborhood relations have often been viewed in terms of the social interaction and/or sociodemographic characteristics of the residential occupants, with the spatial dimension taken as a given. The larger unit of urban space, the city, has experienced a similar theoretical problem. In creating city typologies, the residents' characteristics formed a database from which induction types have been created, for example, predominantly industrial city, service city, university town, based on the proportion of population engaged in different occupations. Density and heterogeneity, as characteristics of urban places, have spatial links and are included when speaking of urbanization as a process.

The problem is, however, as Gottdiener (1991, p. 295) points out that, "The city as a form of socio-spatial organization has always figured prominently in the analysis of society. In the main, however, it has been treated as a container for social processes whose origins lie elsewhere."

Wirth's (1938) "urbanism as a way of life" is different from the concept of urbanization, but has no verb form in the English language. Perhaps this is due to the fact that both processes occurred simultaneously and together with industrialization so that the conceptually different processes were not made apparent, which is reflected by the language use.

In contrast, industrialization, particularly heavy industry in Finland, was a late comer, largely pushed by the war reparations demanded by Russia as condition of the peace treaty between the two countries relating to World War II. Increased industrialization combined with an evacuation and relocation of Viipuri (then one of Finland's three largest cities) caused rapid urbanization. In the 1940s to 1950s the state radio in Finland had a humorous program focusing on "city-cousin" and "country-cousin." In the postwar period, schools made annual class trips to the capital, Helsinki, to expose the country-cousins to the parliament buildings (Eduskuntatalo), presidential palace, and national and art museums. Jalmari Finne's Kiljusen Herrasvaet was a popular children's reader focusing on this rural-urban shift. The Finnish language reflects the shifts and changes of that time period by having two words, one referring to the process of a spatial place becoming city like, (kaupungistuminen) corresponding to the English urbanization, and another referring to the process of the residents of these cities becoming like city dwellers (kaupunkilaistuminen), for which the English language has no verbal equivalent, only the noun reflecting the end product urbanism as a way of life (Wirth 1938). Just as on the larger scale, there is a spatial and social dimension to urban location, there are separate spatial and social dimensions to the residence-neighborhood interface. It is hoped that by creating a typology of these relationships on the neighborhood level, space can become an organizing tool of analysis in urban sociology.

RESIDENCE-NEIGHBORHOOD INTERFACE

I have chosen to focus on the residence-neighborhood interface as the spatial anchor of household residents. As Gottdiener (1991, p. 302) points out, "recently a number of social theorists have turned to the concept of space and incorporated it in their understanding of society" (Foucault 1979; Giddens 1984; Lefebvre 1974). Gottdiener and Lagopoulos (1986) extended the discussion to the relation between "mental maps, culture, and space." In fact, Gottdiener (1991, p. 305) says that "urban sociology and community studies should be redefined in terms of a sociology of space and place." Some form of physical relationship is implied by the concept neighborhood itself. What the social interactions between neighbors as spatial proximates are, is a different dimension from the structural dynamics of the neighborhood setting. Some social interactions are direct and immediate, others are structured by rules having normative or legal status, imposed by either the local community or a larger societal entity. For example, some residential areas, particularly apartment complexes and walled-in communities, permit no door-to-door salesmen while there are communities where the milkman, baker, greengrocer, and knife sharpener used to come to the door (United Kingdom and The Netherlands) and in some places still do. For the elderly, shut-ins, and housewives with small children this service delivery mode lightened the load of maintaining the home and providing food for the household.

By focusing solely on group relationships we may overlook how we actually share social space. While accepting the existence of symbolically constituted new communities (Chekki 1996; Cohen 1985; Calhoun 1991; Elkins 1995) and the possibility of "community without propinquity" (Webber 1963), it is nevertheless acknowledged that there is an important, often taken-for-granted, spatial dimension to our social existence.

The basic underlying assumption is that we are largely what we do in time and space. Our movements are constrained by a complex pattern of life-cycle stages we simultaneously occupy as well as the functional interdependencies we enter into. Spatial connectedness to the residence is seen to vary by the stage in the age, family, education, work, and free-time or leisure life cycles (see Appendix; Dixon-Woudenberg 1993, p. 1513). We get a different picture of community when we focus on the spatial interconnectedness of social actors rather than on existing social groups, but one does not negate the existence of the other.

It is acknowledged by Wellman and Leighton (1979) that "neighborhood as community is very much part of a fundamental sociological issue." They also see that common locality has encouraged the identification of community with neighborhood, but feel that neighborhood is not a community. It would be a similar to say that urbanization and urbanism are conceptually the same, but they are not. If the neighborhood is seen as spatial proximity and community as a social group, they would be interconnected but not the same. In this paper the focus is on spatial connectedness with major emphasis on the local neighborhood, defined as the

Table 1. Residence-Neighborhood Impingement Typology

Impingement Type:	Residence Core/Periphery	
Neighborhood Impact on Residence:		
Audible		
Visible	High/Medium/Low	Positive/Negative
Olfactory		
Touchable		
Residence Impact on Neighborhood:		
Audible		
Visible	High/Medium/Low	Positive/Negative
Olfactory		
Touchable		

residential spatial proximates within hearing, seeing, smelling, and touching distance. This aspect of neighborhood is called "hidden community," hidden because it is often overlooked or taken for granted.

There have been numerous studies of social networks focusing on differing contents of links, such as kinship, friendship, and material assistance (Shulman 1972, p. 19), but without the spatial connection. Among basic human needs (see Maslow's 1997 "hierarchy of needs") are safety and belonging. Home residence partially fulfills these needs. What we do in time and space is divided into obligatory and discretionary time (Chapin 1974). Both are partially shared with others in residential space; few of us live totally alone. Those who do not have human house mates or family members may share space with small animals as pets. This sharing—with humans or animals—involves explicit or implicit rules for behavior inside the home residence and compliance with rules of the external community. Whether we like it or not, this makes us part of a community. The quality of life of the residents depends largely on the relationship with the external community, which involves visual, audible, olfactory, and touching dimensions. How much these impact on us and how much our residential occupation impacts on other community residential owners and occupants depends on what we do in our residences and how much time we spend in them.

To study the residence-neighborhood interface, a typology has been created to be used as a conceptual tool applying it to the environment behavior analysis. Using this typology, the spatial neighborhood environment can be classified along structural dimensions which can be applied cross-culturally. Thus, the neighborhood relations can be analyzed, keeping the spatial and social aspects separate.

The impingement typology is intended to be an objective measurement of the often overlooked dimension of the residence-neighborhood interface. With the household as a unit of analysis, a grid of residence-neighborhood interdependencies can be created. Here are some examples of impingement from outside the residence.

Audible impingement from the outside could be caused by a noisy freeway (often mitigated by the construction of sound barrier walls), railroad, airport, or factory noises. As an example, Abbasiah, Cairo (Egypt) is a residential area where a fly-over one-way street has been built over the original street as a second level road. After the new construction, some of the second floors of the older apartment buildings now have balconies only a few meters away from the traffic. The impingement levels are high on three dimensions—audible, visible and olfactory. I spent a month in Abbasiah and the traffic never stopped (not even at night), except when President Mobarak's motorcade came by and the security patrol cleared the roads hours before his arrival. In the +42°C heat with only a room fan going, the windows had to be kept open, letting in the fumes, road dust and noise. Sitting on the balcony to catch a breeze was only a temporary relief because of the visual stimulus overload. Further aggravation was a barbecue shop on the ground floor which had a substandard, short chimney that reached only to the second floor balcony level, not to the apartment roof top. During Ramadan (the ninth month of the Moslem year, during which strict fasting is observed from dawn until sunset) the barbecuing went on from sunset till late at night, filling the upstairs apartments with nauseous fumes.

Another occurrence of visual impingement would be if the residence would be built on a terraced ocean view property and a neighbor would build a multistory residence next door, effectively obstructing the view. Beach front properties often have legal height restrictions, such to be broken only by special city permits. The functional windmill of Pea Soup Andersons, Carlsbad, California, was permitted to exceed the height restrictions on the condition that it produced a certain amount of electricity.

Examples of impingement on a touchable dimension are cases where flowering shrubs and fruit trees protrude and hang over neighbors' fences. If it is a fragrant lilac, the impingement may be viewed as positive by some, but if it is a mulberry tree dropping highly staining berries onto the neighbor's property, it might be seen as a highly negative impingement causing ill will and disputes. Some touchable impingement may be beyond the resident's control, such as the Laguna Hills, California landslides which, after torrential rains, sent complete houses slipping down the terraced slope into the neighbors' gardens below.

With the residential core is understood the dwelling itself, whether it be a cardboard shack in a favela (Brazilian shantytown), apartment dwelling, or a mansion on hilltop. This core is also the residential area which is potentially most private. With periphery is understood the immediate area surrounding the dwelling, interlaced between the residence and other spatially proximate structures, whether residential dwellings, factories or businesses. The size of this peripheral field may be very narrow, just the brick and mortar between apartments or acres of green space, lawns, gardens, or trees between adjacent residences.

It is interesting to study the cross-cultural similarities and differences of these different types of residence-neighborhood settings. Ethnicity, race, and social class have been studied in the neighborhood context and indexed in various ways. However, the interaction effect of ethnicity, race, and social class with a detailed analysis of the residence-neighborhood spatial dimension is missing. First, what percentage of urban residents[4] of different ethnic, racial and social class background of a given society[5] live in high-medium-low impingement residence-neighborhood settings? Second, how are the degrees of impingement viewed by the residents exposed to impingement on the residence from the outside neighborhood, and how does the outside neighborhood view the impingement of the residence on the neighbors outside? Third, what difference does it make if the impingement typology is applied, using the individual as a unit of analysis, compared with using a social group, such as family as a unit of analysis? Fourth, using a life-cycle form of analysis, some hypotheses can be formulated that relate to the needs of family members sharing residential space. Finally, the impingement typology is viewed in relationship to some neighborhood research and projections are made as to how to use this analytical tool in cross-cultural settings, and what urban planning and policy implications it would have.

RESIDENTIAL IMPINGEMENT TYPOLOGY AND SOCIAL STRATIFICATION

Many different paradigms have been posited as explanations of the urban process, listed by Bourne (1996, p. 4), with classic urban geography, structuration theory, gender and feminist theory, and social and cultural theory among them. Each paradigm tends to produce its own image. Similarly, the impingement typology provides its own view of the urban neighborhood as a subarea of the larger urban community.

Who lives in high-medium-low impingement residence-neighborhood settings? To begin to answer this, it is useful to take a look at the research by Ahlbrandt (1984).[6] His study shows that the local neighborhood is still an important factor in people's daily lives. Almost one-half of the respondents use local shopping, recreation, and religious service facilities near their place of residence. About the same number felt that they could turn to their neighbors in an emergency.

For further analysis, neighborhoods are stratified on the basis of their income. Income was selected as the basis for the stratification because previous analysis has shown that the economic level of the neighborhood is an important explanatory variable for differences among neighborhoods in terms of the composition of the social fabric and the feelings that people have about their place of residence.

The income groups were constructed from the standardized value of each neighborhood's mean household income as determined from the 1980 citizen survey. Neighborhoods were categorized into groups of *high income, middle income, moderate income,* and *low income,* based on mean household income.

The research findings provide ample evidence in support of the "community of limited liability," introduced by Horowitz (1967). The community of limited liability was conceived as an alternative to widespread forecasts of the decline of community, an argument that the local community would simply disappear as the traditional community lost its hold. Repeated findings show that this simply does not happen. Rather, given the choice, some people continue to participate in the local community, to give it their time, their loyalty, their energy. They do so conditionally rather than unconditionally—hence the concept of limited liability (Ahlbrandt 1984).

Interestingly, the percent "attached to neighborhood"[7] is about the same (60-63%) in all income neighborhoods, but percentage "satisfied with neighborhood"[8] is the highest (89%) for the *high income* neighborhood and the lowest (45%) for the *low income* neighborhood in this Ahlbrandt (1984) study. Based on the empirical findings in that study, let us project what the relationships might look like using the impingement typology and life-cycle web as tools. Although

the neighborhood classification in Ahlbrandt's study was based on family characteristics of household income, the other variables appeared to have the individual
respondent as a unit of analysis (see note 6).[9] Having the same neighborhood classification scheme as a starting point and separating the neighborhoods into high,
medium, and low income neighborhoods based on the family household income,
the analysis will proceed with the household as the unit of analysis.[10]

The strategy is to separate the structural, more objectively quantifiable aspects
of the physical residence into degrees of impingement along the visual, auditory,
olfactory, and touchable dimension shown in Table 1. The impingement from the
outside neighborhood on the residential space is measured first. Next, the
life-cycle configuration of each current resident is mapped out. Their involvement
in the various life cycles of age, family, education, work, and free-time/leisure
(see Appendix for operational definitions of these concepts) are then anchored
into the residential location by the amount of time actually spent in the residential
space (including both core and periphery). Given that the residence-neighborhood
interface has never been studied in this way, the suggested relationships are meant
as starting points for future empirical research which will either support or refute
the validity of this frame of reference. Also, the impingement includes only the
actual intrusion factors of proximate residential households, whether emanating
from the core or periphery. A conscious effort will be made to avoid confusing the
racial, ethnic, age, and gender characteristics of the proximate neighbors with
their behavior. It is the spatial structures and the behavior of the residents, not
their demographic characteristics, which will impinge on the neighboring house-
hold(s). It was the noise and fumes of dozens of fire crackers set off from my Chinese neighbor's balcony (in Surinam, South America) on Chinese New Year that
impinged on my residence, not the fact that the neighbors happened to be Chinese.
Similarly, if we had a loud pool party of rambunctious teenagers, it would not be
their skin color or ethnicity, but their noisy laughter and the sound of splashing
water that would intrude into the neighbor's residential space, and if we were in
an Arabic country, probably the view of the bikini clad bodies as well, unless the
pool was well secluded.

Although it is theoretically possible to have residences with a core surrounded
by an extended periphery in all kinds of neighborhoods, it is predicted that the
high income neighborhoods, followed by medium income neighborhoods will
have larger peripheral space than the low income neighborhoods, at least in the
urban setting, thus making the more wealthy households less vulnerable to a high
degree of neighborhood impingement.

The wealthy live in low residential core and periphery impingement locations.
Big mansions (residential core), extensive private grounds (residential periphery),
and chauffeur-tinted limousines that carry them in and out of their residences protect them from the various impingement dimensions.

Some of the poorest, high impingement residences can be seen along railroad
tracks (e.g., Tilbury to London, United Kingdom, or terraced housing in industrial

cities or coal mining towns). It is expected that low income housing anywhere would be classified as higher impingement than middle or high income housing, but this remains to be investigated by cross-cultural studies.

Even residence in a high impingement situation may not be so stressful if the impingement is not constant and/or one's time spent in the residence is short and intermittent. The characteristics of the residential space itself are more salient for people in certain life-cycle stages. The very young, not yet in school, and the very old, already retired, are more residentially bound than those who are involved in the education life cycle and work life cycle. Furthermore, some people are made "redundant" even before they have had a chance to enter the workforce. In the modern, industrialized society, there simply is no room for perfect, full employment. The most salient factors of the European work scene are the massive lay-offs and early retirements (Walker 1997). For those already in low income neighborhoods, this may mean an almost total dependence on the residence and immediate neighborhood for quality of life, which may involve a high level of impingement from the outside.

It should also be noted that rather than taking the household as a unit of analysis, impingement typology may be used in another direction as well, from the household to the neighborhood. In fact, residential impingement on the surrounding neighborhood can be positive or negative. Well kept upper-class residences (e.g., Hollywood Hills, California; Windsor Park, United Kingdom; Soestdijk, The Netherlands; Marbella, Costa del Sol, Spain) are shown with pride by locals as examples of positive impingement on the local neighborhood community. Residences with views of oceans, lakes, rivers, mountains, even of the city from a hilltop location, are usually priced out of reach of the average homebuyer in most countries. One is left to wonder how much of the mental health of the upper class is actually influenced by their residential location. Kaplan and Peterson (1993) suggest that some perceptual characteristics of natural areas can play a significant role in reducing stress and other negative aspects of fast-paced *urban* life and aid in recovery from illness (Ulrich 1993; Bixler and Floyd 1997). "Because wildlands can be defined as any large or small unmanicured area, a person's backyard can provide opportunity for daily contact with wildlands" (Bixler and Floyd 1997). However, anecdotal reports of wildland experiences by students indicate that some people actively dislike such environments (Wohlwill 1983). What does this mean in terms of impingement? Are there cultural variations in handling impingement? The last section will give some indications.

DEGREES OF IMPINGEMENT AND CULTURAL VARIATIONS

Until you walk or cycle in a neighborhood, you cannot really observe the residence-neighborhood impingement dimensions of a community. Sidewalks, cycle paths, and train tracks are often at the periphery of the household residence. In many countries, especially in big cities, residents today have intricate alarm systems and try to avoid unwanted physical (touching dimension) impingement into their private space. In the same cities, the homeless are totally at the mercy of their spatial proximates. Rolled up in a blanket in a dumpster or cardboard box, they have completely lost the safety and belonging potentially available to those either owning or even renting a residence.

Residential shelter and the psychological security accompanying it is often taken for granted. But there is also the impact of legal regulations on residential occupancy. For example, some allow no children. In one case, in Los Angeles (in Boyle Heights, 1975) a family with children was unsuccessful in finding an apartment where they would accept children, and finally they became so desperate that they rented one without the landlord being notified of the children's existence. Both parents had to work to support the family and children were left at home by themselves and told to be deadly quiet. Tragically, one time when the mother had locked herself out of the apartment, the children were so afraid that they by accident suffocated the crying baby, hugging it tightly in an attempt to keep the baby quiet. By the time the children realized it was their mother calling behind the door, it was too late. This would not have happened without the residential restrictions. Denton (1998, pp. 38–39) says, "Basic needs are not context dependent, although how one meets basic needs is context dependent," basic needs being defined as "basic objective things to sustain life such as food, shelter, clothing, mobility, physical safety, sexual intercourse, leisure, health, and knowledge."

Hidden in the urban fabric are many homeless youth who run away from stressful family and home living situations. There is now a growing literature that indicates that symptoms of depression are pervasive among homeless youth, with over half of a sample of homeless youth in Los Angeles meeting the DSM-III criteria for clinical depression (Unger, Kipke, Simon, Johnson, Montgomery, and Iverson 1997; Unger, Kipke, et al. 1998).

Wiesenfeld's (1997, p. 210) case study of a Venezuelan "barrio" illustrates the process by which "space becomes a locale, a dwelling becomes a home, a barrio becomes a community." This type of community represents identity; people are connected to it by their own sweat and toil, and the knowledge of having built the community together. At some point along the historical road from colonial city to the modern city, the barrio in the Hispanic American colonial city ceased to function as an integrated social and physical space and acquired a negative connotation in North America.

In Latin America (e.g., San Pedro Sula, Honduras), the street signs still indicate which barrio a given street belongs to. Interestingly, even Toronto still has some indicators of specific parts of the city like "Fashion District" indicated on the street signs. The residents of the Fashion District still proudly tell the newcomer the history of the neighborhood. They have a positive identity.

It will be interesting to compare neighborhoods cross-culturally, along the impingement typology dimensions and to see to what degree and under which circumstances the residential households try to protect themselves from outside impingement. What happens at the periphery, or just outside it? In Amsterdam, The Netherlands, in the section of the city called "Jordaan," I recently noticed signs for supplies of needles for drug addicts. At the same time I noticed that the day care establishment close by had wire netting surrounding the area where children went for recess. One person's freedom in the neighborhood is another person's constraint. Whereas in the 1960s in The Netherlands, an evening walk along the sidewalk, looking in people's picture windows, seeing how the families spent their evenings in their residences was safe, fun, and entertaining, but such activities are becoming a thing of the past.

The media has some influence on how the neighborhood residents share the impingement area of the residence-neighborhood space, "the hidden community" dimensions. Daily news relating muggings, murders and assaults of women, children, and the elderly, create fear and prevent people from venturing into the edge of their peripheral space.

Even "community builders" are not respected. "Nothing has damaged the squatters of Rio de Janeiro more in their quest for dignity than the popular image of vagabonds living off the sweat of other inhabitants of the city" (Pino 1998, p. 18).

Favelas can be success stories too. Not all "hidden communities" are sad cases. In fact, Curitiba, Brazil is the "greenest city in the world," with advanced recycling programs, extensive pedestrian zoned shopping areas, good public non-polluting transportation system, free health care in favela clinics, trading garbage for food (six bags of refuse for one bag of food for favela dwellers), and overall spectacular recycling rates for homeowners (Moore 1994). The man who inspired the people of Curitiba is its former mayor, Jaime Lerner.

Could the success of Curitiba be replicated elsewhere? "Because the neighborhood is so crucial to the quality of urban life, the questions raised by complicated patterns of stability, decline, and rebirth capture the attention of citizens, analysts, and policy makers alike... Will home owners in a given neighborhood maintain their dwellings at constant quality and choose to remain in them for extended periods," (Galster 1987, p. 1) are questions asked by people concerned with home ownership and neighborhood investment. Montgomery (1998) gives a partial answer by stating that city as a phenomenon is one of "structured complexity," which to be successful must combine "quality in three essential elements: physical space, the sensory experience and activity."

Whereas in the historical past, communities were built from scratch, much like urban "favelas" of Brazil are today, the organization of urban space in most societies is very complex indeed. People cannot freely choose the kind of neighborhood they would like to live in. In today's capital-driven economies, money, social class, race, and ethnic origins play a part in a household's chances of being able to occupy their dream home, the one they would be happy with. Most people have to settle for second best, not what they would like, but what they can afford.

The dominant images of urban community research in North America seem gloomy. "The U.S. ghetto today is an outcast ghetto, differing in its definition and role from the historic black ghettos in that its inhabitants are the excluded and the castaway, rather than the subordinated and restricted" (Marcuse 1997, p. 229). In European communities there are the poor and those "made redundant" living off social assistance, but those in the American ghettos belong to the hidden community, the outcasts that the society would rather forget exist.

In the 1968 "Report of the National Advisory Commission on Civil Disorder" it was concluded that "our nation is moving toward two societies, one black, one white—separate and unequal...Over 15 percent of central city minorities were unemployed—over twice the rate for whites" (Timilty 1979).

Goldsmith and Blakely (1991) show that "poverty in most U.S. inner cities has worsened." As an example, "many government and private programs have sought to revitalize Baltimore's inner-city neighborhoods, where one in five houses is vacant, 17 percent of residents are unemployed, and half of all adults over age 25 lack a high-school diploma."

The current situation is partly to blame on previous policies. Until 1949, the Federal Housing Administration denied essential insurance to integrated housing. Prior to 1962, the agency had no policy of nondiscrimination. However, the United States should not be considered the dominant model of urban form. Not even all inner cities are doom and gloom environments if one takes a cross-cultural view. In the United Kingdom, for example, centers of historic towns such as Chichester and Horsham are examples of "the best urban environment" (West Sussex County Council 1998). In history, many centralized cities have been populated by both poor and rich, but nowhere did the same distribution observed in U.S. cities exist in other cities, because their elites valued "proximity to the center of power, urbanity, and social interaction above other considerations, and thus settled in central locations" (Lozano 1990, p. 188). Furthermore, today's European cities have excellent public transportation systems which are available to the rich and the poor equally, bringing job markets within easy reach. In North America community facilities and transportation systems appear "only above a certain community size" (Lozano 1990).

There are indicators that some countries have paid more attention to the residence-neighborhood interface than others, to create a more liveable residential community. Holland is an example. In a study of bicycle use by Lowe (1990), The Netherlands is seen as the most "bicycle-friendly of all industrial countries," and having "the Western world's highest densitites of both cars and cycleways (separate paths or special bike lanes in roads)," resulting in 20 to 50 percent of all trips to be made by bicycle in Dutch towns and cities.

A leisurely cycle ride along these paths gives you a pleasant view of the Dutch way of life. Especially in the summer time, you can catch people pottering around in their well-kept gardens, children playing in the yards and on the sidewalks, and mothers sitting on their porches in the afternoon sun. An exchange of an occasional "goede middag" brightens up the ride with the human social touch. Or if you get lost, the people are very helpful in showing you the way through the maze of country-wide cycle paths. This visual and sometimes audible contact with the neighborhood, as you pass by, gives you a feeling of belonging; it is one of the "hidden" community dimensions. It is a pleasant impingement area between a residence and its spatial proximates, not only the other neighborhood residences, but the contact with pedestrian and cycle traffic ways. The Dutch concept "woonerf" ("living yard") (Lowe 1990) allows all means of transport at slow speeds, but "bicyclists and pedestrians have priority and cars enter only as 'guests'" (Lowe 1990). This opens the neighborhood for cars and children to share the road close to their homes as playground and movement area. The children are often within seeing and hearing distance of their parent(s) at home. It is also a more user-friendly urban setting for the handicapped.

CONCLUSION

Whereas theoretically speaking, community dwellers are anchored in urban space through their residences which provide for their basic human need of safety and belonging, the reality is that there are homeless families with children, particularly female-headed families, the fastest growing segment of the homeless population in North America (Butler 1997). Homeless families were virtually unheard of in earlier eras, but now national estimates indicate that 21–28 percent of the homelss are in families (Nord and Luloff 1995); and about 80 percent of these families are headed by single parents, primarily women" (Lindsey 1996).

To make sense of the complexity of residential neighborhood relationships, a residence-neighborhood impingement typology was developed to create an impact assessment of the neighborhood's intrusion on the residential space along the audible, visible, olfactory, and touchable dimensions, as well as a similar impact assessment of that of the residence on the neighborhood.

It is hypothesized that there will be a social class effect, measured by income, so that high income neighborhoods are more likely to be low impingement areas, using households as units of analysis. It is further hypothesized that residence-neighborhood impingement, measured by the typology, will have a differential effect on the members of the household, depending on their web of life cycle involvements. It is expected that the structural constraints of the life-cycles, seen as age, family, education, work, and free-time or leisure life cycles, measured in terms of time and energy spent in each life cycle, will either exacerbate or ameliorate the impact of neighborhood impingement.

The author plans to do pilot research with this frame of reference to be able to further the development of this theoretical approach. Perhaps there will be surprises in store. Could it be that the inner-city households have life-cycle configurations that are compatible with their residential location and the right mix of both translates into hope and satisfaction, given better community planning.

APPENDIX

Age Life Cycle

First stage	Birth to childhood
Second stage	Adolescence
Third stage	Young adult
Fourth stage	Adult
Fifth stage	Middle-aged
Sixth stage	Old
Seventh stage	Old-old
Eighth stage	Dying/dead

Family Life Cycle

01 Childhood home/family of origin/household one is born into
02 Single, never married, not cohabiting/ = alone
03 Couple, cohabiting/married
04 Cohabiting/married with young children
05 Couple, cohabiting/married with mixed age or older children
06 Couple, living together/children launched
07 Single, by widowhood
08 Single, by divorce or separation
09 Single, by disruption of cohabitation
10 Old couple (past retirement age), grandparent stage

Education Life Cycle

Basic (often mandatory education)
01 Kindergarten
02 Elementary education
03 Secondary education

Continuing academic education
04 Undergraduate 1-2 years
05 Undergraduate 3-4 years
06 Graduate studies

Nonacademic education
B4 Terminal degrees
B5 "In house" training by choice
B6 "In house" training/ obligatory
B7 Taking courses of interest

Work Life Cycle

Career-oriented jobs		*Terminal/noncareer type of jobs*	
01	First "job" = nonpaid job experience	B1	First "job" = non-paid job experience
02	Career track entry level job	B2	First paid job
03	Promotion to 1-2-3-related jobs	B3	1-2-3- unrelated but continuous jobs
04	Temporary exit from career job	B4	Temporary exit from dead end job
05	Re-entry to career job	B5	Re-entry to dead end job
07	Timely retirement from career	B7	Timely retirement from dead end job
08	Unpaid home labor	B8	Unpaid home labor
09	Unpaid volunteer work outside home	B9	Unpaid volunteer work outside home
	(professional type of work requiring higher education)		(nonprofessional type of work requiring no higher education)
10	Job-related retirement benefits	B10	Job-related retirement benefits

Leisure Activity Profile

	Mental Dimension	*Physical Dimension*
Active	solitary	solitary
	shared	shared
Passive	solitary	solitary
	shared	shared

(to be measured in quartiles)

NOTES

1. Almost every day after school, I went to the covered market (Kauppahalli in Tampere, Finland) and stood in line queuing up to be served at the small sale booths, only to move on to the next queue when it was almost my turn, just to observe people's interactions.

2. I have moved from place to place over thirty times in my lifetime, not counting short stays of 3-5 weeks for research and vacation purposes. Long-term residence includes places in Finland, Sweden, United Kingdom, The Netherlands, Michigan, Washington, DC., Surinam, California, and Canada. Short-term (3+weeks) includes Spain, Egypt, Brazil, and Central America. Other travel covers most of Western Europe (except Portugal and Greece), Morocco, Israel, Australia, Indonesia, and several Caribbean Islands.

3. Finland is officially bilingual—Finnish and Swedish.

4. This typology could also be applied to a rural setting, but for clarity of discussion this paper focuses on the urban setting.

5.   The unit of analysis can vary from such spatially defined areas as neighborhood, village, town, or country. Expressed in ratios or percentages, it can be applied cross-culturally.

6.   This research was based on a survey of neighborhood residents in the city of Pittsburgh (N = 5,896). The head of household or spouse (18 years of age or older) was interviewed.

7.   This reflects the percentage of respondents strongly or very strongly attached to the neighborhood.

8.   This reflects the percentage of respondents rating the neighborhood a good or excellent place to live.

9.   Variables used in the study were age, household income, race (black or white), length of time in neighborhood, number of children under 18 living in the household, marital status, work status, and sex.

10.   The impingement typology and life-cycle web can also be used with the individual as a unit of analysis, but the structural dynamics and conclusions will be different and following both tracks in this paper would only confuse the issues. The author will pursue this in a future paper.

REFERENCES

Ahlbrandt, R.S. Jr. 1984. *Neighborhoods, People, and Community.* New York: Plenum Press.

Aiken, M., and P.E. Mott, eds. 1970. *The Structure of Community Power.* New York: Random House.

Albrow, M., and J. Eade. 1994. "The Impact of Globalization on Sociological Concepts: Community, Culture and Milieu." *Innovation: The European Journal of Social Sciences* 7(4) 371–390.

Bixler, R.D., and M.F. Floyd. 1997. "Nature is Scary, Disgusting, and Uncomfortable." *Environment and Behaviour* 29(4): 443–468.

Bourne, L.S. 1996. "Presidential Address—Normative Urban Geographies:Recent Trends, Competing Visions, and New Cultures of Regulation." *The Canadian Geographer* 40(1): 2-16.

Butler, E.W. 1976. *Urban Sociology: A Systematic Approach.* New York: Harper & Row.

Butler, S.S. 1997. "Homelessness Among AFDC Families in a Rural State: It is Bound to Get Worse." *Affilia: Journal of Women and Social Work* 12(4): 427–452.

Calhoun, C. 1991. "Indirect Relationships and Imagined Communities: Large-Scale Social Integration and the Transformation of Everyday Life." Pp. 95-130 in *Social Theory for a Changing Society,* edited by P. Bourdieu and J.S. Coleman. New York: Russell Sage Foundation.

Chapin, F.S. Jr. 1974. *Human Activity Patterns in the City.* New York: John Wiley& Sons.

Chekki, D.A., ed. 1996. "The Social Landscape of New Communities in North America." Pp. 3-16 in *Research in Community Sociology,* Vol. 6. Greenwich CT: JAI Press.

Cohen, A.A. 1985. *The Symbolic Construction of Community.* London: Tavistock.

Denton, T. 1998. "Social and Structural Differentiation: Conceptualization and Measurement." *Cross-Cultural Research* 32(1): 37–79.

Dixon-Woudenberg, A.L.S. 1993. "Multi-Tiered Life-Cycle Theory of Aging." Pp. 1513–1516 in *Recent Advances in Aging Science,* edited by E. Beregi, I.A. Gergely, and K. Rajczi. Bologna, Italy: Monduzzi Editore.

Elkins, D.J. 1995. *Beyond Sovereignty: Territory and Political Economy in the Twenty-first Century.* Toronto: University of Toronto Press.

Foucault, M. 1979. *Discipline and Punish.* New York: Vintage.

Freeman, L.C. 1968. *Patterns of Local Community Leadership.* New York: The Bobbs-Merrill.

Galster, G.C. 1987. *Homeowners and Neighborhood Investment.* Durham, NC: Duke University Press.

Gans, H.J. 1962. *The Urban Villagers—Group and Class in the Life of Italian Americans.* New York: The Free Press.

Giddens, A. 1984. *The Constitution of Society.* Cambridge: The Polity Press.

Goldsmith, W.W., and E.J. Blakely. 1991. *Separate Societies.* Philadelphia: Temple University Press.

Gottdiener, M. 1991. "Space, Social Theory, and the Urban Metaphor." Pp. 295-311 in *Current Perspectives in Social Theory,* edited by Ben Agger, Vol. 11. Greenwich, CT: JAI Press.

Gottdiener, M., and A. Lagopoulos, eds. 1986. *The City and the Sign.* New York: Columbia University Press.

Hillery, G.A. Jr. 1963. "Villages, Cities, and Total Institutions." *American Sociological Review* 28(5): 779–791.

Horowitz, M. 1967. *The Community Press in an Urban Setting.* Chicago: University of Chicago Press.

Hunter, A. 1975. "The Loss of Community: An Empirical Test Through Replication." *American Sociological Review* 40(5): 537-552.

Hutchinson, J.F., N. Rodriquez, and J. Hagan. 1996. "Community Life—African Americans in Multi-ethnic Residential Areas." *Journal of Black Studies* 27(2): 201-223.

Kaplan, S., and C. Peterson. 1993. "Health and Environment: A Psychological Analysis." Landscape and *Urban Planning* 26: 17-23.

Karp, D.A., G.P. Stone, and W.C. Yoels. 1977. *Being Urban: A Social Psychological View of City Life.* Lexington, MA: D.C. Heath.

Kennedy, L.W. 1990. "The Changing Role of Communities: Crime, Conflict, and Alternate Dispute Resolution." Pp. 131-146 in *Research in Community Sociology,* Vol. 1, edited by D. Chekki. Greenwich, CT: JAI Press.

Lefebvre, H. 1974. *La Production de L'espace* [The Production of Space]. Paris:Editions Anthropos.

Lindsey, E.W. 1996. "Mothers' Perceptions of Factors Influencing the Restabilization of Homeless Families." *Families in Society* 77: 203-215.

Lowe, M.D. 1990. "Reinventing the Wheels." *Technology Review* 93(4): 60–70.

Lozano, E.E. 1990. *Community Design and the Culture of Cities.* Cambridge: Cambridge University Press.

Marcuse, P. 1997. "The Enclave, the Citadel, and the Ghetto—What Has Changed in the Post-Fordist U.S. City." *Urban Affairs Review* 33(2): 228–265.

Marouli, C. 1995. "Women Resisting (in) the City: Struggles, Gender, Class and Space in Athens." *International Journal of Urban and Regional Research* 19(December): 534-548.

Maslow's Hierarchy of Needs. 1997. http://www.connect.net/georgen/maslow.htm.

Montgomery, J. 1998. "Making City: Urbanity, Vitality and Urban Design." *Journal of Urban Design* 3(1): 93–117.

Moore, C. 1994. "Greenest City in the World." *International Wildlife* 24(1): 38–44.

Nord, M., and A.E. Luloff. 1995. "Homeles Children and Their Families in New Hampshire: A Rural Perspective." *Social Service Review* 69: 461-478.

Pino, J.C. 1998. "Labour in the Favelas of Rio de Janeiro, 1940-1969." *Latin American Perspectives* 25(2): 18–40.

Ross, M.G. 1955. *Community Organization Theory and Principles.* New York: Harper & Brothers.

Salingaros, N.A. 1998. "Theory of the Urban Web." *Journal of Urban Design* 3(1): 53-72.

Shulman, N. 1972. "Urban Social Networks: An Investigation of Personal Networks in an Urban Setting." Unpublished papers, University of Toronto.

Timilty, J.F. 1979. "People, Building Neighborhoods—Final Report to the President and the Congress of the United States." *The National Commission on Neighborhoods.* Washington DC: U.S. Government Printing Office.

Tönnies, F. 1957. *Community and Society (Gemeinschaft und Gesellschaft),* trans. and edited by C.P. Loomis. East Lansing: Michigan State University Press.

Ulrich, R.S. 1993. "Biophilia, Biophobia: A New Research Area in Environmental Education." Pp. 73-137 in *Biophilia Hypothesis,* edited by S.R. Kellert and E.O. Wilson. Washington, DC: Island Press.

Unger, J.B., M.D. Kipke, T.R. Simon, S.B. Montgomery, and C.J. Johnson. 1997. "Homeless Youths and Young Adults in Los Angeles: Prevalence of Mental Health Problems and the Relationship

Between Mental Health and Substance Abuse Disorders." *American Journal of Community Psychology* 25: 371-394.

Unger, J.B., M.D. Kipke, T.R. Simon, C.J. Johnson, S.B. Montgomery, and E. Iverson. 1998. "Stress, Coping, and Social Support Among Homeless Youth." *Journal of Adolescent Research,* 13(2): 134–158.

Vidich, A.J., and S.M. Lyman. 1998. "Qualitative Methods—Their History in Sociology and Anthropology." Pp. 41-109 in *The Landscape of Qualitative Research Theories and Issues,* edited by N.K. Denzin and Y.S. Lincoln. Thousand Oaks, CA: Sage.

Walker, A. 1997. "Age and Employment." Paper presented at the XVIth Congress of the International Association of Gerontology, Adelaide, Australia, August 19-23.

Webber, M. 1963. "Order in Diversity: Community Without Propinquity." In *Cities and Space,* edited by L. Wingo, Jr. Baltimore: John Hopkins University Press.

Wellman, B., and B. Leighton. 1979. "Neighborhoods, Networks, and Communities—Approaches to the Study of the Community Question." *Urban Affairs Quarterly* 14: 363–390.

West Sussex County Council. 1998. *West Sussex Structure Plan,* Chapter 15. http://www. westsussex.gov.uk/pl/structure-plan/chap15.htm#2

Wiesenfeld, E. 1997. "From Individual Need to Community Consciousness—The Dialectics Between Land Appropriation and Eviction Threat." *Environment and Behaviour* 29(2): 198–212.

Wirth, L. 1938. "Urbanism as a Way of Life." *American Journal of Sociology* 44: 1-24.

Wohlwill, J.F. 1983. "Concept of Nature: A Psychologist's View." Pp. 5-35 in *Behavior and the Natural Environment: Human Behavior and Environment: Advances in Theory and Research,* edited by I. Altman and J.F. Wohlwill. New York: Plenum Press.

INDEX